INTEGRALISM AND THE COMMON GOOD

INTEGRALISM
AND THE
COMMON GOOD

Selected Essays from *The Josias*

VOLUME 2

The Two Powers

Edited by
P. Edmund Waldstein, O.Cist.

First published in the USA
by Angelico Press 2022
Copyright © Angelico Press 2022

All rights reserved:
No part of this book may be reproduced or transmitted,
in any form or by any means, without permission

For information, address:
Angelico Press, Ltd.
169 Monitor St.
Brooklyn, NY 11222
www.angelicopress.com

ppr 978-1-62138-878-4
cloth 978-1-62138-879-1
ebook 978-1-62138-880-7

Book and cover design
by Michael Schrauzer

CONTENTS

PREFACE   ix

I. Jurisprudence

1. Notes on Right and Law
   Petrus Hispanus   3
2. Rights and the Common Good
   Edmund Waldstein, O.Cist.   9
3. *Obergefell vs. Hodges* in Light of Catholic Doctrine on Marriage
   James N. Berquist   23
4. The New Natural Law Theory as the Source of Bostock's Error
   James N. Berquist   37

II. Spiritual and Temporal Power

5. Integralism in Three Sentences
   Edmund Waldstein, O.Cist.   53
6. Nature, Grace, and Integralism
   Edmund Waldstein, O.Cist.   54
7. Integralism and Gelasian Dyarchy
   Edmund Waldstein, O.Cist.   74
8. On the City of God Against the Pagans
   Alan Fimister   109
9. The Soul-Body Model of the Relation of Spiritual and Temporal Authority
   Thomas de Vio, O.P., Cardinal Cajetan   126

10. On the Two Powers
    Domingo de Soto, O.P. 129

11. On the Mutual Relations between Church and State
    Tommaso Maria Cardinal Zigliara, O.P. 151

12. Against Political Iconoclasm
    Nathaniel Gotcher 175

13. Integralism Today
    Edmund Waldstein, O.Cist. 183

14. Integralism and the Logic of the Cross
    Edmund Waldstein, O.Cist. 190

15. The Politics of Hell
    Urban Hannon 209

16. St Bernard and the Theology of Crusade
    J. Marlow Gazzoli 230

17. The Catholic State: Anachronism, Archenemy, or Archetype?
    Peter Kwasniewski 243

III. Religious Liberty

18. Religious Liberty in the Light of Tradition
    Edmund Waldstein, O.Cist. 255

19. Vatican II and Crisis in the Theology of Baptism
    Thomas Pink 290

20. A Critique of John Locke's *Letter Concerning Toleration*
    Derek Remus 335

CONCLUSION: An Integralist's Brag
Edmund Waldstein, O.Cist. 373

PREFACE

The relation between the spiritual authority that Christ gave to his Apostles and their successors, and the authorities found within temporal societies, is asymmetrical. "My Kingdom is not of this world," says Jesus before Pilate (Jn 18:36). To the Church that He founded, the kingdoms of this world are of secondary importance. Unlike the first century Judean Zealots, Christ did not want to immediately reestablish the Davidic Kingdom, depriving the Romans and Herodians of their authority. "You would not have had any authority whatever over me, if it had not been given you from above," he tells Pilate, thereby implying that He recognizes that temporal authorities have been established by God, who created man as a political creature, and guides human communities through His wise providence.

But like any part of creation, political life has been wounded, and is in need of healing. In this time between the First and Second Comings of Christ, the Church is not a threat to temporal authorities, but rather the bearer of a message of hope that they can become more fully themselves. Not until the Second Coming will the Kingdom "not of this world" be fully realized, when our political nature will be elevated, fulfilled, and transcended by a higher form of communal life.

In the meantime, the primary demand the Church makes of temporal powers is the *libertas ecclesiae*, the freedom to proclaim the Gospel and to rule her subjects in the Spirit. While it might seem that the most favorable position of the Church is one in which she is being persecuted—since the constant necessity of risking one's life for Christ destroys illusions and purifies the Church of the lukewarm—this has never been the position vis-à-vis the world that the Church herself has sought. God wills all men to come to the recognition of the truth, especially the weak and the miserable, and therefore, His Church desires a tranquil peace with earthly powers:

> So I ask you first of all to make your prayers, entreaties, intercessions, thanksgivings, for all people, for kings and all who are of high degree, so that we may live a quiet and peaceful life in all piety and dignity. This is good and acceptable in the sight of God our savior, who wishes all people to be saved, and to come to the recognition of the truth. (1 Tim 2:1–4)

The nature of the demand for *libertas ecclesiae*, for the greatest freedom of action possible in the given circumstances, explains to a large extent the apparent indifference that the Church has shown to various political forms. As Carl Schmitt pointed out, the adaptability of the Church to various political forms has seemed to her enemies like "limitless opportunism":

> During the Holy Alliance, after 1815, [the Church] became a center of reaction and an enemy of all liberal freedoms, and in other countries an exponent of these same freedoms, especially freedom of the press and freedom of education.... In European monarchies, [she] preaches the alliance of throne and altar, and in the peasant democracies of the Swiss cantons or in North America [she] stands wholly on the side of a firm democracy.[1]

Temporal politics is a secondary concern for the Church of Christ. Christianity is not a religion of law like Islam, whose growth is tied up with the expansion of a particular political and jurisprudential system. But neither are politics and jurisprudence entirely irrelevant to the Church, whose mission is to renew *all things* in Christ. She is constantly calling on temporal powers to recognize the truth about man and the law that his Creator has written into his heart. And her demand for her own liberty ultimately implies that earthly authorities should recognize the basis of that liberty: that she is a necessary society founded by God, endowed by Him with the authority to pursue the supernatural good—an authority higher than any merely temporal authority—and with an infallible teaching office that extends to even the most humble of natural moral truths.

---

1 Carl Schmitt, *Roman Catholicism and Political Form*, trans. G. L. Ulmen (London: Greenwood Press, 1996), 4.

Preface

Brought to its ultimate conclusion, the demand for *libertas ecclesiae* is the demand for the stance known as "integralism." As St. John Henry Newman put it, a temporal society must either reject the Church's claims or submit itself to them:

> As [the Church] resisted and defied her persecutors, so she ruled her convert people. And surely this was but natural, and will startle those only to whom the subject is new. If the Church is independent of the State, so far as she is a messenger from God, therefore, should the State, with its high officials and its subject masses, come into her communion, it is plain that they must at once change hostility into submission. There was no middle term; either they must deny her claim to divinity or humble themselves before it,—that is, as far as the domain of religion extends, and that domain is a wide one. They could not place God and man on one level.[2]

The relation between apostolic authority and the authority of temporal rulers and governments is, therefore, asymmetrical. If the Church can look with indifference on various political forms, it is not true conversely that the political communities can look with indifference on various forms of "religion."

The first volume of selected essays from *The Josias* was largely concerned with man's social nature, the fact that the highest goods that he pursues are social goods.[3] This second volume is concerned largely with what follows from that social nature when it comes to man's *social duties* toward the true religion. Pope Leo XIII gave classic expression to those duties in the encyclical *Immortale Dei* (n. 6):

> Since, then, no one is allowed to be remiss in the service due to God, and since the chief duty of all men is to cling to religion in both its teaching and practice—not such religion as they may have a preference for, but the religion which God enjoins, and which certain and most clear marks show to be the only one true religion—it is a public crime to act as though there were no God. So, too, is it a sin for the State not to have care for religion as

---

2   John Henry Newman, *A Letter Addressed to His Grace the Duke of Norfolk on Occasion of Mr. Gladstone's Recent Expostulations* (London: Pickering, 1875), 22.

3   See *Integralism and the Common Good: Selected Essays from* The Josias, vol. 1: *Family, City, and State*, ed. Edmund Waldstein, O.Cist. and Peter A. Kwasniewski (Brooklyn: Angelico Press, 2021).

a thing beyond its scope, or as of no practical benefit; or out of many forms of religion to adopt that one which chimes in with the fancy; for we are bound absolutely to worship God in that way which He has shown to be His will.

Societies are bound to worship God according to the truth He has revealed, and this is done principally by recognizing and supporting the Church He has founded. Thus the two powers—the temporal power of earthly rulers and the spiritual power of the Apostles and their successors—are meant to enter into an ordered relation. Each has its own proper concern. The temporal society is concerned with the common good of a "temporal" society, a society belonging to the present order of time, that is destined to pass away. The spiritual power is concerned with the common good of an eternal city not of this world, although it is already present in mystery in this world. And yet, as Pope Leo points out, since both of these powers are from God and both rule over the same subjects, there must be an order between them (see *Immortale Dei*, n. 13). The essays in this volume defend this teaching and draw out its conclusions.

My thanks are due to Ethan Mack for technical assistance; our publisher John Riess of Angelico Press; and Peter Kwasniewski, who was of great help in editing the volume for publication. Above all, I thank the contributors to this volume, who have truly been friends in the common pursuit of truth. Together with the contributors I thank the wider group of friends behind *The Josias,* to whose discussions the thoughts in our contributions owe so much. We thank especially I.B., J.B., S.B., W.B., A.D, M.D., S.D., T.D., A.F., C.F., N.G., P.J.I., J.K., D.L., E.L., B.M., P.d.M., C.P., G.P., A.S., P.J.S., J.T., Z.T., A.V., A.G.V., M.W, R.W. We thank also the past and current editors of *The Josias*—E.M., Joel Augustine, Jonathan Culbreath, and Daniel Whitehead.

This preface was written on a pilgrimage undertaken with theology students to the Shrine of Our Lady at Fátima. The Apparitions at Fátima can be seen in part as a supernatural response to the persecution of the Church unleased by the violently anti-clerical, liberal Revolution of 1910 in Portugal and its 1911 Law of Separation of Church and State. The calls for penance and reparation at

Preface

Fátima can be seen to include the call to atone for the many sins committed in the name of the ideology of secularism by liberals and by the socialists and communists who followed in their footsteps and shared their ideological commitment to the separation of Church and state. May the essays in this volume help Catholics to understand the reasons why the principle of separation of Church and state—the fundamental principle of both liberalism and communism—is false, and may it help them thereby to act more effectively for the Social Kingship of Christ and for the peace of the world.

Edmund Waldstein, O. Cist.
Fátima, Portugal
Ember Friday of September
September 23, 2022

I
JURISPRUDENCE

1

Notes on Right and Law

Petrus Hispanus

1. The words *right* and *law* refer to related realities. Their meaning is derived from the Latin *ius* and *lex*. The more fundamental of these is *ius*, as regards both the nature of the virtue of justice generally, and the juridical order specifically. In English, this is obscured by the predominance of the words "law" and "legal" to designate that order and the framework within which "rights" exist.

2. The first and foundational meaning of *ius* is as the object of justice, which is the habit of giving or rendering to each what is his own: *ius suum cuique tribuere*. Thus, *ius* is the *suum, that which is owed*, referring to the thing or action that is due to someone by virtue of any number of titles that sustain his claim to them.

3. The scope of the virtue of justice is universal, such that one can properly speak of "rights" in any context where human (and indeed more than human) action is involved. Thus, one can properly speak of general or political justice, the ultimate object of which is the common good of the political community, as it refers to the rights that are owed to the community (or to its ruler, as appropriate) by virtue of the demands of that common good. These rights are therefore supreme in the order of justice, subject only to the rights due to God himself (by individuals and by the community as a whole), which are the object of the virtue of religion, a species of the virtue of justice. Below them, we find the rights owed between individual persons. We can therefore classify the orders of justice with regard to the dignity of the creditor: individuals, the political community, and God.

4. In the sphere of particular human relationships, the study of the object of justice has traditionally been the province of jurists,

who have provided us with the most complete and precise notion of "right." For this reason, we now turn to their insights.

5. Before getting into the subject-matter itself, a historical point is in order regarding the use of these words. The connection between right and justice outlined above, and particularly between the juridical order and justice, which in classical thought is necessary, is denied by most modern jurists. Justice, for the moderns, is not the virtue of giving what is owed to others; that is, it is not concerned with action and thus with the good, but is at best either an ideal—a political "value" or ideological Omega point of sorts—or a mere procedure. It is telling, for example, to find in the rulings of entities like the International Court of Justice, when referring to the fundamental or non-negotiable aspects of what they call "natural justice," that this includes little more than a schematic summary of due process.

6. In Roman law, *ius* classically referred to the (usually physical) object owed to someone. The paradigmatic case is property or ownership, where my right (*ius*) simply *is* the thing I claim as mine. There is no distinction between a right and its object, for what I am owed is precisely the object itself and not only a claim over it. In the case of rights less absolute than ownership, such as usufruct or use, my right is also the thing, but only to a certain extent or under certain conditions. The same thing happens with rights over persons, such as any form of debt, where what is owed is an action, such as the action of returning what has been loaned. (To ensure this right over persons did not devolve into servitude, the Romans sagely permitted compensation in case of breach, to be rendered in the form of *pecunium*—i.e., money.)

7. The *basis* of rights is found in what can be called the *distribution* of things. If something is owed to someone as his own, it is only because he first received it from another. The only holder of absolute rights is therefore God, Who alone can claim not to have received what is His from any other. For this reason, ultimately all rights must derive in some fashion from the divine ordinances. However, in the vast majority of cases, this ultimate origin is mediated by secondary causes, which can be summarized in the two categories of (a) nature and (b) human will, from which much of the distribution of things can be discerned.

8. The discernment of the *content* of these distributions is the primary task of the jurists and is the proper object of jurisprudence. The fruit of this effort is the determination of what the jurists have called the *titles* of rights. The title of a right is what determines its scope, its content, its measure, and its effects.

9. Thus, some titles are found directly in nature, such as the title that gives a father the right to (claim as what is due to him) the obedience of his family. Others are found in acts of the human will, either as regards the care of private things or the care of the common good. An example of the first is the title by which a man grants someone the right to live in his house in exchange for periodic payments. An example of the second is the title by which the sovereign may exact a fine from a subject for violating a traffic regulation. Further, the titles derived from the human will can also be distilled from more diffuse expressions of that will as exercised over time and space, as in the form of customs or the common practices of the nations.

10. To summarize, we can say that the two sources of rights are nature and human will, which in turn devolve into the two sources of contract and human law. However, the care of private things is subject to the care of the common good, so rights derived from contract are also subject to human law. Therefore, we can say that rights are in reality derived from two basic sources: nature and human law. This is where the traditional distinction between natural and positive rights finds its origin.

11. However, the distinction between natural and positive rights is not helpful when used to mean that the two spheres are unrelated. In fact, many, if not most, positive rights derive their ultimate legitimacy from the order of nature. For example, the right of the sovereign to place a murderer in jail or execute him is not a merely positive right. It is more helpful to say that in most cases, although the existence of a right may be found in nature, its specifications may be due to human ordinance (such as the decision of when murder should be punishable by prison or by death). There are also many natural rights that are simply recognized in human law, such as the father's right to *patria potestas* mentioned above.

12. The second meaning of *ius* refers by analogy to the *order* (or, as the moderns prefer to say, the *system*) constituted by the web

of rights derived from the titles found in nature and in human law. Thus, according to their source, we can distinguish, as the Romans did, between a *ius naturale* (natural right), a *ius civile* or *ius quiritium* (civil right), and a *ius gentium* (the right of nations), each referring to the juridical orders constituted by the rights derived from nature, the ordinances of the city, and the common practices of the nations.

13. In all these cases, the foundational reality of *ius* remains the same: what is owed to each according to the distributions to be discerned in nature and in the ordinances of the human will. The main reason to distinguish between the various orders then is political, for while a Parthian or a Goth may be entitled to his rights derived from nature and from the common practices of the nations, he is certainly not entitled to the rights derived from the laws of the Roman People.

14. Thus, it is not that these are parallel orders, but, as noted above, they express merely the openness of the juridical order to not only the product of the human will, but also to nature itself. They are all in fact a single order, having application at the same time in any given case. Only in this sense can the juridical order be a true *order*. Without reference to a criterion transcending the human will, any juridical system would be little more than a self-referential mechanism. A good illustration of this is that it is simply not possible to make sense of the basic concepts of juridical thought (such as, for example, the doctrine of the capacity of legal subjects, the requirements of valid consent, or the diverse mental states relevant in criminal law) without reference to nature.

15. The third meaning of *ius* designates the practical science by which the jurists have derived the various rights in question. Thus, the Romans also spoke of *ius* as the *ars boni et aequi* (the art of the good and the equitable) and as *divinarum atque humanarum rerum notitia, iusti atque iniusti scientia* (the knowledge of matters divine and human, and the science of what is just and unjust), referring to the work of the jurists itself and to the scientific synthesis they formulated for it. The science of right—*jurisprudence*—is the order of definitions, categories, arguments, and methods employed by the jurists to discern, in each particular case, what is owed to

the parties involved—that is, their rights. To study *ius* is, thus, to study this science.

16. As a practical science, jurisprudence is not concerned exclusively with the rigor of formal and logical structure and argument. Its end is action, specifically just action. For this reason, it is dialectical and contingent. The basis for a jurisprudential determination is the contrasted validity and persuasiveness of the juridical arguments posed by the claimant and the respondent in a case, but it is always only probable, relative, and conditional, for the possibility remains ever open that once a determination is made in favor of one person, a third party may arrive with a better claim over the same thing. A juridical absurdity, therefore, is not necessarily only a logical absurdity; rather, it is an unjust determination. The modern confusion of juridical science with its method (as in Kelsen, for example) is thus erroneous, or at least incomplete, in so far as it closes it off from its end as a practical science, the just action.

17. These three meanings of *ius* or right were known to St Thomas,[1] who synthesized them from the various sources the classical tradition had bequeathed, especially the sayings of the Roman jurists contained in the *Digest* of the *Corpus Iuris Civilis*.

18. Second, Scholasticism added two new meanings of *ius* not found in the classics or in St Thomas, but which are not at odds with them. Francisco de Vitoria taught that a fourth analogical meaning of right is *lex*, that is, law. The reason is that the law is a primary source of right, for when we speak of natural rights or positive rights, we are in fact speaking of the rights to be derived from the titles found in the natural and positive laws. St Thomas considered this argument in the context of his discussion of right as the object of justice and taught that law can be called an expression of right, but not a species of it.[2] Vitoria can therefore be considered to be already moving in a more or less legalistic understanding of right, even if he was not a legalist himself.

19. In turn, Francisco Suárez stated that *ius* also means analogically the faculty or power over something, in the sense that it is owed

---

1 St Thomas Aquinas, *Summa theologiae* [hereafter *ST*], II-II, qq. 57, 60.
2 *ST* II-II, q. 57, a. 1, ad 2.

to someone that the exercise of that faculty or power over an object or person be respected. To have a right in this last sense means that one's sphere of action over the object must not be violated. This meaning of right is the most widespread today, especially in English, where "right" is hardly intelligible in the first three meanings mentioned above (or in Vitoria's fourth). Perhaps the reason for this is that Suárez's work was a principal source for the understanding of natural right in Locke, arguably (and lamentably) one of the most influential natural right thinkers of the modern age.

20. Be that as it may, Suárez's notion is not incorrect, in so far as we understand (as he did) that it is analogical and derivative. I can have the right to exercise a power over a thing or person only if that thing or person is itself, in the first place, my right. In other words, right as a power or faculty is already virtually contained in the first, principal meaning of right sketched out above.

21. To conclude, a word about the meaning of *lex*. In Latin, as in most Romance languages, this word refers specifically to the ordinance of reason, issued by one who has care for the common good and promulgated. This refers to the generally binding decrees of those who have the legislative power: in Rome, the Roman People and later the emperors, today, a parliament, congress, or national assembly. A *lex*, therefore, is technically a specific form of public decree.

22. In English, the word "law" may also be used with this meaning, but more commonly it means *ius*, understood in the second and third meanings summarized above, that is, as an order and as a science. Thus, one speaks of "obeying" or "applying the law," and of "studying law," or making a "legal" argument. As noted by Vitoria, the analogical use of the word *lex* to mean *ius* is not incorrect, but it can be confusing at best when it gets out of this limited scope and loses sight of the more foundational meanings. The reason for this is that the use of the word "law" to designate right threatens to place too much emphasis on the voluntaristic and (in a secularized culture) merely positive aspects of the juridical. Ontologically, however, the heart of the juridical is its relationship with the virtue of justice, which is clearly expressed in the primary meaning of *ius* as that which is owed.

2

Rights and the Common Good*

Edmund Waldstein, O.Cist.

1. Beginning with the obvious

Some things are difficult to understand because they are very abstract, separated from the concrete and sensible realities surrounding us—this is a difficulty that we experience, for example, in the consideration of the most universal predicates. Other things are difficult to understand because they are so exalted, existing on a higher level of perfection than us—this is the difficulty we find, for example, in understanding the hierarchy of the angels. Yet other matters are difficult to understand because they are so complicated, involving so many parts and elements and influences that it is difficult to keep them all in our minds at once—for example, the politics of Bosnia and Herzegovina.

But there are some things which we find difficult to understand because they are more concrete, lowlier, and simpler than we expect. Our minds fly at once to vague abstractions and lofty ideals, and we suspect complexity and complication when, in fact, the truth is concrete, close at hand, and simple. This, I think, is the difficulty in understanding rights. Many of the difficulties that people get into in thinking about rights stem from a lack of the patience necessary to begin with the first and most basic notion of rights, which is also the most concrete. Only by patiently considering the most basic and concrete rights, the rights that lie, so to speak, at our feet, can we see the order in which the notion can then be extended analogously. The most basic notion of a right is, I will argue, the "object of justice," or "the just thing."

---

* The following paper was first delivered as a lecture at the Adenauer Forum, ITI Trumau, January 27, 2022. My thanks to John Hennenfent for the invitation.

I will presently explain what that means. Before doing so, however, I will consider the role that rights have played in the debate on liberalism in recent decades. That debate shows the importance of a proper understanding of rights, and also some of the difficulties involved in understanding them.

2. Strauss and MacIntyre on Rights and Liberalism

The political system that has been dominant in many parts of the world since the nineteenth century is liberalism. Liberalism traces its philosophical influences back to the Enlightenment thinkers of the seventeenth century—especially in England and Scotland. But in the decades following the French Revolution it was "moderate" supporters of the ideals of the Revolution in continental Europe who popularized the term and formed liberalism as a powerful political movement.[1]

Now, from the first, liberalism has had many critics from many different traditions—Neoscholasticism, Marxism, Romanticism, reactionary monarchism, natural law jurisprudence, and others. I want to turn particularly to the critique made from within the Socratic tradition of political philosophy—the philosophy of Plato and Aristotle, and their many followers.

In the past seventy years or so, two of the most trenchant critics of liberalism from within the Socratic tradition have been Leo Strauss (1899–1973), a German-Jewish philosopher who emigrated to the United States, and Alasdair MacIntyre, born in 1929, a Scottish philosopher, who also emigrated to the United States, and is now a Catholic.

Both of these thinkers criticize the role that "rights" play in liberal theory and practice. In his 1953 masterpiece, *Natural Right and History*, Strauss argued that liberalism can be defined by the role that it gives to rights:

> If we may call liberalism that political doctrine which regards as the fundamental political fact the rights, as distinguished from the duties, of man and which identifies the function of the state

---

[1] See Helena Rosenblatt, *The Lost History of Liberalism: From Ancient Rome to the Twenty-First Century* (Princeton: Princeton University Press, 2018).

Rights and the Common Good

with the protection or the safeguarding of those rights, we must say that the founder of liberalism was Hobbes.[2]

Strauss contrasts this centrality of rights in the tradition of politics inaugurated by Hobbes with what he sees as the marginality of rights in the Socratic tradition:

> The premodern natural law doctrines taught the duties of man; if they paid any attention at all to his rights, they conceived of them as essentially derivative from his duties. As has frequently been observed, in the course of the seventeenth and eighteenth centuries a much greater emphasis was put on rights than ever had been done before. One may speak of a shift of emphasis from natural duties to natural rights.... The fundamental change from an orientation by natural duties to an orientation by natural rights finds its clearest and most telling expression in the teaching of Hobbes, who squarely made an unconditional natural right the basis of all natural duties, the duties being therefore only conditional.... The profound change under consideration can be traced directly to Hobbes's concern with a human guaranty for the actualization of the right social order or to his "realistic" intention. The actualization of a social order that is defined in terms of man's duties is necessarily uncertain and even improbable; such an order may well appear to be utopian. Quite different is the case of a social order that is defined in terms of the rights of man. For the rights in question express, and are meant to express, something that everyone actually desires anyway; they hallow everyone's self-interest as everyone sees it or can easily be brought to see it. Men can more safely be depended upon to fight for their rights than to fulfil their duties. In the words of Burke: "The little catechism of the rights of men is soon learned; and the inferences are in the passions."[3]

Strauss goes on to argue that the consequence of this shift is modern individualism. The ancients (meaning Plato, Aristotle, and Cicero, not, say, Lucretius) had been convinced that man can reach his *telos* only as part of a city, and that the common good of the city is therefore teleologically prior to the private good

---

2 Leo Strauss, *Natural Right and History* (Chicago: The University of Chicago Press, 1953), 181.

3 Strauss, *Natural Right*, 182–83.

of the individual. Man's duties towards the city and his fellow citizens are, as a consequence, prior to any claim of rights against them. But for liberalism, the individual is prior to the community; the community is established for the sake of defending the individual's rights; any rights of the state or the sovereign are derivative from the rights of the individual, as are any duties the individual may have towards state or sovereign. This individualism of liberalism remains even when its notion of rights goes through great changes. Hobbes and Locke derived rights from nature. Modern liberals, however, "became impatient of the absolute limits to diversity or individuality that are imposed even by the most liberal version of natural right, they had to make a choice between natural right and the uninhibited cultivation of individuality. They chose the latter."[4]

This choice of individuality is often taken in the name of "tolerance" which is a quality on which liberals pride themselves. But the result is (paradoxically) intolerance: "Liberal relativism has its roots in the natural right tradition of tolerance or in the notion that everyone has a natural right to the pursuit of happiness as he understands happiness; but in itself it is a seminary of intolerance."[5]

A reason for this paradox (if I may slightly modify Strauss's argument) is that radical individualism sees itself threatened by ways of thinking or living that assume that there is some more objective measure for human life than individual choice. Thus, the securing of the right of each one to choose his own final end necessitates vigorous attacks on anyone who calls such a right into question. We can see this very clearly today, for example, in the LGBTQ+ movement, which attacks and denounces anyone who refuses to agree that homosexual perversion is good for homosexuals, or that a transvestite is a woman.

Alasdair MacIntyre, the second of the critics of liberalism that I want to bring up, is often thought of as being very far from Strauss. This is because MacIntyre is (in some sense) a man of the left, whereas Strauss was seen as being on the right wing of the political spectrum. Moreover, Strauss was (at least exoterically) a

---

4 Strauss, *Natural Right*, 5.
5 Strauss, *Natural Right*, 6.

strong critic of historicism, whereas MacIntyre appears to be an historicist. But the difference is much less than appears.[6] As far as their critique of liberalism, and the role that rights play in that critique, go, Strauss and MacIntyre are very close.

In his 1981 book *After Virtue*, MacIntyre argues that modern moral and political philosophy is an incoherent collection of concepts divorced from their original context in societies which saw their goal in leading human beings as they are in their "untutored state" (slaves of their passions) to a perfected state in which they reach the *telos* of their essential nature through the virtues that perfect that nature.[7] In such older societies,

> the individual is identified and constituted in and through certain of his or her roles, those roles which bind the individual to the communities in and through which alone specifically human goods are to be attained; I confront the world as a member of this family, this household, this clan, this tribe, this city, this nation, this kingdom.[8]

In such non-individualistic societies, justice is a matter of what is owed to others on account of my and their role in society. Rights are not important, although MacIntyre recognizes that they exist, "conferred by positive law or custom on specified classes of person."[9] But in modern society, rights take on a new importance, and a new concept of universal rights is developed "alleged to belong to human beings as such" and as providing reasons for "their pursuit of life, liberty and happiness."[10] These kinds of rights MacIntyre takes to be a moral fiction invented to try to make sense of a morally incoherent society:

> It would of course be a little odd that there should be such rights attaching to human beings simply *qua* human beings in light of the fact ... that there is no expression in any ancient or medieval language correctly translated by our expression "a right" until

6 Cf. Nathan J. Pinkoski, "Alasdair MacIntyre and Leo Strauss on the Activity of Philosophy," in *The Review of Politics* 82 (2020): 97–122.
7 Alasdair MacIntyre, *After Virtue: A Study in Moral Theory*, 3rd ed. (Notre Dame, IN: University of Notre Dame Press, 2007), 53.
8 MacIntyre, *After Virtue*, 172.
9 MacIntyre, *After Virtue*, 67.
10 MacIntyre, *After Virtue*, 68–69.

> near the close of the middle ages: the concept lacks any means of expression in Hebrew, Greek, Latin or Arabic, classical or medieval, before about 1400, let alone in Old English, or in Japanese even as late as the mid-nineteenth century. From this it does not of course follow that there are no natural or human rights; it only follows that no one could have known that there were. And this at least raises certain questions. But we do not need to be distracted into answering them, for the truth is plain: there are no such rights, and belief in them is one with belief in witches and in unicorns. The best reason for asserting so bluntly that there are no such rights is indeed of precisely the same type as the best reason which we possess for asserting that there are no witches and the best reason which we possess for asserting that there are no unicorns: every attempt to give good reasons for believing that there are such rights has failed.[11]

Macintyre is thus even more critical of the liberal idea of rights than Strauss.

3. Tierney and Legge: Questioning MacIntyre and Strauss

The critique of liberal conceptions of rights that we find in Strauss and MacIntyre has been questioned by a number of writers who have pointed to the role that the notion of rights did in fact play in medieval thought. The historian Brian Tierney sought to show that the idea of rights in fact had deep roots in medieval jurisprudence and theology. Far from being contrary to older understandings of human morality, Tierney argues, rights are correlative to natural law. The Latin word *jus*, according to Tierney, could mean an objective moral order, or a moral precept, or finally it could also mean a moral faculty or power, a "right" in the modern sense—and these three meanings are not only compatible, they are the same thing viewed from different perspectives:

> The various senses of *ius*... are not contradictory concepts. Rather they are correlative. In considering Aquinas and the canonists we suggested that the concepts of *ius* as objective right order and as moral or legal precept are not intrinsically incompatible with one another. Now we can add that both concepts are compatible with

---

11 MacIntyre, *After Virtue*, 69.

the idea of individual rights. (We can define the relationship of parents and children in terms of an objectively right order. Or we can define it in terms of moral precept—"Honor thy father and thy mother." But we could also define the same relationship by saying that parents have a right to the respect of their children.) As for individual rights and *ius naturale* considered as meaning what is objectively right: to affirm a right ordering of human relationships is to imply a structure of rights and duties. In propounding a system of jurisprudence one can emphasize either the objective pattern of relationships or the implied rights and duties of persons to one another—and then again one can focus on either the rights or the duties. The emphasis can fall in different ways depending on social and economic and political circumstances and on the temperament of a particular author. (It will probably have little to do with his abstract metaphysics.) The resulting works may be very different in tone and spirit, but the different emphases do not necessarily imply logical contradictions.[12]

The distinctions that Tierney raises here between different senses of the Latin *jus*, and between "objective" and "subjective" right, are very important, although I think that Tierney misunderstands them.

A similar but (in my opinion) stronger argument has recently been advanced by the American theologian, Dominic Legge, O.P. He argues that (contrary to MacIntyre's assertion that there was no concept of rights before the fourteenth century) St Thomas Aquinas had a concept of subjective rights. Nevertheless, Legge argues that there was an important shift between St Thomas and later scholastics, such as William of Ockham and Francisco Suárez, and the many modern neoscholastics influenced by Suárez. For St Thomas, "law and justice, and consequently any theory of natural rights, should always be understood in terms of an over-arching order to the good."[13] This dimension was, however, eclipsed by Ockham and Suárez, who, in their respective accounts of law, justice, and right, put more emphasis on the will of the lawgiver (human or divine).

---

12 Brian Tierney, *The Idea of Natural Rights: Studies on Natural Rights, Natural Law, and Church Law 1150–1625* (Grand Rapids: Eerdmans, 1997), 33.

13 Dominic Legge, O.P., "Do Thomists Have Rights?," in *Nova et Vetera* Eng. ed. 17.1 (2019): 127–47, at 129.

4. What Strauss and MacIntyre, Tierney and Legge Get Right, and What They Get Wrong

I believe there is something true about all of the positions that I have discussed: Strauss, MacIntyre, Tierney, and Legge (although Tierney less than the others). I think Strauss's insight into the function of rights in modern political philosophy and practice is particularly important. There is indeed something new about the predominance of rights in modernity. And it is indeed connected to modern moral pessimism about man's achieving perfection as a common good, and is therefore bound up with modern individualism. MacIntyre's arguments confirm these insights. But I also agree with Tierney and Legge that the history of rights is not quite as simple as Strauss and MacIntyre make it out to be. And particularly, I agree with Legge that there is a concept of subjective right in St Thomas, and that the most important shift is that from a view which sees rights as integrated into an overarching order to the good, to one that sees them more in terms of the will of the ruler.

On the other hand, I think that all of these accounts miss something. I think that Strauss's account misses how the notion of objective right is a middle term between duty and subjective right. That is, the shift that he correctly identifies is not just a shift from a primacy of duty to a primacy of right, but also a shift of priority between two senses of right. For his part, I think Legge slightly misunderstands the notion of objective right and its relation to law, and therefore does not see how important the reversal in the order between objective and subjective right is to the shift he correctly identifies between right understood as part of an overarching order to the good, and right not so understood.

5. On Justice, Law, and the Common Good

At the beginning of this lecture I said that the most basic notion of a right is the "object of justice," or "the just thing." I am almost ready now to discuss what that means. But an essential preliminary to understanding the object of justice is to understand justice, so I will first indicate some things about justice, and its relation to law and the common good, before, finally, turning to right.

Rights and the Common Good

Father Legge, in the article I have already cited, argues that St Thomas sees justice as connected to a wise understanding of the good. He points to the following text from the *Prima Pars:*

> Since the object of the will is the good as understood, God cannot will anything other than what conforms to the *ratio* [rational order] of His wisdom. For the *ratio* of His wisdom is, as it were, the law of justice, in accord with which His will is right [*recta*] and just [*justa*]. Hence, God does justly whatever He does in accord with His will, just as we ourselves do justly whatever we do in accord with the law. But we act in accord with a law that is given to us by some superior, whereas God is a law for Himself.[14]

As Fr Legge points out, this means that justice follows from a prior wise ordering of all things by God, whereby He gives every thing its proper goodness, which in various ways tends toward Himself as the highest good and last end of all things:

> For Aquinas, law is not primarily the expression of God's will, but rather, the wisely ordered plan of creation in God's intellect is like the "law" that guides the perfectly just willing of God. Law is an expression of reason, an ordering according to reason, even in God. And so justice results from rightly willing according to the wise or reasoned ordering of all things to God.[15]

It is important to note here that, according to St Thomas, there are different senses of "justice." There is "general justice," also called "legal justice," which is what establishes right order in man's actions toward the common good of society. And then there is particular justice (further divided into commutative and distributive), which establishes right order in men's relation among themselves. Particular justice is a particular virtue, but general justice, since it establishes order in view of the common good, includes acts of all the virtues:

> Now it is evident that all who are included in a community, stand in relation to that community as parts to a whole; while a part, as such, belongs to a whole, so that whatever is the good of a part can be directed to the good of the whole. It follows therefore that

---

14   *ST* I, q. 21, a. 1, ad 1.
15   Legge, "Do Thomists Have Rights?," 130.

the good of any virtue, whether such virtue direct man in relation to himself, or in relation to certain other individual persons, is referable to the common good, to which justice directs: so that all acts of virtue can pertain to justice, in so far as it directs man to the common good.[16]

Recall that in the text from the *Prima Pars* St Thomas says that the *ratio* of God's wisdom is like a "law of justice." Law is what determines what is truly for the common good. Hence, general justice is also called "legal justice." In subjects it consists in obeying the law, and in rulers it consists in laying down the law in a wise manner, so as to help the whole community achieve its good.

St Thomas defines law as follows: "Law is an ordering (*ordinatio*) by reason, directed toward the common good, made by one who is in charge of the community, and promulgated."[17]

Of particular importance for us are reason and the common good. Law is something reasonable, something based on understanding of the good. And the good in question is the *common good*. In St Thomas's understanding, the common good is not a merely instrumental or useful good. It is not a means to individuals attaining purely individual goods. Rather, the common good is a common end communicable to many, not instrumental. *The common good, St Thomas argues, is identified with the end of human life as such*:

> As has been explained (a. 1), by virtue of the fact that law is a rule and measure, it has to do with the principle of human acts. Now just as reason is the principle of human acts, so too within reason itself there is something which is the principle with respect to everything else. Hence, this must be what law is chiefly and especially concerned with. Now in actions, which practical reason is concerned with, the first principle is the ultimate end. But, as was established above (q. 2, a. 7), the ultimate end of human life is happiness or beatitude. Hence, law must have to do mainly with an ordering that leads to beatitude. Again, since (a) every part is ordered toward its whole in the way that what is incomplete (*imperfectum*) is ordered toward what is complete (*perfectum*),

---

16 *ST* II-II, q. 58, a. 5.
17 *ST* I-II, q. 90, a. 4.

and since (b) a man is part of a complete community, law must properly be concerned with the ordering that leads to communal happiness (*ad felicitatem communem*). Hence, in the definition of legal affairs alluded to above, the Philosopher makes mention of both happiness and political communion. For in *Ethics* 5 he says, "The laws (*legalia*) we call 'just' are those that effect and conserve happiness and its elements within the political community." For as *Politics* 1 puts it, a city is a complete community.[18]

St Thomas is here clearly within the Socratic tradition of political philosophy, which, as Strauss wrote, "had assumed that man cannot reach the perfection of his nature except in and through civil society and, therefore, that civil society is prior to the individual."[19] If the Socratic tradition is right on this point, and I think it is, then what follows for our understanding of rights?

6. On Rights[20]

The English word "right" is derived from the Indo-European root "reg," meaning straight (and hence, to move in a straight line, to lead straight, to put right, to rule, etc.). "Right" is the etymological equivalent of the Latin *rectitudo*. But in our context "right" translates another Latin word, namely *jus*. *Jus* has a variety of analogically related meanings. The primary meaning, I claim, is the "object of justice," or "the just thing." What does this mean?

Many modern writers have misunderstood what is meant, because they assume it means something very lofty and universal, such as an objective moral order. *Jus* can certainly also be used in that sense. But "the object of justice" is much more concrete. It is something so concrete, particular, and banal that at first glance it seems hardly worth mentioning. This is the problem that I brought up at the beginning: some things are so obvious that they are easily misunderstood. The virtue of justice is the firm will to give to each his due. Thus, an *object* of justice is *what is due*, the *thing*

---

18   ST I-II, q. 90, a. 2.
19   Strauss, *Natural Right and History*, 183.
20   The following section is based in part on my essay "Hard Liberalism, Soft Liberalism, and the American Founding," in *Integralism and the Common Good: Selected Essays from* The Josias, vol. 1: *Family, City, and State*, ed. Edmund Waldstein, O. Cist. and Peter A. Kwasniewski (Brooklyn: Angelico Press, 2021), 286–305.

or action due to another. Thus an "objective right" is nothing more than a thing or action due to another. For example, a fair share of the spoils of battle is due to Achilles—it is his *right*. Or, money is due to the baker who gives me a loaf. The money is his *right*. Or the cantor's singing of an antiphon is due to the cathedral chapter which has appointed him—the singing of the antiphon is the chapter's *objective right*. The spoils, the money, and the singing are themselves the objective rights. That is, it is not primarily that Achilles *has* a right to the spoils, but rather that the spoils *are* his right.[21]

Now what determines what is due to another? Justice. But, as we saw, justice is connected to a sapiential order to the good. And it is above all law, "the law of justice," that determines what is just. That is, law makes a certain distribution of things, of objective rights, *for the sake of the common good*. This distribution of things is made in the first place by God's eternal law with a view to the universal common good of all things—both the intrinsic common good, the harmonious order of the whole of creation, and the extrinsic common good, God Himself as the object of happiness. The objective rights distributed by natural law can be called "natural rights." In this sense, therefore (*pace* MacIntyre) there are indeed rights that "belong to human beings as such," or rather that belong to them as members of the order of the whole of creation.

In the second place, the distribution of things is made by human custom and law for the sake of the common good of temporal happiness and peace. Law is, as St Thomas puts it, the *"ratio iuris"*: it gives the reason why some thing is due to someone.[22] Legge mistranslates this to say that "law is a kind of expression of *ius*."[23] Clearly, he is thinking of *jus* here in the sense of an overarching order of rights. That is indeed a sense of *jus*, but it is not what St Thomas means in the passage in question. Rather, he means *jus* in the sense of the just thing. The just thing is an expression of *lex*, because *lex* is the *ratio* of the just thing. Literally translated, the passage says, "law is the reason of right." But this does indeed confirm

---

21   See chapter 1.
22   *ST* II-II, q. 57, a. 1, ad 2.
23   Legge, "Do Thomists Have Rights?," 131.

and strengthen Legge's more fundamental point, that everything goes back to wisdom about the common good, and what serves it.

The consequences of St Thomas's view on the relation of rights to law (and therefore the common good) are far reaching. For example, the distribution of private property will be regulated with a view to what serves the common good. Therefore, the law can put limits on the acquisition of wealth, if it judges that too great an acquisition damages social peace. Or it can forbid certain kinds of contracts or loans that are judged to be prejudicial to civic friendship.

Now, the modern sense of "right" as a *moral power*, that is, *what someone ought to be allowed to do without interference*, was originally an analogical extension of *jus* (anticipated already in St Thomas, as Legge shows,[24] but fully developed by later Scholastics), and originally meant that if a thing is one's right, then the power or license that one has to do certain things to or with the thing is also due to one, i.e., one's right. For example, if a piece of bread is someone's *ius*, then eating the bread is also his *ius*. That is, he ought *to be allowed* to eat the bread.

This analogical extension would be unobjectionable in itself. Such moral powers do indeed have some foundation in reality, and it makes sense to extend the name *jus* to them. But in the course of the extension, a fatal reversal takes place. The analogical extension of *jus*, right as a power, comes to be seen as the *prime analogate*, and objective right, the object owed to the other, as an analogical extension. On the basis of this reversal, Suárez and his Enlightenment imitators hold that something is due to another, *because* of the inviolable moral power that he has of demanding it, *rather than* the power being an effect of his being owed something. Henri Grenier explains the consequences with his customary concision:

> If objective right is understood as right in the strict sense, it follows that subjective right, i.e., right as a power, is measured by the just thing, according to conformity to law. Moreover, since law is an ordinance for the common good, it follows that the whole juridical order is directed to the common good. But, if subjective right is understood as right in the primary, strict, and formal meaning of

24 Legge, "Do Thomists Have Rights?," 133.

the term, it follows that the juridical order consists in a certain autonomy, independence, and liberty. For subjective right is not measured by the just thing, but the just thing is measured by the inviolable faculty, which is a certain liberty. Therefore, according to moderns, the juridical order is directed to liberty rather than to the common good. This gives rise to errors among moderns, who speak of liberty of speech, liberty of worship, economic liberty — economic liberalism — without any consideration of their relation to the common good.[25]

Here we can see why Strauss is right to say that the primacy of *rights* in modern politics is essentially liberal. It leads to an instrumental understanding of the common good. For liberals the common good is not that in which the members of society find their flourishing and happiness, but rather an order instrumental in bringing about the liberty of all. The true goal is not an actual good, but the maximum freedom for each to determine his good. If tyranny is defined by subordinating the common good to the private good, then the liberal order is a tyranny in which everyone is a tyrant.[26]

---

25 Henri Grenier, *Thomistic Philosophy*, vol. 4, *Moral Philosophy*, trans. J. P. E. O'Hanley (Charlottetown: St Dunstan's University, 1950), §950.
26 Cf. St Thomas, *De Regno*, I.2.

3

Obergefell vs. Hodges in Light of Catholic Doctrine on Marriage

James N. Berquist

The Supreme Court's 5-4 decision legalizing homosexual marriage carries with it many questions varying in nature. One set of questions the ruling brings into high relief for Catholics concerns the relationship of state-sanctioned civil marriage to sacramental marriage. To what extent (if any) and in what ways should the state regulate marriage, and given other legal practices such as divorce and contraception, does this ruling (or rulings about homosexual marriage in general) change anything significantly?

There are several ways one might answer these questions (for instance, considering and applying natural law), but the first thing faithful Catholics must do is turn to the teachings of the Church in this matter for direction. We are fortunate to live in a time where the Church has given a good deal of pertinent direction for just this sort of situation. We have, among many other resources, three encyclicals in recent history devoted to elucidating the Catholic teachings on marriage or particular aspects of marriage: Leo XIII's *Arcanum Divinae*, Pius XI's *Casti Connubii*, and Paul VI's *Humanae Vitae*.

Based upon these (*Casti Connubii* most of all), we Catholics must recognize three things at least which we are bound to hold according to the doctrines of our Faith. First of all, we are bound to defend the proposition that the nature of marriage, both natural and sacramental, is not under the authority of the state. Secondly, the state is obliged to protect and preserve the set-apart character of the family, and this for the sake of the state itself. Thus a civil institution usurping the place of the family is of grave import. Finally, based upon the nature of true marriage, we must recognize the full breadth of the problem presented by the legalization of gay marriage. While the legalizations of contraception and divorce diminish our nation's capability of understanding marriage—and while abortion is a greater evil in itself—the recognition and legalization of homosexual marriage *destroys* our nation's capability to understand the nature of marriage. When accepted by the culture and sanctioned by law, the former errors definitely oppose the ends of marriage, but the latter error actively denies the essential nature of the marital union itself.

The following essay does *not* argue to particular remedies or policies that need to be adopted. It is ordered to the Catholic reader who wants to see more precisely, in light of magisterial teaching, what the problems with the ruling are, why they are problems, and the general principles which will underlie any particular remedies.

The Nature of Marriage

The Catechism of Trent, using Scripture and St Augustine as guides, declares that marriage is an institution created by God, not man,[1] and that it is ordered to the goods of offspring, conjugal faith (or spousal fidelity), and the sacrament—the signification of Christ's love for the Church.[2] The encyclicals we are examining clarify and further define this teaching.

1) Marriage is instituted by God

Pius XI first notes that this is indeed the Catholic understanding:

> Matrimony was not instituted or restored by man but by God.... This is the doctrine of Holy Scripture; this is the constant tradition of the Universal Church; this the solemn definition of the sacred Council of Trent, which declares and establishes from the words of Holy Writ itself that God is the Author of the perpetual stability of the marriage bond, its unity and its firmness.[3]

A few paragraphs later, he states this again while explaining man's role:

---

[1] The Council implies it at the beginning of Session Twenty-Four, and the Catechism of Trent states it explicitly in the section "The Sacrament of Matrimony."
[2] Again, this is explicitly found in the Roman Catechism (the Catechism of Trent).
[3] *Casti Connubii* 5.

Obergefell vs. Hodges *in Light of Catholic Doctrine on Marriage*

From God comes the very institution of marriage, the ends for which it was instituted, the laws that govern it, the goods[4] that flow from it; while man, through generous surrender of his own person made to another for the whole span of life, becomes, with the help and cooperation of God, the author of each particular marriage, with the duties and goods annexed thereto from divine institution.[5]

Marriage is not something man-made; it is not something merely constructed by society for some level of convenience and stability (though it is a principle of stability). Rather, the Creator establishes it, and as such His are the laws that govern its nature even *before* Christ raises it to the level of a sacrament.

This is not to say, of course, that man's will is of no consequence whatsoever in marriage. Man's will is indeed involved through the "generous surrender of his own person to another for the whole span of life." But this is to be a cooperating author with God in *this* or *that* particular marriage, not an originator or definer of marriage compacts. Man's will is important in the institution of a particular marriage, because he must freely will to enter it, but he has no say over what marriage is and what it is ordered to.[6]

Thus, all marriage, even the natural marriage, is of divine institution, its essence beyond man's power or authority to define.

2) *Marriage is ordered to offspring*

Of the three aforementioned goods (offspring, spousal fidelity, and the sacrament), the fundamental one is offspring:

---

4   I use the English translations taken from the Vatican website. However, I have substituted "good" as a translation of the Latin *bonum*, which was rendered in the original with the word "blessing." While I think *bonum* can be translated as "blessing," it loses something of the notion of an *end*, which is fundamental for understanding what the pope will later be talking about.

5   *Casti Connubii* 9.

6   This does not, by the way, make marriage a non-natural relationship, for it arises out of that love which is "according to nature" and a "naturally indivisible union" (*Arcanum* 9). The union is a "foreshadowing of the Incarnation," in which there is something "holy and religious...implanted by nature" (*Arcanum* 19). This will be clearer when considering some of Paul VI's passages later on, but in proving that marriage is instituted by God, the popes are not so much declaring it outside of nature as they are showing that it is part of the fundamental nature of things.

The child holds the first place. And indeed the Creator of the human race Himself, Who in His goodness wishes to use men as His helpers in the propagation of life, taught this when, instituting marriage in Paradise, He said to our first parents, and through them to all future spouses: "Increase and multiply, and fill the earth."[7]

This good is not to be understood to be completed in procreation, but rather:

> Something else must be added, namely the proper education of the offspring. For the most wise God would have failed to make sufficient provision for children that had been born, and so for the whole human race, if He had not given to those to whom He had entrusted the power and right to beget them, the power also and the right to educate them.[8]

And thus it is clear that of the goods of marriage the child has priority, and not just the conception of the child, but his *perfection* as well. Moreover, this perfection is the responsibility of parents. They have the "power" and "right" to be the educators. This is true, again, even in the natural marriage. *The perfection of offspring is the first good of any marriage, and the first responsibility of the parents.* It is not to the state that we must look for the primary educators of children, but to the parents. This authority is theirs according to the nature of the institution.

3) Marriage is ordered to spousal fidelity

The second good of marriage is that of the fidelity of the spouses. Again, Pius XI explains:

> The second good of matrimony... is the good of conjugal honor which consists in the mutual fidelity of the spouses in fulfilling the marriage contract, so that what belongs to one of the parties by reason of this contract sanctioned by divine law, may not be denied to him or permitted to any third person; nor may there be conceded to one of the parties anything which, being contrary to the rights and laws of God and entirely opposed to matrimonial faith, can never be conceded. Wherefore, conjugal faith, or honor, demands in the first place the complete unity of matrimony which

---

[7] *Casti Connubii* 11.
[8] *Casti Connubii* 16.

the Creator Himself laid down in the beginning when He wished it to be not otherwise than between one man and one woman.[9]

Marriage, every marriage, is definitively between one man and one woman; it is therefore both an *exclusive* union of two spouses, and a union only of man and woman. The pope's aim in this part of the encyclical[10] is primarily to demonstrate from Scripture and Tradition that polygamy is not allowed to the Christian—or to the marriage instituted by God and restored by Christ—but he is also stating that one cannot have marriage without the complementarity of man and woman. Other popes repeatedly confirm this point,[11] as does Trent.[12]

Complementarity is important in its own right, inasmuch as it demonstrates that Catholics must indeed defend the truth that marriage can take place only between a man and a woman, of course; but it is also significant in that it denotes the *unity* of matrimony is first characterized by male-female complementarity.

Paul VI clarifies the nature of this complementarity by considering the nature of the marital act in particular.

> The fundamental nature of the marriage act, while uniting husband and wife in the closest intimacy, also renders them capable of generating new life—and this as a result of laws written into the actual nature of man and of woman. And if each of these essential qualities, the unitive and the procreative, is preserved, the use of marriage fully retains its sense of true mutual love and its ordination to the supreme responsibility of parenthood to which man is called.[13]

The union of husband and wife is a relationship uniquely oriented precisely insofar as it is a union that in its expression, its "making manifest" the *nature* of the unity in question, renders the two capable of generating life. *The unity of spouses is defined according to its natural openness to new life.*

---

9 *Casti Connubii* 19–20.
10 *Casti Connubii* 20–21.
11 *Arcanum* 5, 9, 24; *Humanae Vitae* 8–9, 11–12.
12 Council of Trent, Session 24, Doctrine; Roman Catechism, Definition of Matrimony.
13 *Humanae Vitae* 12.

Moreover, as Paul is clear to state, this unity is ordered to not just procreation, but "responsible parenthood." The perfection, not simply the existence, of the child is the end of the union. Paul confirms Pius's earlier argument: the union of marriage brings with it the responsibility of *perfecting* offspring.

None of this is to deny that the love of spouses is for the sake of the spouses, or that their unity is not for their own sakes. The popes are adamant that this fidelity is for the sake of the spouses, for they are bound by it "to give one another an unfailing and unselfish help."[14] The popes, however, are concerned to make a deeper point. The unity of spouses, which is the good of conjugal fidelity, is *in itself* an openness to new life. The desire for the good of one's spouse cannot be intrinsically separated from the good of offspring.[15]

It must here be remarked that infertile spouses, while their situation is deeply regrettable for accidental reasons, still have that unity "written into the actual nature of man and woman." Infertility, even when it is foreseen, *does not alter the nature of man and woman, nor of this man and this woman* (husband and wife), and therefore it does not alter the *nature* of their relationship.[16] It is merely an impediment beyond anyone's will that makes it impossible for them to conceive. Moreover, since as they are indeed man and woman, their unity can be ordered to the generation of life and therefore its perfection.[17]

Thus, to follow out the popes' teachings in respect to the second good, we see that it connects to and completes our understanding

---

14   *Arcanum Divinae* 11.

15   The depth of this conjugal love is infinitely deepened by the sacrament, and it is in the sacrament that one best understands the good of conjugal faith. For, as all the popes point out, the Christian couple images Christ's relationship to His Body, the Church. Thus, the *Christian* couple is ordered to the spouses' mutual salvation, and through that ordination they also intend, not accidentally, the salvation of new life.

16   *Humanae Vitae* 11.

17   It is in these points that one must recognize the essential, natural law problem with homosexual activity. The agents are attempting to express a unity their act simply and by its "nature" cannot express. There is no impediment, for there is no marital complementarity in the agents. No matter how much one may *want* it, it is intrinsically absent. Thus, when one also considers the good of children and the perfection of children, it is clear that a homosexual couple cannot parent. Their relationship cannot be the life-generating unity context that children are to be raised in. The love that members of the same sex can have for each other, while great, cannot be the love of parents.

of the first. *The unity of spouses in any marriage is to be understood as that sort of unity that according to its nature renders the agents capable of generating and perfecting new life. The spouses' love for each other and their conjugal faith is to be understood according to its life-giving and life-perfecting complementarity.*

4) Marriage is ordered to the Sacrament

Finally, marriage is a union ordered to the *sacrament* of marriage. What does this mean? It means that Catholics must understand even the natural marriage in light of and for the sake of the sacrament whereby the spouses symbolize the union of Christ and His Church. Pius XI argues this by first clarifying what Augustine and Trent mean by saying that "the sacrament" is a good of marriage.

> But this accumulation of benefits is completed and, as it were, crowned by that good of Christian marriage which in the words of St Augustine we have called the sacrament, by which is denoted both the indissolubility of the bond and the raising and hallowing of the contract by Christ Himself, whereby He made it an efficacious sign of grace.[18]

This indissolubility, to be clear, is characteristic of all marriages (even non-sacramental). Pius first notes that there is an inviolable bond which belongs to every marriage:

> And this inviolable stability, although not in the same perfect measure in every case, belongs to every true marriage, for the word of the Lord: "What God hath joined together let no man put asunder," must of necessity include all true marriages without exception.[19]

Immediately after this, he points out that the seeming "exceptions" to this permanent character (he is thinking of the Petrine and Pauline Privileges) do not contradict the inviolable stability *in the nature* of all true marriages:

> And if this stability seems to be open to exception, however rare the exception may be, as in the case of certain natural marriages between unbelievers, or amongst Christians in the case of those

---

18 *Casti Connubii* 31.
19 *Casti Connubii* 34.

marriages which though valid have not been consummated, that exception does not depend on the will of men nor on that of any merely human power, but on divine law, of which the only guardian and interpreter is the Church of Christ. However, not even this power can ever affect for any cause whatsoever a Christian marriage which is valid and has been consummated, for as it is plain that here the marriage contract has its full completion, so, by the will of God, there is also the greatest firmness and indissolubility which may not be destroyed by any human authority.[20]

Hence, even natural marriages cannot be dissolved by any natural authority. Catholics must recognize that the consummated, sacramental marriage is the *completion* of the marriage contract and is indissoluble simply speaking, but even the natural marriage is unable to be dissolved by any human authority and therefore indissoluble by any natural power.

The indissoluble character of *all* marriages is explained by the good introduced when Christ raised marriage to the level of a sacrament, since it is in the raising of the institution to the level of a sacrament (and to the "mystical signification of Christian marriage") that one sees the "intimate reason"[21] in the decree. All true marriages, in other words, are in themselves naturally inviolable for the sake of making marriage a fit institution to bear the sacramentality Christ now bestows upon it in a Christian context.

Thus it is clear that even the natural marriage is in itself inviolable, and Christians must see the good of the sacrament in all marriages. Even the true marriage of unbelievers bears a certain implicit testament to the relationship of Christ and his Church (though it does not symbolize this relationship).

5) Marriage defined

The four points above set out a definition of marriage that is totally beyond the power/authority of man. *Marriage is the naturally indissoluble institution, established by God through the wills of the spouses, wherein a man and a woman are made one in such a way as to render them capable of generating and perfecting life, for*

---

20 *Casti Connubii* 35.
21 *Casti Connubii* 36.

the sake of offspring, conjugal fidelity, and the sacrament. Without all these aspects being respected (at least implicitly), there is no marriage, natural or sacramental.

The Authority of the State

6) The State has no authority over the nature of any true marriage

It is evident from the above that the nature of marriage is in no way under the authority of man, for it is established by God. Whatever authority man has, it is as a *participating* agent in God's plan.

The popes also argue that the authority of the state extends neither over the nature of marriage, nor over rights of individual men and women seeking real marriages. Recall, first of all, that the perpetual bond of any true marriage is beyond the power of civil law:

> In such a marriage, inasmuch as it is a true marriage, there must remain and indeed there does remain that perpetual bond which by divine right is so bound up with matrimony from its first institution that it is not subject to any civil power.[22]

The perpetual bond of marriage is beyond civil power *because* it is bound up with the very institution of marriage. The civil power, in other words, does not extend to the nature of the institution of marriage. Furthermore: "To take away from man the natural and primeval right of marriage, to circumscribe in any way the principal ends of marriage laid down in the beginning by God Himself in the words 'Increase and multiply' (Gen 1:28) is beyond the power of any human law."[23] So also, then, the ends of marriage—the goods and purposes for which it exists according to the nature of its institution—are similarly beyond the power of the state.

Finally, Pius XI states that a civil power that seeks to claim authority over the faculty of marriage is in reality "arrogat[ing] to itself a power over a faculty which it never had and can never legitimately possess."[24] Thus, the state has no power to *define* marriage (for it is only God's to define), it has no power to circumscribe the ends of marriage, and it cannot claim authority over the faculty

---

22 *Casti Connubii* 34.
23 *Casti Connubii* 8.
24 *Casti Connubii* 68.

of marriage. Therefore, Catholics must recognize that the intrinsic goods of marriage (offspring, spousal fidelity, and the sacrament) cannot be stripped away from any true marriage and that the state has no power to do so or to re-define the marital union (whether it be the natural or the sacramental union).

7) The State has authority to act against the vices opposing marriage

Yet, the state does have obligations in regards to this holy institution. For, while it has no power over it or the marriage faculty, it *does* have authority to preserve and protect society. And the popes clearly argue that marriage and family are the *foundation* of society.

> Just laws must be made for the protection of chastity, for reciprocal conjugal aid, and for similar purposes, and these must be faithfully enforced, because, as history testifies, the prosperity of the State and the temporal happiness of its citizens cannot remain safe and sound where the foundation on which they are established, which is the moral order, is weakened and where the very fountainhead from which the State draws its life, namely, wedlock and the family, is obstructed by the vices of its citizens.[25]

Leo XIII also points out that the effects of marriage must be protected, to ensure that no harm comes to the children.[26] The perfection of offspring is the principle of conjugal unity; it is the *responsibility* and therefore *the right* of conjugal pairs to work for that perfection. The very union of marriage is ordered to the upbringing of children, and therefore the formation of citizens. *This means the state must take an interest in the safety and security of marriage, if only for the sake of its own stability.* It has no authority over the essential nature of marriage, as demonstrated above, so its power lies in protection. The moral law must be promoted; vices must be opposed, especially those vices and anything else that threaten the life of marriage and the family.

Leo XIII further clarifies the basis of the state's authority in relation to marriage by noting that it consists first and foremost in a state's recognition of *true* marriages: "Further, the civil law can deal with and decide those matters alone which in the civil order

---

25 *Casti Connubii* 123.
26 *Arcanum Divinae* 40.

spring from marriage, and which cannot possibly exist, as is evident, unless there be a true and lawful cause of them, that is to say, the nuptial bond" (*Arcanum*, 40). The state is concerned with those aspects of marriage that connect to civil order, but the state must order itself to the nuptial bond *as it is in itself*; any laws for the sake of civic order must be based upon a recognition of the *truth*.

In sum, though the state cannot assume authority over the essence of the institution, it must strive to preserve and protect it insofar as it may. The popes urge, first and foremost, that laws be made that protect chastity and aid conjugal fidelity (some easy examples of such laws would be anti-pornographic laws, or laws against prostitution). Furthermore, any legitimate authority the state has in relation to marriage must begin with a *recognition* (in the laws themselves) of the true nuptial bond.

The Significance of the Legalization of Homosexual "Marriage"

In light of these statements and reasons, Catholics must recognize the grave dangers this ruling compounds, and those it introduces.

8) The state's legal recognition of homosexual "marriage" confirms and adds to the errors already present in our culture

The state has long been failing in its duty inasmuch as the legalization of such things as divorce, contraception, and abortion solidifies and lends credence to *false notions* of marriage. Among other moral problems, these notions make it harder for true marriages to be entered into by would-be spouses who are formed according to these errors. The state should be defending the institution precisely against these errors, but we find in our nation that the laws rather confirm them. Since the culture of the nation supposes that marriage is what it is not, these would-be spouses' wills have obstacles to true union. For example, if one goes into a "marriage" with the explicit notion that it is dissolvable, or explicitly intending never to have children, one is not truly married.

For all this, however, a non-believer who goes into a marriage intending it to be for the rest of his life and for the sake of raising children still aims to enter that union which renders him generative and perfective of life. The basic *character* of marriage is retained in the midst of the errors promoted by divorce and contraception. The non-believer may not fully grasp what he is doing, but he may indeed intend the reality.

The acceptance of homosexual "marriage," however, compounds and adds to these errors against the holy institution by putting forth the notion that the complementarity of the sexes is not intrinsic to the sexual union. The marital act, and through it the marital union, is stripped of all the intrinsic characteristics that allow for the direct link to acting with God in *generating* new life, and therefore also the intrinsic responsibility and right for *perfecting* new life. Thus, not only is marriage seen to be merely a state-sanctioned promise of living together and sharing in sexual matters (and in other vague ways), but society explicitly loses sight of the sacred, set-apart union responsible for the upbringing of *children*. The state again fails in its duty to protect marriage by confirming society in this error, and it sets the nation against true marriage in an even more fundamental way by denying the life-giving nature of the marriage union.

The "spouses" (even those who are male-female) set in this false understanding will not be intending to have the *sort* of union that is the context for the family. *They may want a family, but the mutual promise comprising their union will not be defined according to the end of family.* The will of man works through his understanding (we can only desire what we in some way know), and thus when one's understanding of the character of marriage is so flawed as to admit of a relationship totally devoid in itself of openness to new life (and of the perfection of new life), one's will is severely impeded in making the vows of a true marriage.

Hence, the errors of earlier legalizations are compounded and added to (i.e., a difficulty for would-be spouses to enter into marriage).

9) The legal recognition of homosexual marriage directly opposes the security of the family

Further, in damaging the notion of marriage so profoundly, the legalization of homosexual marriage directly opposes the correct understanding of the role of husband and wife as parents and primary educators of their children. The popes (as shown above) all point to the connection between the generation and the perfection of offspring. Insofar as the perfection of children is the *first* responsibility of married couples according to the nature of marriage, the state must see itself as secondary to the parents in regard to the education of children, and this because of the nature of the institution of marriage.

Yet, as soon as one denies the essential connection between marriage and the rights and responsibilities of parenthood, there is no longer an intrinsic protection of these rights and responsibilities. As marriage becomes (in the view of the state) an institution without intrinsic connection to the generation and perfection of children, the parents' role with their children is no longer clear. The state must be concerned with the welfare of children, since children are citizens in need of formation. With a healthy understanding of marriage and the family, the state can recognize its secondary role with respect to children's formation. But insofar as marriage is no longer considered to be an institution beyond the authority of the state, the state has no clear limits in its authority over the formation of children. The parent is no longer seen as intrinsically the primary educator.

In brief, as society further holds (beyond the errors of divorce and contraception) that the homosexual union is a marital union, it cannot but abandon the most basic good of marriage, namely the generation and perfection of offspring. The essence of marriage, whereby it is the origin of the family, consists in its being the sort of union that renders the spouses capable of generating life. With that generation comes the right and responsibility of raising children as the primary educator. If one denies by law this aspect of marriage, one denies the rights and responsibilities of parents, and directly opposes the security of the family. *Consequently, the security of the family is not merely attacked by this law as by previous laws and permissions, but in a real sense destroyed.*

Conclusion

This much, then, Catholics must in conscience hold concerning civil and sacramental marriage, and particularly the recent ruling on marriage. (a) The state cannot determine the nature of marriage, and (b) it is in fact *bound* for its own sake to preserve the institution as inviolate. (c) Finally, the Supreme Court's decision directly violates the principles enumerated above. It assumes an authority not its own, and it acts directly against what is — as indicated by the Church — the very foundation of society and the state. Not only, then, is the truth at stake, but the truth about the first principles of society. Catholics must recognize and work assiduously to combat these errors, which are of enormous significance. The Church's teaching explicated above does not, perhaps, give us all the precise laws (or remissions of laws) concerning marriage that we should promote, but it does give us the general principles according to which we must apply ourselves. And it demonstrates the significance of the evil we are faced with. This recognition must be clarified to our brothers and sisters in Christ, and through them to our nation.

4

The New Natural Law Theory as the Source of Bostock's Error

James N. Berquist

Bostock vs. Clayton: The Arguments of Gorsuch and Alito in Brief

If you have ever wondered what practical significance the understanding or misunderstanding of the natural law presented by the New Natural Law (NNL) theorists might have in public life, look no farther than the strange arguments presented in the majority's opinion in *Bostock vs Clayton*. Neil Gorsuch, a student of John Finnis (a founder and chief proponent of NNL theory), argues the following:

> If the employer intentionally relies in part on an individual employee's sex when deciding to discharge the employee—put differently, if changing the employee's sex would have yielded a different choice by the employer—a statutory violation has occurred.... An individual's homosexuality or transgender status is not relevant to employment decisions. That's because it is impossible to discriminate against a person for being homosexual or transgender without discriminating against that individual based on sex.[1]

> Consider, for example, an employer with two employees, both of whom are attracted to men. The two individuals are, to the employer's mind, materially identical in all respects, except that one is a man and the other a woman. If the employer fires the male employee for no reason other than the fact he is attracted to men, the employer discriminates against him for traits or actions it tolerates in his female colleague. Put differently, the employer intentionally singles out an employee to fire based in part on the

---

1 See p. 9 of the majority opinion. This—along with the dissents of Alito and Kavanaugh—can be found at https://www.supremecourt.gov/opinions/19pdf/17-1618_hfci.pdf.

employee's sex, and the affected employee's sex is a but-for cause of his discharge.[2]

He completes his argument by means of another example:

> A model employee arrives and introduces a manager to Susan, the employee's wife. Will that employee be fired? If the policy works as the employer intends, the answer depends entirely on whether the model employee is a man or a woman. To be sure, that employer's ultimate goal might be to discriminate on the basis of sexual orientation. But to achieve that purpose the employer must, along the way, intentionally treat an employee worse based in part on that individual's sex.[3]

So, to sum it up: to discriminate on the basis of sexual orientation necessitates that one discriminate on the basis of sex, because if—in a thought experiment—the same inclination were present while the sex of the employee were changed, then the reason for discrimination would appear or disappear, respectively. Robert loves Susan (and openly lives in accordance with that inclination), and the employer is fine with that, but if Robert were actually Roberta, then the employer would fire her. It is all about the sex of "Robert(a)."

Alito is more than surprised at this line of argumentation and, in particular, the last example cited:

> This example disproves the Court's argument because it is perfectly clear that the employer's motivation in firing the female employee had nothing to do with that employee's sex. The employer presumably knew that this employee was a woman before she was invited to the fateful party. Yet the employer, far from holding her biological sex against her, rated her a "model employee." At the party, the employer learned something new, her sexual orientation, and it was this new information that motivated her discharge.[4]

Yes, but Gorsuch would say that while the information was new, it was only relevant *because* of the sex of the employee. So, Gorsuch would say, it all comes down to the sex, and is therefore in violation of Title VII.

---

2 See pp. 9–10 of the majority opinion.
3 See p. 11 of the majority opinion.
4 See pp. 11–12 of Alito's dissent.

The New Natural Law Theory as the Source of Bostock's Error

The key question, as both Alito and Gorsuch understand it, is what *motivates* the firing of the employee. Alito says it is the sexual orientation that motivates the firing, Gorsuch says that it is the sex *plus* the orientation that so motivates, and all that is needed (to be in violation of Title VII) is a "but-for" condition. Even while the employer focuses on the same-sex orientation, the fact remains that if the sex of the employee had been different, so also would the employer's attitude.

Alito backs up his explanation with the following argument:

> The problem with this argument is that the Court loads the dice. That is so because in the mind of an employer who does not want to employ individuals who are attracted to members of the same sex, these two employees are not materially identical in every respect but sex. On the contrary, they differ in another way that the employer thinks is quite material. And until Title VII is amended to add sexual orientation as a prohibited ground, this is a view that an employer is permitted to implement.[5]

So, Alito is saying, the difference between a man attracted to women (erotically, and acting from that attraction) and a woman so oriented is not simply that one is a man and the other a woman, but rather that one is erotically inclined to members of the same sex, and the other is erotically inclined to members of the opposite sex. Gorsuch, Alito is implying, is treating the "erotic inclination to women" as if it is predicated univocally of both men and women, but it is not. Thus, the motivation is not about the sex, it is about the different kinds of erotic orientation.

Alito's charge is absolutely correct. It would be helpful, however, to explain more clearly *why* one cannot predicate the particular orientation univocally of men and women. Gorsuch's mistake, which is absolutely typical of the NNL theorists in general and Finnis in particular, is that he attends to reality as if things existed in reality in the same way they exist in thought. In our thoughts, we can abstract and separate things that cannot be separated in reality. The NNL theorists and, again, Finnis in particular tend to treat of things separated in thought as if they could be separated

---

5 Alito's dissent, pp. 14-15.

in reality. This can be a danger in speculative understanding, to be sure, but it is deadly in questions of motivation, action, and practical reasoning in general. For we can separate good things in thought and then treat of their goodness or desirability as if they could also be parceled out, as it were, according to the separations or abstractions in our mind.

This must be further explicated. I do so by analyzing Gorsuch's particular error, and then showing the same kind of error in the principles of the NNL theory, and Finnis's work on fundamental human goods specifically. Finally, I show the danger to any judicial theory subject to these errors.

Gorsuch's Particular Error Examined

Let me give an example parallel to Gorsuch's "fateful party" example. Let us suppose that Robert invites his boss to his home for a party and introduces his boss to his "spouse," x. Is x male or female? The fate of Robert depends upon the answer. To use Gorsuch's mode of interpretation, this means that the action of the employer—and thus the motivation of the employer—will spring from the sex of the spouse. If "x" is Susan, the employer will be fine and happy. If "x" turns out to be Charles, the employer will be motivated to fire Robert. Thus, but for the sex of x, Robert would be fine. It seems that the motivation for firing depends upon sex, specifically the sex of the spouse.[6]

I don't offer this example facetiously, or to score any cheap points. I am sure Gorsuch's response would be that the sex of Robert was just as informative of the situation. But in reframing the example slightly, I am pointing out the kind of argumentation that Gorsuch is employing. He is saying that the motivation of the action on the part of the employer comes down to the information that leads to the understanding of the situation. The

[6] One could push the original example further in other directions. For example, as pointed out to me by Richard Berquist, could one not make the same kind of argument that Gorsuch suggests with reference to a man (not a transgender man, to be clear) being "discriminated" against because of his sex when he isn't allowed into a women's locker room? I presume Gorsuch would distinguish the examples, but one would have to say by the same line of reasoning that he presents in the majority opinion that the sex of the man is a "but-for" condition. Take the same example and change the sex of the individual, and no one has a problem.

employer learns of the orientation of his employee by understanding the sex of his employee plus coming to know the sex of his employee's "spouse."

This is true as stated, but the point in question is not what information leads to an understanding of the whole situation, but rather what is the reality of the situation, and in particular what is the reality of the *love* that is being talked about. I may say that I do not understand that a person is living a homosexual lifestyle until I see that he is erotically inclined and acting upon that inclination to individual men. I thus see *that* he is homosexual when I consider his sex plus his erotic inclination and action upon this inclination to other men. But at that moment, my understanding of "attracted to men" is differently said of this situation than it would be in the case of a woman "attracted to men." And that is because I hold that erotic love is only naturally ordered when it is between men and women. Thus, while my understanding of the reality comes from the putting together of terms in the way Gorsuch sets out, my understanding of the terms themselves changes as they come together. I cannot predicate/say "attracted to men" in the same way of men and women unless I am merely attending to the reality according to the abstraction and separation in my mind. Thus, the employer really can be motivated by the orientation as opposed to the sex, to complete Alito's argument, because it is not important whether the employee is a man or woman; what matters to the employer is the reality of erotic love, and he wants his employees to live in accordance with that reality.

Gorsuch is doing something the NNL theorists do consistently (if usually more broadly) and especially in their accounts of the principles of human agency. He is analyzing a situation abstracted from concrete reality, separating terms, and then saying that the agent is motivated according to this abstraction and separation of terms. Gorsuch thus considers a situation wherein a man is attracted to men (in the relevant ways) and separates the terms "man" and "attracted to men" as if the understanding of what it means to be "attracted to men" is something that can be understood so abstracted and applied univocally in reality. But "attracted to men" does not exist in a vacuum; it only exists in this or that individual, or you can say it exists in the mind of one considering it abstractly. However, the point is that it does not exist in reality in the same way that it exists in the mind. In the latter, it is predicable of either men or women, and thus it exists in the mind abstracted from proper or improper orientation. By itself, it indicates neither. That is *why* it can be said of both. But it exists in men (and in *this* man) as an improper orientation—i.e., not in accordance with nature, and in women (and in *this* woman) as a proper orientation—i.e., in accordance with nature. It is therefore the inclination *as it exists in the subject* that is pertinent. The employer is concerned not about the sex, but the *proper* or *improper* orientation of the individual employee regardless of sex.

To get technical,7 this is why logic and metaphysics (and also natural philosophy) are not the same science—in the scholastic sense—and why logic is an art rather than a science. Logic concerns the existence things have in the mind and the production of intentions, statements, and syllogisms, while metaphysics considers being *as such* (and natural philosophy considers *natural* being specifically). For the logical intentions exist in the mind and we incline to the reality through logical intentions. And thus while we use them in every science, we must recognize when we are considering the reality in itself, or considering it according to the logical abstraction through which we incline to the actual subject. It is not bad to do the latter; we do it of necessity, as the above examples indicate. But we must not confuse the abstraction's existence with the reality's existence, or the kind of predication that works univocally *in* abstraction with the analogical or equivocal predication that obtains in reality. This is the case in both speculative and practical matters, but perhaps there is a special urgency

---

7   To see a more technical account of the sort of distinctions that Gorsuch and the NNL theorists tend to miss, see Aristotle's distinction between the subject genus and the predicate genus in his *Metaphysics* (Bk. 5, 1024b1–20) as well as Aquinas's commentary on these passages (*Sententia Libri Metaphysicae*, Lib. 5, lect. 22, nos. 6–9 [Marietti]). Also, in the *De Ente et Essentia*, ch. 3 (Leonine ed., 43:374–75), Aquinas details the way essence is in the logical intentions, and thus also the ways in which a logical definition is helpful but not sufficient for science. The logical intentions always treat according to a certain level of imprecision, and this why they can be predicated univocally, because the differences between things are explicitly left out. Gorsuch is bringing logical intentionality to a fight over the nature of things, you might say.

in practical matters where what is important to the agent is what his action is about *in reality*.

Gorsuch's argument is practical (in kind) inasmuch as he is talking about the way reason shapes action. Again, he argues that *because* the employer would act differently based upon whether or not the employee is a man or woman who lives out an erotic attraction to women or men, therefore the *reason* for the employer's action in part comes down to sex. But this is to claim that *action is rooted not in being as it is in things, but rather as it is in the mind*. While it is true to say that we cannot desire what we do not know, and to this extent it must be in our mind, it is foolish to say we want things according to the existence they have in the mind. When we incline to a thing, we want *it*, not the thought of it. When we make something (and this the NNL is better about), we want the being of the thing in reality and not merely in our mind. But the being that we want (or don't want) is always the existence outside of the mind. As Aristotle and Thomas consistently say, goodness is in things.

So, to close off this section on Gorsuch's error, we should emphasize that the employer who is concerned that his workplace respect the natural order, and therefore wishes to prevent any scandal in regards to the true ordination of erotic love, is not concerned with the sex of his employees even in part. He is focused upon the good of the natural law and order regardless of a person's sex. Whether or not the employee is a man or a woman, the employer simply requires that the same reality be respected.

John Finnis and the (Lack of a) Hierarchy of Goods

In the next section, I detail the general version of Gorsuch's error that permeates the most basic principle of the NNL theory. To do so, let's first examine an identical mode of argumentation and confusion in John Finnis's work. In his influential book, *Natural Law and Natural Rights*, Finnis argues that there is not an intrinsic hierarchy amongst the basic or fundamental goods of human life.

To understand his position adequately, we should first explain what is meant by "basic" or "fundamental human goods" in NNL theory. Inasmuch as something can be listed as desirable for its own sake such that one need not reference anything further in order to explain its desirability, that something is called a basic or fundamental human good. Christopher Tollefsen gives a nice summary of the basic goods position of the NNL theorists:

> Practical reason, that is, reason oriented towards action, grasps as self-evidently desirable a number of basic goods. These goods, which are described as constitutive aspects of genuine human flourishing, include life and health; knowledge and aesthetic experience; skilled work and play; friendship; marriage; harmony with God, and harmony among a person's judgments, choices, feelings, and behavior. As grasped by practical reason, the basic goods give foundational reasons for action to human agents. Moreover, they are recognized as good for all human agents; it is equally intelligible to act for the sake of the life of another as for one's own life.[8]

The actual list of goods has been something the NNL theorists have gone back and forth on, but they remain consistent in claiming that the basic goods are those that can be reasons for action all by themselves. Anything that is desirable for its own sake (such that one need look no further for a reason for action) is a basic good or the instantiation of one.

John Finnis argues, in line with the rest of the NNL theorists, that these goods have no *intrinsic* order amongst themselves, since they can all be "good for their own sakes." Here is how Finnis defends the position in a critical passage in *Natural Law and Natural Rights*:

> If one focuses on the value of speculative truth, it can reasonably be regarded as more important than anything; knowledge can be regarded as the most important thing to acquire; life can be regarded as merely a precondition, of lesser or no intrinsic value; play can be regarded as frivolous; one's concern about "religious" questions can seem just an aspect of the struggle against error, superstition, and ignorance; friendship can seem worth forgoing, or be found exclusively in sharing and enhancing knowledge; and so on. But one can shift one's focus. If one is drowning, or, again,

---

8 Christopher Tollefsen, "The New Natural Law Theory," *Lyceum* X, no. 1 (Fall 2008): 2.

if one is thinking about one's child who died soon after birth, one is inclined to shift one's focus to the value of life simply as such. The life will not be regarded as a mere precondition of anything else; rather, play and knowledge and religion will seem secondary, even rather optional extras. But one can shift one's focus, in this way, one-by-one right round the circle of basic values that constitute the horizon of our opportunities.[9]

It all depends on what one focuses on in the moment or a given set of circumstances. Each basic good can be seen to be more important than the others, or perhaps one set over another. To present a parallel example, if one witnesses another person drowning, in that moment, the goodness of life will seem more important than the goodness of knowledge. But in a moment of persecution, one might recognize that one should be willing to stand up for the worth and goodness of truth even if it means risking or losing one's life.

But this mode of argumentation—while presenting the truth in part—is *exactly* like Gorsuch's insofar as he tries to make a conclusion about the order of goodness by an analysis according to the existence things have in the mind. Finnis's—where one's analysis of the situation rests upon certain concepts separated from others in thought (health and the further perfection of truth)—shows that one thinks about the situation through these concepts, and then concludes that in the given situation under consideration, one's desire and motivation for action is in accordance with that separation. In the struggle for life that occurs when one is drowning, one aims at the goodness of life, and probably doesn't even think about the goodness of knowledge in any explicit way. Yet, if I take a step back, is it not evident that even the drowning man desires life or health for what it is in *reality* and not according to the kinds of separation that occur in his mind? He may not attend to the fact that being alive and healthy makes him able to pursue the truth (or any number of other goods—indeed, all of them!), but what he wants in reality *is* a condition for the pursuit of these other more perfect goods, for that is what life *is*. If we recognize,

---

9 John Finnis, *Natural Law and Natural Rights* (Oxford: Oxford University Press, 2011), 92–93.

as we should, that man is ordered to the contemplation (knowledge and love) of the supreme truths—for it is man's intellect and rational will that distinguish him from all other creatures in the visible world—then we see that life and health are ordered to the knowledge and love of truth. There is an order *in reality*, and we desire goods according to that reality.

Whatever Finnis makes of Gorsuch's argument (and I suspect that NNL theorists could still object to Gorsuch's argument on other grounds, such as claiming that this sort of ruling violates the human ordination to all the basic goods—especially to the good of marriage—and also the genuine political harmony required for pursuing the basic goods), it is evident that Gorsuch is falling prey to the same kind of confusion found in the Finnis example.

The Broader Confusion in NNL Principles

To be clear, the problem here is not what I will call the "logical analysis" of the situation. Our actions are rooted in such analysis inasmuch as we come to know the situation in light of these separations in thought. This is what makes the NNL approach potentially more dangerous than most errors; it is so close to the truth in a certain respect. For it is true that in a moment of decision the agent will categorize and compare his options through such separations in thought. If I am thinking about eating some ice cream, I will likely in some respect weigh the good of health over against the good of sweetness and pleasure, etc. In that moment, the desirability of health can be considered apart, as Finnis says, from the goodness of knowledge or marriage or harmony amongst my inner passions, etc. But none of this analysis actually explains the motives of action, for it does not address the *kind* of desire. I may desire health itself for all sorts of reasons, or at least three, finally.[10] I may desire it because it is useful for many other activities, as Finnis first intimates. Or I may desire it because it is pleasurable (for instance, when one feels ill and in pain, the desire for health may be mostly about a desire to be free from pain). Or, I may recognize that my life according to my nature—and thus also all human life—and all other life in its own measure is a share in the

---

10   The useful, the pleasant, and the honest/honorable good. See *ST* I, q. 5, a. 6.

divine, as Aristotle puts it,[11] and thus something to be loved for its own sake. The point is that the *kinds* of desire are not identical with distinctions in the *kinds* of things. We desire many things and can desire them for diverse reasons. The basic goods are rooted in a division of *things*, but diverse motivations for action are finally explained according to a proper division of *goods* as such.

As one becomes more familiar with the NNL theory, there is a kind of irony here. For the NNL theory is predicated upon the division between the speculative order (knowledge for its own sake) and the practical order (knowledge ordered to action).[12] From the beginning, the key NNL point has been that the practical order has its own first principles that are parallel to the speculative first principles and totally underived.[13] One does not act except insofar as something is seen to be *good*. We only move toward something insofar as we are focusing upon its goodness. Thus, they argue continually, and with some real truth, that a good explanation of action must remain in the realm of practical truths which are all about the *good* that moves desire. And yet, the kind of analysis we see above is not in the practical realm, for it abstracts from an account of goodness as such. I do not incline to health according to the separation made in my mind, or knowledge cut off from life. To desire the truth *presupposes* the goodness of life. Even when I think it worth sacrificing my life for the truth, I am desiring in my final acts to adequate my mind to the reality, and that adequation presupposes my life. Desire does not follow the separations in thought and get cut off from what—in reality—is not separate.

---

[11] See in particular his *De Anima*, Bk. II, ch. 4 (415a26–415b2), where Aristotle reflects that the preservation of the individual and the species is the way in which each material life inclines towards the divine, since it is that share in immortality and life that is possible to the material being's activity. Rational beings have a higher participation, as one sees in the *Nicomachean Ethics*, Bk. X, ch. 7 (1177b26–1178a9) and the *Eudemian Ethics*, Bk. 8, ch. 3 (1249a22–1249b25) in particular.

[12] For an introduction to this notion, one could look directly to *ST* I-II, q. 94, a. 2. But I suspect a more worthwhile introduction could be found in *ST* I, q. 79, a. 11, which, along with much more (such as I-II, q. 3, a. 5), Aquinas expects the reader to have under his belt, so to speak. Practical reason is reason ordered to *action*, and thus practical truths are truths that are or can be the basis of the reasoning that goes into setting one's course.

[13] Again, see Tollefsen ("The New Natural Law Theory," 2–3) for an excellent summary of this point.

And this allows us to see the broader error in the principles of the NNL theory. Consider its beginning. The NNL began as an interpretation of Aquinas's article on natural law in the middle of his discourse on law in the *Summa theologiae*.[14] The first precept of the natural law, which is also the first principle of all practical reasoning, is that *good is to be done and pursued, and evil shunned*.[15] This good is the *end* or *goal* of action inasmuch as in practical things the end or goal is the principle of action and thus of reasoning about action.

Here is how Grisez interprets this in his foundational article. He holds that the first precept directs man to his ultimate end—which Thomas is absolutely clear about—but argues that this end is nothing definite:

> The will necessarily tends to a single ultimate end, but it does not necessarily tend to any definite good as an ultimate end. We may say that the will naturally desires happiness, but this is simply to say that man cannot but desire the attainment of that good, whatever it may be, for which he is acting as an ultimate end. The desire for happiness is simply the first principle of practical reason directing human action from within the will informed by reason. Because the specific last end is not determined for him by nature, man is able to make the basic commitment which orients his entire life. The human will naturally is nondetermined precisely to the extent that the precept that good be pursued transcends reason's direction to any of the particular goods that are possible objectives of human action.[16]

In other words, Grisez is making the same general sort of error we saw in Gorsuch and Finnis. The beginning of practical reasoning, he is arguing, is not goodness as it is in reality, but rather a non-determined "goodness," a logical concept of goodness that is open to all kinds of goods precisely because it is in fact none of them. There is a separation in thought, a separation that allows for universal predication, so that the principle of action is in things

---

14 *ST* I-II, q. 94, a. 2.
15 "Hoc est ergo primum praeceptum legis, quod bonum est faciendum et prosequendum, et malum vitandum."
16 Germain G. Grisez, "First Principle of Practical Reason," *Natural Law Forum* 107 (1965): 168–200, here 199–200.

insofar as "good" is predicable of them. Gone is the notion that the principle of action is the *source* of all goods, God Himself.[17] The NNL bases action on the *conceptual* good rather than the *final cause*. The good that grounds action is the good abstracted.

Aquinas explicitly rejects this notion of the end when he talks about how the final cause of any law is the common good. When considering the objection that law must order particular actions, Aquinas responds: "Operations indeed pertain to particular matters: but those particulars are referable to the common good, not as to a common genus or species, but as to a common final cause, according as the common good is said to be a common end."[18] Aquinas sees that actions are not ordered to *generic* good, but the actual common good. Action is all about ordering our lives to the ultimate final cause. For a rational creature, this must be, finally, God Himself.[19] Grisez thinks of the good of the first precept as a mere generic orientation, not as the actual good itself. For him the ultimate end must be something constructed and based upon a vague orientation. For the NNL theorists, goodness is in the mind, not in things — not because they think anything so silly as that we want things merely to exist in the mind, but rather because the desirability that motivates action follows the rational operations rather than preceding them.

One can see in all this the NNL's need for the basic goods, since the "good" of the first precept is insubstantial. And in the spelling out of these goods, we see the same general, logical error brought to fruition in the notion that there is no longer an intrinsic hierarchy of goods because all analysis of action and goodness comes down to the predicability that is rooted in the abstract separation of "good." Actions and things that are in reality ordered to one another are no longer so ordered, because their goodness is considered according to a separation in thought that allows for universal predication precisely because it refrains from precision.

17 See, for example, *Quaestiones Disputatae de Veritate*, q. 22, a. 2 (Leonine ed., 22:617.54–71). God is sought in every action implicitly because just as he is the first efficient cause that grounds all other causes, so is he the last end that grounds all other ends.

18 *ST* I-II, q. 90, a. 2, ad 2: "...operationes quidem sunt in particularibus, sed illa particularia referri possunt ad bonum commune, non quidem communitate generis vel speciei, sed communitate causae finalis, secundum quod bonum commune dicitur finis communis."

19 See *ST* I-II, q. 3, a. 8, corp. in particular.

In Sum

This kind of error is by no means unique to the NNL theorists.[20] And, indeed, because the NNL theory is rightly grounded in the absolute importance of truth, its supporters avoid many erroneous conclusions about human life. Grisez for instance saw the problematic character of contraception before it was clearly understood by many.[21] And in general, because they are so focused upon the logical analysis, the NNL theorists do an admirable job, often, of breaking a situation down into its parts.[22] But they never explain the actual agency of the agent, for they do not consider goodness *as such*. Rather they remain in the realm of "things that can be called good."

While I suspect that most of the NNL theorists themselves would find ways to avoid the conclusions of Gorsuch, we see in his opinion the same fundamental error of logical analysis. It's a perfect example of how this kind of reasoning—which orders desire and motivation according to the separation of concepts in the mind as opposed to the reality being analyzed by such separations—leads to absurdities in practical application. One loses sight of the real.

---

20   Perhaps the single best illustration of this error is seen in the Epicureans and the Utilitarians. They confuse the pleasurable and the honest good throughout all their treatises. They implicitly see that both are delightful, but are then unable to see that there is a fundamental difference in each case with respect to *where* the will rests. They thus confuse the motive of action with the predication that can be common even though in reality there is a fundamental difference of motivation.

21   See his comments to Fr Ford (who was on the commission set up by John XXIII and continued by Paul VI before *Humanae Vitae*), and, in particular, his first set of responses. These may be found at http://twotlj.org/BCCommission.html and http://twotlj.org/Critique-2-papers.pdf.

22   Robert George, *In Defense of the Natural Law* (Oxford: Oxford University Press, 1999), 46–48.

II
SPIRITUAL AND TEMPORAL POWER

5

Integralism in Three Sentences

Edmund Waldstein, O.Cist.

Catholic Integralism is a tradition of thought that, rejecting the liberal separation of politics from concern with the end of human life, holds that political rule must order man to his final goal. Since, however, man has both a temporal and an eternal end, integralism holds that there are two powers that rule him: a temporal power and a spiritual power. And since man's temporal end is subordinated to his eternal end, the temporal power must be subordinated to the spiritual power.

6

Nature, Grace, and Integralism

Edmund Waldstein, O.Cist.

If patriotism and love of liberty[1] are beautiful things when well ordered, they are remarkably ugly when disordered. John Brungardt has asked me to respond to a particularly outrageous example of disordered love of liberty from John Zmirak.[2] Zmirak attacks what he calls "illiberal Catholicism"—a name which he applies to (among others) Michael Baxter (for agreeing with Dorothy Day), Cardinal Dolan (for wanting universal healthcare), and Thomas Pink (or those who follow him, for reading *Dignitatis Humanae* with a hermeneutic of continuity). He then proceeds to call all of these good people "bleeping crazy" (or at least to claim that calling them that would be forgivable), and to compare their political principles to those of Hitler and Stalin. He then musters all the clichés of old-fashioned anti-Catholic polemics, and says that said clichés are all justified to the extent that Catholicism does not embrace the principles of the Enlightenment. Such an embrace he sees as having been developed in the USA, brought to its apex in Fr John Courtney Murray, S.J., and accepted by the whole Church at Vatican II. But this acceptance he sees as being under threat from the likes of Patrick Deneen and Thaddeus Kozinski.

Zmirak is evidently what children and journalists nowadays call a "troll," so I hesitated before responding, especially since many other blogs have already sprung to the defense of "illiberal Catholicism."[3]

---

1 See "Saint Severinus of Noricum and Arthurian Republicanism," *Sancrucensis*, January 8, 2014.
2 See John Zmirak, "Illiberal Catholicism," *Aleteia*, December 31, 2013.
3 For example, New Catholic, "Editorial Note: After 'reactionary,' 'illiberal,'" January 4, 2014; Artur Rosman, "Contra Zmirak: In Praise of the Inquisition," *Cosmos The In Lost*, January 2, 2014. Gabriel Sanchez also made a reply shortly after Zmirak's original piece

But then on its being pointed out to me that lots of our friends basically agree with Zmirak—even though they would not express themselves in such outrageously offensive fashion—I decided to write something after all. Zmirak refers to a group of Catholic thinkers much more worthy of being taken seriously—"men like John Courtney Murray, Michael Novak, Robert George…"—and so I will take this as an opportunity to address once again what I think is wrong with the project of "neoconservative Catholicism," or (to use my favorite term) "Catholic Whiggery."[4]

David Schindler's Critique of Liberalism

This time I want to look at a critique of Catholic Whiggery developed by a theologian who has devoted careful thought to the task, and who has entered into direct debate with Weigel, Novak, et al.—namely, David Schindler. Schindler's articles in *Communio*, and especially his strange and beautiful book *Heart of the World, Center of the Church*, have influenced my own thinking on these things a lot, but I have come to think on the one hand that Schindler doesn't quite follow his insights to their logical conclusion, and on the other hand that there are certain philosophical imprecisions in his account. His unwillingness to follow all the way through seems to come from a misguided fear of integralism and an acceptance of the common misreading of *Dignitatis Humanae*.[5] The imprecisions are a bit more complicated, and have to do with being, relation, and the good, and the order of the natural to the supernatural. If I find anything to criticize in the *nouvelle théologie* it is usually due to its exponents putting their speculative seven-league boots on when baby steps would be helpful. I shall try to indicate a little that the truths Schindler is driving at can be teased out more precisely with the help of some patient Thomism-of-the-strict-observance from Ronald McArthur and Charles De Koninck.

---

but it has since disappeared; nevertheless many relevant pieces on "illiberal Catholicism" may be found at Sanchez's blog *Opus Publicum*.

4 See Michael Novak, "The Return of the Catholic Whig," *First Things*, March 1990, online at www.firstthings.com/article/1990/03/the-return-of-the-catholic-whig.

5 A misreading corrected by Thomas Pink: see his "What is the Catholic doctrine of religious liberty?," available at www.academia.edu/639061/What_is_the_Catholic _doctrine_of_religious_liberty.

It is worth going back to Schindler's essay "Is America Bourgeois?,"[6] the opening salvo, as it were, of his attack on the Catholic Whigs. I remember coming across this essay by chance one day in college, and being carried away by the power of the argument, and even by its rhetorical skill. For Schindler, though his prose sometimes reads like a too-literal translation from German, is quite a rhetorician. Schindler was responding to an article by George Weigel that defended American culture from the charge of being "bourgeois," a charge implicit in a remark of Cardinal Ratzinger's.[7] Weigel had argued that far from being pusillanimous, selfish, and irreligious, American culture was in fact marked by generosity, devotion to the common good, and growing religiosity (this was the 1980s). Schindler responds that Ratzinger's charge had to be understood at a much deeper level. At the level of morality American culture might indeed be marked by generosity and community, but at the level of its deepest order and "onto-logic" it is marked by an anthropological atomism. Religiosity and generosity are (in such a culture) understood as a matter of persons' self-determination, extrinsic to their deepest being. Weigel's very framing of the argument, Schindler argues, instantiates this problem:

> [Weigel's implicit] view that relation emerges first at the level of action and thus is most properly a matter of the self's liberty entails a denial that relation emerges first and most properly at the level of being. But this is just to say that the self, at the level of its being, is precisely unrelated, is just so far atomic (simply an individual). In short, Weigel's conception of the problem ipso facto instantiates—already as a matter of principle implies—the claim that the relation of others to the being of one's self is external.[8]

Such an implicit anthropology makes religion, generosity, etc. a matter primarily of outward-directed *achievement*. A truly Catholic view on the other hand sees the persons as related to God and others in their deepest depths, and thus gives more importance to interiority and receptivity:

6 David L. Schindler, "Is America Bourgeois?," *Communio* 14.3 (1987): 262–90.
7 George Weigel, "Is America Bourgeois?," *Crisis Magazine*, October 1, 1986.
8 Schindler, "Is America Bourgeois?," 272.

[The] primary and deepest activity of a human being is to receive, to bring within, which is to say to interiorize, the relation to God and to all men in God which establishes us in being. In short, Mary's Fiat ("let it be done unto me"), understood in all of its ontological force, exemplifies the most proper activity of human being.[9]

This primacy of receptivity is rooted in the fact that we are created through the Word, the Son of God, who is entirely from and toward the Father. The Christian life is being like the Son. In the words of Joseph Ratzinger, alluded to by Schindler:

Being a Christian means being like the Son, becoming a son; that is, not standing on one's own and in oneself, but living completely open in the "from" and "toward." Insofar as the Christian is a "Christian," this is true of him. And certainly such utterances will make him realize to how small an extent he is a Christian.[10]

Schindler then goes on to argue (quite powerfully) that American culture shows an anti-interior ontological individualism in its capitalist economic structures, its Cartesian intellectual life, and in the legalization of abortion in the name of "the *right* to choose."

The Question of Religious Liberty

Schindler's essay led to an exchange between Schindler, Weigel, and others.[11] Weigel initially accused Schindler of wanting to go back to the "monism" of the pre-Vatican II papal magisterium, which Weigel takes to have been definitively rejected by the affirmation of religious liberty in *Dignitatis Humanae*. In a number of essays Schindler defended himself from this charge while attacking the account of religious liberty popularized by Fr John Courtney Murray. I want to look at one of these,[12] which

---

9 Schindler, 270.
10 *Introduction to Christianity*, trans. J. R. Foster (San Francisco: Ignatius Press, 2004), 187. See Schindler, "Is America Bourgeois?," 268.
11 Summarized by Mark Lowery in "The Dialogue Between Catholic 'Neoconservatives' & Catholic 'Cultural Radicals': Toward a New Horizon," *Catholic Social Science Review* 3 (1998): 41–61, online at www.scribd.com/document/294534729/M-Lowery-The-Dialogue-Between-Catholic-Neoconservatives-Catholic-Cultural-Radicals.
12 "Religious Freedom, Truth, and American Liberalism: Another Look at John Courtney Murray," *Communio* 21 (Winter 1994): 696–741, online at www.communio-icr.com/files/Schindler1994Communio.pdf.

later formed the first chapter of *Heart of the World, Center of the Church*. I think Schindler's own reading of *Dignitatis Humanae* is slightly wrong, but his critique of the Whig Catholic reading is brilliant and illuminating.

Murray's theory of religious liberty, which was indeed highly influential in the drafting of *Dignitatis Humanae*, is one that he sees as embodied in the First Amendment to the American Constitution. Murray sees the First Amendment's exclusion of the confessional state as fundamentally different from the laicist/anticlerical secularism of continental Europe. For Murray the First Amendment is an article of peace; it is purely formal, having no religious content, merely limiting the power of the state in such a way as to allow for the freedom of all religions. At the Council Murray argued that the Fathers should endorse religious liberty in that sense. Murray reads *Dignitatis Humanae* as doing just that, as affirming a purely formal, negative "freedom from." He considers the parts of the document that do not fit this reading to be to have been inserted for pastoral reasons, or by fathers who did not understand the main argument: "One might question... the prominence given to man's moral obligation to search for the truth, as somehow the ultimate foundation of the right to religious freedom."[13]

Schindler attacks Murray's position here with a very MacIntyrean argument; he shows that the supposed neutrality of such a formal, negative religious liberty is not really neutral at all. In fact in conceals an ideology: liberal ideology. "The liberal appeal to religious pluralism hides its own 'monism'; the liberal appeal to religious freedom hides its own definite truth about the nature of religion."[14] Schindler shows this in a number of ways; I want to pick out one of them:

> The simple but crucial point here is that a primitively negative relation (indifference) to God is not for all that neutral; on the contrary, it already differs from a primitively positive relation to God. A negative relation, for all of its being negative, nonetheless and for all that remains a relation which bears a definite meaning,

---

13 Cited in *Heart of the World, Center of the Church: Communio Ecclesiology, Liberalism, and Liberation* (Grand Rapids: William B. Eerdmans, 1996), 61.
14 Schindler, "Religious Freedom," 697.

one which excludes the priority of a positive relation. Murray's proposal thus serves as a matter of (juridical) principle to disfavor those religions which understand the human act to be first "full" of relation to God — to be positively ordered from the beginning, *in its very constitution as a creaturely act*, toward God.... The human act in its basic structure, for purposes of the constitutional ordering of society, is understood to be silent about God (cf. "articles of peace"). But this means that, when theists go on to fill this silence with speech, they must now do so precisely by way of *addition* and in their capacity as *private* members of society. Non-theists, in contrast, have merely to *leave* the state's formally-conceived human act *as it is*, namely, in the primitive emptiness which has already been accorded *official-public* status. Worldviews that favor silence about God in the affairs of the earthly or temporal order therefore always retain an *official-public* theoretical advantage over worldviews that favor speech about God.[15]

Schindler sees the root of this problem in the defective, atomistic view of the person implicit in liberal thought, and in an extrinsic/additive account of the order between nature and grace that follows from this. He appeals here to Henri de Lubac's famous thesis about a false view of the nature-grace distinction leading to secularism. What does this mean for the relation of the Church and the state? Schindler quotes de Lubac:

> It is from within that grace seizes nature, and, far from diminishing nature, raises it up, in order to make it serve its (grace's) own ends. It is from within that faith transforms reason, that the Church influences the state. As the messenger of Christ, the Church is not the guardian of the state; on the contrary she ennobles the state, inspiring it to be a Christian state and thereby more human.[16]

In other words, Schindler argues that the form of religious liberty promoted by the Catholic Whigs leads in fact to indifferentism and secularism — the very accusations that Lefebvrites bring against *Dignitatis Humanae* itself — and he even calls for a "Christian state." But Schindler is very careful to distinguish himself from "integralism" in the Lefebvrite sense:

---

15   Schindler, 721-22.
16   Cited in Schindler, 732.

Murrayites and Lefebvrites, however much they do so for opposite reasons, nonetheless converge in their apparent conviction that clear priority of religious truth is incompatible, or at least strongly in tension, with a principled commitment to religious liberty. In what sense is this the case?... Let me first of all repeat what was stated earlier: Vatican Council II unequivocally affirmed religious freedom and thereby unequivocally rejected "integralism"; and the importance of Murray in these conciliar achievements is indisputable.

Schindler thinks that *communio* ecclesiology offers a way of escaping both liberalism and integralism. It is worth quoting from his argument at length:

> If the state and the Church are to remain ever distinct as juridical entities, they nonetheless maintain this distinctness now only from within nature's internal relation to grace.... [The] whole world [must] be inserted within the mission of Jesus Christ: that the whole world thus become a "civilization of love." This intrinsic subordination of the world to the finality given in grace must always be maintained simultaneous with the juridical distinctness of state and Church. The former subordination without the latter distinctness entails "integralism"; the latter distinctness without the former subordination entails secularism.... [This] dynamic for the world's—and, in the way qualified, including also the state's—conversion does not deny but on the contrary affirms freedom, and indeed makes it possible. The religious truth that is now given priority is the truth of *communio*, and thus of love. This truth is not a juridical thing which can be imposed; nor is it first a string of propositions to be believed or a moral code to be enforced. It is first the person of Jesus Christ, as revealer of the Trinitarian God. Conversion therefore must take the path of discipleship: of our own relating to Jesus Christ, and of inviting others to share in this relationship. To be sure, this relationship bears an inner movement from and toward the Church in her reality as juridical organization, as dogma, as morality. But these have their primary meaning themselves only in terms of the love revealed by the Trinitarian God in Jesus Christ. It is the way of this love precisely to be free and to make free (Jn 8:32), and not to coerce. The way of the Church in her mission to the world can therefore never, insofar as the Church's deepest reality

remains that of *communio*, be to employ the mechanical-coercive methods of the state, even should she succeed in Christianizing the state's constitutional interpreters.[17]

There is much to be affirmed in this, of course, but I find the meaning that Schindler gives here to "integralism" questionable. He takes "integralism" to mean that the state is subordinated to the Church *without juridical distinction*, but in fact authentic integralism has always been about a form of subordination that presupposes distinction. Thus the Magna Carta of integralism, Pope Boniface VIII's Bull *Unam Sanctam* of 1302, is as much about the distinction of the two powers as about the subordination of the one to the other. Pope Boniface's argument for *juridical* subordination is precisely the subordination of nature to the finality of grace that Schindler wants to preserve:

> For, according to the Blessed Dionysius, it is a law of the divinity that the lowest things reach the highest place by intermediaries. Then, according to the order of the universe, all things are not led back to order equally and immediately, but the lowest by the intermediary, and the inferior by the superior.

Of course, Schindler's concern with juridical subordination is really that the splendor of the Gospel will be tarnished by association with worldly power.[18] Schindler is right to emphasize that freedom flows from love,[19] and that the Church's mission in the world cannot be marked by force and coercion. Nevertheless, as Thomas Pink has shown,[20] the Church does have the authority, and at times the duty, to coerce her own children. To think that love excludes *any and all* uses of coercion is (to reverse a charge usually made against integralists) "immanentizing the eschaton." "The use of the rod can actually be a service of love," as Pope Benedict XVI said in a sermon cited by Pink. "The Church too

---

17 Schindler, 737–39.
18 See my post "Tarnishing the Splendor of Truth," *Sancrucensis*, January 2, 2014.
19 See Fr Mauro Giuseppe Lepori, O.Cist., Letter from the Abbot General for Christmas 2013, "You Have Broken My Chains!," https://lnx.ocist.org/pdf/EN-Christmas.pdf.
20 See the aforementioned essay by Pink, "What is the Catholic doctrine of religious liberty," as well as "Conscience and Coercion," *First Things*, August 2012, online at www.firstthings.com/article/2012/08/conscience-and-coercion.

must use the shepherd's rod, the rod with which he protects the faith against those who falsify it, against currents which lead the flock astray."[21]

Dignitatis Humanae was careful not to contradict the integralist teaching of the papal Magisterium from St Gregory VII and Boniface VIII to Leo XIII and St Pius X. It explicitly states that it is addressing the native power of the civil authority in religious matters, not the power it might have as an agent of the Church: "Therefore it leaves untouched traditional Catholic doctrine on the moral duty of men and societies toward the true religion and toward the one Church of Christ."[22]

Pink shows that the lack of a native authority in the state to coerce in matters of religion has to do with the fact that in Christ religion orders us to an end which transcends the natural order—an end to which we are ordered by the authority of the Church, not that of the state. (And the Church claims this authority only over the baptized.) Pink shows how this teaching is already present in scholastic thinkers, and how it was very highly developed by such Baroque scholastics as Francisco Suárez. And yet, he shows there is a difference between the Suárezian doctrine and the doctrine of *Dignitatis Humanae*. Suárez had argued that the civil power did have authority to coerce in matters of *natural religion*. He thought that since man is ordered to the worship of the one God already by nature, and not only by grace, the civil authority had a *native* authority to forbid idolatry and such things contrary to natural religion. *Dignitatis Humanae* rejects this teaching, and the reason has to do with the question of the relation of nature and grace.

The *Natura Pura* Debate

Central to Schindler's interpretation of *Dignitatis Humanae* is the account of the relation of nature and grace worked out by Cardinal de Lubac. De Lubac was certainly no integralist in the ordinary sense of the word, but he was concerned with the *integration of*

---

[21] Homily of His Holiness Benedict XVI, June 11, 2010, www.vatican.va/content/benedict-xvi/en/homilies/2010/documents/hf_ben-xvi_hom_20100611_concl-anno-sac.html.
[22] *Dignitatis Humanae* 1.

nature and grace.²³ De Lubac's concern was with an account of the relation of nature and grace that separated them too much — a view of nature that saw it as a closed system to which grace was merely added on in an extrinsic way. Some of de Lubac's critics have suggested that he was chasing after shadows, but Schindler provides some startling evidence that the problem with which de Lubac was concerned is quite real. Schindler quotes Fr Leon Hooper, S.J., a follower of John Courtney Murray, as follows:

> [In] this world there are two sources of moral authority. Early on these were for Murray the state and the church, or, more generally, the natural law and the revealed law. Later they became civil societies and religious communities, or the secular and the sacred. Each of the two orders is differently based (in creation and redemption) and is directed toward different ends (civic friendship and eternal beatitude). Each can legitimately claim its own autonomy.²⁴

This is a shocking view of things indeed, according to which the natural order seems to be a system running merrily along on its own steam toward its own (earthly) end established in creation, while the order of grace is another system, added by the redemption (!), which does not interfere with the natural order, but adds an extra other-worldly goal to human life.

De Lubac definitely saw a real problem, but I don't think that he got every element of his account of that problem and its origins right. According to de Lubac the problem arose with the doctrine of "pure nature," worked out in late scholasticism by the likes of Suárez, Cajetan, and Bellarmine. Pure nature refers to nature *in abstraction from grace*. According to Suárez et al., one can consider nature apart from grace and understand it in itself, as it would be without grace. In the actual dispensation of Providence man is ordered through grace to a supernatural end, an end which exceeds his natural powers, namely the vision of God in God's own essence. But if one abstracts from grace, the late scholastics hold, one can see the end which is proportionate to man's nature.

---

23 For this reason, some, like Bernard Mulcahy, like to call him an integralist, reserving the term "integrist" for Marcel Lefebvre-style integralism.
24 Schindler, "Religious Freedom," 730.

Of course Suárez and Cajetan are not Hooper; they realize that in a way this end is the same as the supernatural end, namely God, but they hold that the proportionate end is God attained to by natural contemplation rather than by the beatific vision. Moreover, the proportionate natural end of man is not (on de Lubac's reading of Suárez et al.) replaced by the supernatural end, but rather the supernatural is added to the natural.

De Lubac argues that the late scholastic account of pure nature has the effect of separating nature and grace too much, of making nature a complete system in itself, thus preparing the way for secularism. But what distresses him most about the idea of pure nature is that it seems (to him) to exclude the beatific vision from being that for which man's human heart is restless, that for which his whole being longs. When man encounters God it stirs in him a deep "memory," the *anamnesis* of his origin;[25] he *recognizes* in God that good from which every fiber of his being comes, and he longs for him with a longing that goes to the marrow of his bones, to the depths of his soul, to the pinnacle of his mind; but (this seems to be de Lubac's point) if that longing can already be satisfied by the attainment of God proportioned to human nature, what need does man have of elevation through grace? Or if on the contrary that desire is really a desire that comes from grace, and leaves intact another, natural desire, then it doesn't really comprehend the whole man.

De Lubac's position has come under a lot of criticism recently by Thomists such as Steven Long.[26] I think that Long et al. show convincingly that the concept of *natura pura* is a necessary one for understanding (among other things) the gratuity of grace. Nature is indeed intelligible even in abstraction from grace. Nevertheless, I do not think that Long has satisfactorily solved the problem as to how the natural and the supernatural end relate in the actual order of Providence. De Lubac is surely right that the Suárezian position on this keeps the two ends too distinct. I think this is shown by the disagreement between Suárez and *Dignitatis Humanae*

---

25 See my post "Nostalgia for a Time that Never Was: Natural Law and Anamnesis," *Sancrucensis*, March 15, 2013.

26 See Steven Long, *Natura Pura: On the Recovery of Nature in the Doctrine of Grace* (New York: Fordham University Press, 2010).

mentioned in the last section. Suárez thinks that the state has right *derived from natural law* to regulate natural religion, that is, the relation to God proceeding from *natura pura*, whereas *Dignitatis Humanae* rejects any such right, and this implies that Suárez did indeed separate the two ends too much.

Long argues that while the natural end attains to God materially, it does not attain to Him formally. That is, the objects of the natural and the supernatural desire are formally *distinct* objects. He illustrates this with the example of seeing someone in a raincoat and desiring to meet him, not knowing that he is a great scientist:

> But to desire to know God in Himself under the *ratio* of "cause of the world" is somewhat like the desire to know Einstein under the *ratio* of "man wearing a raincoat." As "man wearing a raincoat" is an accidental denomination vis-à-vis Einstein, so to desire God as cause of the world is strictly speaking not truly to desire *God*, Who is infinitely more than cause of the world.[27]

I don't agree with Long here. In the Q & A of a lecture of Long's given at my alma mater Thomas Aquinas College, someone argues (and I think convincingly) that the relevant distinction between objects of natural and of supernatural desire is not matter and form, but rather confused and distinct.[28] That is, to desire God based on one's natural knowledge of Him through His effects is really to desire *God*, in Whom those effects really participate. Here the Platonic notion of *anamnesis* that Ratzinger takes up (in a text very dear to David Schindler) is extremely helpful. When one comes to know God by natural reason, one "recognizes" in Him the infinite ocean of perfection in which one's own and all created being participates. But of course this knowledge is very imperfect, confused knowledge; the light of faith gives a much more distinct knowledge of Whom it is that one desires. But of course it still does not follow (as de Lubac seemingly holds) that the natural desire is a desire *for the beatific vision*, because one can still distinguish between the end as the object itself desired

27 Long, *Natura Pura*, 20.
28 The full recording may be accessed at "The Loss of Nature as a Normative Principle in Catholic Thought," https://archive.org/details/674TheLossOfNatureAsANormativePrincipleInCatholicLife.

(God), and the end as *my attainment of the end*. Long's argument that by nature it is not possible to desire to attain to God by a mode that transcends nature is entirely convincing. Nevertheless, the natural desire to attain to God is really a desire to attain *to God*, and thus the desire given by grace really perfects, elevates, and completes that desire by revealing both more about Who God is, and by revealing an unspeakably perfect and beatifying mode of attaining to Him; it does not add another, independent desire.

Thus the natural order and the supernatural order can indeed be "integrated." As a great late scholastic thinker, Cornelius a Lapide, wrote, nature is *for the sake of grace:* "God's creation has been ordained, as to its end, to the justification and glorification of the Saints... for the order of nature has been created and instituted for the order of grace... that is to say, this universe has been created so that the Saints delight in grace and glory..."[29]

Nature, the Angels, and the Common Good

Steven Long argues that de Lubac's blaming of *natura pura* for playing into the hands of secularism by cutting nature off too much from the supernatural is really a misplaced accusation. The real problem, and what really plays into secularist hands, Long argues, is the evacuation of nature, the loss in the account of nature of its theonomic-teleological structure. While I have argued that de Lubac is right that the Suárezian account of *natura pura* is defective, I do think that he exaggerates the importance of that error, and underestimates the importance of the philosophy of nature itself in coming to (or missing) a truly integral, theocentric view of reality.

The main problem here is the view of nature formulated by Bacon, Descartes, and other Enlightenment philosophers, who stripped nature of its internal ordering to God, its teleology, and its participated forms.[30] But here too Suárez's late scholasticism is not entirely without blame. Post-Suárezian scholasticism obviously did not accept the full-blown Cartesian account of nature, but it

---

29 Cited in my post "Elaboration on the Foregoing: the Predestination of Christ and Our Lady as the Final Cause of Everything," *Sancrucensis*, December 21, 2010.

30 Br. Peter Totleben, O.P. has summarized this very well in a single comment: https://web.archive.org/web/20140409082113/http:/modestinus.wordpress.com/2013/10/10/orthodoxy-and-natura-pura/#comment-4764.

moved closer to that account than it ought to have done. The great Thomist Charles De Koninck in his work *The Cosmos* has some very harsh things to say about Suárez's corrupt late scholasticism, but he blames him not for separating nature too much from grace, but rather for separating the spiritual and the material too much in the natural order itself:

> Some are reluctant to see in nature a generalized ascending movement from imperfect forms towards forms more and more perfect. St Thomas did not hesitate. (See *De Potentia*, q. 4, a. 1.) The reluctance of modern Schoolmen is easily explained. Since the time of Suárez they have boxed in the universe. They want to explain everything in nature by intra-cosmic causes. By denying the demonstrative value of the arguments of St Thomas to prove in a strictly rational way the existence of pure spirits, Suárez cut asunder every essential link between the cosmos and the created spiritual world.[31]

The "created spiritual world" to which De Koninck here refers is the hierarchy of the angels. St Thomas does not think that the material cosmos can be understood without the agency of universal causes.[32] This doctrine of universal *agent* causality is of the greatest importance for understanding the hierarchy of *final causality* in creation. The picture of the natural universe that one gets in St Thomas is one suffused with meaning and order. The whole natural order is an image of the beauty of the Creator, and this order is restored, elevated, and perfected by grace.[33] The common good of temporal society is nothing other than a participation (a partial sharing in) that universal order. Hence the profound truth of de Lubac's statement: "It is from within that grace seizes nature... it is from within that... the Church... ennobles the state, inspiring it to be a Christian state."

---

[31] Excerpts from *The Cosmos* (1936) published at www.goodcatholicbooks.org/dekoninck/world/lecosmos-extracts.html; trans. slightly modified.

[32] See Ronald McArthur, "Universal *in praedicando*, universal *in causando*," *Laval théologique et philosophique* 18 (1962): 59–95, online at www.scribd.com/document/137090495/Ronald-McArthur-Universal-in-Causando.

[33] See my essay "What is the Primary Intrinsic Common Good of Political (or Imperial) Community?," *Sancrucensis*, May 31, 2013, https://sancrucensis.wordpress.com/2013/05/31/what-is-the-primary-intrinsic-common-good-of-political-or-imperial-community/.

The doctrine of universal causality is of great importance for understanding St Thomas's doctrine of the common good. While the angels are universal causes in the order of *agent* causality, the common good is a universal cause in the order of *final* causality. Understanding what that really means is I think the key to deepening and clarifying Schindler's critique of Whig Catholicism.

On the Difference Between Just Being and Being Good: Why Rights Are Not the First Principles of Political Life

Recall Schindler's main critique of Weigel et al. He argued that Weigel has an implicitly atomistic view of man. Relation and communion are matters of extroversion, of man going outside himself, on his own free initiative; matters of his achievement. Man's dignity on this account comes from his freedom and initiative, his ability to achieve. Schindler contrasts this extroverted view of man with the Christian view of the human person, which sees the dignity of the person in her receptivity, in her interiority, which flows from her receptive relation to the Creator, which is itself caused by (and in a weak sense) reflects the receptive relation of the eternal Son to the Father.

Unfortunately Schindler sometimes (with his speculative seven-league boots on) speaks as though the root of this difference is that the extroverted view sees man as substance, whereas the interior/receptive view sees him as being "constituted by relation" in such a way as to be *almost* a subsistent relation. As Michael Waldstein (my father) has pointed out, that can't be quite right.[34]

St Thomas's teaching on the order of final causes is very helpful in understanding better the truth that Schindler is trying to get at. As I have argued at length before,[35] one of the most misunderstood principles in Thomistic philosophy is this: "The good is that which all things seek, insofar as they seek *their own* perfection." What is meant by their *own* perfection for beings who participate being? St Thomas teaches that there is an order of senses in which this can be taken. At the summit of this order is God Himself: that

---

34 See Michael Waldstein, "'Constitutive Relations': A response to David L. Schindler," *Communio* 37 (Fall 2010): 1–23, online at www.academia.edu/15827163/Constitutive_Relations_Response_to_David_Schindler.

35 See my "Thomism, Happiness, and Selfishness," *Sancrucensis*, September 21, 2012.

perfection in which my perfection is a *participation* (*partem-capio*). Since creatures have being by participation in God, their *own* perfection is found *more* in Him than in their individual substantial existence. It is thus natural for creatures to love God more than themselves. When St Thomas teaches that God is the final cause of the whole universe, this is not to be taken in an extrinsic way, as though things where ordered externally to God's glory; it means that for every creature and for creation as a whole, God is really *their good*, not their good in the sense that they can enjoy Him (only rational creatures can do that), but in the sense that *their own perfection* is found primarily in Him. Thus the *elicited* desire for God in rational creatures is founded in the natural, ontological ordering toward God of their very being. The shock of love that follows the "recognition" of God in rational creatures is first of all a love of God *for His own sake*, although of course the desire to attain to God through contemplation follows immediately on this.[36]

At the next level *one's own perfection* is found in the common good of the whole universe, that good which most fully reflects the divine perfection. At yet another level it refers to the angels who are one's universal causes. At another level it refers to the common good of the human species. At yet another level it refers of the common good of a "perfect" human community — that is the common good of "civil society." As De Koninck shows at great length in his masterpiece *On the Primacy of the Common Good*, my *own* perfection is found more in the common good of the city than in my individual substance. The common good of the city is more lovable than my particular good because of its place in the order of final causality. (From this De Koninck immediately draws an integralist conclusion, which I shall take up below.)

So on Thomas's account one can see very clearly that from the very depths of our participated being as created things we are called to be like the Son, "not standing on one's own and in oneself, but living completely open in the 'from' and 'toward'" (to quote a Ratzinger text cited by Schindler).

36 On these various points, see Peter A. Kwasniewski, *The Ecstasy of Love in the Thought of Thomas Aquinas* (Steubenville, OH: Emmaus Academic, 2021); idem, "The Foundations of Christian Ethics and Social Order," in Waldstein and Kwasniewski, *Integralism and the Common Good*, 1:31–48.

In his original attack on Weigel, Schindler makes a very insightful comment on rights:

> A right in and of itself is a claim I have on another. As such a right is by definition self-directed or self-centered. Nonetheless it is often asserted that such self-centeredness is overcome when and in so far as this notion of right is universalized: when it is urged that everyone has rights. But a brief look at what is actually occurring here will reveal that such a procedure does not at all entail a transformation or reversal of self-centeredness. On the contrary the procedure merely—exactly—universalizes self-centeredness.[37]

St Thomas's teaching on the different levels of a thing's "own perfection" can help to show just how profoundly true this point of Schindler's is. Charles De Koninck in his reply to Eschmann's attack on the primacy of the common good states a fundamental principle of philosophical anthropology and politics that follows from a thing's own perfection being found primarily outside itself:

> Ultimately, person and society are not to be judged by what they are absolutely, but by what is their perfection, i.e., by what is their good; that is the only way in which Aristotle and St Thomas ever discussed this problem. To look upon the absolute comparison of person and society as the most basic consideration is distinctly modern. It is also distinctly modern to accord absolute priority to the subject and to believe, with Spinoza (who, in this respect, follows in the footsteps of David of Dinant) that "to be absolutely" is "to be good absolutely," i.e., that "ens simpliciter" is "bonum simpliciter".... From such a point of view, the problem of person and society quite naturally becomes the question: is the person better than society? instead of: is the proper good of the person better than his common good? When the problem itself has been so distorted, what can be expected in the solution?[38]

Ronald McArthur, a student of De Koninck and my *beau idéal*

---

37 Schindler, "Is America Bourgeois?," 283.
38 Charles De Koninck, *On the Primacy of the Common Good*, trans. Sean Collins, in *The Aquinas Review* 4.1 (1997), 319–21. An alternate translation was prepared by Ralph McInerny and published as *The Writings of Charles De Koninck*, vol. 2: *On the Primacy of the Common Good* (Notre Dame, IN: University of Notre Dame Press, 2009). Herein, the Collins translation will be cited, unless otherwise noted.

of an integralist,[39] wrote an important essay[40] in which he draws out the implications of this statement of De Koninck's with respect to the primacy of rights in modern political discourse. He unfolds the distinction to which De Koninck refers above between "to be absolutely" and "to be good absolutely." St Thomas of course teaches that being is really convertible with goodness; to be is to be good. But in created things there is this difference: a thing there is said just to be because of its substantial existence, simply because it is. How much of a thing is, or what color or shape it is, or whose brother it is, or where or when it is, are not simply speaking what make it to be rather than not be. Hence they are called "being in a certain respect," rather than just "being" or "being simply" (*ens simpliciter*). But with the good exactly the reverse is true. A thing is not called "good" simply speaking just because it exists; this makes it only "good in a certain respect"—good, one might say, in scare quotes—namely, insofar as it is. But it is called "good simply" (*bonum simpliciter*) because it has attained its perfection. And it attains "its own perfection," both by realizing that perfection as much as is possible in itself (through virtue), and by attaining to that perfection as it (more eminently) exists in its cause, by knowing and loving the cause.

The dignity of the human person does not consist in her substantial existence (just being), but in the perfection to which she is ordered (being good). Thus De Koninck can write:

> God's dignity is the only dignity which is identical to his Being, and hence infallible. Because no other agent is its own ultimate end, and because the proper end of all other beings can be ordered to a higher end, the rational creature is fallible and can lose its dignity; its dignity is not assured except insofar as it remains in the order of the whole and acts according to this order. Unlike irrational creatures, the rational creature must keep itself in the order which is established independently of itself; but to remain in this order is to submit oneself to it and allow oneself to be

---

39 See my post "Ronald McArthur and Authentic Catholic Integralism," *Sancrucensis*, November 8, 2013.

40 "The Rights of Man and the Tyranny of Law," www.scribd.com/document/182571048/The-Rights-of-Man-and-the-Tyranny-of-Law; a recording of an abridged version may be found at https://archive.org/details/Rights.

measured by it; dignity is thus connected to order, and to place oneself outside of it is to fail of one's dignity.[41]

That being so, McArthur argues, one can see how perverse the modern conception of politics is. In the modern conception man's dignity is seen as being derived from his simple, substantial existence. "Rights" are thought to inhere in man just because of what he is. And the order of politics, far from being recognized as a participation in a higher perfection *to which man is ordered*, is seen as an instrument *ordered to the preservation of his rights*. Thus we see the profound truth of Schindler's statement that the universalization of rights is the universalization of self-centeredness.

The Integralist Thesis

John Zmirak (remember him?) writes that the "Church inherited from pagan thinkers such as Plato and Aristotle a top-down philosophy of government, which centered on the 'rights' of lawgivers and rulers to enforce their vision of the Good in citizens' lives instead of the rights of citizens against the powers of the State."

This shows just how trapped in the modern discourse of rights Zmirak is. The philosophies of Plato and Aristotle do not "center" on rights at all; they center on the good. The fact that "liberal" philosophy does not center on the good shows how deeply illiberal "liberalism" really is—closed off to the truth that liberates.

The dignity of the common good of political life is intelligible only through its place in the order of final causes; as soon as it is removed from this order it becomes a monstrosity. To see this truth is to become an integralist. Charles De Koninck expresses this in a wonderful passage which has long been my favorite statement of the integralist thesis:

> When those in whose charge the common good lies do not order it explicitly to God, is society not corrupted at its very root?... Political prudence rules the common good insofar as the latter is Divine. For that reason Cajetan and John of St Thomas held that the legal justice of the prince is more perfect than the virtue of religion.... The ordering to the common good is so natural that a pure intellect cannot deviate from it in the pure state of nature.

---

41 De Koninck, *Primacy*, 42.

In fact the fallen angels, elevated to the supernatural order, did turn aside from the common good but from that common good which is the most Divine, namely supernatural beatitude, and it is only by way of consequence that they lost their natural common good. The fallen angels ignored by a practical ignorance (*ignorantia electionis*) the common good of grace; we, on the other hand, have come to the point of being ignorant of every common good even speculatively. The common good, and not the person and liberty, being the very principle of all law, of all rights, of all justice and of all liberty, a speculative error concerning it leads fatally to the most execrable practical consequences.[42]

---

42 De Koninck, 69–71.

7

Integralism and Gelasian Dyarchy*

Edmund Waldstein, O.Cist.

1. Introduction: Three Theories

Political philosophy or politics, according to Aristotle, has an architectonic role in the practical order because it is concerned with the highest good.[1] All other practical sciences and arts are ordered to it, because their goals are sought for the sake of the goal of politics, but the goal of politics is sought only for its own sake. Politics is concerned with the final end, and hence it is the final judge of good and bad, of what is to be sought and of what is to be shunned. It is politics that judges something to be good without qualification, and not only in some respect.[2]

Aristotle sees this as following from the very notion of the good as a final cause. In order to desire anything at all, one must see it as tending toward one's end, one's perfection. Most goods are desired for the sake of something else; food, for example, is desired for the sake of preserving life, and the preservation of life is desired for the sake of other activities such as festivity and philosophy. But such a chain of ends cannot go on forever. There must be some *final* end that is desired for its own sake. If there were no such final end nothing could be desired at all; human desire would make no sense. Nor can there be more than one final end, since in that case there would be no rational way of choosing

---

* My thanks especially to Alan Fimister for his critique of my account of *potestas indirecta*. I would also like to thank James Bogle, Fr Hugh Barbour, O.Praem., and John Milbank for their comments.

1   *Nicomachean Ethics*, 1094a–b.
2   *Nicomachean Ethics*, 1152b.

between different goods—the human will would be radically split and turned against itself.[3]

And this final end, which Aristotle calls *eudaimonia* (blessedness), is not only the goal of man merely considered as an individual, but even more his goal as a part of political society: "For even if the end is the same for a single man and for a state, that of the state seems at all events something greater and more complete."[4] That is to say, the final end of man is a common good, a good that is shared in by all without being divided or diminished.[5] And Aristotle sees this common good as being the good of the city-state, which he thinks of as a "perfect society" (to borrow a later term): a society whose end is man's complete good, and which includes all other societies (such as the family, the village, and voluntary associations) as its parts. Thus politics has the role of ordering and integrating all of human life, both individual and corporate, by guiding it toward its final goal. Politics is not a violent imposition of power, but a legitimate and binding authority that aids human persons in the achievement of their true end.[6]

Aristotle's marvelously simple account of politics and the good seems to be challenged, or at least complicated, by Christianity. "*Duo... sunt*": there are two by which the world is chiefly ruled, Pope St Gelasius wrote in his classic letter to the Emperor Anastasius, which was to be endlessly cited and interpreted by subsequent popes:

> There are two, august Emperor, by which this world is chiefly ruled, namely, the sacred authority (*auctoritas sacra*) of the

---

[3] Cf. James Chastek, "Christ's Pluralism," *Just Thomism*, April 22, 2012, https://thomism.wordpress.com/2012/04/22/christs-pluralism/: "Aristotle no doubt thought [this opinion] was logically necessary: if we lack one single court of final appeal, how will we avoid chaos and anarchy? If one person or body is not ultimately in charge, how is anyone in charge? Admitting two 'final judges' means that some disputes are unresolvable even in principle—unless we are so polyannic as to assume that they will never come into conflict."

[4] *Nicomachean Ethics*, 1094b.

[5] Cf. Henri Grenier, "The Dignity of Politics and the End of the Polity," in *The Josias*, June 17, 2015: https://thejosias.com/2015/06/17/the-dignity-of-politics-and-the-end-of-the-polity/; Edmund Waldstein, O. Cist., "The Good, the Highest Good, and the Common Good," in Waldstein and Kwasniewski, *Integralism and the Common Good*, 1:7–30.

[6] Cf. Edmund Waldstein, O. Cist., "The Politics of Nostalgia," in Waldstein and Kwasniewski, *Integralism and the Common Good*, 1:267–85.

priests and the royal power (*regalis potestas*). Of these, that of the priests is weightier, since they have to render an account for even the kings of men in the divine judgment. You are also aware, most clement son, that while you are permitted honorably to rule over human kind, yet in divine matters you bend your neck devotedly to the bishops and await from them the means of your salvation. In the reception and proper disposition of the heavenly sacraments you recognize that you should be subordinate rather than superior to the religious order, and that in these things you depend on their judgment rather than wish to bend them to your will. If the ministers of religion, recognizing the supremacy granted you from heaven in matters affecting the public order, obey your laws, lest otherwise they might obstruct the course of secular affairs by irrelevant considerations, with what readiness should you not yield them obedience to whom is assigned the dispensing of the sacred mysteries of religion?[7]

The so-called "Gelasian dyarchy" of pontifical authority and imperial power, of spiritual and temporal power, was deeply rooted in Scripture and tradition.[8] From the beginning Christianity did not deny the legitimacy of the existing political order; it recognized therein an authority founded in God's creation and granted by His providence. But it saw the political, like any part of creation, as wounded by sin and in need of healing in the present, and of elevation, fulfillment, and transcendence in the eschatological future, by a higher form of communal life. The order of creation was seen as a good but temporary and preliminary order—a sign of a yet better order to come. The Lord's famous dictum according to which one must render unto Caesar the things that are Caesar's, but unto God the things that are God's (Mt 22:21) did not at all conform to expectations about the Messiah. The Messiah was expected to end Roman rule and reestablish the rule of God. But our Lord does not immediately destroy the existing order; instead He plants the kingdom of God as a seed that is to grow in the midst of that existing order. Only at His triumphant

---

7   Pope St Gelasius I, *Famuli vestrae pietatis* (also known as *Duo sunt*), in Andreas Thiel (ed.), *Epistolae Romanorum Pontificum*, Vol. 1 (Braunsberg: Eduard Peter, 1868), 349–58, at 350–51; trans. John S. Ott, http://www.web.pdx.edu/~ott/Gelasius/.

8   The rest of this paragraph is taken from my essay "Religious Liberty in the Light of Tradition," found in chapter 18.

Integralism and Gelasian Dyarchy

return at the end of time will He replace earthly powers with the New Jerusalem.

There are many different ways of understanding the Gelasian dyarchy. I will discuss only three of them: Augustinian radicalism, integralism, and Whig Thomism. My main focus will be on what I term *integralism*, which I will argue is the only adequate understanding of Gelasian dyarchy. Integralism reads Gelasius in the light of the unfolding of his teaching in the magisterium of the popes of the High Middle Ages—from St Gregory VII to Boniface VIII—and in the light of the opposition to modern liberalism in the popes of the nineteenth and twentieth centuries. Integralism sees the two distinct powers as being harmonized by the explicit subordination of the temporal to the spiritual.

Integralism has fallen out of fashion since the teaching Church ostensibly abandoned it at Vatican II, and opinion is now divided among various alternative positions. I shall argue, however, that Vatican II did not and could not abandon the essence of integralism. Nevertheless, I shall unfold my thesis chiefly by considering two of the many alternate understandings of dyarchy. The two that I consider are not necessarily the most important, but I consider them because they formulate clarifying objections to integralism, and because they contain important insights that have to be integrated into integralism.

What (for lack of a better term) I call *Augustinian radicalism* comes close to abandoning the idea of dyarchy altogether. It takes a highly pessimistic view of earthly power, which it associates with Augustine's city of man; it emphasizes the *temporal,* passing nature of such power, and sees a quasi-inevitable conflict between it and the Church. The Church on this account should reject the coercive means used by earthly power, and by already living in an anticipatory fashion the peace of the heavenly Jerusalem, serve as a sign of contradiction to the powers that are passing away. This position comes in many forms and degrees. The writers of whom I am thinking in particular are Stanley Hauerwas, Michael Baxter, John Milbank, and William T. Cavanaugh as well as Dorothy Day, whose practical example serves as an inspiration to many of the others.

Spiritual and Temporal Power

Whig Thomism, on the other hand, takes a much more positive view of temporal power. The Whig Thomists emphasize the distinction between the two powers. Welcoming a certain form of the separation of Church and state, they reject any juridical subordination of the state to the Church, and hold that the influence of the Church on the state should come only through the Church's influence on the consciences of individual citizens. By far the most eloquent and insightful expositor of Whig Thomism was John Courtney Murray, S.J.

The question of the relation of spiritual to temporal power is intimately connected to the question of the relation between nature and grace. Christianity is able to distinguish between the two powers because it is a religion of grace, which does not destroy the order of nature, but presupposes, elevates, and perfects it. I shall argue that Augustinian radicalism tends to exaggerate towards a monism of grace, in which the natural loses all standing. Whig Thomism, on the other hand, tends to exaggerate the distinction, not sufficiently understanding that nature is for the sake of grace. Only integralism fits well with a fully satisfactory account of the elevation and perfection of natural teleology in grace.

The question of dyarchy is not, however, reducible to the problem of nature and grace. Insofar as the relation of the two powers is a political question, it depends on an account of the common good. Augustinian radicalism's theology of grace leads to an inability to see the transcendence of the natural common good of political life, and thus to a misunderstanding of what it means for political authority to be derived from God. Hence its excessively negative judgment on all coercive power, a judgment that is ultimately irreconcilable with magisterial teaching on political authority. Whig Thomism adopts a "personalist" account of the good, reducing the common good to a mere instrumental/useful good, and adopting a liberal misunderstanding of the role of political authority. This misunderstanding is at the root of the Whig Thomists' erroneous notion that the indirect influence of the Church on the temporal order through the consciences of individual citizens is enough to fulfill the demands of the Social Kingship of Christ.

2. Augustinian Radicalism

2.1 The Two Cities

The establishment by Christianity of an authority distinct from earthly power without the immediate destruction of earthly power can be seen as necessarily causing a violent conflict.[9] I have called the position that tends in that direction "Augustinian radicalism." The term "radicalism" is meant to suggest that it sees Christianity as challenging the roots of earthly power, and as having revolutionary social implications. "Radicalism" is also meant to suggest affinities with certain "radical" secular political movements such as anarchosyndicalism, with which Augustinian radicalism often shares an approach to concrete social problems, but Augustinian radicalism is itself thoroughly antisecular.

A figure often held up as an example by Augustinian radicals is the founder of the Catholic Worker movement, Dorothy Day. Michael Baxter describes Day's movement as follows:

> The ethos of the Catholic Worker may be summed up as a commitment to embodying the lesson in the parable of the last judgment. In that parable, the Son of man is identified as a king and the virtuous enter eternal life by putting into practice the works enumerated by the king: feeding the hungry, clothing the naked, visiting the sick, and caring for prisoners. Thus, performing these practices is what it means to live under the Kingship of Christ.... Thus the concrete embodiment of this christologically-formed politics has ranged widely over the years: fighting for housing rights for the poor; supporting labor, such as striking sailors and farm workers; setting up work camps for conscientious objectors

---

9 James Chastek once put the problem as follows: "Admitting two 'final judges' means that some disputes are unresolvable even in principle—unless we are so polyannic as to assume that they will never come into conflict. And yet this crazy pluralism is exactly what strikes Christians as necessary and reasonable since we recognize the necessity of civil society while at the same time having no religious civil code, even while we claim to make final and definitive pronouncements affecting the civil order. I have usually read Christ's claim that he 'brought not peace, but a sword' as simply another way of his restating that he is a 'sign of contradiction,' but I wonder now if there is not a more radical sense to it: Christ insisted on the integrity and even autonomy of civil power and his Church, even though he knew that one need not wait long to hit upon some point upon which they disagree.... Christ describes the world (before his return) as a 'house divided.' This strikes a very ominous note, given that Christ is very clear that such a house cannot stand since it is set in fundamental contradiction with itself" ("Christ's Pluralism").

during World War II; protesting against nuclear weapons; organizing resistance to the draft and the Vietnam War; harboring Central American refugees; and so on.... The Catholic Worker takes *Rerum Novarum* and *Quadragesimo Anno* in a distributist or decentralist direction, which results in a "localist politics" that provides an alternative to the depersonalizing bureaucracy of the modern liberal nation-state.[10]

Dorothy Day was deeply mistrustful of the nation-state. She often quoted St Hilary as saying "the less you have of Caesar's the less you have to give him."[11] That is, she wanted to accept as little as possible from the state so as not to be in a relation of dependence on it. If one accepts coins from Caesar, one must render taxes to Caesar, but if one makes no use of money, then one is not bound to pay taxes. Day wanted to begin living another kind of society within the "shell" of the old society: a new kind of cooperative society that would live entirely without coercion, applying the teachings of the Sermon on the Mount as literally as possible. The hope was that this new society would slowly begin to replace the old, violent, coercive, acquisitive society. As she put it:

> But, and I cannot stress this enough, we must never forget our objective, which is to build that kind of society "where it is easier for people to be good."... We must keep in mind the fact that we are active pacifists and anarchists. Or peacemaker personalists. Or libertarians, pluralists, decentralists — whatever you want to call it. It certainly needs to be presented in many lights, this teaching of revolution, non-violent social change. We begin now within the shell of the old to rebuild society.[12]

The new society that is growing within the old is a sort of anticipation of the eternal city; the old is passing away. It is not clear whether the old society will pass away entirely before the Second Coming. Baxter and the Protestant theologian Stanley Hauerwas, in a notable paper they coauthored, write that the old society will to

---

10   Michael Baxter, "'Overall, the First Amendment Has Been Very Good for Christianity'—Not!: A Response to Dyson's Rebuke," *DePaul Law Review* 43.2 (1994): 425–48, at 444–45.

11   Dorothy Day, "Sanctuary," in *The Catholic Worker*, February 1969, online at www.catholicworker.org/dorothyday/articles/895.html.

12   Ibid.

some extent endure till the ἔσχατον, and that therefore the tension between the societies will remain. Significantly, Baxter and Hauerwas identify the new society with the Church herself, which they describe as a form of political life. Therefore, they can describe the enduring tension as a tension between Church and state: "Christians are called first and foremost not to resolve the tension between church and state, but to acknowledge the kingship of Christ in their lives, which means leaving church-state relations profoundly unresolved, until the day when He comes again in glory."[13]

I have called Augustinian radicalism "Augustinian" because its proponents often use St Augustine's *City of God* to describe the relation between the old and the new. The "shell of the old society" is identified with the city of man, while the new society that is being built by the practice of the Gospel is identified with the City of God. Thus the Anglican Augustinian radical John Milbank writes:

> In Augustine, there is, disconcertingly, nothing recognizable as a "theory of Church and State," no delineation of their respective natural spheres of operation. The *civitas terrena* is not regarded by him as a "state" in the modern sense of a sphere of sovereignty, preoccupied with the business of government. Instead this *civitas*, as Augustine finds it in the present, is the vestigial remains of an entire pagan mode of practice, stretching back to Babylon. There is no set of positive objectives that are its own peculiar business, and the city of God makes a *usus* of exactly the same range of finite goods, although for different ends...[14]

It is hard to see how such a reading that identifies earthly power as such with the *civitas terrena*, and thus sets up an inevitably antagonistic relation between the Church and earthly power, is reconcilable with the Gelasian *duo sunt*. Of course, as an Anglican, Milbank need not scruple at rejecting the Gelasian teaching. Catholic Augustinian radicals, however, ought to do so. Surprisingly, however, Catholic theologian William T. Cavanaugh seems to argue that there is an opposition between the Augustinian and Gelasian positions, and that the Augustinian position is the correct one:

---

13 Stanley Hauerwas and Michael Baxter, "The Kingship of Christ: Why Freedom of 'Belief' Is Not Enough," *DePaul Law Review* 42.1 (1992): 107-27, at 126.

14 John Milbank, *Theology and Social Theory: Beyond Secular Reason*, 2nd ed. (Oxford: Blackwell, 2006 [1st ed.: 1991]), 410.

Spiritual and Temporal Power

The problem can be seen in considering the difference between Augustine's "Two cities have been formed by two loves" and Pope Gelasius I's famous and influential dictum "Two there are...by which this world is ruled." For Augustine church and coercive government represent two cities, two distinct societies which represent two distinct moments of salvation history. There is not one society in which there is a division of labor. In Gelasius' words half a century later, there is one city with two rulers, "the consecrated authority of priests and the royal power." The eschatological reference is not absent; for Gelasius, the distribution of power between priest and king is a sign that Christ's coming has put a check on human pride. Nevertheless, the element of time has been flattened out into space. The one city is now divided into "spheres," and, as Gelasius says, "each sphere has a specially qualified and trained profession."[15]

There is an important element of truth in what Cavanaugh is saying, as well as a subtle misreading of Gelasius (to both of which I will return), but first it is important to note his identification of "coercive government" with the city of man.

Although there are many differences between different proponents of Augustinian radicalism, they all share a profoundly negative view of coercion. Stanley Hauerwas is of course a pacifist. Following the Mennonite theologian John Howard Yoder, he claims that Christian theological justifications of coercive power are all betrayals of the Gospel aimed at making Christianity acceptable to rulers.[16] John Milbank's view is more subtle. He notes that St Augustine sees coercion as an effect of the fall, but that St Augustine also teaches that the City of God makes "use" of the peace established by earthly coercion, ordering that superficial peace to the peace of the Heavenly City, and that she can even make a "pastoral" use of coercion herself.[17] But Milbank sees this position as the "most problematic" element of Augustine's social thought.[18]

---

15   William T. Cavanaugh, "From One City to Two: Christian Reimagining of Political Space," in *Political Theology* 7.3 (2006): 299–321, at 309.
16   See, for example, Stanley Hauerwas, "A Christian Critique of Christian America," in *The Hauerwas Reader*, ed. John Berkman and Michael Cartwright (Durham: Duke University Press, 2001), 459–80.
17   Milbank, *Theology and Social Theory*, 410–11.
18   Milbank, *Theology and Social Theory*, 411.

Milbank argues that given Augustine's own principles even a "pastoral" use of coercion cannot escape the taint of sin:

> The revolutionary aspect of [Augustine's] social thought was to deny any ontological purchase to *dominium*, or power for its own sake: absolute *imperium*, absolute property rights, market exchange purely for profit, are all seen by him as sinful and violent, which means as privations of Being. But his account of a legitimate, non-sinful, "pedagogic" coercion partially violates this ontology, insofar as it makes some punishment positive, and ascribes it to the action of divine will. This is inconsistent, because in any act of coercion, however mild and benignly motivated, there is still present a moment of "pure" violence, externally and arbitrarily related to the end one has in mind, just as the school-master's beating with canes has no intrinsic connection with the lesson he seeks to teach.... Because punishment must, by definition, inflict some harm, however temporary, it has an inherently negative, privative relationship to Being, and cannot therefore, by Augustine's own lights, escape the taint of sin.[19]

The position that we see emerging from the Augustinian radicals is of an insoluble conflict between the City of God and any coercive earthly authority. All earthly powers belong to a tragic drama of sin that is passing away. The role of the City of God is to enact on the same stage a comic drama, through a practice of entirely non-coercive social life generously giving without expectation of repayment, and suffering evil without murmur or retaliation. In an evocative and amusing comparison, Cavanaugh compares the city of man to Ariadne in Richard Strauss's opera *Ariadne auf Naxos*, and the city of God to Zerbinetta, disrupting Ariadne's *opera seria* with an improvised *opera buffa*.[20]

2.2 An Integralist Critique of Augustinian Radicalism

There is much truth in Augustinian radicalism. It is quite right to emphasize that there is no third city between the City of God and the city of man.[21] I can even agree with Milbank's words:

---

19 Milbank, *Theology and Social Theory*, 426.
20 Cavanaugh, "From One City to Two," 315–18.
21 See Tracey Rowland, "Augustinian and Thomist Engagements with the World," *American Catholic Philosophical Quarterly* 83.3 (2009): 441–59.

"insofar as *imperium* lies outside *ecclesia*, it is an essentially tragic reality."[22] Augustinian radicalism is right to resist an exaggerated distinction between nature and grace (as the discussion of Whig Thomism below will demonstrate). Its own account of the relation of nature and grace, however, goes too far in the opposite direction. In following Henri de Lubac's teaching on natural desire for the supernatural, Augustinian radicals tend to evacuate the theonomic structure of natural teleology.[23] Grace elevates and perfects nature, but does not replace it. Divine charity does not invalidate the demands of natural justice. The supernatural end of the City of God is indeed the absolutely final end to which all other ends must be in some way subordinate; but it does not do away with a common good of temporal life that is final in its own order. And crucially, it does not do away with the coercive methods of natural political authority, even while it subordinates them (in some sense) to a higher authority.

The coercive authority of temporal rule derives from the primacy of the common good, from the fact that the common good is more divine than any good of an individual as an individual. Human persons are not parts of a community the way that parts of a body are parts. Nevertheless, they do relate to the common good in a way similar to the way parts relate to a whole. They *participate* (share in a partial way) in that good, as a good which is for them better than any private good of their own. The common good is really the good *of* the citizens (they are the subjects who attain to it), but it is not ordered to them as its end. Rather they are ordered to it as their end. Created perfection is a *participation* in the perfection of God, who is the most universal common good. That is, a creature's *own good* is found more in God than in itself, and all creatures *by nature* (not only by grace) tend more toward God than toward themselves. But God is not the only common good. In the order of nature, God's perfection is participated in most fully by the universe

---

22 Milbank, *Theology and Social Theory*, 425. It is not clear whether this is actually Milbank's own position, since he is merely trying to tease out the implications of Augustine's position in the text cited. But in any case, my analysis has shown that this is the direction in which Augustinian radicalism tends.

23 I have unfolded this point in more detail in chapter 6, and in "De Lubac and His Critics Make the Same Error," *Sancrucensis*, July 20, 2014.

as a whole. Thus the order of the universe is for any creature a *better* good than its own private good, a better good *for which it can give up any private good*. And, again in the natural order, the highest created common good attainable by human action is the common good of a perfect human society, which is a microcosm of the common good of the universe, and a higher good than any good belonging to individual men as individuals.[24] Thus Hauerwas is completely wrong to suppose that the Catholic tradition's acceptance of political uses of coercion (including capital punishment) is a watering down of Christian ethics to make them acceptable to rulers. Rather, that tradition is a recognition of the fact that even the temporal common good transcends all individual goods. The use of the sword by temporal rulers is therefore not violence done by one individual against another, but rather the exercise of an authority granted by God (cf. Rom 13) through the common good, which is "more divine" than any private good. Similarly, Milbank is wrong to suggest that any punishment must be sinful because its violence is only extrinsically related to the good to which it is trying to lead the sinner. In view of the common good, the authoritative use of the sword is really like a surgeon cutting the body for the sake of health — the violence, though a physical evil, is a moral good because it is intrinsically demanded by justice.

Cavanaugh writes: "the Church is not a merely particular association, but participates in the life of the triune God, who is the only good that can be common to all."[25] This amounts to saying that God *as directly attained to by grace* ("life of the triune God") is the *only* common good. This is an unacceptable monism of grace, totally unreconcilable with the Catholic tradition (as reiterated for instance in *Gaudium et Spes*).[26] Nevertheless, Cavanaugh's

24 See Waldstein, "The Good, the Highest Good, and the Common Good."
25 William T. Cavanaugh, "Killing for the Telephone Company: Why the Nation-State is Not the Keeper of the Common Good," *Modern Theology* 20.2 (2004): 243–74, at 274.
26 "Now many of our contemporaries seem to fear that a closer bond between human activity and religion will work against the independence of men, of societies, or of the sciences. If by the autonomy of earthly affairs we mean that created things and societies themselves enjoy their own laws and values which must be gradually deciphered, put to use, and regulated by men, then it is entirely right to demand that autonomy. Such is not merely required by modern man, but harmonizes also with the will of the Creator.

position has a certain plausibility derived from his critique of the modern liberal state, which he argues is not really ordered to any common good, and does not see itself as so ordered.[27] Cavanaugh's portrait of the modern liberal nation-state is highly persuasive, and it raises serious questions about the legitimacy of the political authority exercised by such states—questions similar to those raised by Augustine in his critique of the Roman Empire as being ordered to a false illusion of justice. To the extent that political authorities do not subordinate the temporal common good to the eternal common good they almost inevitably are sucked into the sinful dynamic of the city of man. All of earthly reality must be subjected to the kingship of Christ.

But how does such subordination take place? Not by replacing natural coercive power with a Christian anarchosyndicalism, but rather with a (moderate version) of what Henri-Xavier Arquillière controversially called "political Augustinianism."[28] Political Augustinianism differs from Augustinian radicalism in that it recognizes the legitimacy of coercive political power, but sees the need of integrating that power into the Church. Political authority thus integrated is not a separate city opposed to the City of God, but rather a particular order *within that city*, one in which the laity rather than the clergy exercise authority, an authority that they receive through the natural law and the temporal common good (at least on the moderate interpretation of the theory),[29] but which they must exercise to serve the eternal common good that is under the authority of the clergy. But that, simply put, is integralism. And it is the interpretation that the Church has always given to the dyarchy of powers.

For by the very circumstance of their having been created, all things are endowed with their own stability, truth, goodness, proper laws and order" (*GS* 36).

27 Cavanaugh, "Killing for the Telephone Company," *passim*.

28 Arquillière's book *L'augustinisme politique: Essai sur la formation des théories politiques du Moyen Âge* (Paris: Vrin, 1955) argued that the hierocratic political theory of the High Middle Ages was a development out of premises found in Augustine. This notion was vigorously disputed by other writers, who argued that the hierocratic theory is totally irreconcilable with Augustine himself. See Michael Bruno, *Political Augustinianism: Modern Interpretations of Augustine's Political Thought* (Minneapolis: Fortress, 2014), ch. 1.

29 The extreme version of the theory sees temporal power as being delegated by the spiritual power. I will show the problems with such a theory below.

3. The Integralist Reading of Gelasian Dyarchy

Catholic integralism (not to be confused with secular movements such as integral nationalism) was a name first applied in the nineteenth and early twentieth centuries to Catholics who defended the antiliberal and antimodernist teachings of the popes.[30] Particularly integralism came to be associated with a defense of pontifical teachings against the separation of Church and state, and the claim that the Social Kingship of Christ demands an explicit subordination of all areas of human social and political life to God through His Church.[31] But the roots of the Catholic Social teaching that integralism defends reach much further back than the antiliberal teachings of the nineteenth-century popes. They reach back to the counterreformation political theology to which those popes appealed, and even further to the development of Gelasian dyarchy in the teaching of the medieval popes.

In his classic study of the relation of lay and clerical power in the Middle Ages, Walter Ullmann argues that the medieval papacy's claims to authority show "a unity of themes and a consistency of principles" that were detectable even in late antiquity, before the name "pope" began to be used. And the most fundamental theme of these claims was the theme of the Church.[32] The Church was understood not as a purely invisible, spiritual community, but as a visible society:

> The Church designates the corporate union of all believers in Christ, as it was so manifestly made clear in Pauline doctrine. But this doctrine also makes it clear that this body, the *unum corpus*, is not merely a pneumatic or sacramental or spiritual body, but also an organic, concrete and earthy society. This dual nature of

---

30 For the history of the term in a Catholic context, see Christopher van der Krogt, "Catholic Fundamentalism or Catholic Integralism?" in *To Strive and Not to Yield: Essays in Honour of Colin Brown*, ed. James Veitch (Wellington: Victoria University, 1992), 123–35.

31 See Gabriel Sanchez, "Illiberal Catholicism One Year On," *The Front Porch Republic*, January 26, 2015; idem, "Catholic Integralism and the Social Kingship of Christ," *The Josias*, January 23, 2015. Note that "integralism" is used in by some authors in quite a different sense. John Milbank, for instance, uses "integralism" to refer to the *nouvelle théologie's* integration of nature and grace, and uses the term "integrism" for what I will be calling integralism. See Milbank, *Theology and Social Theory*, 206–7.

32 Walter Ullmann, *The Growth of Papal Government in the Middle Ages: A Study in the Ideological Relation of Clerical to Lay Power*, 2nd ed. (London: Methuen, 1962), 1.

the *corpus Christi* is of fundamental importance: the element, however, which brings this concrete body into existence, which makes the union a corporate entity, is the spiritual element of the Christian faith: this element alone gives this body its complexion. As a body the *corpus Christi* is in need of direction and orientation: although the many constitute this *unum corpus*, not all have the same functions within it. There are gradations of functions within this body...[33]

Given this account of the visible Church, papal authority had political arguments, and Ullmann shows that the arguments for papal authority can be understood as political arguments along the following lines:

In the realm of government the teleological principle upon which any society must needs rest, operates through the principle of functional qualification. For society and its government are two complementary concepts. The latter directs the former in accordance with its underlying purpose or aim, its "finis" or "telos." Only those who are qualified, claim to be entitled to govern; and the qualification depends upon the nature and purpose of society. The function of rulership presupposes the fulfilment of certain qualifications. He who is qualified to translate the purpose for which society exists, into concrete terms and measures, acts in the capacity of a ruler: he functions as a ruler, because he is appropriately qualified. This principle of functional qualification is operative in any society. The form of rulership or government, whether monarchic or oligarchic or aristocratic and so forth, may vary, but this does not affect the general principle.[34]

Membership in the Church was conferred by baptism, but membership did not of itself grant the necessary qualification for governing the Church:

Another element, namely ordination, was needed to secure, according to papal views, the right to direct the Church. The distinction between ordained and unordained members of the Church, between clerics and laymen, was the distinction which was not only to give medieval society its peculiar imprint, but also to

33 Ullmann, *Growth of Papal Government*, 2-3.
34 Ullmann, *Growth of Papal Government*, 2.

make the problems of this society, that is, of Latin Christendom, accessible to understanding. The distinction—not between Church and State, but between clergy and laity as parts of one and the same unit—is a thread that runs throughout the medieval period.[35]

The one qualified to rule the whole Church on earth was the bishop of Rome, as was already clearly expressed by Leo the Great:

> When Pope Leo I spoke of himself as functioning on behalf of St Peter—"cuius vice *fungimur*"—he succinctly expressed the principle of functional qualification in monarchic form. By virtue of succeeding to the chair of St Peter, Leo claimed that he alone was functionally qualified to rule the universal Church, that is, to rule it on the monarchic principle. This designation by Leo of the pope as "Vicar of St Peter" was new; the idea which it embodied was not. The formula chosen by Leo was the dress in which the idea of the *principatus* of the Roman Church was clothed. The idea embodied in the term *principatus* belongs to the realm of government. And government concerned the direction and orientation of the body of Christians, that is, of the universal Church.[36]

The conception of the Church that Ullmann lays out here seems to be monarchical rather than dyarchical; it seems to be a Christian, universalist version of the Aristotelian theory of the *polis*. And yet, Ullmann sees the basic lines of this theory as being already taught by St Gelasius in the very *locus classicus* of dyarchy:

> Since the pope alone has the *principatus* over the Christian body, the emperor, according to Gelasius, must be directed by the *sacerdotium*. The secular power has not only no right to issue decrees fixing the faith, since the emperor is no bishop, but he also must carry out his government according to the directions given to him by the priesthood.... Again, considering the nature and character of [the] Christian *corpus*, Gelasius's claim that the priesthood must direct royal power, is self-evident.... Consequently, in this Christian world, in the "mundus," the secular power has a mere "potestas," whilst the *principatus* of the pope expresses itself in the Pontifical *auctoritas*. And this *auctoritas* being divinely conferred for the purpose of governing the Christian body corporate, is

---

35 Ullmann, *Growth of Papal Government*, 1–2.
36 Ullmann, *Growth of Papal Government*, 2.

logically enough *sacrata*, whilst the emperor's power is a simple "regalis potestas." This is a thoroughly juristic terminology employed by Gelasius. *Auctoritas* is the faculty of shaping things creatively and in a binding manner, whilst *potestas* is the power to execute what the *auctoritas* has laid down. The Roman senate had *auctoritas*, the Roman magistrate had *potestas*.... Whilst, however, this fundamental difference between the pontifical *auctoritas* and the imperial *potestas* was clear to anyone versed in Roman juristic terminology and ideology, Gelasius superimposed a typical Christian argument upon it: in a Roman-Christian world, the sacred Pontifical *auctoritas* is all the greater, as it has to render an account even for the doings of the kings themselves on the Day of Judgment.... And since rulership comes from God...God's priests are particularly concerned with the emperor's exercise of the (divinely conferred) rulership: and since in a Christian society, of which the emperor through baptism is a member, every human action has a definite purpose and in so far has an essential religious ingredient, the emperors should submit their governmental actions to the ecclesiastical superiors and should not order the latter about, since they alone know what is, and what is not, divine and therefore Christian: they alone have *auctoritas* within a Christian body corporate.[37]

Ullmann's reading of the *auctoritas/potestas* distinction has been criticized from an historical-critical perspective, with critics arguing that he anachronistically reads Gelasius in the light of the popes of the High Middle Ages.[38] I think that Ullmann makes a fairly strong case for his reading even on historical-critical grounds. But, in any case, a theological reading of a magisterial text has to go beyond mere historical criticism and interpret the teaching in the light of other Church teachings.

In his interpretation of another important Gelasian text, *Tractate IV*, Ullmann gives a reading of the task of the imperial power that makes it seem similar to the task given to the deacons in Acts 6:[39]

37 Ullmann, *Growth of Papal Government*, 20–22.
38 See, for example, Alan Cotrell, "*Auctoritas* and *Potestas*: A Reevaluation of the Correspondence of Gelasius I on Papal-Imperial Relations," *Medieval Studies* 55 (1993): 95–109.
39 Fittingly the Holy Roman Emperor would later serve as a deacon or a subdeacon in certain liturgical celebrations. See Marc Bloch, *The Royal Touch: Sacred Monarchy and Scrofula in England and France*, trans. J. E. Anderson (Abingdon: Routledge, 2015 [1971]), 117.

Integralism and Gelasian Dyarchy

According to Gelasius, Christian emperorship originates in Christ Himself. Christ was the last *Rex et Pontifex*, the last Melchisedek, and by "a marvelous dispensation" He had discerned between the functions of the royal and of the sacerdotal power. Since the time of Christ no emperor had arrogated to himself the title of a pontiff and no pontiff had claimed the height of royal power, although the pontiffs were actually, through Christ's generosity and in a very special sense, both royal and priestly. But Christ, "mindful of human fragility" had discerned between the functions of each power: "discrevit officia potestatis utriusque." His reason for so doing was twofold. On the one hand, it is written that no one warring for God should be entangled with secular things. The *raison d'être* of the royal power was to relieve the clerics of the burden of having to care for their carnal and material wants. For the temporal necessities the pontiffs indeed need the emperors, so that they can devote themselves to their functions properly and are not distracted by the pursuit of these carnal matters, but the emperors, Christian as they are, need the pontiffs for the achievement of eternal salvation. On the other hand, Gelasius introduces the very important and fruitful principle of functional order operating within society. To each part of an organic whole is assigned a special function and each member should adhere to the scope of functions allotted to him: then there will be order, or as Gelasius put it, human haughtiness—*humana superbia*—will be prevented from coming into its own again. This principle of functional order is a principle which is necessitated by the manifold functions which a body has to perform in order to be an integrated whole: it is a principle which will play a major part in the fully developed hierocratic ideology.[40]

---

40 Ullmann, *Growth of Papal Government*, 24-25. The key passage of Tractate IV that Ullmann is interpreting runs as follows: "For Christ, mindful of human frailty, regulated with an excellent disposition what pertained to the salvation of his people. Thus he distinguished between the offices of both powers according to their own proper activities and separate dignities, wanting his people to be saved by healthful humility and not carried away again by human pride, so that Christian emperors would need priests for attaining eternal life, and priests would avail themselves of imperial regulations in the conduct of temporal affairs. In this fashion spiritual activity would be set apart from worldly encroachments and the 'soldier of God' (2 Tim 2:4) would not be involved in secular affairs, while on the other hand he who was involved in secular affairs would not seem to preside over divine matters. Thus the humility of each order would be preserved, neither being exalted by the subservience of the other, and each profession would be especially fitted for its appropriate functions." In Hugo Rahner, S.J.,

An important point that emerges from Tractate IV is that the functional dyarchy of powers arises from "human pride," that is, from sin. Without the effects of sin, temporal matters would not be a distraction from sacred matters, and there would be no need to distinguish them. Because, however, we live in a fallen world, it is necessary for the spiritual power to be freed of care for earthly matters. This "diaconal" or "ministerial" understanding of the temporal power was to be taught very explicitly by Gregory the Great. In a letter to the Byzantine Emperor Maurice, Gregory writes: "Power over all people has been conceded from on high to the one who governs, such that the earthly kingdom would be a service which subordinates itself to the heavenly kingdom."[41] Gregory was certainly influenced by Augustine in this regard,[42] and, like Augustine, he sees the necessity of temporal power particularly for curbing sin. As Arquillière puts it, Gregory the Great

> speaks of the pontiff who, with the help of princes, is concentrated on the restriction of the reign of sin and the promotion of the action of grace. The mission of the religious king had, by its very nature, become paramount in a Christianized society. It captures, from the beginning, the confusion of powers which would mark the Middle Ages, the essentially spiritual character of pontifical intervention.... [By] inculcating the duty of kings with the discipline of the Church, Gregory opened an unlimited opening for the interventions of the Holy See.[43]

Arquillière's reference to "confusion of powers" points to his main thesis: that the political Augustinianism of the medieval popes absorbed the temporal order too much into the spiritual order, thus destroying the legitimate autonomy of earthly authority. Douglas Kries, commenting on Arquillière's thesis, claims that Augustine's "obfuscation of the boundary between the natural and

---

Church and State in Early Christianity, trans. Leo Donald Davis, S.J., Kindle e-book (San Francisco: Ignatius Press, 2006 [1992]).

41   *Epist.* III,65, translated in Martin Rhonheimer, *The Common Good of Constitutional Democracy: Essays in Political Philosophy and on Catholic Social Teaching*, ed. William F. Murphy (Washington: The Catholic University of America Press, 2012), 7.

42   See, e.g., *Civ. Dei* V,24 and XIX,17.

43   Arquillière, *L'augustinisme politique*, 40, cited and translated by Bruno, *Political Augustinianism*, 37.

the supernatural" did provide the premises for the strictly monarchical view of spiritual power developed by consistent medieval hierocrats.[44] This is very similar to my critique of Augustinian radicalism above. But the traditional political theory of the medieval popes is not quite so simplistic.

In Ullmann's portrayal, the medieval papal theory seems monarchical, not dyarchical. There is one body of Christians ordered to the end of eternal life. The ruler of this body is the pope. Temporal rulers are ministers of the pope with care of mundane matters. And yet the dyarchical element, derived from Gelasius, was always preserved: on account of human pride, God has established two powers. At times, the medieval popes seem to deny the Gelasian teaching by saying that the temporal power is derived not immediately from God, but rather mediately *through* the spiritual power. A careful reading, however, shows that this is not the case. The temporal power is derived *from God*; it can only have legitimacy, however, if it submits itself to the spiritual power, which has care of the final end. That is, the temporal power inevitably serves the city of man if it is detached from the spiritual power, but if it subordinates itself to the spiritual power it can play a helpful role in the city of God.

Innocent III in one text compares spiritual and temporal power to the sun and moon:

> Just as God, founder of the universe, has constituted two large luminaries in the firmament of Heaven, a major one to dominate the day and a minor one to dominate the night, so he has established in the firmament of the Universal Church, which is signified by the name of Heaven, two great dignities, a major one to preside — so to speak — over the days of the souls, and a minor one to preside over the nights of the bodies. They are the Pontifical authority and the royal power. Thus, as the moon receives its light from the sun and for this very reason is minor both in quantity and in quality, in its size and in its effect, so the royal power derives from the Pontifical authority the splendour of its dignity, the more of which is inherent in it, the less is the light

---

44 Douglas Kries, "Political Augustinianism," in *Augustine through the Ages: An Encyclopedia*, ed. Allan D. Fitzgerald (Grand Rapids: Eerdmans, 2009), 657, cited in Bruno, *Political Augustinianism*, 39.

with which it is adorned, whereas the more it is distant from its reach, the more it benefits in splendour.[45]

At first sight this text would seem to be in tension with the Gelasian dyarchy; if the temporal power "derives from the Pontifical authority," how will the "human pride" of pontiffs be curbed? But at second glance one sees that the tension is maintained. It is indeed God who has "constituted two large luminaries." And therefore Innocent, in another text, teaches that the spiritual power only intervenes in earthly affairs *"ratione peccati,"* by reason of sin. Thus he writes:

> No one, therefore, may suppose that we intend to disturb or diminish the jurisdiction or power of the illustrious king of the French just as he himself does not want to and should not impede our jurisdiction and power; as we are insufficient to discharge all our jurisdiction, why should we wish to usurp that of someone else?... For we do not intend to render justice in feudal matters, in which the jurisdiction belongs to him, unless something may be detracted from the common law by some special privilege or contrary custom, but we want to decide in the matter of sins, of which the censure undoubtedly pertains to us and we can and must exercise it against any one. In this, indeed, we do not lean on human constitutions, but much more on Divine law, because our power is not from man but from God: any one who has a sound mind knows that it belongs to our office to draw away any Christian from any mortal sin and, if he despises the correction, to coerce him with ecclesiastical penalties.[46]

Similarly, Pope Boniface VIII, in a speech to French ambassadors, defended himself against the accusation of contradicting the Gelasian teaching:

> We have been learned in the law for forty years, and we know very well that the powers established by God are two. How should or can anyone suppose that anything so foolish or stupid [as the contrary] is or has been in our head? We declare that we do not wish to usurp

---

[45] Innocent III, *Sicut universitatis conditor*, November 3, 1198, in Sidney Z. Ehler and John B. Morrall, eds., *Church and State through the Centuries: A Collection of Historic Documents with Commentaries* (London: Burns and Oats, 1954), 73.

[46] Innocent III, *Novit ille* (1204), in Ehler and Morrall, *Church and State through the Centuries*, 69–70.

the jurisdiction of the king in any way... But the king cannot deny that he is subject to us *ratione peccati*... Our predecessors deposed three kings of France... And although we are not worthy to walk in the footsteps of our predecessors, if the king committed the same crimes as those kings committed, or greater ones, we should, with great grief and sadness, dismiss him like a servant.[47]

One could read Boniface as merely paying lip service to the dyarchy, while interpreting the power *ratione peccati* so broadly as to effectively make the pope a universal monarch. But this is not how the Catholic tradition developed the teachings of Boniface and his predecessors.

The key to understanding the dyarchy comes from the elaboration of the hierarchy of ends in scholastic theology. An important point is the distinction between two different kinds of happiness to which man can attain, one in the natural order, and one in the supernatural. St Thomas Aquinas writes:

> Now man's happiness is twofold, as was also stated above. One is proportionate to human nature, a happiness, to wit, which man can obtain by means of his natural principles. The other is a happiness surpassing man's nature, and which man can obtain by the power of God alone, by a kind of participation of the Godhead, about which it is written that by Christ we are made "partakers of the Divine nature." And because such happiness surpasses the capacity of human nature, man's natural principles which enable him to act well according to his capacity, do not suffice to direct man to this same happiness.[48]

Now, there is clearly an order between these two kinds of happiness. Natural happiness is ordered to supernatural happiness, as St Thomas teaches in the *De Regno*:

> Through virtuous living man is further ordained to a higher end, which consists in the enjoyment of God, as we have said above. Consequently, since society must have the same end as the individual man, it is not the ultimate end of an assembled multitude

---

47 Boniface VIII, *Licet haec verba* (1302), in *Giles of Rome's "On Ecclesiastical Power": A Medieval Theory of World Government*, ed. and trans. R. W. Dyson (New York: Columbia University Press, 2004), xv–xvi.

48 *ST* I-II, q. 62, a. 1.

to live virtuously, but through virtuous living to attain to the possession of God.[49]

If the supernatural final end could be attained by the power of human natural activity, then the temporal rulers would have the care of it. But since it cannot be so attained, the final end is under the care of the spiritual power. The powers are distinct, but the lower is ordered to the superior:

> Thus, in order that spiritual things might be distinguished from earthly things, the ministry of this kingdom has been entrusted not to earthly kings but to priests, and most of all to the chief priest, the successor of St Peter, the Vicar of Christ, the Roman Pontiff. To him all the kings of the Christian People are to be subject as to our Lord Jesus Christ Himself. For those to whom pertains the care of intermediate ends should be subject to him to whom pertains the care of the ultimate end, and be directed by his rule.[50]

The temporal is, however, not entirely swallowed up in the spiritual. It does receive its authority from God (through the natural law), not from the spiritual authority. As the young Thomas taught in the *Commentary on the Sentences*:

> There are two ways in which a higher power and a lower can be related. In one way, the lower power may be completely derived from the higher, and the whole power of the lower will then be founded upon the power of the higher; in which case we should obey the higher power before the lower simply and in all things.... In this way... is the power of the emperor related to that of the proconsul.... In another way, a higher and lower power can be such that each arises from some supreme power which arranges them in relation to each other as it wishes. In this case, the one will not be subject to the other save in respect of those things in which it has been subjected to the other by the supreme power; and only in such things are we to obey the higher power before the lower.... Spiritual and secular power are both derived from the Divine power, and so secular power is subject to spiritual power insofar as this is ordered by God: that is, in those things which pertain to the salvation of the soul. In such matters, then,

---

49 *De Regno ad Regem Cypri* I,15.
50 *De Regno* I,15.

the spiritual power is to be obeyed before the secular. But in those things which pertain to the civil good, the secular power should be obeyed before the spiritual, according to Matthew 22:21: "Render to Caesar the things that are Caesar's."[51]

On the high-medieval view that I have elaborated, therefore, both powers are within the City of God. The temporal power must be subordinate to the spiritual power, or else it will become mere violence, and yet it does not derive its authority from the spiritual power: it derives its authority from God through the natural law. Nature is not destroyed by grace, and yet nature must be subordinated to grace.

This medieval view was, however, to become partially obscured in the context of the post-Reformation "confessional state." Baroque scholasticism tended to treat the question not as a question of two powers within the one City of God, but rather as a question of the relation of two (relatively) perfect societies: the Church and the state. There was a tendency here to slightly exaggerate the distinction between nature and grace, and not to see the extent to which nature is for the sake of grace.[52]

One can see the slight exaggeration of the autonomy of the natural in later scholastic manuals. In his twentieth-century manual, the great neo-Thomist philosopher Henri Grenier argues that temporal happiness is not strictly speaking a means to the end of

---

51 *In II Sent.*, dist. 44, q. 3, a. 4, in R. W. Dyson, ed. and trans., *Aquinas: Political Writings* (Cambridge: Cambridge University Press, 2002), 277–78. Thomas makes an exception, however, for the pope, whom he sees as having supreme temporal as well as supreme spiritual authority: "Unless perhaps the spiritual and secular powers are conjoined, as in the pope, who holds the summit of both powers: that is, the spiritual and the secular, through the disposition of Him Who is both priest and king" (ibid.). But that exception is not necessarily demanded by the popes' own teachings, as we have already seen. The pope can be seen as holding the summit of the spiritual power only, and having authority over the temporal only insofar as the temporal is subordinated to the spiritual. Even Boniface VIII's *Unam Sanctam*, the most extensive claim of authority on the part of the pope, is consistent with this view. Boniface writes: "Both, therefore, are in the power of the Church, that is to say, the spiritual and the material sword, but the former is to be administered by the Church but the latter for the Church; the former in the hands of the priest; the latter by the hands of kings and soldiers, but at the will and sufferance of the priest." That is, the temporal sword is in the power of the pope, but not in the sense that the pope himself wields that sword.

52 I am grateful to Alan Fimister for correcting an earlier version of this essay with regard to this point, as well as with regard to the discussion of Grenier below.

eternal happiness, because no natural operation can be a direct means to the supernatural end:

> The end of civil society, i.e., of the State, is the temporal happiness of this life. But the temporal happiness of this life is a complete good in its own order: for it is not a part of eternal happiness, nor is it of its nature a means of directly attaining eternal happiness, for there can be no natural proportion between natural good and supernatural good.[53]

Now it is true that there is no proportion between natural good and supernatural good, but the acts in which temporal happiness consists may themselves be elevated by grace to become such means.

Grenier concludes from his position that the Church is not one all-encompassing perfect society; that there are two societies, one ordered to the temporal good and one to the eternal, the polity and the Church; and that *neither of these societies is, absolutely speaking, a perfect society*:

> Neither the Church nor the State [i.e., the political community], from the point of view of the moral order, may be called a perfect society, as we have already seen. For a perfect society is a society whose end is man's complete good, and which embraces all other societies as its parts. But the Church does not embrace all other societies as its parts—civil society is not a part of the Church; and its end is not man's complete good, but rather his highest good.[54]

Grenier does, however, hold that both Church and state are "juridically perfect," that is, that each has everything necessary to attain its goal, and that the goal of each is supreme in its own order.[55]

Now, in one sense Grenier is right. If by "the Church" he means the hierarchy of the spiritual power, then indeed it does not embrace the temporal order as a part. But a more proper meaning of "the Church" is simply the City of God, and in this sense the Church includes both the temporal and the spiritual powers as its parts. The City of God is indeed an all-embracing community, ruled by Christ the King.

---

53 Henri Grenier, *Thomistic Philosophy*, vol. 3, *Moral Philosophy*, trans. J. P. E. O'Hanley (Charlottetown: St Dunstan's University, 1949), 474.
54 Grenier, 3:471.
55 Grenier, 3:472–74.

While the reasons that Grenier gives are not quite right, his practical conclusions tend to match those of the medieval popes: the temporal power is subject to the spiritual power *ratione peccati*. Later, however, the neoscholastic framing of the question in terms of Church and state as juridically perfect societies, with only indirect subordination of one to the other, lent itself to erroneous interpretations. Thus Grenier's fellow Laval School Thomist Charles de Koninck was to write:

> The distinction between State and Church is radical. The ends that define these societies are different; and these societies can be called perfect to the extent that they are sufficient unto themselves.... I do not believe that it is henceforth permitted to maintain that the State can again consent to be the secular arm of a religious society.... To be the secular arm of the Church appears to me to be contrary to the nature of the State as complete society, sovereign and autonomous.[56]

Such misunderstandings could have been avoided by a more careful reading of the teachings of Pope Leo XIII, who gave a very full account of the relation of the two powers. In *Immortale Dei* Pope Leo writes:

> The Almighty, therefore, has given the charge of the human race to two powers, the ecclesiastical and the civil, the one being set over divine, and the other over human, things. Each in its kind is supreme, each has fixed limits within which it is contained, limits which are defined by the nature and special object of the province of each, so that there is, we may say, an orbit traced out within which the action of each is brought into play by its own native right. But, inasmuch as each of these two powers has authority over the same subjects, and as it might come to pass that one and the same thing related differently, but still remaining one and the same thing might belong to the jurisdiction and determination of both, therefore God, who foresees all things, and who is the author of these two powers, has marked out the course of each in right correlation to the other. "For the powers that are, are ordained of God."... There must, accordingly, exist between these two powers a certain orderly connection, which

---

56 Charles de Koninck, "What is Caesar's," trans. David Quackenbush, online at www.scribd.com/doc/200567591/What-is-Caesar-s.

may be compared to the union of the soul and body in man. The nature and scope of that connection can be determined only, as We have laid down, by having regard to the nature of each power, and by taking account of the relative excellence and nobleness of their purpose. One of the two has for its proximate and chief object the well-being of this mortal life; the other, the everlasting joys of heaven. Whatever, therefore in things human is of a sacred character, whatever belongs either of its own nature or by reason of the end to which it is referred, to the salvation of souls, or to the worship of God, is subject to the power and judgment of the Church. Whatever is to be ranged under the civil and political order is rightly subject to the civil authority.[57]

Like his medieval predecessors, Leo frames the question as a question of the relation of two powers. Each of the two powers is instituted by God, and each has a certain legitimate sphere. But the temporal power can only live properly if it is subordinated to the spiritual power, which is like its soul.

Leo XIII's position is that such integration should have juridical form—that is, that the earthly power should explicitly and officially recognize the authority of the Church, and form its laws in accordance with Church law. But we now turn to another theory of how the primacy of the spiritual should be realized: Whig Thomism.

4. Whig Thomism

The term Whig Thomism refers to various writers who agree with Lord Acton that the first Whig was St Thomas. That is, they try to show that there is harmony between the Whig strand of Enlightenment liberalism and the political philosophy of St Thomas.[58] Notable examples are Michael Novak, George Weigel, and Richard John Neuhaus, all of whom have been deeply influenced by Fr John Courtney Murray, S.J.[59]

---

[57] Leo XIII, *Immortale Dei* 13–14; cf. Thomas Pink, "Opening Address," Pink-Rhonheimer debate on the interpretation of *Dignitatis Humanae*, University of Notre Dame, November 20, 2015: https://www.academia.edu/19136187/Pink-Rhonheimer_debate_at_Notre_Dame_on_the_interpretation_of_Dignitatis_Humanae_-_opening_address, 2–5.

[58] See Michael Novak, "The Return of the Catholic Whig," in *First Things*, March 1990, online at www.firstthings.com/article/1990/03/the-return-of-the-catholic-whig.

[59] See Tracey Rowland, *Culture and the Thomist Tradition: After Vatican II* (London: Routledge, 2003), 16.

Unlike some of his later followers, John Courtney Murray was careful to try to avoid contradicting any element of authoritative Catholic Social Teaching. He did not, however, succeed. In an important essay, written over a decade before Vatican II, he proposed that the American model of Church-state relation escaped condemnation since it is able to preserve the primacy of the spiritual:

> What the First Amendment fundamentally declares, as the constitutional will of the American people, is the "lay" character of the state, its non-competence in the field of religion, the restriction of its competence to the secular and temporal. There is here a unique historical realization of the "lay" state—unique because this lay state is not laicized or laicizing, on the Continental model. This lay state does not pretend to be The Whole—an absolutely autonomous, all-embracing religio-political magnitude with its own quasi-religious content—such, for instance, as the Third Republic was in the minds of the small knot of men who shaped it. On the contrary, there is in the First Amendment a recognition of the primacy of the spiritual—a recognition that is again unique, in that it is a recognition of the primacy of the spiritual life of the human person, as a value supreme over any values incorporated in the state. There is too an implicit recognition that this region of man's spiritual life is the source from which the state itself receives its ethical content, its moral purpose, and the higher norm that governs the operation of its political processes.[60]

For Murray, the primacy of the spiritual power is thus realized not by an official recognition of the authority of the Church, but rather by a recognition on the part of the state of the authority of the individual consciences of its citizens, who are to form the state according to the dictates of those consciences through democratic processes. Thus, according to Murray, the Catholic citizens of such a state can subordinate its end to the final end, by making sure that its laws are in accord with the law of God. Murray argues that this amounts to a new application of the Gelasian teaching on dyarchy:

60 John Courtney Murray, S.J., "Contemporary Orientations of Catholic Thought on Church and State in the Light of History," *Theological Studies* 10 (1949): 177–234, at 188–89.

Its premise is the Christian dualist concept of man; and it recognizes that a dyarchy therefore governs the life of man and of society. However, this dyarchy has not the form that prevailed in the Middle Ages—the dualism of *auctoritas sacrata pontificum* and *regalis potestas* (with its oscillations between caesaropapism and hierocratism). Nor is it the dyarchy constituted in the so-called confessional state of post-Reformation times—the juridically established co-partnership in society of state and Church (Catholic or Protestant—the Protestant form being the "Church-state" of Erastian tendency, and the Catholic form being the "state-Church" with boundaries of jurisdiction laid down chiefly by concordat). The terms of the dyarchy visible in the First Amendment are not state and Church (that manner of dyarchy is constitutionally excluded by the provision against "establishment of religion"), but state and human person, *civis idem et christianus* (to adopt Leo XIII's phrase).[61]

The reference to Leo XIII's *Immortale Dei* is crucial to Murray. He puts much weight on Leo XIII's teaching that spiritual and temporal power come into contact because they rule over the same persons. Seventeen years later he was to claim that Vatican II's *Dignitatis Humanae* adopted a "personalist" account of society that supported his thesis:

> The Declaration embraces the political doctrine of Pius XII on the juridical state (as it is called in Continental idiom), that is, on government as constitutional and as limited in function—its primary function being juridical, namely, the protection and promotion of the rights of man and the facilitation of the performance of man's native duties. The primacy of this function is based on Pius XII's personalist conception of society—on the premise that the "human person is the foundation, the goal, and the bearer of the whole social process," including the processes of government.[62]

The main problem that I have with Murray's position is with his understanding of the "personalist" conception of society (supposedly)

---

61 Murray, "Contemporary Orientations," 189.
62 John Courtney Murray, S.J., "The Issue of Church and State at Vatican Council II," in *Religious Liberty: Catholic Struggles with Pluralism*, ed. J. Leon Hooper (Louisville: Westminster/John Knox Press, 1993), online at www.library.georgetown.edu/woodstock/murray/1966h.

taught by Vatican II and Pope Pius XII. In the previous chapter, I unfolded David Schindler's profound critique of Murray's teaching on religious liberty. Schindler argues that the sort of separation of Church and state found in the First Amendment to the American Constitution actually involves an implicit theory of religion:

> The human act in its basic structure, for purposes of the constitutional ordering of society, is understood to be silent about God (cf. "articles of peace"). But this means that, when theists go on to fill this silence with speech, they must now do so precisely by way of *addition* and in their capacity as *private* members of society.[63]

In the last chapter I discussed how Schindler shows that Murray separates nature and grace too much, taking insufficient account of the way in which nature is ordered to grace. But here I want to attend to Murray's problematic account of the common good to which Schindler's critique also alludes. Note Schindler's emphasis on the *private* nature of the influence of the spiritual power on society through the consciences of its citizens in Murray's account.

Murray's "personalist" understanding of human society is "personalist" in the precise sense of that term so ably attacked by Charles de Koninck in *On the Primacy of the Common Good: Against the Personalists*. On Murray's account the political community is ordered not to the greatest temporal good of man, but simply to "the protection and promotion of the rights of man and the facilitation of the performance of man's native duties."[64] But this is to fundamentally misunderstand that man's chief temporal good is the *common good* of natural happiness. And since the primacy of the common good is based on the fact that *even in the natural order* it is a greater participation in the divine good than any merely private good, it is necessary that those who have charge of the common good order it *explicitly* to God. As de Koninck argues:

> When those in whose charge the common good lies do not order it explicitly to God, is society not corrupted at its very root?... If, in truth, the politician must possess all the moral virtues and

---

63 Schindler, "Religious Freedom," 722.
64 My account of Murray here is admittedly somewhat simplistic. A fuller account would have to show that Murray's distinction of civil society and the state is finally incoherent, and thus cannot be the means of allowing him to escape the errors of personalism.

prudence, is this not because he is at the head and must judge and order all things towards the common good of political society, and the latter to God?[65]

This is true even on the natural level. But, according to the consistent magisterium of the popes from Gelasius I to Leo XIII, the coming of Christ means that the ordering of the temporal common good to God must be achieved by the one who has care for it submitting to the *auctoritas sacrata* of the Church.[66] Thus Leo XIII writes in *Immortale Dei*:

> Men living together in society are under the power of God no less than individuals are, and society, no less than individuals, owes gratitude to God who gave it being and maintains it and whose ever-bounteous goodness enriches it with countless blessings. Since, then, no one is allowed to be remiss in the service due to God, and since the chief duty of all men is to cling to religion in both its teaching and practice—not such religion as they may have a preference for, but the religion which God enjoins, and which certain and most clear marks show to be the only one true religion—it is a public crime to act as though there were no God. So, too, is it a sin for the State not to have care for religion as a something beyond its scope, or as of no practical benefit; or out of many forms of religion to adopt that one which chimes in with the fancy; for we are bound absolutely to worship God in that way which He has shown to be His will.[67]

The consistency of this teaching with *Dignitatis Humanae* has been amply demonstrated by Thomas Pink.[68] As a matter of policy, the Church does not currently make use of the state as an instrument for coercing her members, but this does not affect the duty of the state to recognize the true religion. As *Dignitatis Humanae* itself declares: "Religious freedom...leaves untouched traditional Catholic doctrine on the moral duty of men *and societies* toward the true religion and toward the one Church of Christ."[69]

---

65   De Koninck, *Primacy*, 69.
66   Sadly, de Koninck does not seem to have quite understood this further point. Hence his denial of the right of the Church to use the state as a secular arm. See De Koninck, "What is Caesar's."
67   *Immortale Dei* 6.
68   See my discussion of Pink in chapter 18.
69   *Dignitatis Humanae* 1.

Integralism and Gelasian Dyarchy

In 1951, Fr F.J. Connell criticized Murray for not leaving traditional Catholic doctrine on the duty of societies toward the true religion untouched.[70] Connell gave the usual account of Church-state relations found in neo-Scholastic manuals of the day. But Murray lashed back in an angry reply, in which he accused Connell of being a "crypto-monarchist,"[71] and argued that Connell's position on the duties of the temporal power would make sense only in the most extremely paternalistic form of absolute monarchy:

> Perhaps Fr. Connell is not a conceptualist in his political philosophy. Perhaps when he speaks of "the state" he may actually, if unwittingly, mean the unlimited monarch, the king in the tradition of the French classical monarchy, who was also "Father of the People," possessed of the total *ius politiae*, and therefore the single source of law and governmental decision.... Clearly, if the term, "the state," really means a *regimen regale* in the technical sense, a monarchic state governed singly from the top down, with unlimited power centered in the hands of "the civil ruler," the king, it might become possible to make sense out of Fr. Connell's theory of the obligations of "the state." The obligation to investigate the claims of the Church and to permit her to preach could be exactly located—in the king; for nothing that concerns the state lies outside his official duty, and there are no limits to his functions.... This leads to an important conclusion. In the logic of Fr. Connell's theories there is inherent a denial of the transcendence of the Church to political forms—the principle that occupied so central a place in the doctrine of Leo XIII.[72]

Now, I am by no means a *crypto*-monarchist (having always been quite open in my monarchism), but the question of monarchism is entirely irrelevant, and is raised by Murray merely to throw dust in his readers' eyes. Nothing prevents a political community with a democratic, republican, or mixed form of government from fulfilling its obligations toward the true religion in the manner described by Connell.

---

70 F. J. Connell, "The Theory of the 'Lay State," *The American Ecclesiastical Review* 125.1 (1951): 7–18.

71 John Courtney Murray, "For the Freedom and Transcendence of the Church," *The American Ecclesiastical Review* 126.3 (1952): 28–48, at 43.

72 Murray, "Freedom and Transcendence of the Church," 37–38.

The reason why it would be difficult for the United States of America to fulfill those obligations is *not* because they form a republic, but because (at least as Murray understands them) they have enshrined a liberal conception of political life in their constitution.[73] The American Republic (at least by Murray's time) does not see itself as ordering itself to the common good of earthly happiness, but rather to securing the God-given rights of its citizens. And that is precisely the problem. Murray's reference to Leo XIII's teaching on the Church's official indifference to different political forms is stunningly inapposite, because Leo explicitly teaches that all such forms can be legitimate *on the condition that they serve the common good*. And, in fact, Leo concludes from that principle that any society must have some (whether one or many) who have charge of the common good and order the whole society to it:

> A society can neither exist nor be conceived in which there is no one to govern the wills of individuals, in such a way as to make, as it were, one will out of many, and to impel them rightly and orderly to the common good; therefore, God has willed that in a civil society there should be some to rule the multitude.[74]

The reason why Murray's Whig Thomism fails is that by taking an overly personalistic view of political community, he does not understand the transcendence of the temporal common good, and therefore cannot understand how that good is to be ordered to the eternal good.

5. Conclusion: A Practical Synthesis

One reason why in our day Augustinian radicalism and Whig Thomism seem more plausible to many than integralism is that the first two seem to offer much clearer guidance on what practical steps to take in our current historical situation. There is no country on earth today where an integralist program is likely to

---

73 One may question whether all of the American founders would have accepted Murray's liberal reading of the constitution. There was certainly a liberal element in the founding, but there was also an older, classical republican element with a robust account of the common good. See Felix de St Vincent, "'In Dread of Modernity': Republican Liberty and the Common Good in the American Tradition," *The Josias*, May 18, 2015.

74 *Diuturnum Illud* 11.

have any immediate success. But the Christian anarchosyndicalist projects of Augustinian radicalism can be started at any time. And nothing prevents one from making the Whig-Thomist attempt at influencing the laws of one's country through democratic procedure. What is an integralist to do?

In part I think that an integralist will do both what Augustinian radicals do and what Whig-Thomists do, but he will do them in a way formed by integralism. In the wasteland of late-capitalist society there is certainly a great need for the sort of alternative communities advocated by Augustinian radicals, communities in which virtues can be fostered and common goods achieved. Integralists form such communities too. But they form them knowing that they cannot attain to the most complete common good of the natural order, the common good that can be achieved only by a *societas perfecta*. Moreover, they form them in a way that takes a more realistic attitude toward coercion. Integralists are often to be found in Benedictine monasteries (especially in the Congregation of Solesmes), but Benedictine monasteries include coercive punishments in their way of life—at least the sort of punishments that are possible for a voluntary community. Contrast the strict rule of Benedictine life with the following description of events in a community founded by Dorothy Day:

> William Gauchat who headed the house of hospitality, furnished an apartment for single women in need, and a married couple arriving first, were sheltered there. But when Bill wanted to put a few single women into the empty bedrooms, the couple announced that they had possession and refused to allow them entrance. Our guests know that we will not call upon the police to evict them, that we are trying to follow the dear Lord's teachings, "If anyone take your coat, let go your cloak also to him...." When another family came to Maryfarm, we explained that we were trying to open a retreat house and that we did not have room for them. It was the family of one of our own willful leaders who "loved God and did as he pleased." He did not wish to remain on a farm belonging to his father, where he was forced to work too hard. He and his wife refused to listen and unpacked their things to stay with us. First they took over the lower farmhouse. After a few conflicts due to their possessing themselves of retreat

house goods (as common goods) they moved to the upper farm to join Victor. For the following year they continued their guerrilla tactics from the upper farm, coming down to make raids on the retreat house food and furnishings, explaining to retreatants that they were true Catholic Workers and that the retreat house was a perversion of the movement.[75]

Now, I mean no disrespect to Dorothy Day (who was certainly a great saint), but a well-ordered community needs authority with the power to enforce rules, and integralists recognize that fact.

And of course, integralists can participate in democratic politics, trying as much as possible to shape the laws according to the natural law. This was the whole point of Pope Leo XIII's policy of *ralliement*. Critics of *ralliement* argue that this policy leads to its practitioners being corrupted by liberalism.[76] But this can be avoided, as Leo XIII intended, by keeping hold of a thoroughly antiliberal political philosophy, and never forgetting that the current liberal order of political life is profoundly disordered.

---

75 Dorothy Day, *The Long Loneliness* (San Francisco: Harper, 1997 [1952]), 261–62.
76 See Edmund Waldstein, O.Cist., "Catholic Action and Ralliement," *The Josias*, February 13, 2016.

8

On the City of God Against the Pagans

Alan Fimister

The doctrine of the two cities, which finds its greatest expression in the work we are to examine, is not the construct of some theologian, however great. It is an essential element in God's revelation to mankind, vital to the correct understanding of the personal and institutional history of each individual and society and of every book of scripture from Genesis to Revelation. The great Pope Leo XIII frequently alluded to this doctrine in his encyclical letters, not least in the thundering opening of *Humanum Genus* promulgated in 1884:

> The race of man, after its miserable fall from God, the Creator and the Giver of heavenly gifts, "through the envy of the devil," separated into two diverse and opposite parts, of which the one steadfastly contends for truth and virtue, the other for those things which are contrary to virtue and to truth. The one is the kingdom of God on earth, namely, the true Church of Jesus Christ; and those who desire from their heart to be united with it, so as to gain salvation, must of necessity serve God and His only-begotten Son with their whole mind and with an entire will. The other is the kingdom of Satan, in whose possession and control are all whosoever follow the fatal example of their leader and of our first parents, those who refuse to obey the divine and eternal law, and who have many aims of their own in contempt of God, and many aims also against God. This twofold kingdom St Augustine keenly discerned and described after the manner of two cities, contrary in their laws because striving for contrary objects; and with a subtle brevity he

expressed the efficient cause of each in these words: "Two loves formed two cities: the love of self, reaching even to contempt of God, an earthly city; and the love of God, reaching to contempt of self, a heavenly one." At every period of time each has been in conflict with the other, with a variety and multiplicity of weapons and of warfare, although not always with equal ardor and assault.

The doctrine of the two cities also underlies a key paragraph in the 1992 *Catechism of the Catholic Church*, one of the foremost jewels in the crown of Pope John Paul II's magisterium, for which we are daily made more grateful:

> 2244. Every institution is inspired, at least implicitly, by a vision of man and his destiny, from which it derives the point of reference for its judgments, its hierarchy of values, its line of conduct. Most societies have formed their institutions in the recognition of a certain preeminence of man over things. Only the divinely revealed religion has clearly recognized man's origin and destiny in God, the Creator and Redeemer. The Church invites political authorities to measure their judgments and decisions against this inspired truth about God and man. Societies not recognizing this vision or rejecting it in the name of their independence from God are brought to seek their criteria and goal in themselves or to borrow them from some ideology. Since they do not admit that one can defend an objective criterion of good and evil, they arrogate to themselves an explicit or implicit totalitarian power over man and his destiny, as history shows.

In order to understand *The City of God* by St Augustine of Hippo one needs to understand the event which inspired it.

On August 24 in AD 410, the City of Rome which had remained unconquered for 800 years was captured and sacked by King Alaric of the Visigoths and his followers. Even when Rome had been sacked in 390 BC by the Gaulish chieftain Brennus, the Capitoline Hill seat of the chief shrines of Roman Paganism had not fallen. The sacred geese of Juno alerted the defenders to the sneak attack and prevented its capture. If the sack of 390 BC is therefore deemed incomplete, Rome had never fallen in its entire history from 753 BC to AD 410 — 1,163 years. That the defenders in 390 should have been aroused by creatures sacred to Juno was particularly significant, as according to its civic mythology Rome was founded by descendants of the exiles of Troy whose city was put to the sword by Greeks inspired by the wrath of Juno and whose people were driven across the Mediterranean by the same jealousy until they settled in Latium. Thus even the goddess least well disposed to the Roman people had by 390 BC apparently got with the project. Rome had a lot for which to thank her gods. They had, as Virgil reminded every Roman school boy, promised her *imperium sine fine*—empire without limit—and they had delivered. For the last five hundred years one quarter of the human race had lived under the dominion of the Roman People. The vast majority of those beyond (so far as the Romans knew) lived in misery and squalor in desolate lands unworthy of the attentions of the Roman army. Edward Gibbon plausibly imagined the motivations of the Romans in omitting to invade the country now known as Scotland: "The masters of the fairest and most wealthy climates of the globe turned with contempt from gloomy hills, assailed by the winter tempest, from lakes concealed in a blue mist, and from cold and lonely heaths, over which the deer of the forest were chased by a troop of naked barbarians."

The people of the Roman Empire had no desire for independence. They were Romans, an identity which from the beginning had a civic rather than an ethnic basis. As the poet Claudian explained just before the catastrophe of 410, Rome:

> Took the conquered to her bosom,
> Made mankind a single family,
> Mother not mistress to the nations,
> Conquering the world a second time by the bond of affection.

And the Romans enshrined in the heart of their commonwealth the most eloquent possible reminders that failure to maintain the favor of the gods could have the most catastrophic consequences. The Temple of Vesta, goddess of the hearth, in the center of the Forum preserved the Palladium, the sacred image of Athena, that Aeneas, last member of the Trojan royal house, had borne from the ruins of Ilium, and forever tended by its virgin priestesses was the perpetual flame ignited by the prince from the fires that consumed his city and carried before him to Italy in the course of his founding migration.

Spiritual and Temporal Power

The idea that religion might be a special separate sphere to the life of the city (or indeed the tribe or kingdom) was unthinkable to the peoples of the ancient world. In classical mythology the concept of an afterlife of bliss or indeed punishment was remote and exceptional. The vast majority of the dead, good or bad, inhabited a shadowy half-life of memories and regrets. Happiness, if it was on offer, was on offer in this life of love and laughter, flesh and blood, here and now under the sun. If prosperity in this life was to be secured then the propitiation of the powers was its first and indispensable requirement. The highest official of the Roman Republic was the Pontifex Maximus — the high priest or bridge-builder in chief, supreme practitioner of the Roman religion. This ancient office was held in his lifetime by Julius Caesar and then by his great nephew and adopted son Augustus and by every Roman Emperor after him.

The concern of the Roman authorities was that the gods be propitiated for the good of the empire. They did not care which gods were propitiated so long as each of their subjects gave due honor to the gods to whom they owed honor and so preserved the good of the lands subject to Rome and so long as the citizens of Rome gave due honor to the gods of Rome herself. Impiety and atheism ought to be punished and it was the Roman magistrate's business to punish them should they come to his attention; but *systematically* to seek out and punish impiety was a duty only in respect of Roman citizens. At least, that is, until 212, when the emperor Caracalla extended citizenship to all freeborn men in the empire.

The persecution of the Church in the empire had up to this moment been sporadic. Now, the elimination of the Christian impiety was a grave duty incumbent upon any emperor with a serious concern for the preservation of the state. At the same time, the character of Roman paganism underwent a dramatic transformation.

Up to this moment the Romans desired only that each one worship his ancestral gods. The Jews' insistence that their God was the only God might be distasteful and gauche but there was a place in the Mediterranean syncretism for their national traditions, if only perhaps a despised place. The Christians were another matter entirely. By seeking to win the Emperor's subjects and fellow citizens away from the gods of their ancestors, they struck at the roots of Roman prosperity. They already threatened the stability of his dominions before 212, but now that a vastly greater multitude were citizens of Rome herself the Christians threatened the very survival of the Republic.

Before the third century, philosophy had been generally critical of traditional religion. Whatever the plebeian adherent of the gods might seek, the philosopher, particularly the Platonist, sought eternal life in a better and higher world. As Gibbon delightedly and admiringly observed: "The various modes of worship, which prevailed in the Roman world, were all considered by the people, as equally true; by the philosopher, as equally false; and by the magistrate, as equally useful. And thus toleration produced not only mutual indulgence, but even religious concord." In the second century St Justin Martyr's account of Platonism as the penultimate stage on his journey to the Gospel could hardly be more positive. The journey to the Gospel for Justin is the journey to the true philosophy. With the rise, in the third century, of Neo-Platonism the philosophers no longer considered paganism to be false, but rather as a picture language for the higher mysteries of which they were the guardians. Far from merely useful, the maintenance of traditional religion was seen by the Neo-Platonists as vital for the preservation and perfection of an empire reenvisaged as the political manifestation of the ontological unity of the cosmos. Christianity in contrast they saw as a dangerous rival, mumbo-jumbo that threatened the social, political, and intellectual integralism which was so tantalizingly close to realization under the reforming government of the Emperor Diocletian.

Of course, this conception of Christianity was quite absurd. It was Neo-Platonism that represented the novelty in the third century. Its attempt to marshal Imperial autocracy, classical myth, and pagan ritual into a coherent body of belief and practice underpinned by a mighty systematization of Platonic thought was a direct response to the imminent prospect of Christian triumph. The Neo-Platonic project was concocted in imitation of the Church and bore no resemblance to traditional paganism. The Great Persecution of 303 to 313 was the terrible offspring of this last desperate attempt to prevent the conversion of the Roman Empire. It failed. Constantine embraced the Gospel. He took the Palladium away with him to his new capital of Constantinople. The Church was compensated for its material losses under persecution. Her clergy were given the privileged status of the pagan priesthood. The privileges and subsidies of the traditional religion were withdrawn one by one. In 380 the Catholic Faith was decreed to be the religion of the Roman Empire. The title of Pontifex Maximus was transferred to the Bishop of Rome. The altar of victory was removed from the Senate House and finally in 394 the vestal fire itself was extinguished by the Emperor Theodosius. At the First Council of Nicaea Constantine read out Virgil's Fourth Eclogue, his ecstatic vision of the coming of a divine child who would redeem the world. Far from being the great enemy of the Roman Empire, the Church was the reason the One True God had created Rome in the first place.

As Prudentius, a statesman and liturgical poet in the administration of Theodosius, explained:

> What is the secret of Rome's historical destiny? It is that God wills the unity of mankind, since the religion of Christ demands a social foundation of peace and international amity. Hitherto the whole earth from east to west had been rent asunder by continual strife. To curb this madness God has taught the nations to be obedient to the same laws and all to become Romans. Now we see mankind living as citizens of one city and members of a common household. Men come from distant lands across the seas to one common forum, the peoples are united by commerce and intermarriage. From the intermingling of peoples a single race is born. This is the meaning of all the victories and triumphs of the Roman Empire: the Roman peace has prepared the road for the coming of Christ.

In his *Oration in Praise of Constantine* Eusebius of Caesarea had already provided the perfect triumphalist synthesis of Imperial political theory and Christian ecclesiology.

> No mortal eye has seen, nor ear heard, nor can the mind in its vesture of flesh understand what things are prepared for those who have been here adorned with the graces of godliness; blessings

which await you too, most pious emperor, to whom alone since the world began has the Almighty Sovereign of the universe granted power to purify the course of human life: to whom also he has revealed his own symbol of salvation, whereby he overcame the power of death, and triumphed over every enemy. And this victorious trophy, the scourge of evil spirits, you have arrayed against the errors of idol worship, and hast obtained the victory not only over all your impious and savage foes, but over equally barbarous adversaries, the evil spirits themselves. For whereas we are composed of two distinct natures, I mean of body and spirit, of which the one is visible to all, the other invisible, against both these natures two kinds of barbarous and savage enemies, the one invisibly, the other openly, are constantly arrayed. The one oppose our bodies with bodily force: the other with incorporeal assaults besiege the naked soul itself. Again, the visible barbarians, like the wild nomad tribes, no better than savage beasts, assail the nations of civilized men, ravage their country, and enslave their cities, rushing on those who inhabit them like ruthless wolves of the desert, and destroying all who fall under their power. But those unseen foes, more cruel far than barbarians, I mean the soul-destroying demons whose course is through the regions of the air, had succeeded, through the snares of vile polytheism, in enslaving the entire human race, insomuch that they no longer recognized the true God, but wandered in the mazes of atheistic error. For they procured, I know not whence, gods who never anywhere existed, and set him aside who is the only and the true God, as though he were not.

Indeed, Eusebius explains, while the pagan theorists saw the Roman polity as the one universal legitimate commonwealth, in fact legitimacy belongs exclusively to that polity which worships the One True God in the manner He has appointed.

Truly may he deserve the imperial title, who has formed his soul to royal virtues, according to the standard of that celestial kingdom. But he who is a stranger to these blessings, who denies the Sovereign of the universe, and owns no allegiance to the heavenly Father of spirits; who invests not himself with the virtues which become an emperor, but overlays his soul with moral deformity and baseness... surely one abandoned to such vices as these, however he may be deemed powerful through despotic violence, has no true title to the name of Emperor. For how should he whose soul is impressed with a thousand absurd images of false deities, be able to exhibit a counterpart of the true and heavenly sovereignty? Or how can he be absolute lord of others, who has subjected himself to the dominion of a thousand cruel masters? A slave of low delights and ungoverned lust, a slave of wrongfully-extorted wealth, of rage and passion, as well as of cowardice and terror; a slave of ruthless demons, and soul-destroying spirits?

And yet, even as Theodosius extinguished the Vestal Hearth there were signs that the immortal empire was imperiled. In 376 a vast host of Goths had appeared at the Danube on the Imperial frontier. They were seeking permission to migrate to the Empire for fear of the Huns, an Asiatic tribe that had driven them from their homes above the Black Sea. The Romans had little interest in settling barbarian auxiliary troops on a frontier they were only crossing in terror of the very tribes against which they would be expected to defend it. On the other hand, they had arrived in worrying numbers. The Romans resolved to pretend that they were acceding to the Goths' petition, invite them across the Danube, isolate their leaders at a banquet, murder them and then massacre the rest at leisure. Unfortunately for the peace of the world this desecration of sacred hospitality was detected in time by the Goths who rose up in fury, rampaged across the Balkans, and defeated and slew the Emperor Valens at the Battle of Adrianople in 378.

It was in response to the chaos engendered by this defeat that Theodosius himself was raised to the purple. He managed to restore order to the frontier but there was no crushing victory. The Goths were bought off. On December 31, 406, in the reign of Theodosius's sons Arcadius and Honorius, the other great European frontier river of the Empire froze solid and a vast host of Vandals, Alans, and Suebi poured into Gaul across the Rhine. The Empire never recovered. It was in the midst of the ensuing anarchy that Alaric and his Visigoths resolved to blackmail the Western Emperor by laying siege to the Eternal City itself. They assumed their demands would be met and that Honorius would never allow the capital to be desecrated. Honorius in turn assumed the Goths would starve before they were ever able to breach the Aurelian walls. They were both wrong and, as Jerome put it, "The City which had taken the whole world was itself taken."

Rome herself was a bastion of Paganism. Despite being the seat of the first of bishops and the resting place of the prince of the apostles the capital was also the residence of the greatest patrician families of the empire, the people whose ancestors had built the temples and held the sacred offices of the pagan priesthood. They protested strongly against the disestablishment of the Roman religion. The removal of the altar of victory[1] had occasioned a long struggle between the leaders of the Senate and St Ambrose, bishop of Milan (the city where the emperor actually resided at the time). Although Rome had long ceased to be the habitual residence of the Emperors who needed to station themselves much closer to the frontiers, this had only served to strengthen its sanctity and greatness in the minds of men.

The reaction of the pagan aristocrats of Rome can easily be imagined. A mere sixteen years after the quenching of the Vestal fire, Rome had fallen. What more eloquent testimony to the madness of Constantine need there be? The promise of his vision that the Triumphant Cross would be the guarantee of endless victory had been cast into the ashes of the Capitol. The pagan account of human history had been vindicated.

It was in response to this catastrophe that St Augustine wrote his greatest work. The *magnum opus et arduum* was the twenty-two books concerning *The City of God, Against the Pagans*.

Augustine was of course a native of North Africa. It is a constant frustration to the modern historian that we do not know whether the ancient Punic language was his mother tongue (or even if he spoke it at all). He was raised and educated most thoroughly in the classical style until he ate, drank, dreamed, and breathed the words of Cicero, Virgil, Caesar, and Sallust. And yet, he was a native of the land of Rome's greatest enemy and we may suspect that he allowed himself a little more emotional distance from the calamities of 410 than the majority of his contemporaries.

How most of Augustine's fellow Christians reacted to the charge

---

1 See Epistle XVII by St Ambrose, in Latin and English: https://thejosias.com/2016/11/17/the-altar-of-victory.

that they had deprived the empire of its genius and fortune we shall never know but it is often supposed that their answer may have resembled that implied by Augustine's friend and admirer Paul Orosius in his *Seven Books of History Against the Pagans*. Orosius sought to show that worse disasters had befallen man in the past when paganism prevailed everywhere outside of Israel and thus, placed in perspective, the vicissitudes of the present time could not be laid as a convincing charge against the truth and efficacy of the Gospel.

Augustine's approach was altogether more radical. Already the title *De Civitate Dei* implied that the great African would refuse to accept the assumptions behind the question posed to him by his pagan opponents. The purpose of history and of God's providential guardianship thereof was not, Augustine argued, to preserve and glorify the temporal commonwealth of the Roman people, nor was that commonwealth, even as transfigured by its acceptance of the Christian Revelation, the supreme community of man and final recipient of his loyalty. This honor belongs by right and alone to the Catholic Church—the City of God. Thus the argument of the work is phrased as a defense of this eternal city against those who disparage it and the good for which it is established in favor of the temporal good of the city of Rome or any other earthly polity.

The work is divided into two parts corresponding, in reverse order, to the subjects indicated in its title: *On the City of God, Against the Pagans*. The first part consisting of the first ten books may be designated "Against the Pagans" and the second part "On the City of God." Part one is further divided in two. Books one to five refute the arguments of those who prefer the earthly city to the City of God because they seek in it and in its gods temporal happiness. Books six to ten refute the argument of those who prefer the earthly city and its gods because they seek from them happiness in the life to come. That is, the first five books are a refutation of the more traditional paganism of the ancient world while the next five are a refutation of the newly minted Neo-Platonic version in which Augustine was well schooled as it had played a decisive role in his own journey to Christianity.

Augustine has a number of effective rhetorical opening salvos. If the Roman gods were so wonderful, why did they abandon

Troy, forcing the Trojans to migrate to Italy in the first place? The pagans of Rome who never embraced Christianity anyway can hardly blame it for their own misfortune. They were however happy to shelter in the churches and basilicas of the faithful during the sack where they were left unmolested by the Goths who, having been converted to the Arian form of Christianity, did not wish to desecrate these shrines. Where, Augustine wonders, is it recorded in the history of earlier times and the annals of pagan warfare that such scrupulosity was maintained by the conquerors of a fallen city?

Even by their own lights the pagans knew that true happiness, even in this life, is the reward of, indeed is to be identified with the exercise of, virtue. Such virtue as the pagans boast is not truly worthy of the name because it is not, in fact, directed towards the true glory prepared for man with God in eternity. It is practiced for the sake of pride and earthly glory. But the Lord is as good as His word. As He says "they have had their reward." While the Romans practiced this simulacrum of true virtue God gave them temporal prosperity. But even the pseudo-virtue practiced in the service of demons whose every fable, rite, and ritual is bent towards the moral destruction of their worshipers cannot long endure, and Augustine chronicles the moral and civil decline of the Roman people even by the corrupted light of natural reason until the final demise of the Republic amidst the incessant civil war and personal squalor of the first century before Christ. By the time the Savior entered the world to establish the universal boundaries of His City, the Roman commonwealth and the virtues it claimed had already by the testimony of their own greatest authors (overwhelmingly republicans) perished from the earth. In truth, the sort of earthly peace the pagans of the more recent centuries really desire is the minimum of security and wealth necessary to indulge an empty hedonism unmolested by external interference. To be deprived of this kind of peace is a blessing.

Augustine has much fun describing the lurid details of popular superstition and the clumsy and self-contradictory efforts of pagan authors to rationalize the members of the traditional pantheon. As he passes on to the second section of part one—against those who worship the pagan Gods for happiness in the next life—he finds no more difficulty in destroying the attempts of the Neo-Platonists to reconcile traditional religious practice with their hierarchies of emanations. Why would such entities, if they are the pure angelic beings the Neo-Platonists allege, wish to be honored with sacrifices and spectacles inextricably bound up with the treacheries, lusts, and perversions recounted of Jupiter, Venus, Mars and their gang? Why would pure angelic beings desire to usurp the worship of the One God? Why would they encourage the foolish blasphemies of magicians and sorcerers? Insofar as there are benign entities corresponding to the beings the Neo-Platonists postulate, they are the angels of the True God who have no desire to be worshiped by men and who will assist their Lord in punishing such idolatry at the end of time. Insofar as there are invisible beings who do indeed approve of the practices that the pagan philosophers seek to salvage with their speculations, they are the unclean demons fallen from the divine service at the beginning of time and tireless in their determination to involve mankind in their rebellion and their ruin.

All of which brings us neatly to the second part of the City of God, books eleven to twenty-two, divided into three sets of four, dedicated to the exposition of the origin, progress, and destiny of the heavenly City and its rival, the diabolical city of the world. For the two cities were divided at the dawn of history when the Devil and his confederates fell from the worship of God. This catastrophe was recapitulated in the Fall of Man and although Adam and Eve were repentant, the consequences of their fall endured and were manifested in the murder of Abel by Cain. Cain and Seth thereafter became the founders among men of the rival cities already established in the angelic realm. Augustine notes the numerous earthly achievements of Cain's descendants recounted in Genesis, starting with Cain himself, literally the founder of the first human city. Like the pagan Romans they have their reward in this life. Their concern is here on this earth with the proud achievements of their own hands, not with the gift of God that surpasses all human understanding. He traces the destruction of the antediluvian world to the intermarriage of the sons of God (descendants of Seth) and the daughters of men (descendants of Cain). Hitherto the two cities had been socially segregated; their unification spelled the triumph of the earthly city, the extraction of a remnant of eight souls, and the destruction of the primeval world. But even before the murder of Abel, within the very flesh of the repentant Adam and Eve raged the war between the penitent spirit, the principle of life and redemption, and the downward pull of delinquent creation. The waters of the flood had no power to end this war or cure man's essential malady. Once more the bulk of human society was swept into the cause of the earthly city and God extracted in the person of Abraham the remnant from which He fashioned the people of election from which the Savior would be born.

The Doctor of Grace and Love lays down the path of the two cities through the histories of the Jewish people and the great Empires identified in the visions of the prophet Daniel. Above all, however, he focuses on the first and fourth, Babylon and Rome. Babylon as the original postdiluvian geopolitical expression of the earthly city represents a type of which Rome was the fulfilment. In the story of Romulus and Remus Augustine sees a crucial echo of the history of Cain and Abel. As the two cities were separated at the beginning of human history by one innocent and one fratricidal brother, so the supreme expression of the earthly city was founded by two equally fratricidal brothers. For the peace of the earthly city is a mere truce of convenience; it is only their pragmatic pact to secure the perishing goods of this world which prevents its citizens from turning on each other. Likewise, the faculties and desires of the citizens of the mystic Babylon are perpetually at war with each other, for without harmony between God and man there can be no harmony within man himself.

At last Augustine turns to the eternal destinies of the two cities. Strictly only the Heavenly City has such a destiny. For, when the elect depart from it, the earthly city and the flesh of its citizens will turn in upon itself and devour itself and it will no longer be a city. And yet, Augustine writes,

> not even the saints and faithful worshippers of the one true and most high God are safe from the manifold temptations and deceits of the demons. For in this abode of weakness, and in these wicked days, this state of anxiety has also its use, stimulating us to seek with keener longing for that security where peace is complete

and unassailable. There we shall enjoy the gifts of nature, that is to say, all that God the Creator of all natures has bestowed upon ours — gifts not only good, but eternal — not only of the spirit, healed now by wisdom, but also of the body renewed by the resurrection. There the virtues shall no longer be struggling against any vice or evil, but shall enjoy the reward of victory, the eternal peace which no adversary shall disturb. This is the final blessedness, this the ultimate consummation, the unending end. Here, indeed, we are said to be blessed when we have such peace as can be enjoyed in a good life; but such blessedness is mere misery compared to that final felicity. When we mortals possess such peace as this mortal life can afford, virtue, if we are living rightly, makes a right use of the advantages of this peaceful condition; and when we have it not, virtue makes a good use even of the evils a man suffers. But this is true virtue, when it refers all the advantages it makes a good use of, and all that it does in making good use of good and evil things, and itself also, to that end in which we shall enjoy the best and greatest peace possible.

And it is in the contemplation of this peace, when the City of God alone remains, transfigured in the glory of the Eternal Jerusalem, that Augustine ends his great work.

It would be no exaggeration to say that as Marx's *Das Kapital* was to the Soviet Union and the other Communist tyrannies of modern times, so was the *City of God* to Mediaeval Christendom — but with results that could hardly be more different. The patriarch of the Mediaeval West, Charlemagne, kept his copy of the *City of God* beside his bed. St Thomas More lectured on it to the Carthusians of London as he discerned his vocation as the last great statesman of Catholic England — the very same Carthusians who would precede him to martyrdom at the hands of the tyrant who restored his country to the dominion of Babylon.

Central to its political power is Augustine's republicanism. The term *Res Publica* remained the official designation of the Roman state into Augustine's own time. The first emperor had claimed not to be founding a monarchy but restoring the republic. The pretense was officially maintained largely until the end of the third century when the Neo-Platonic totalitarianism took over and still in some part up to and beyond Augustine's own time. But Augustine and the other great Latin writers of antiquity knew all the same that it was a pretense. Augustine relied on the republican writers who witnessed the last embers of Roman liberty, Sallust and Cicero, for his claim that the Roman commonwealth had perished before the coming of Christ. We know from his other writings that, while he held there was place for monarchy, he saw it as a sign of a degenerate age. As he writes in *De Libero Arbitrio*,

> Human beings and peoples [do not] belong to the class of things that are eternal, and can neither change nor perish...[but are] changeable and subject to time...Therefore if a people is well-ordered and serious minded, and carefully watches over the common good, and everyone in it values private affairs less than the public interest, is it not right to enact a law which allows this people to choose their own magistrates to look after their own interests—that is, the public interest?...But suppose that the same people becomes gradually depraved. They come to prefer private interest to the public good. Votes are bought and sold. Corrupted by those who covert honors they hand over power to wicked and profligate men. In such a case would it not be right for a good and powerful man (if one could be found) to take from this people the power of conferring honors and to limit it to the discretion of a few good people, or even to one?

But the credentials of the Republic to be a true city bound together by justice and the common good are only in a very secondary sense founded for Augustine on the external liberty of its political institutions. Far more fundamentally they are rooted in the liberty of grace, the glorious liberty of the sons of God.

For this argument, which really is the central argument of the *City of God*, Augustine is reliant on a key definition of Cicero's as to the nature of a Republic. Literally, of course, a republic is "the public thing," that which belongs to the people as a whole and thus presupposes the existence of a people—not a mere multitude, but a rationally ordered multitude, or, as Cicero defines it, "a multitude united in association by a common sense of right and a community of interest." This common sense of right or *ius* cannot exist without justice, *iustitia*, defined by the ancients as "the constant and perpetual resolve to render unto each one that which is his due."

The first requirement of justice is therefore that we render what is due to the One to Whom we owe most, indeed to Whom we owe all things. The first requirement of justice is that we worship the One True God in the manner He has appointed. For "kingdoms without justice," Augustine declares, "are but *latrocinia*," criminal gangs, multitudes of thieves united in association by a common agreement on the objects of their brigandage and the division of the loot. As the first deceiver stretched out his hand to take the divine likeness as if his by right rather than humbly receiving it as God's gift, so all those who have followed him on the road to eternal ruin are thieves and brigands. But only one community is authorized, only one community is able, to worship the One True God in the manner He has appointed through the offering that He Himself made as man on our behalf upon the Cross. For, as Augustine concludes, "there is no justice save in that republic whose founder and ruler is Christ." When Romulus founded Rome he gathered its citizens by proclaiming to the outlaws and criminals of the world that they could gather in his city and start afresh as citizens. Here, as in the splendid vices the Romans took to be virtues, we see a shadowy figure of the true Eternal City gathered together by the new song of the Gospel, fashioned by sinners washed clean in the blood of the Lamb.

The virtues of the pagans are but splendid vices. They are truly vices but they are truly splendid. For the Romans to embrace the heavenly city and its path is to find everything they wrongly imagined to be great in their earthly republic restored, purified and made true in the grace of God. St Augustine calls out to them:

> In former times you had glory from the peoples, but, through the inscrutable decision of divine providence, the true religion was not there for you to choose. Awake! The day has come. You have already awakened in the persons of some of your people, in whose perfect virtue we Christians boast, and even in their suffering for the true faith; they have wrestled everywhere against hostile powers, have conquered them by the courage of their deaths, and "have won this country for us by their blood."
>
> It is to this country that we invite you, and exhort you to add yourself to the number of our citizens. The refuge we offer is the true remission of sins. Do not listen to those degenerate sons of

yours who disparage Christ and the Christians, and criticize these times as an unhappy age, when the kind of period they would like is one which offers not a life of tranquility but security for their vicious pursuits. Such satisfactions have never been enough for you, even in respect of your earthly country. Now take possession of the Heavenly Country, for which you will have to endure but little hardship; and you will reign there in truth and for ever. There you will find no Vestal hearth, no Capitoline stone, but the one true God, who fixes no bounds for you of space or time but will bestow an empire without end.

9

The Soul-Body Model of the Relation of Spiritual and Temporal Authority*

Thomas de Vio, O.P., Cardinal Cajetan

St Thomas, *Summa theologiae* II-II, q. 60, a. 6, obj. 3 and ad 3:

Obj. 3: Moreover, spiritual power is distinguished from temporal power. But sometimes prelates having spiritual power involve themselves in those matters which pertain to the secular power. Therefore usurped judgment is not unlawful.

Ad 3: To the third, it should be said that the secular power is subject to the spiritual power as the body to the soul. And thus judgment is not usurped if a spiritual prelate involves himself in temporal matters so far as concerns those matters in which the secular power is subject to the spiritual, or which are granted to the spiritual power by the secular power.

Commentary of Cardinal Cajetan, in IIamIIae, q. 60, a. 6

Having omitted the fifth article, the matter of which (as regards subjects) has been discussed in the preceding Book; in the sixth article, in the response to the third objection, note that the Author, assuming from the decretal *Solitae benignitatis, de Maiorit. et Obed.* that the temporal power is subject to the spiritual as the body to the soul, assigns two modes in which the spiritual power involves

---

* Thomas de Vio, O.P., Cardinal Cajetan (1469–1534) was one of the most important commentators on the *Summa theologiae* of St Thomas, whose teachings he defended against Scotists, Renaissance Humanists, and Protestant Reformers. In the following passage he explicates St Thomas's use of the traditional likeness of the subjection of temporal to spiritual power to the subjection of the body to the soul. Translated by Timothy Wilson.

itself in temporal things: the first of which belongs to the spiritual power from its nature; while the second belongs to it from another, namely, from the secular power itself.

Now, for evidence of this assumption, know, from the *De anima* bk. II,[1] that the soul acts upon the body according to three kinds of cause: namely, effectively, because it effects the corporeal motions of the animal; formally, because it is its form; and finally, because the body is for the sake of the soul. And it is similar, proportionally speaking, regarding the spiritual power in respect of the secular power: indeed, it is as its form and mover and end. For it is manifest that the spiritual is formal in respect of the corporeal: and by this, the power administering of spiritual things is formal in respect of the power administering of secular things, which are corporeal. It is also indubitably clear that corporeal and temporal things are for the sake of spiritual and eternal things, and are ordered to these as an end. And since a higher end corresponds to a higher agent, moving and directing; the consequence is, that the spiritual power, which is concerned with spiritual things as its first object, moves, acts, and directs the secular power and those things which belong to it to the spiritual end. And from this it is clear that the spiritual power, of its very nature, commands the secular power to the spiritual end: for these are the things in which the secular power is subject to the spiritual. The text intends this specification with the words: *so far as concerns those matters in which the secular power is subject to the spiritual.* The Author observes by this, that the secular power is not wholly subject to the spiritual power. On account of this, in civil matters one ought rather to obey the governor of the city, and in military matters the general of the army, than the bishop, who should not concern himself with these things except in their order to spiritual things, just as with other temporal matters. But if it should happen that something of these temporal things occurs to the detriment of spiritual salvation, the prelate, administering of these things through prohibitions or precepts for the sake of spiritual salvation, *does not move the sickle unto another's crop*, but makes use of his own authority: for as regards these things, all secular powers are subject to the spiritual power.

---

1 *De Anima* 415b8–12; St Thomas, *In libros de anima*, lib. II, lect. vii.

And thus, besides the thing assumed, the first mode by which the spiritual power judges of temporal things is clear.

And the second mode, namely, from the concession of the secular power, is quite sufficiently clear in prelates who have both jurisdictions in many places, as gifts from princes.

10

On the Two Powers*
Domingo de Soto, O.P.

Whether the ecclesiastical power is supreme in such wise, that the civil power depends upon it, as its delegate.

We have considered it worthwhile to treat, at the end of this matter of orders, the question of the ecclesiastical power in respect of the civil, divided into two articles. The first of which is, whether the ecclesiastical power is supreme, in such a way, that the civil power depends upon it as its delegate.

For the affirmative, one may argue thus:

[First,] Christ instituted the Church as the best commonwealth: but the best commonwealth is that which, after the manner of a kingdom, is governed by one supreme head, as the Philosopher says in the *Politics*, bk. II: but there cannot be a supreme head in the Church, unless the civil power be wholly subject to the ecclesiastical, so that the pope is the lord of all, as much temporal as spiritual. Otherwise there would be two heads, which the Philosopher condemns in the *Metaphysics*, bk. XII. And it is confirmed from

---

* Domingo de Soto (1494–1560) was a prominent Dominican of the sixteenth century in Spain. One of the foremost Thomist philosophers and theologians of his time, he occupied a chair of theology at the famous University of Salamanca from 1532 to 1545, and then held the principal chair of theology there from 1552 to 1556. In 1545 he was selected by Emperor Charles V as imperial theologian to the Council of Trent, where he labored much in drawing up decrees and answering the principal heresies of that age. He is perhaps best known for his treatise *De natura et gratia* in three books, which he composed during the Council of Trent and in which he expounded the Thomist doctrine regarding original sin and grace; but he left a great many other able works, including the large and worthy treatise *De iustitia et iure* in ten books, commentaries upon several of the works of Aristotle, a commentary upon St Paul's letter to the Romans, and two volumes of commentary upon the fourth book of Peter Lombard's *Liber Sententiarum*. The translation presented here is from *In IV Sent.*, dist. 25, q. 2 (On the ecclesiastical power, and the exemption of clerics), a. 1. Translated by Timothy Wilson.

Romans 12 and 1 Corinthians 12, where Paul says, that Christians are all one body consisting of diverse members: and there must be a single head of one body, lest it be monstrous. Jerome declares this with the example of bees, can. *In apibus.* 7. q. 1.

Secondly: Christ left to his vicar that power which he himself had: but he, even insofar as he is man, was not only Lord of the kingdom of heaven in spiritual things, but also king of temporal things: for he says, in the final chapter of Matthew, *All power is given to me in heaven and in earth:* for which reason in Apocalypse 19 he is called the King of kings, and Lord of lords.

Thirdly, it is gathered from Canon law, for in any cause whatsoever, one may appeal from any secular judge to the apostolic see, 11. q. 1. can. *Quicumque litem,* and the pope can depose kings: for Pope Zachary deposed the king of the Franks as harmful to the kingdom, 15. q. 6. can. *Alius,* and Innocent deposed Frederick, dist. 96. can. *Duo sunt.*[1]

But to the contrary, there is the authority of Pope Pelagius[2] in the same cited can. *Duo sunt,* where he says: *Two there are, emperor Augustus, by which this world is ruled, the sacred authority of the pontiffs, and the royal power.*

Concerning this dispute, as Turrecremata says in bk. 2. cap. 113, there are two diametrically opposed opinions, between which there is a middle opinion, which shall be established as the catholic. For there are those who, out of an enthusiasm and (as they think) a zeal for religion, attempt to extol the apostolic dignity, so that they think the Roman Pontiff to be the supreme judge as much in temporal as in spiritual matters, and thus it pertains to him to institute kings and secular princes, who thus are as his vicars delegate. Augustinus de Ancona partakes of this opinion in his *Tractatus de potestate ecclesiastica,* whom Sylvester followed, at *Papa* §2. Panormitanus is also a patron of this opinion, as well as many other jurists. Others, having sunken to the other extreme, withdraw from the Supreme

---

1 An obvious error; evidently Soto refers here to Innocent IV's *Ad apostolicae,* de sent. et re iud. in 6.—Trans.

2 Another obvious error; but this error seems to have been somewhat common around that time. One finds a similar attribution of the can. *Duo sunt* to Pelagius in Turrecremata, Guarnieri, and Marchese, to name a few. Tom. I of the 1578 Venetian edition of Turrecremata's commentaries on the *Decretum* of Gratian, in a marginal note, observes that "a more modern codex ascribes this *capitulum* to Gelasius."—Trans.

Pontiff absolutely any temporal power; no indeed, in temporal matters they subject him entirely to the civil power, and permit no exemption of clerics to be of divine law. Concerning this latter heresy, we shall speak at greater length in the following article.

To the present question, therefore, a response is made in five conclusions.

The first [conclusion]: The ecclesiastical power and the civil are two and distinct. This assertion is from Pelagius [*recte*: Gelasius] in the cited can. *Duo sunt*. But because this matter touches upon divine law, it is to be gathered from the testimonies of sacred scripture. For, because (I plead your good indulgence) it has not been granted to the interpreters of the sacred Canons to treat of the divine and natural law with precision, it is no wonder that they prate idly in this present matter. For the sacred Canons which speak of this matter shall have to be elucidated through sacred scripture, from which they are collected.

Thus the conclusion is proved: as the Philosopher says in *Ethics*, bk. II, potencies and arts differ through actions, and actions through the objects and ends whither the actions are directed: but in the mystical Christian body there are two ends, the one natural, whither civil administration tends, namely, the peace and tranquility of the republic: and the other supernatural, which is occupied in the divine consideration, which, as Paul says, neither eye hath seen, nor ear heard: therefore there are diverse powers for pursuing those ends. The reason is that of Hugo, part. 2 *de sacramen.*, where he says, that since there are two lives, the one terrestrial and the other spiritual, in order that both be preserved in justice, and that utility prosper, there is necessary a twofold power for the conservation of justice: one, which presides over terrestrial things to govern the civil life, and the other, which presides over spiritual things to order the spiritual life.

Now the same truth is proved, secondly. The ecclesiastical power is the faculty of the keys of the kingdom of heaven, as is clear from Matthew 16 and 18, and likewise of the remission of sins, as is had in John 20, and moreover, the power of consecrating the true body and blood of Christ: but this faculty has not been conceded to the civil power: therefore there are two powers.

Thirdly, because in order to move men to ends of this sort, there are diverse laws, namely, in respect of the temporal end there are laws entirely human and civil, but in respect of the supernatural end, the supernatural mandates of the sacraments are also used: likewise there are also diverse swords: namely, diverse punishments: for civil punishments are consummated in the death of the body, nor are they extended further: while the ecclesiastical power uses a sword moreover spiritual: namely, excommunication, and other censures.

Fourthly, and finally: the spiritual power is referred proximately to souls, and it is incumbent upon it to examine and consider the divine laws, and is concerned with divine worship, and thus it institutes pontiffs and priests, which functions do not belong to kings, but the rights of emperors are to negotiate and to create praetors and other magistrates. There are diverse hierarchies, therefore, and thus diverse powers; and moreover, not only in the Mosaic law but also in the law of nature, the priests were different from the other magistrates, and to them was entrusted the summit of religion and divine worship. For as we have demonstrated in dist. 1 q. 2, under every [condition of] law there was always some supernatural and necessary revelation of faith, which pointed out the necessary worship of God. No indeed, even in the state of nature these two powers would have flourished, although in that case no sacraments would have been necessary. But it is not proper to this place to discuss this further.

But perhaps one might argue to the contrary. The end of the civil commonwealth is, as Aristotle says in the same place, to make the citizens good, and well-instructed: now none is good but he who would be a friend of God, which friendship suffices for eternal life: whence it is gathered, that civil laws suffice for the obtaining of eternal life. And it is confirmed from Matthew 22, *If you wish to enter into life, keep the commandments*, where he was speaking of the commandments of nature, *Thou shalt not kill, Thou shalt not steal*, etc., which if it be true, the end of the civil and ecclesiastical power is one, and not many, and thus there is but one power. But the heretics of this age gather, that the spiritual power, along with the civil, lies with kings and the civil republic. This heresy, though it is the most recent of all, never heard of before our age, yet is the most pestilential.

It is responded, therefore, that although the commands of the natural and civil law be referred to the order of eternal felicity, still they are not sufficient for obtaining it: for where Aristotle says that it is the purpose of the ruler to make the citizens good, he spoke only of moral goodness, but the moral duties do not suffice for the friendship of God without infused charity, without which no man is either called or is good, nor any work good. For this reason, beyond the natural and civil law, there is required, in the first place, the special help of God, and the laws of the sacraments, which are supernatural: for *unless a man be reborn of water and the holy Spirit, he cannot enter into the kingdom of God*: and *except you eat the flesh of the son of man*, it is said, *you shall not have life in you*. This power, therefore, which Christ committed in the first place to his vicar and through him to the Church, is more exalted than the civil.

But if you should ask again, surely God could have comprehended both through a single power and a single head: namely, that the king (just as has been imagined recently amongst the English) would administer all things pertaining as much to divine worship as to the civil commonwealth, or that the pope would do both alone? It is responded, that it is not our concern to dispute on the absolute power of God; yet because, as it says in Wisdom 7, *[wisdom] ordereth all things sweetly*, and it is the task of wisdom, as Aristotle says in the Metaphysics, to order and govern all things in an orderly and apposite manner according to their ends, it was not seemly to commit such diverse offices to one power alone, for the ecclesiastical and civil administrations are very much different. Indeed, the one is administered by secular magistrates, who have wives and children, while the other is appropriate to none but men free from the burden of a wife: for as the Apostle says in 1 Corinthians 7, he who has a wife seeks how he may please her, and they who are without a wife, seek how they may please God. If, therefore, the same power were to lie with the same supreme governor, it would be impossible for everything not to be jumbled, and thus subject to many perils. For this reason it was necessary that diverse heads be determined for matters so diverse, and that the Church would be as a queen seated at the right hand of the ruler, clothed round about with variety, and that the mystical body of Christ be compacted from various members, as Paul says in 1 Corinthians 10.

The second conclusion: The spiritual power is more excellent than the civil. Their very names declare this conclusion, as Innocent says in the capit. *Solitae* de maior. et obedien. The pontiff in that place reprehends the Emperor of Constantinople, who, on account of the testimony in 1 Peter 2: *Be ye subject therefore to every human creature for God's sake: whether it be to the king as excelling; or to governors as sent by him for the punishment of evildoers*, etc., opined that the royal power was more excellent than all others. He reprehends him, I say, objecting that in that place the Apostle only signifies the excellence of kings in temporal matters, in respect of dukes and others, who receive those offices from him. But nevertheless, the pontiff prevails in spiritual matters, which are as much worthier than temporal matters, as the soul surpasses the body. And so, just as the soul is that which vivifies the body, and the spirit is the commander of the body: so also the spiritual power ought to be preeminent over temporal things. To this he also joins another and most apt similitude, that God instituted the pontifical and regal authorities as two great lights, namely the Sun and the Moon, for just as the Sun presides over the day, so also the pontiff over spiritual things: and just as the Moon presides over the night, so also the king over temporal things, which take the likeness of the night. Moreover, just as the Moon receives light from the Sun, so also does the civil power receive light from the spiritual: for the king ought so to rule and govern temporal matters, that they serve spiritual religion.

This is proved secondly from the end of both powers: for as the Philosopher says in the *Ethics*, bk. I, the order between ends is such as that between faculties and arts which have them as their set ends. On account of this, the equestrian art is more excellent than the bridle-making art, and the nautical art more excellent than the art of making ships, because the ends of the former are superior to the ends of the latter: and thus the equestrian art commands the bridle-making art as to how it ought to fabricate the bridle, and the nautical art the shipmaking art as to how it ought to make a ship: since therefore the end of the spiritual power is, as we have said, eternal beatitude, and the end of the secular power is the tranquil state of the republic, which is referred to that supernal beatitude, it happens that the ecclesiastical power is higher.

Furthermore, this is proved by the example of Paul in Hebrews 7, where he proves that the priest Melchisedech was superior to the secular Abraham, because, as it is read in Genesis 14, Melchisedech blessed Abraham, and (says Paul) without doubt he who blesses is greater than he who is blessed.

The third conclusion: The excellence of the ecclesiastical power, in respect of the civil, is not of this sort, that the pope is the lord of the whole earth in temporal things. We do not speak of a particular kingdom, whether the Supreme Pontiff is truly the temporal king of those cities and provinces of which he holds supreme dominion in temporals, since in these he knows no superior on earth. So much do we not deny this, that we think it pertains to his defense and splendor. But we speak of the universal kingdom of the world, whether the whole world, or the Christian world. This conclusion follows from the first: for if the pope were supreme lord of all things, there would not be two powers, but one: for then, just as all prelates are subject to the supreme pontiff, and dukes to the king, by the same reason and in the same manner, kings would be subject to the Supreme Pontiff, and would depend upon him entirely in the same way: for this reason, just as the ecclesiastical power is one, and the whole civil power one, in like manner then the two would be simultaneously one.

So that this conclusion and those subsequent might be known through their first foundation, it should be noted, that Christ left no other power to his vicar than that which he himself received insofar as he was man and redeemer of the world: yet he took up no temporal kingdom, but that precise dominion of temporal things which was necessary for the end of redemption. I have said, insofar as he was man: for inasmuch as he was God, it is entirely acknowledged and accepted by all mortals, and not merely Christians, that he is by right of creation the absolute Lord and king of the world. For, as the Psalm has it, *the earth is the Lord's, and the fulness thereof*: and as it is read in Proverbs 8, by him *kings reign, and lawgivers decree just things*. For this reason, John Faber, who in his commentary upon *c. de summa Trinitate* attempts to show that Christ was a king because he was God, produces nothing of relevance. For we dispute of him insomuch as he was man. But insofar as he was man, he could indeed, if he had wished, have taken up even universal secular dominion of the world. And yet it is the case, as we have asserted, that he did not accept a dominion and kingdom of this sort, but only spiritual, and accepted of temporals only so much as was necessary for that spiritual dominion. For the spiritual kingdom is that which, as we have said above, has eternal life for its proximate end: and the temporal kingdom is that which is concerned with the peaceful status of the Republic. The conclusion is therefore proved, firstly. In the whole of the gospel, there occurs no mention of the temporal kingdom of Christ: it is therefore vain, lest I say temerarious, to assert it: for if a thing of such importance were true, the Evangelists never would have been silent upon it: but they pay heed only to the spiritual kingdom, which is called the kingdom of heaven. For this reason, the *protheme* of the preaching of John the precursor, and then of Christ, was, as in Matthew 3, *Do penance: for the kingdom of heaven is at hand*, and Matthew 5, *Blessed are the poor in spirit: for theirs is the kingdom of heaven*, and many other things of that sort.

Secondly, it is confirmed by plain reason. Christ, who, since he was God, as David says, had no need of our goods, put on our humanity for that reason and end only, that he might bring about our redemption: for this reason, he preached the faith to us, and instituted laws, and created Apostles and pontiffs, who would be our shepherds, that they might lead us to that beatitude: therefore, since Christ took up nothing superfluous, and the temporal power of a kingdom, so broadly and absolutely patent in secular kings, was not necessary to him for that end, the consequence is, that he by no means took it up.

But the patrons of the contrary opinion say, that Christ seized royal power of the whole world on account of his outstanding excellence and dignity. Yet reason stands to the contrary, because this pertained not at all to that same excellence of his. For, I ask, what increase of honor would accrue to Christ, since he was God *per se*, and, insofar as he was man, king also of the kingdom of heaven, if he had taken up temporal dominion and kingdoms, that is, their power? None, certainly. No indeed, how much more loftily is his majesty then commended, that, aside from that which was necessary for his office, he scorned the whole world: for he lived in poverty, and chose for Apostles men abject and humble, and ever preached against the glory and pomp of the world: poverty, and humility, and repudiation of the world he both taught and extolled with praise. Life of this sort, after the fall of Adam, is best, and suffers fewer perils. Whence Paul says, Philippians 3, that he considers all these things as dung.

Thirdly, it is argued thus: Christ never discharged this office of royal power, no indeed, he always removed himself from the use of the same, which the partisans of the contrary opinion are unable to deny: for as he himself says, John 3: *God sent not his son into the world, to judge the world, but that the world may be saved by him.* And when the adulterous woman was brought before him [in John 8], whose cause he would judge, he passed no sentence as judge, by which he would either condemn or absolve her, but he only explicated the natural and divine law, *He that is without sin among you, let him first cast a stone at her.* And when the coin of the census was offered to him, he refused to judge whether or not the tax was due to Caesar, but left that to their judgment: only commending the natural and divine law, that if something be owed to Caesar, it be rendered to him, just as to God that which is his. And when others came to him, that he would sit as judge between them, he disparaged it as something lesser, saying, *Who hath appointed me judge over you?* Therefore, if he never discharged the office of king, it happens that he never took up such power: for that power is redundant and vain, which is never reduced to act. Sight or hearing accrue no dignity to man, except on account of their use. For this reason, if Christ was never to use that power, no dignity accrued to him from thence. Moreover, since power is made known through its acts, if the Gospel teaches us that he had neither the use nor the splendor of royal power, it is asserted without foundation that he took it up. For if he had taken it up on account of his dignity, he would have had to make it visible to men through its use. This was so far from his intent, that when the crowds set off to make him king, he withdrew himself from their attempt. A futile device, then, is that charming opinion of some, who say that in Christ there was royal power, but not its use.

A fourth and more evident argument. Christ, as we are taught by the evangelical testimony, was naught but king of the Jews: but the king of the Jews was not to be a king of temporal goods, but of a spiritual and sempiternal inheritance: therefore he was not a king in temporals, as are secular kings. This is plainly confirmed from John 18, where, when Christ, who had been accused by them before Pilate of making himself a king, was asked by the governor whether he was a king, he asked him in turn whether he had said so from himself, or whether others had told it of him: as if to ask, of what kingdom he meant it: of that secular kingdom, by which the Romans and other nations rule, or another and higher? And when Pilate responded that he had said it not from himself, but from the relation of the Jewish nation: Christ, conceding that he is the king whom they awaited, adds, that his kingdom is not of this world, that is, of that sort which are temporal and perishable kingdoms. Hence the governor, not understanding that mystery, absolved him of the crime presented. And afterward, as if by a prophetic spirit, he affixed that epitaph to the Cross, *Jesus the Nazarene, King of the Jews.*

And if we consult the ancient testimonies of the prophets, they plainly manifest this. For he himself says through the prophet, Psalm 2: *But I am appointed king by him* (namely, God) *over Sion his holy mountain* (namely, the Church), *preaching his commandments.* Behold, he established his kingdom in the preaching only of the faith of the celestial kingdom. This is consonant with Matthew 28, where he says: *All power is given to me in heaven and in earth. Going therefore, teach ye all nations; baptizing them,* etc., where he affirms, that no other power was given him, than that which pertains to the celestial kingdom. And Jeremias 23: *Behold the days come, saith the Lord, and I will raise up to David a just branch: and a king shall reign, and shall be wise ... In those days shall Juda be saved,* that is, there will only be a king in order to save Juda. And Isaias 9: *He shall sit upon the throne of David, and upon his kingdom, to establish it ... from henceforth and forever.* Thus David speaks of his offspring, Psalm 144: *Thy kingdom is a kingdom of all ages:* because it is not brought to an end, as the secular kingdom is, through the elapsing of mortal life, but without interruption endures forever. The Angel expounded this to Mary, saying: *The Lord God shall give unto him the throne of David his father, and he shall reign in the house of Jacob for ever. And of his kingdom there shall be no end.*

Some have imagined that he was a king by paternal right: for Joseph descended from David through Solomon, and the blessed Virgin through Mathan; but this is not pertinent. Firstly, because that kingdom was peculiar only to that province: but we speak of a universal kingdom of the whole world. Moreover, that temporal kingdom of David was entirely extinguished in Sedecias,[3] as is written in 4 Kings 24, according to the prophecy of Jeremias 22. Wherefore Ambrose, in bk. 3 *super Lucam* says, that although Christ the king descended from Jechonias, to whom it was threatened by the prophet that none of his offspring was to be king, yet (he says) there is no contradiction: because he did not rule with secular honor, nor sit in the seat of Jechonias, but in the seat of David. No indeed, although Jechonias had sat in the seat of David, yet not in the same seat as Christ: the latter had an eternal kingdom, which sort David himself did not have.

Finally, the same truth is confirmed by the testimony of all the holy fathers, for whom the thing was ever undoubted, that Christ took up no other kingdom than the spiritual kingdom of heaven. Whence Augustine, *Book of 83 Questions*, q. 61, and wherever else he discusses this matter, says nothing but that Christ was our king, for that he gave to us an example of battling and conquering, by whose leadership we are liberated from Egypt, and brought into the heavenly Jerusalem, as into the land of promise.

But if someone should object to us blessed Thomas, in *opusculum* 20, lib. 3, cap. 13 [i.e., *De Regno*], where it appears to some that he taught the contrary opinion, it is responded, that it shall be clear to no one reading him attentively that he was of such an opinion. For there he establishes only that Christ was monarch of the whole universe, which he deduces from Psalm 8, *Thou hast subjected all things under his feet*, and from Malachi, *From the rising of the sun to its setting, great is his name.* Now these testimonies are

---

3 In other translations, Zedekiah.

understood only of his heavenly kingdom, in respect of which all things are subject to him. Which St Thomas himself acknowledges, adding, that that dominion and kingdom of Christ is ordered to the salvation of the soul, and to spiritual goods, although temporal things are not excluded from it insofar as they are ordered to spiritual things. He does not, therefore, affirm that he was a king in temporals except precisely in the order to spiritual things. And thus to be understood are his final words *in II Sent.*

But Burgensis, *addit. 2 super Matt. 1*, contrives the contrary opinion, namely, that he was king in temporals, although he admits that it cannot at all be gathered from the testimonies of the prophets, who ascribe only an eternal kingdom to him. But he says that because the Jews were anticipating him to be a temporal king also, God ordained that Christ would have the same dignity. Now this conjecture is so tenuous, that it rather confirms our opinion. For that opinion of the Jews was false and erroneous: for aside from the testimonies cited, they had the clear witness of Zacharias, *Behold thy king will come to thee, the just and savior: he is poor, and riding upon an ass,* by whom they were taught that he would come without royal pomp. It was not fitting, therefore, that Christ take up a temporal kingdom on account of that error.

Let the good reader consult whether I have confirmed this foundation of truth with so many things. We now turn to the confirmation of the third conclusion. And indeed, should Christ have taken up a temporal kingdom: yet it would not immediately follow thence, that he committed an equal power to his vicar, for we could say that such pertained to his power of excellence, just as does his power to institute sacraments, and to confer grace without these, which function he did not commit to the pope. But since neither did he take up royal power, it is most plain, that neither did he commit it to his vicar.

But furthermore, the same truth shines forth from what Christ says, Matthew 20 and Luke 22, *You know that the princes of the Gentiles lord it over them; and they that are the greater, exercise power upon them. It shall not be so among you: but whosoever will be the greater among you* (namely, Peter, who was to be the head of the Church), *let him be your minister. Even as the Son of man is not come to be ministered unto, but to minister, and to give his life a redemption for many.* Which place Bernard introduces, *De consideratione* lib. 2, and says: "For what else has the Apostle given to you? *What I have*, he says, *I give thee*. What is that? One thing I know, it is not gold or silver. Albeit you claim these things to yourself for any other reason: but not by Apostolical right; for he could not give to you that which he had not: that which he had, he gave, as I have said, the solicitude over the church[es].[4] Can it be that he says domination? Hear him. *Neither as lording it over the clergy*, he says, *but being made a pattern of the flock*. And lest you think this said in mere humility, and not truth also, it is the words of the Lord in the Gospel, *The kings of the Gentiles lord it over them; and they that have power over them, are called beneficent:* and he continues, *But you not so*. It is plain: lordship is forbidden to the Apostles. Go, then: try, if you dare, to take up the office of an Apostle as one who dominates, or to exercise lordship as an Apostle. Plainly you are prohibited from one or the other. If you should wish to have both at once, you shall lose both. Do not think yourself excepted from the number of those of whom God speaks thus: *They have reigned, but not by me; they have been princes, and I knew not*. This is the apostolical pattern: mastery is forbidden, ministry is enjoined." And below: "Go out into the field (the field is the world): go out not as a master, but as a servant." Thus Bernard. With Bernard as interpreter, Christ could not have removed this temporal dominion from the apostles in a more splendid manner. Hence it is a fiction to say that the pope has the power of this dominion without its use. For that a power is vain which cannot be reduced to act, is proven much more efficaciously of this, than of Christ.

Likewise. If he had such a power, the pope would also be able to usurp the jurisdiction of princes without injury, and to remove and institute kings even outside of causes of faith: which the most holy pontiffs, whatever their flatterers should say, certainly have never dared to attempt. Indeed Innocent,[5] in the cited can. *Duo*

---

4 The 1560 edition of de Soto's commentary, from which we translate, here reads *super ecclesiam* in his quotation of Bernard; the 1538 Lyon edition, and the 1701 Paris edition, reads *super Ecclesias*. — Trans.

5 Here de Soto seems once again to misattribute the can. *Duo sunt* to Pope Innocent IV; see note 1. — Trans.

sunt, recognized that the two powers of the emperor and the pope are distinct. Nor does he attribute any power of the pope over kings other than that of a pastor, such that he can excommunicate them, and remove them by reason of the faith.[6] And the can. *Si imperator* says that the Emperor has the privileges of his power, which he has obtained divinely for the sake of administering the public laws. And in the cap. *Per venerabilem*. qui filii sunt legitimi, he frankly says that he does not have power in temporals over the king of France. And whatever others might dream up, he understood that of all kings. And in can. *Cum ad verum*, Nicholas expressly says that neither has the Emperor seized the rights of the pontificate, nor the pontiff the Imperial name: since the mediator of God and man Christ Jesus has divided the offices of both powers with their own proper acts and distinct dignities.

Moreover, these things are more clearly confirmed. The administrations of the ecclesiastical and the civil republic are so different, that the ecclesiastical is impeded most of all by secular business: for this reason all the canon laws admonish the clerical order not to mix themselves up in secular affairs. Because of this, it was most just that they be most removed from marriage: for as Paul says, they who have wives, seek how they may please the wife. Certainly for this reason, in the same can., Nicholas says that just as the Emperor ought not to mix himself up in divine affairs, so also the pope, soldiering for God, ought not to entangle himself in secular business, lest he seem to preside, not over divine things, but secular.

But in order that these things might become even clearer, it is argued, again. Power, as much civil as ecclesiastical, is divinely instituted: for *there is no power but from God*, as the Apostle says in Romans 13: *and those that are, are ordained of God: and therefore, he that resisteth the power* whether civil or ecclesiastical, *resisteth the ordinance of God*. Yet God wisely has appointed these in different ways: for he has granted to each and every republic the civil power through the law of nature, of which he is the author, as we have demonstrated copiously in *De iustitia et iure*, lib. IV, q. 4. a. 1: for to each and every republic there pertains the governance of itself,

---

6 This is the conclusion that may be drawn, not from the can. *Duo sunt* of Gelasius, but from the cap. *Ad apostolicae* of Innocent IV; see note 1.—Trans.

as it belongs to all things to preserve themselves: namely, that they rule themselves either by the power of *optimates*, or of the people, or of a king: for which reason the people voluntarily transfer to the ruler all their authority and power, as is read in l. *Quod principi de constitu. principum.* ff. But Christ by himself conferred the ecclesiastical power to his vicar. The royal power, therefore, is derived from God through the republic: in which sense the text of Proverbs 8 is understood, *Through me kings reign, and lawgivers decree just things:* but the ecclesiastical and evangelical power was committed by Christ to Peter: therefore, the secular dominions of kingdoms were not simply committed either to Peter, or to his successors.

According to these it is then plainly argued. The law of faith does not destroy the law of nature, but perfects it: but kings ruled prior to the coming of Christ by the law of nature and the law of nations, which derive from the eternal law of God: whence it is read in Daniel 2, that the God of heaven gave to Nabuchodonosor power and a kingdom: and Christ responded to Pilate, *Thou shouldst not have any power against me, unless it were given thee from above*: therefore Christ did not change the kingdoms, whence the Apostle says in Romans 13, speaking universally of the potentates even of the infidels, *Let every soul be subject to higher powers*: to which he urges that tribute be paid. And in 1 Peter 2, Peter commands all Christians to *be subject to every human creature for God's sake*, whether *to the king*, he says, *as excelling*. And after: *Servants, be subject to your masters with all fear, not only to the good and gentle, but also to the froward*: whence it is gathered, that Christians ought to obey even infidel kings, so long as they rule without peril to the faith and injury to the Savior: much more freely, therefore, do the kings of Christians enjoy their power by themselves independently from the pope, so long as they inflict no injury upon the faith.

It is therefore an unvarnished invention, to constitute the pope thus as the ordinary judge of temporal kingdoms, and of kings, just as he is the supreme judge of the things of the church, and its prelates, or as the secular king is the judge of his dukes, and counts, and other vassals. Hence not all jurists hold to that opinion. For Ioannes Andreae, Hugo, and others think with us. Nor should Sylvester have adhered to the contrary opinion, since blessed Thomas (whose disciple he was), although he was a most studious defender of the Apostolic See, nowhere left such an opinion.

On that account, the aforementioned patrons of this opinion provide even less reason for its probability, saying that the donation made to Sylvester by Constantine (if such existed) or by king Philip, was not a donation, but a restitution. And *vice versa*, that Sylvester, for the good of peace, gave to Constantine the eastern empire. Likewise that the pope, if he does not use the administration of temporal goods in the whole Christian world, does so not from a lack of power which he truly has, but for the sake of confirming tranquility and peace with his sons. No wonder, therefore, if others, being more sensible, reject these as trifling nonsense. For if he had simply and absolutely the right of all temporals, he could have the use thereof without injury, which none of them dares to assert.

The fourth conclusion. Not only is the pope not the lord of temporal kingdoms, no indeed neither is he their superior such that he can institute kings: indeed, someone could perhaps say, that although he is not the lord simply speaking of temporal kingdoms, yet he can in an ordinary way institute kings everywhere, just as he institutes bishops, although he is not the lord simply speaking of episcopates, or just as a king institutes dukes and magnates, although he is not simply speaking the lord of their patrimonies: but this conclusion of ours asserts the contrary. Hence he cannot act as judge between kings in an ordinary way absent causes of faith, just as between ecclesiastical prelates, or between dukes. Unless perchance their quarrels incline to the detriment of the faith or of religion: for then he can very rightly do so, not only by way of fraternal correction, as Innocent says, cap. *Novit.* de iudic., but also with coercive judgement. This is gathered from what was said above: for either power is sufficient of itself, and divinely instituted in a different way, such that any king is, in temporals, made by his commonwealth the supreme judge in his own kingdom. Hence in the same cap. the same pontiff protests that he does not involve himself in order to usurp the judgment of kings. And Alexander III, cap. *Causam.* in 2. qui filii sunt legitimi, declares that judgment regarding possessions pertains, not to the church, but to the king.

From these, finally, the consequence is, that though the king were to break out into tyranny: absent injury to the faith, it is incumbent upon, not the pontiff, but the republic to expel him from the kingdom.

In sum, in the pope there is no merely temporal power, as there is in kings, except in the lands secularly subjected to him. This is what Cajetan, that loyal defender of the Apostolic See, asserted in his *Apologia de potestate papae*, cap. 6. And the reason is, that temporal power of this sort is simply not necessary for the government of the church.

Yet for greater clarity and firmness regarding these things, a fifth and likewise catholic conclusion is given against the heresy of those who deny *all* temporal power to the pontiff. Any civil power whatsoever is so subject to the ecclesiastical in the order to spiritual things, that the pope can, through his own spiritual power, as many times as regard for the faith and religion should require, not only act against kings by means of the buffets of ecclesiastical censures, and coerce them, but also deprive Christian princes of their temporal goods, and even proceed to their deposition. I have said, through his own spiritual power: because the power of the pontiff, insofar as he is pontiff, is not merely temporal, but he uses the temporal as minister of the spiritual. But this conclusion is not the same as the second: the latter only asserted that the ecclesiastical power is superior. Wherefore perhaps someone would merely conclude that the secular prince is bound to measure his laws and acts according to the spiritual end and to obey the pontiff in spiritual censures. But this [fifth] conclusion asserts moreover, that the pope can use temporal goods for his end and spiritual purposes, and can coerce princes by temporal punishments.

To elucidate this, it should be noted, that the ecclesiastical power is not only more excellent than the civil, for that its end, which is eternal beatitude, is more perfect and more exalted than civil felicity: but also for the reason that civil felicity is not sufficiently perfect in itself, and thus it is *per se* ordered and related to celestial beatitude. I wish to say, that there are not two commonwealths, entirely distinct and diverse, neither of which depends upon the other, of which sort are those of the French and the Spanish, or of which sort were the Roman and Athenian, for of these, even if one were more excellent and more perfect than another, yet neither was bound to serve the other. I say that the spiritual and civil powers are not to be compared thus: but the civil, whatsoever it be, is referred to the spiritual, which is unique to all Christians, because human felicity is of itself ordered to the divine. They are not as two arts wholly different, namely, as ironworking and woodworking, but as armor-making is ordered to the military art, and shipmaking is ordered to the art of navigating: the inferior of which is bound to make arms and ships in such a way, that they not deviate from the end of the superior art, and thus, as the Philosopher says in *Ethics* bk. I, the superior artisan commands the inferior artisans how they ought to work, because he is the judge of the inferior arts. In like manner, the civil commonwealth is referred to the spiritual: for both are simultaneously bound together into one mystical body, which is composed of both, as Paul luculently declares in Romans 12 and 1 Corinthians 12. Now in one body, all the members ought to be referred to one head, but spiritual things are not ordered to temporal things, which latter are less perfect, therefore on the contrary, temporals ought to be subject to the judgment of spirituals. Whence the same Apostle, in 1 Corinthians 2, comparing the temporal faculty to the spiritual, says that *the animal man perceiveth not these things which are of the Spirit of God,* but *the spiritual man judgeth all things, and he himself is judged of no man.* Nor is this opposed by what we have said above: namely, that the king has supreme power in temporals, because it lies with [the temporal power] to be subordinate to the spiritual in such a way that it must not deviate from it.

This foundation having been laid down, the argument is as follows. For the due government and administration of the spiritual commonwealth, it is necessary that all secular power obey it: therefore, also necessary thereupon, in the spiritual ruler, is the faculty of using temporals insofar as they are necessary for his end, and thus of coercing princes when it should be needed, even to the point of their deposition, as of members which are now putrid and pestiferous. Now Christ was not lacking in those things which were worthwhile to his Church; therefore not only did he take up in himself this sort of temporal power related to the spiritual, but also thereafter committed it to his vicar.

It is argued secondly for the same truth. The chief pontiff was constituted by Christ as the supreme and universal shepherd of the whole Christian flock. Now it is the office of the shepherd to recall to the way errant sheep, of whatever order and dignity they be, and to compel them in any regard: therefore, through that pastoral power, he can use temporals when there is need for it. And Innocent equipped himself with this reason against the Emperor of Constantinople, in the cap. *Solitae* de maior. & obedien. in order to coerce him. He says, "To Us in blessed Peter have the sheep of Christ been committed," with no difference placed between these [sheep] and those: and excepting nothing, as Christ said to Peter, *Whatsoever thou shalt bind*, etc. And in the same sense must Pope Nicholas be understood, cap. *Omnes*. 22 distin. where he says, that Christ "committed to blessed Peter, the key-bearer of eternal life, at once the laws of earthly and celestial authority." By the laws of earthly authority, he means the earthly power of temporal goods and princes, not absolutely, as the authors cited above falsely think, but in the order to spiritual things. And thus is the Gloss to be understood, so that it be in agreement with the truth which it thence collects, that the pope has both swords: because he can depose kings, as in 15. q. 6. can. *Alius*, and 96 dist., can. *Duo sunt*.[7] And with the same moderation should the text of Boniface be taken, in Extravag. *Unam sanctam*, de maiorit. & obedien. where he says, that the two swords, namely, the spiritual and the temporal, are in the power of the Roman Pontiff. Although, when he ascribes this sense to that word of the apostles in Luke 22, *Behold, here are two swords*, he does not mean to make such a sense an article of faith: for perhaps there Christ, when he said, *He that hath not, let him buy a sword*, meant nothing other than the calamity which threatened them. Hence Peter, who, taking it to be about the material sword, cut off the ear of Malchus, was reprehended. Nevertheless, it is still rightly adapted to our proposal. For this reason, kingdoms have never been changed by the pontiff except by reason of the faith: for this reason Pope Stephen transferred the empire from the

---

7 See the preceding note.

Spiritual and Temporal Power

Greeks to the Germans, as is clear in cap. *Venerabilem.* de electione, and cap. *Licet*, de foro competenti. And Innocent IV prohibited to the king of Portugal the administration of the kingdom, as in cap. *Grandi.* de supplenda negligentia praelatorum libro sexto.

But it is necessary to explain the difference between this conclusion and the two prior ones by way of examples. For however much the king administers the government of the kingdom in other kinds of offenses outside of peril to the faith, nothing falls to the pope, except by way of fraternal correction. But if, for example, the Christian king were to make laws to the detriment of the faith: namely, laws adverse to the sacraments, or to the Christian religion in any way, or if the pope were to call a Council, which the king impeded wrongly and contrary to right, or if he were to furnish aid to heretics, and infidels opposing our faith, or to schismatics, or move any other sort of mischief against the Apostolic See or the Church, then the pope would be able to act against him, not only with the spiritual sword, but with the temporal also.

But you might argue the contrary, firstly. Would it not be enough to hurl at them the fulminations of the spiritual sword, namely, of anathema and other censures? For [the Church] seems to have no other arms: for as Paul says in 1 Corinthians 10, *The weapons of our warfare are not carnal*, but are spiritual. It is responded, that the Church would not have been sufficiently provided for unless, when she is afflicted in her affairs by secular potentates, and spiritual arms do not suffice, she be able to compel them with the temporal sword also: because otherwise she would not have wholly coercive force, of the sort which is necessary for her.

But again, someone might ask whether in events of this sort the pope, omitting the spiritual sword, would be able to employ the temporal? For it seems that he could, because he has both equally. It is responded, that it neither befits him, nor is it licit, unless there were imminent peril, since the ordinary way of the pontiff is the pastoral rod: while the secular sword is extraordinary. Now the ordinary way ought to precede, nor ought he to use the temporal sword, unless there be urgent need that requires it: namely, when, having attempted spiritual force, he recognizes that this is not sufficient for the matter at hand. No indeed, unless it were in his own lands, of which he is the temporal lord, in order to defend them, but in others it does not befit the pope to wage war by himself, but when there is a prince of the Church rebellious and injurious to the faith, he ought to present the business of arms to another prince. For so far is what Paul says true, that the arms of Christian warfare are not carnal, although the legitimate sense is of the combat which each man sustains against the demons and his own flesh.

But because we have said that the pope can abrogate laws which would be harmful to the faith, it should be understood to mean, when they would cause manifest destruction. For that law of princes, that a testament is not valid unless confirmed by five witnesses, contradicts absolutely no word of sacred scripture in Matthew 18 and John 8, *That in the mouth of two or three witnesses every word may stand*: for that is understood where the sincerity of the human race flourishes: since, where human trust is so corrupted, it is not repugnant to those words to require more witnesses: because that Evangelical law does not forbid it. Likewise, the law which, in matters of cheating within a half of the just price, does not permit action, as in l. 2. C. de rescinden. venditio. and cap. *Cum dilecti* and cap. *Cum causa* de emptione et venditione, is not contrary to justice: because it does not absolve the one cheated in the forum of conscience, but it only intends to put quarrels to rest. But if the king were to make a law, so that a *possessor malae fidei* prescribes,[8] that would be both contrary to conscience and the nurse of many frauds and deceits: which would thus have to be abrogated by the pontiff: just as one reads it was abrogated in cap. *Vigilanti* and cap. ult. de praescriptionibus.

The solution to the first argument, therefore, is gathered from the foregoing. The civil and ecclesiastical power are two and distinct, as has been said: but Christ established only the ecclesiastical under one head of the whole earth: while he left the civil derived from the divine and natural law, so that each kingdom would have its own head: but he willed the civil to be subordinated to

---

8 Soto here makes reference to the second *regula iuris* of the Liber Sextus of Boniface VIII, *Possessor malae fidei ullo tempore non praescribit*; and to the Roman legal concept of *praescriptio longi temporis*, which established that a person who possessed something which did not in fact belong to him could lawfully gain ownership of it if it remained in his possession for a set amount of time and if he had originally obtained it in good faith.

the ecclesiastical such that its laws would not be opposed to the faith and the law which he himself preached: and in this manner is the pontiff the unique head of all Christian kings. And that is the sense of Paul when he says, that all Christians are the one mystical body of Christ. For nothing concerns the pope in regard to the infidels, other than to send preachers to them, who convince them of the faith in a legitimate manner and order. But this does not concern the present discussion, nor does the question of whether there is one emperor of the whole world: which we have discussed at length in *De iustitia et iure*, lib. IV.

To the second, a sufficient response is, that Christ assumed naught but a spiritual kingdom, and of temporals, only so much as was necessary for the former. And this is what the cited sacred testimonies teach.

To the third, finally, it is responded, that that canon, *Quicumque litem*, 11. q. 1, has been abrogated, as the Gloss says, which it proves with many decrees, such as cap. *Si duobus*, de appellationibus, and 2 quaestione sexta, can. *Non ita*, and many others. Indeed, that text is not a sacred determination of the Church, but of the emperor Theodosius, who wished to show his great affection toward the Apostolic See. At present there is no need of appealing from civil causes to the Church.

But if you should argue: the pope is the judge of all sins: it is responded, that this is true in the spiritual forum, but in the exterior forum he is only the judge of ecclesiastical causes, while civil causes are to be judged by the civil laws; unless no agreement could be reached between kings after all civil laws had been consulted: for then, the pope could interpose himself by way of fraternal correction, according to the tenor of cap. *Novit*. extra de iudiciis.

11

On the Mutual Relations between Church and State*

Tommaso Maria Cardinal Zigliara, O.P.

The nature of the Catholic Church having been set forth, and its power, consequently it remains to speak of the mutual relations existing between the Church and the civil State. And indeed it is proper to the Catholic Church, that it have members in every part of the world, and thus would rule over subjects of all nations; whence it comes about, that its power is found in intimate relation with civil States. It is necessary, therefore, that we speak of these mutual relations between the Church and the civil State. Indeed it is a difficult subject, not by its nature, but on account of the injustice of times and the malice of men. But that we might plainly determine the aforesaid relations, we begin from more remote principles, inquiring firstly *of political atheism*: whether indeed the political State is able to conduct itself as if no religion existed, and as if God did not exist;—secondly, *of liberty of conscience*, as they call it;—thirdly, *of liberty of cult*;—fourthly, *of liberty of teaching*;—fifthly, *of the subordination of the State to the Church*.

* Tommaso Maria Cardinal Zigliara was a prominent Thomist philosopher and theologian in the latter half of the nineteenth century. Among many other accomplishments, he was closely involved with the preparation of the Leonine edition of the Angelic Doctor's *Opera Omnia* and assisted in preparing the encyclicals *Aeterni Patris* and *Rerum Novarum*. The articles translated here are taken from chapter 5 of book two of the third part of Zigliara's widely circulated *Summa philosophica* (14th ed., 1910). Having treated of domestic, civil, and religious society in their principles and particulars in the preceding books and chapters of this part, he now sets himself the task of treating in brief the relations which should obtain between those two perfect societies, the Church and the State. Translated by Timothy Wilson.

ARTICLE 1
On Political Atheism

I. The notion of political atheism. Earlier in our treatise we distinguished atheism into the species of *theoretical* and *practical*, insofar as either the existence of God is positively denied, or life is conducted as if God did not exist. In this second sense do we inquire concerning political atheism. For the elements of society are two: the governing element, in which there rests social authority, and the governed element, or the subjects, who are ordered by the ruler to the common good. And with respect to the governing element—whether he be called a prince, or is called by another name—is he able, in the drawing up of laws, in their execution, or in exercising judiciary power, to act as if God did not exist, and consequently to have no regard for divine laws, whether natural or positive? Behold the question.

II. The principles of political atheism. To the question proposed, the political atheist responds affirmatively; it is not difficult to assign the erroneous principles from which it is logically inferred: for they are both designated and proscribed many times in the lauded *Syllabus*, delivered by the authority of our most holy lord Pope Pius IX. Accordingly, whether the existence of God is denied; or, as with pantheism, his nature is confounded with the nature of the world; or, the existence of God having been posited, His divine providence is denied—God is always excluded from the world, such that "any action of God upon men and the world is to be denied" (*Prop.* 2). From this it follows, 1° that "Human reason, having no regard at all for God, is the single arbiter of the true and false, good and evil; it is a law unto itself, and suffices, by its natural powers, for procuring the good of men and peoples" (*Prop.* 3).—2° Thus, "They derive all truths of religion from the native force of human reason; hence reason is the chief norm by which man may be able and ought to arrive at knowledge of all the truths of any sort of knowledge whatsoever" (*Prop.* 4).—3° Therefore "the laws of morals by no means require divine sanction, and it is not at all necessary, that human laws should be conformed to the law of nature, or that they should receive binding force from God" (*Prop.* 56).—4° Therefore "Knowledge of philosophic and moral matters, and likewise civil laws, are able and ought to decline from divine and ecclesiastical authority" (*Prop.* 57).—5° "Therefore the State, as the origin and font of all rights, enjoys a certain right circumscribed by no bounds" (*Prop.* 39).—6° Therefore "right consists in material fact, and all duties of men are a hollow name, and all human deeds have the force of right" (*Prop.* 59).—7° Therefore "the chance injustice of a deed causes no harm to the sanctity of right" (*Prop.* 61).—8° Therefore "Authority is nothing other than the sum of number and material powers" (*Prop.* 60).—Errors of this sort, as anyone may see, are connected: for from the denial of God, descending, one arrives at materialism, and material force is opposed to individual right, and the despotism of the stronger to social right. Behold political atheism, both in its principles, and in its inferences proved by fact itself. Bayle, with whom Voltaire himself disagreed concerning this matter, dreamt of an atheistic society; Rousseau, for the most part, consented to Bayle in Book IV, ch. 7 of the *Social Contract*; both are more or less followed by those politicians who argue for the absolute separation of the State from the Church. Against all these, the conclusion is set forth:

III. Political atheism is absurd. It is proved. Political atheism dissolves society itself: because it is directly opposed as much to the *end* as to the essential *elements* of society. Therefore political atheism is absurd.—The *antecedent* is proved.

It is directly opposed to the end of society. The end of society is the perfection of the citizens, to be obtained through means which each and every person is not able to have from himself, and has from society; which perfection consists chiefly in the knowledge of one's proper duties, and in the virtue by which those duties are carried out. But we have proved (32, IV) that the more principal duties of religion are the fundament of all other duties.[1] Therefore

---

[1] Zigliara here makes reference to earlier sections in the *Ethica* (lib. I, cap. 1, a. III, no. III; cap. 2, a. I, no. IV) where, treating of right, duties, and religion considered in itself as a virtue, he writes:

III. Nevertheless, in a created moral person, duty is more prior than right. And in fact, the first thing which is found in an existing man (and the same is said of any other created moral person) is the creaturely *esse*, which essentially implies a dependence, physical as well as moral, upon the Creator, so that the creature might observe the laws of the Creator, pursuing faithfully the order to the end set in place by Him. This primitive and essential duty having been posited, there spring

in society, and from society, the citizens principally ought to have the means by which they might carry out the duties of religion. But political atheism is either the denial of those things which pertain to religion, or at least an indifference and carelessness concerning the same, as it indeed defines itself. Therefore political atheism is directly opposed to the more principal end of human society. Wherefore Rousseau himself, in the text cited, against Bayle and indeed against himself, acknowledges that *never was there any State founded, the basis of which was not religion*. But if religion is the basis of society, then religion having been expelled, it is necessary that human society should collapse.

It is opposed to the essential elements of society. The elements of this sort, as has been said, are the sovereign and the subjects: the former commands; the latter should be subject to him by the laws. Again, according to the hypothesis of political atheism, social authority depends upon no moral fundament and has no reason for existing. And this is indeed the case. Social authority is not the sum of number and material powers (51, V), but is something essentially moral, claiming for itself the right of ruling the human multitude. And thus it is not from the individual reason, to which

---

forth the rights of preserving and defending life, of employing means necessary for perfecting themselves and for achieving their end, and others of this sort; but, that primitive and essential duty having been removed, all rights crumble because destitute of rational fundament: which is also clear from other quarters from the things said before (29, II). Whence that is to be retained as an unshaken principle: *Human rights proceed from duties toward God....*

IV. The duties of religion are the chiefest duties, and are the fundament of all duties. This proposition is the corollary of the preceding. For the duties of religion emerge from the very essence of man, and from the very essence of God, as we have proved in no. II. Therefore they are the chiefest. — In addition, God having been removed by hypothesis, there also perishes by that very fact the reason for any duty whatsoever. Therefore religion, which implies an ordering to God, as has been said, is the fundament of all duties. Let St Thomas be heard, who, by reason of the *end*, to which the virtues are ordered, infers that religion is preeminent among the other moral virtues, and consequently that the duties of religion are chief among all our other duties: "Those things which are for an end, draw their goodness from the order to the end; and thus, however much they are nearer to the end, so much are they better. But the moral virtues, as has been said above, are concerned with those things which are ordered to God, as to an end. Now religion approaches more nearly to God than the other moral virtues, insofar as it works those things which *directly and immediately are ordered* to the divine honor. And thus religion is preeminent among the other moral virtues" (*ST* II-II, q. 81, a. 7).

no command or authority belongs of itself over other men, nor from an *impersonal* source, which is something abstract and fantastical, but is immediately from God, as a derivation or participation of the divine authority (*ibid.* IV). Therefore, political authority is not able to call itself atheistic, lest by this very act it necessarily and essentially negate itself. — The same result comes to pass if social authority were considered with respect to setting forth laws. For civil laws are naught except either proclamations of the law of nature, or determinations of that law of nature (25, VIII): but the law of nature is nothing other than a participation of the eternal law, from which every other law has its force. In consequence, political atheism is the denial of authority in itself; it is the denial of human legislation, which is null, for according to this hypothesis, it has no moral force to obligate. — Finally it should be added, that political authority, if it moves away in whatever degree from God, should be said to depend on nothing other than itself. But this is *State-theism*, or, as it is called in the vulgar tongue, *il Dio Stato*, which in fact is able to be nothing other than the individual reason or will of rulers, governed not by a moral and superior principle, but by the force of arms and a supremely powerful ruler. Evidently, in political atheism, human society is not ruled by moral authority, but by the will and violence of individual reason, in that manner by which brute animals are governed.

The same conclusion is entirely proved, if we should consider the *subjects*. For these are men, that is, moral beings, to be directed in their course not through violence, but through law. Seeing, therefore, that the political authority professing atheism depends upon no moral principle, and the laws drawn up by it rest upon no principle superior to the individual reason, the citizens, reasoning in an *ad hominem* manner (41, XI), are not able to consider the authority as morally superior to themselves, and its laws as having the force of moral obligation; but they oppose individual reason to the individual reason of the one ruling. The material force which prevails in the ruler remains, but material force is not a social bond of men. It can be avoided through wickedness, and even overcome; and thus impious and foolish rulers can, through force brought to bear by the citizens, be despoiled of the dignity [i.e., the sovereignty] which they abuse against God. And so it happens, that the political authority which rises up against God in a most impious manner sees its own subjects rising up against itself.

I do not speak of the impiety of political atheism: for this is clear in itself. For if it is impious that a citizen deny to God the duties of religion, it is most impious among those who rule society. For these latter are men, and so are obliged to fulfill those things which are man's duty before God; they are rulers, and so ought to lead the way for all their subjects in the example of virtue and religion; they are for the good of society, and so ought not to subvert or subordinate religion, but ought, with all their powers, to promote it, so that men might not draw detriment from society—from which they have the right of aspiring to moral perfection—in those things which chiefly look to perfection, that is, religion and the eternal salvation of the soul.

ARTICLE 2
On Liberty of Conscience

I. The notion of liberty of conscience. Everywhere today, all who profess liberalism proclaim that liberty of conscience is necessary; and not a few Catholics, from the *liberal school*, as they call it, who thus call themselves liberal Catholics, are of the same mind with the liberal rationalists. But what is liberty of conscience? Generally, according to its defenders, it can be called *the faculty of thinking and doing those things which are more pleasing in those matters which relate to God and religion*. We ask, therefore, whether man enjoys this right, or this liberty of conscience: and note the words of the question, for we inquire concerning the *right*.

II. First preliminary note. In the first place, I say that *faith* is able to be imposed upon no unbeliever through violence, which faith he refuses to admit; because *to believe is of the will*, as St Thomas says in II-II, q. 10, a. 8. Wherefore the Council of Toledo commanded these things: "But concerning the Jews, the holy Synod commands, that force be inflicted upon no man in order that he believe; for God shows mercy to whom He wills, and hardens whom He wills."[2] Whence they indeed calumniate the Catholic Church, who say that

---

2 Cf. Francisco Victoria, *Relect.* V. de *Indis*, §XV.

she does violence to consciences in order to obtain the faith of Christ. Certainly, there has been, and is, violence—but the Church has suffered it and indeed now suffers it; she has not inflicted it, as the history of the martyrs and persecutions manifestly attest.

III. Second preliminary note. For our purposes, so that the exercise of true liberty may be had, it is necessary that it disparage no duty: for liberty is not for evil, but for good (Ps 50:14).[3] Therefore as often as a man abuses it for evil, it ought not to be called liberty, but more truly license. To ask, therefore, whether liberty of conscience is licit, is the same as to ask whether the liberty of thinking and doing those things, which are more pleasing in matters which are concerned with God and religion, disparages the duties toward God Himself. This precisely is the sense of the question, and under this aspect it is to be solved; and its solution is easy.

IV. Third preliminary note. In truth, this question, posed in this manner, is able to be defined 1° *absolutely*, or liberty of conscience considered in itself; 2° *relatively*, or liberty of conscience considered with respect to social cooperation: under which latter aspect it is chiefly defended by the adversaries.—Let the first conclusion, therefore, be stated.

V. Liberty of conscience, considered in itself, is entirely impious. And indeed, man, by a most strict duty of nature, is held to think rightly of God, and of those things which look to religion, both speculative and practical (33, II). But voluntarily to make resistance to a most strict duty is license, not liberty; and if the discussion, as in our argument, is concerned with the voluntary transgression of a duty toward God, the aforementioned license is an impiety. Since, therefore, through liberty of conscience, a right is given to man of thinking of God as it more pleases him, this liberty, this right is a true impiety.—But, because this first conclusion is hardly examined by the adversaries, the things already said suffice for its proof; and I arrive at the second part of the question. And thus let the second conclusion be stated.

VI. Liberty of conscience, socially considered, if it is able to be tolerated in given circumstances, yet never is to be approved, much

---

3 It is not easy to see what Zigliara could be referring to with this citation of Ps 50:14, "Restore unto me the joy of thy salvation, and strengthen me with a perfect spirit"; 1 Pet 2:16 seems more apropos.

Spiritual and Temporal Power

less to be protected or inculcated. That it is able to be tolerated in given cases is easily admitted: for many other evils are *tolerated*, or are not punished (for to tolerate is not *to approve*, nor simply *to permit*, but only *not to punish*) — no indeed, it sometimes happens that they ought to be tolerated in society, for otherwise worse evils would follow. But this tolerance ought not to be approbation, nor protection, nor inculcation. — The thesis is proved. Liberty of conscience, socially considered, is founded in nothing other than political atheism: it is most pernicious to society, and self-contradictory. Therefore liberty of conscience, socially considered, is in nowise able to be approved. The *antecedent* is proved.

It is founded in political atheism alone. And indeed, as has been said in the preceding number, liberty of conscience is a right, conceded to individuals, of thinking of God as they should please, or of submitting those things which are of God and religion, and the duties following from these, to the definition and arbitration of individual conscience, which thus is constituted as the *criterion* of religion. But just as in many other things, man not only errs from ignorance, but also from malice, so in the things which pertain to religion; nay more, in these more than in others, for religion imports more severe duties, to which the depraved passions make resistance: which errors, both speculative and practice, yet constitute an impiety in the religious order. But because, as has been said, in liberty of conscience, the criterion is the individual reason, the right of liberty of conscience is truly a right to error and impiety: which right indeed is not able to be approved in society and by society, unless at the same time there be set in place religious skepticism or political atheism.

It is most pernicious to society. For, as long as actions remain in the conscience, they are proper to the individual, and do not fall under judgment except that of God. But by the very fact that they are manifested, they have relation to the members of society, and consequently, when they inflict evil upon the members of society, they fall under the purview of the social authority. Now just as men suffer either scandal or any other injury whatsoever from the improbity of other men, so *a fortiori* they suffer scandal and injury from public and unpunished improbity, and much more from the permitted and approved dissemination of error and impiety, by which the intellectual and moral perfection of men is directly impeded. Therefore not to impede, nay more, indeed to approve these scandals, these injuries, more grave than corporal injuries, is not only impiety toward God, but is a perversion of the social order itself.

It is self-contradictory. And in fact, either liberty of conscience is a right, or it is not. If it is not, why is it noisily proclaimed? But if it is a right, why is it limited? In this limitation is clearly found the contradiction of the defenders of liberty of conscience. Indeed, not only do they prescribe religion, but they also forcibly impose in regard to civil laws, in regard to the king, etc. But neither civil laws, nor the king, nor society itself are above God, Who being removed, all other things topple, and all morality is either absurdity or the animal law of the stronger (29, II). Therefore if liberty of conscience is a right with respect to the duties of religion toward God, and political authority is scrupulous in preserving this right inviolate, the political authority itself is not able to impede it, without manifest contradiction and without open violence, so that that right is exercised fully with respect to royal power, with respect to civil laws, and finally, with respect to civil society itself. — And if it be said, that liberty of conscience should be restrained, such that duties toward society are not harmed; I rejoin, therefore much more ought, not liberty, but rather license of conscience to be restrained, lest the duties toward God be abused — which duties are more weighty than social duties, such that the latter do not exist, nor are able to exist, without the former.

VII. Corollary. Rightfully therefore are the following propositions condemned in the Syllabus of Pius IX, which propositions affirm both liberty of conscience and *indifferentism:* "Every man is free to embrace and profess that religion which, led by the light of reason, he shall consider true" (*Prop.* 15). "Men are able to find the way of eternal salvation in the worship of any religion whatever, and therein to attain eternal salvation" (*Prop.* 16).

VIII. Note. A difficulty is resolved. The things which present-day liberals teach concerning liberty of conscience in the social order are not new — indeed, Rousseau had already given them in his *Social Contract*, Book IV.8. Let us therefore hear this sophist, that from his mouth we might become acquainted with the arguments of the others:

> Subjects are not obliged to render a reason to the civil power concerning their opinions, except so far as these are referred to the community. But it is in the interest of the State, that each and every citizen profess a religion which impresses upon him a love of his duties; but the dogmas of this religion concern neither the State nor its members, except so far as they are referred to morals and to the duties which the citizen is obliged to fulfill toward others.[4]

That these things were written by Rousseau in hatred of the Catholic Church is manifest from the things which he invents with respect to the will in the chapter cited. Next in order, we shall see the contradictions and absurdities which we encounter throughout his words and in those of his imitators.

Without doubt, so long as religion is shut up in the interior conscience, it lies hidden from both the civil and ecclesiastical power; and consequently God alone is the judge of it. But when religion becomes the rule of morals, by this very fact it is referred to the community. In this sense, Rousseau thought the State to be present so that each citizen might profess that religion which impressed upon him a love of his duties. But only true religion impresses upon citizens a love of their duties. Therefore, contrary to what Rousseau illogically concludes, it ought entirely to be said, that even from his principles, it is not only fitting to the State that the true religion be at least externally observed by all the citizens, and the propagators of irreligion or of false dogmas be restrained, but it is incumbent upon it as a most grave duty of carrying out that which is proper to it.

All of which things are in such wise true, that Rousseau himself, who defends liberty or license of conscience against the Catholic Church, utterly destroys it after the words just cited by making firm the omnipotence of the State, or Statolatry:

---

4 This is our direct translation of the Latin text given by the Cardinal. The 1782 translation by G. D. H. Cole from the French renders it thus: "The subjects then owe the Sovereign an account of their opinions only to such an extent as they matter to the community. Now, it matters very much to the community that each citizen should have a religion. That will make him love his duty; but the dogmas of that religion concern the State and its members only so far as they have reference to morality and to the duties which he who professes them is bound to do to others."

On the Mutual Relations between Church and State

Therefore there ought to be admitted a purely civil profession of faith, the right of determining the articles of which belongs to the Sovereign, not [framing them] as dogmas of religion, but as sentiments of sociability without which it is impossible that a man be a good citizen and faithful subject. The Sovereign has no faculty for imposing faith in articles of this sort but he is yet able to make an exile of him who does not believe them — not as one who is impious but as one who is unsociable and incapable of sincerely loving the laws and justice, and of pouring out one's life, if necessary, for the carrying out of a duty. And if a man were publicly to admit the aforementioned dogmas yet led a life as if he did not believe them, let him be punished by death: for he perpetrates the greatest crime, because he has spoken falsely before the law (*qu'il soit puni de mort: il a commis le plus grand des crimes, il a menti devant la loi*).[5]

Thus speaks Rousseau, and thus speak they who follow after his sophisms. They set out from the principle: *Nothing pertains to the Sovereign concerning the religious opinions of the subjects*, so long as their exterior life is conformed to social duties, but immediately it is added, that *a code of religion ought to be rendered by the Sovereign*, which ought to encompass positive dogmas, that is, the existence of God, the future life, rewards for good deeds, and punishments for bad; and negative dogmas, which Rousseau reduces to *intolerance alone*. Finally, it is concluded that those citizens ought not to be tolerated — and indeed ought to be expelled from the State or punished by death — who do not hold to this civil religion, even if in other quarters they observe all those things which pertain to duties toward others. That is, religion is excluded from the State by reason of *liberty of conscience*, as if the principles of *true* religion should in fact be of no concern to the State; by reason of *sociality*, religion itself is submitted to the arbitrary will of the Sovereign; and by the

---

5 Cole renders it: "There is therefore a purely civil profession of faith of which the Sovereign should fix the articles, not exactly as religious dogmas, but as social sentiments without which a man cannot be a good citizen or a faithful subject. While it can compel no one to believe them, it can banish from the State whoever does not believe them — it can banish him, not for impiety, but as an anti-social being, incapable of truly loving the laws and justice, and of sacrificing, at need, his life to his duty. If any one, after publicly recognizing these dogmas, behaves as if he does not believe them, let him be punished by death: he has committed the worst of all crimes, that of lying before the law."

arbitrary will of the Sovereign, the citizens, in admitting religion, ought to comply in a blind fashion, under pain of exile or death!

Nor could any other conclusion have been reached. For liberty of conscience, once admitted, just as it is opposed to *true* religion, is opposed to the *true* felicity of the State; because there is no morality without God, and no duty without religion. But if regulation in those matters which pertain to religion is taken away from the Church of God, it is necessary that it be given over to the arbitration of the civil power: which, lacking authority in religion, imposes its own tyranny upon consciences; and thus the true *liberty of souls* is oppressed by means of the same principles with which the false *liberty of conscience* is proclaimed by Rousseau and his followers.[6]

ARTICLE 3
On Liberty of Cult

I. The notion of liberty of cults. Liberty of cult is intimately involved with liberty of conscience. For if each and every citizen is free to decide upon a religion for himself according to his will, since religion implies also an external cult, each and every citizen ought to be free to profess his religion by any extrinsic cult whatever: and because the State is not able to offend against liberty of conscience, so neither may it prohibit liberty of cult; no indeed, it ought to sanction it by its laws. Thus teaches liberalism, the opinion of which the Church has condemned, as has been related in no. VII of the preceding article. Since, therefore, the liberty of cult is wholly founded in the liberty of conscience, it is to be refuted by the same process and with the same principles which we have laid down against liberty of conscience. Therefore let the first conclusion be set forth:

II. Liberty of cult, considered in itself, is absurd. This proposition remains proved in the first place from the things said above. For liberty of cult is inferred from the liberty of conscience. Because, therefore, this latter is absurd, the former ought also to be called absurd. — But furthermore: liberty of cult having been conceded to

---

6 Cf. Honoré Torombert et al., *Principes du Droit politique mis en opposition avec le Contrat social de J.-J. Rousseau* (Paris: Rey et Gravier, 1825), 335.

man, there is removed from God the power of assigning a determinate cult to men, and there is imposed upon God an obligation of accepting or at least approving any cult shown to Him by human reason. And indeed, if God is able to command a cult, if it is clear that He has prescribed a determinate cult, if He is held by no reason to accept the arbitrary cults of men, men are not able, without manifest irreligion or impiety, to oppose the commands of God, and their cult is an arbitrary and true mockery of God, and liberty of cult is superstition and an impiety. But it is an impiety to deny to God the ability of determining cult, and to impose in any way the duty of approving any cult whatsoever indiscriminately. Therefore liberty of cult is absurd. — In addition, let the second conclusion be stated:

III. Although the civil social authority is able at times to tolerate liberty of cult, yet it is in no way able to sanction it by any law. There is nothing to be added concerning tolerance after the things said concerning tolerance of liberty of conscience. And so the thesis is proved with respect to approbative or prescriptive law. We have proved above that political atheism is entirely repugnant. Therefore, just as any citizen, so also society itself, endued as it is with the nature of a moral person, is obliged to the duties of religion, and of true religion, by a most strict precept of nature. But religion implies external cult. Therefore the civil authority, to which it belongs to direct society, is most strictly obliged to observe, inculcate, and promote this external cult: I say that the civil authority is held to a cult consentaneous to the nature of sociality, that is, public, social, and finally, proper to society as it is society, or as a public and moral personality. But a false cult is not religion, but superstition and consequently error and impiety. Therefore to sanction liberty of cult, is to sanction impiety, but the denial of some social *cult* is the negation of religion in society *qua* society. Therefore social authority, although at times it is able to tolerate liberty of cult, yet is in no wise able to sanction it in law. — These things seem to me to be evident, and I wonder that they are denied not only by the rationalists — who, since they either explicitly deny God or retain Him in word only, logically reject any religion by the individual and from society — but by the liberalism which wishes to be called Catholic. For a Catholic would know that God ought to be worshiped with a true cult, and thus a false cult is not able to be endorsed; that God has spoken to men, has commanded a determinate cult, has constituted the Catholic Church as the sole *magistra* in those matters which pertain to religion—and hence there ought not to be approved any cult but that ordained by the Church, commanded by God Himself.

IV. Note. A difficulty is resolved. You may say: by means of liberty of cult, the Catholic Church also is able freely to practice its worship, while on the contrary, this liberty having been removed, the Church loses even her juridical liberty.—I respond, that this sort of argument effects a sham, and confounds things which, among themselves, are distinct and ought to be distinguished. For we are able to speak in a twofold manner concerning liberty of cult, *relatively* and *absolutely*.[7] *Relatively*, against those who proclaim liberty of cult and yet (just as we have heard from Rousseau concerning liberty of conscience) plague the Church, and prohibit her from practicing her worship, we argue in this manner: Either liberty of cult is to be admitted as a true social principle, or not. If it is to be admitted, therefore unjustly and irrationally are Catholics prohibited from profiting by their liberty; but if not, therefore liberty of cult is merely proclaimed by means of a solemn lie. This argumentation is indeed right, and strikes against the adversaries: wherefore also the Catholic Church does not scornfully reject it, but urges it so that she might defend the claims of her liberty.—But this does not imply that the liberty of cult is able to be defended *absolutely* by Catholics. For liberty of cult, considered in itself, is absurd and impious, as has been proved. Therefore it is absurd and impious to defend it in an absolute manner. And although from such liberty there sometimes arise goods, namely the liberty of Catholics,

---

7 The Cardinal here refers to vol. 1 of his manual, *Logica: Dialectica* III, cap. 4, a. II, no. XI, where, delineating kinds of demonstration, he writes: "Absolute demonstration, and relative demonstration or ad hominem. The first is that which proceeds from premises, the truth of which is admitted by us and is assumed for inferring something absolutely: as when we demonstrate the real existence of God from the contingency of creatures, and other things of this sort. A relative or ad hominem demonstration is that which proceeds from principles admitted by an adversary and assumed by us in order to refute him, an abstraction having been made from the truth of those principles; as if someone were to assume principles admitted by materialists or rationalists, in order to convince them of the falsity of their doctrine."

Catholics are not for this reason able to teach or defend it; for it is not licit to speak error for the apparent defense of truth: "For if the truth of God hath more abounded through my lie, unto his glory, why am I also yet judged as a sinner? And not rather (as we are slandered, and as some affirm that we say) let us do evil, that there may come good? whose damnation is just" (Rom 3:7–8).

ARTICLE 4
On Liberty of Teaching

I. Question. Simultaneously one with liberty of conscience and of cult, there is proclaimed by the more recent liberalism a liberty of teaching, particularly with respect to the means with which it is principally exercised, namely, with respect to liberty of the press (*la libertà della stampa*). We ask, therefore, whether this liberty is upright, and to be approved by the civil authority. Here again I caution that the discussion is concerned, not with tolerance, but with approbation: evils indeed are able to be *tolerated*, yet naught but goods ought to be *approved*.

II. First preliminary note. It has been said more than once by us, that man is born for society, and cannot have the helps for perfecting himself except in society and from society. But the perfection of man chiefly is found in the intellective part of him, to which it is proper *to know* and *to love*: to know the truth, and to love the good. Thence it is, that to impede man from the acquiring of truth and the virtues is in a certain way to kill him intellectually.

III. Second preliminary note. However, there is a certain doctrine which does not instruct minds but perverts them, insinuating error under the guise of truth. On account of which, seeing that man by his nature is drawn to the truth and has the right of seeking it and the duty of shunning error, he has the right that others not induce him into error under the guise of truth. Therefore just as the liberty *of truth* is honorable, so the liberty of error is the *death of the soul*, as St Augustine says, and does not merit the name of liberty, but of license.

IV. Point of the question. Therefore the entire question concerning the liberty of *teaching* does not touch upon the true liberty of teaching the truth, but the *liberty* of teaching as it encompasses the instruction both of truth and of error. Is this liberty able to be permitted by the civil authority? To this question, defined in this fashion, I respond with the following conclusion:

V. Liberty of teaching, whether spoken or written, is intrinsically absurd and disgraceful. For it is intrinsically absurd and shameful to concede the same rights to truth and to error; it is intrinsically absurd and shameful that the civil authority should not preserve voluntarily the citizens from the corruption of mind and heart; it is intrinsically absurd and shameful that the civil authority should permit that which it is itself compelled to condemn and punish. But liberty of teaching is of this sort. Therefore it is intrinsically absurd and shameful. — The *minor* is proved.

Liberty of teaching concedes the same rights to truth and to error. This is included in the very nature of liberty of teaching, as it is understood by liberalism. For it includes in its scope the right of striking down things pertaining as much to the world as to God, religion, morals, individual life, and social life. Now it is not necessary to prove, that men may err in the gravest of matters, which matters natural reason itself commands to be altogether defended and most firmly held. The faculty of teaching therefore having been granted, the same right is conceded to error which is conceded to the truth, that it might propagate itself, to the detriment of truth: no indeed, error would enjoy a greater right than truth. For the truth cannot but employ those means which are honest and worthy, while on the contrary error holds all means as licit. No one of sound mind does not see how absurd and disgraceful are all of these things: for the right is truth; therefore just as error is the lack of truth, so is it the lack of right.

Liberty of teaching works to the corruption of the mind and heart. I assume two things for demonstrating this: 1° that men, from the corruption of nature, are wont to accept theories which favor their passions; 2° that most men by themselves are incapable of freeing themselves up [i.e., making time] for the pursuit of knowledge, and of extricating themselves from false reasoning and the sophisms of error. He who would deny these two things, would deny a fact which is at once constant and manifest to all. But: 1° from the liberty of teaching there arises the liberty of error, as has been said above, through which the passions are favored and excited against the intellective part—and, the intellective part erring, it cannot happen that the whole man be not corrupted; 2° on account of the liberty of teaching, men are exposed daily to the danger of erring in those things which they are held to know and about which they are held to think truly—such as the matters which have to do with God, the human soul, morals, and religion—when through false teachers, truths of this sort are assailed with impudent license, and which the greater part of humanity is not able to defend from sophisms. Wherefore, a proclivity toward evil being supposed on one hand, and an impotence for reasoning scientifically on the other, it cannot happen that the liberty, or more truly the license, of teaching does not entirely and efficaciously work to the corruption of the minds and hearts of the citizens.—But it is the right of the citizens that the civil authority defend them from so great a calamity, nor is this authority able to abandon this duty without thereby committing a crime. How much more shameful and absurd it is, then, that the civil authority should proclaim in its laws this deformity, which through an intolerable abuse of words is called the liberty of teaching?

Liberty of teaching is simultaneously approved and punished by the civil authority. On the one hand, liberty of teaching is established, and on the other, they are punished who abuse the press in order to circulate things which in fact are, or are judged to be, opposed to the civil authority. But, either the liberty of teaching in word or writing is to be proclaimed in its whole extension; or on the contrary, it is to be confined within limits lest it lead to evil. But if it ought to be admitted in its full extension, why therefore are they who use and abuse it punished? If it ought to be constrained within certain limits, lest it devolve into license, then: 1° it is able to be limited so that it does not work evil (*la revisione preventiva*), just as it is punished after evil has been perpetrated; no indeed, it would be more prudent to obstruct it, for most often the evil is irreparable; 2° these limits are to be defined only according to truth and integrity; wherefore, just as liberty of teaching is condemned and punished by the civil authority when it inclines to the detriment of the same authority, so *a fortiori* it is to be condemned and punished whenever the same liberty sallies forth against God, religion, morals, and the true liberty of citizens: because the civil authority is not superior to God, religion, morals, and truth, nor is it more serious to disparage the Rulers of cities and kingdoms, than to disparage God and religion and truth, without which no authority commands and no society stands.

VI. Note. Difficulties are resolved. *First objection.* There is in man an innate desire of communicating to other men the discoveries of his own talent. But this natural desire is not satisfied, except by means of liberty of teaching. Therefore liberty of teaching corresponds to natural human desire.

I respond. I distinguish the *major:* there is in man an innate desire of communicating the discoveries of his own talent within the limits of truth, *I concede;* outside the limits of truth, *I deny.* — I distinguish also the *minor:* this natural desire is not satisfied except by means of liberty of teaching rightly understood, that is, through true liberty which is not contrary to truth, *I concede;* it is not satisfied except through liberty badly understood, that is, through license which is contrary to truth, *I deny.* — Nature does not give an inclination to error, just as it does not give inclination to evil; wherefore, just as the inclination to evil, which is from the corruption of nature, ought to be checked, so also the perverse inclination to error. — But the liberty of error is not true liberty, but the abuse of liberty, and is license, to be detested and curbed.

Second objection. By reason of liberty of teaching, whether in word or writing, opinions are considered and the truth is more and more made clear. But that which is of this sort not only contains nothing of evil, but indeed confers the greatest good. Therefore liberty of teaching ought very much to be supported.

I respond. In the first place, the adversary concludes, from the fact that there may be some good had from liberty of teaching, to the goodness of this liberty; which conclusion we have proved is not able to be had from this aforementioned good alone, in no. IV of the preceding article. I respond secondly, by distinguishing the *minor:* Something of this sort contains nothing evil if, through liberty of teaching, only opinions are considered, and errors are not defended, *I concede;* if error is defended against truth, *I deny.* — It has been said that error lacks right, and indeed is the lack of right.

Where the liberty of teaching is conceded to error, therefore, there is no right, but manifest injustice against truth, which in this case is not elucidated, but is denied.

Third objection. Liberty of teaching having been denied, the State is constituted as the judge of teaching, and additionally, there is conceded to it a monopoly on teaching. But the State is not the judge of teaching, and is not able to arrogate to itself the monopoly on teaching without the greatest tyranny. Therefore liberty of teaching is entirely to be permitted.

I respond. I deny the *major*, I concede the *minor*, and I deny the *consequence*, liberty having been accepted as it is at once a right of truth and error, as it is taken by the adversaries. — I concede that there belongs to the civil State no authority concerning teachings: but it is not necessary that one be endowed with this governance of teaching, or *magisterium*, in order to discern those things which are manifestly evil, so much in themselves as in relation to civil society, so that the former might be able to be inculcated and the latter prohibited; just as, if one were to defend an innocent from a manifest unjust aggressor, he would not thereby be constituted judge between the two; but the innocent has a manifest right, and in order to defend him from an unjust attacker in the act of aggression, one is able to seek out the help of another. But in the order of teaching, there are certain vices, that is, manifest errors, which indeed the State is able and ought to know and punish, just as other vices, without seizing for itself the teaching magisterium. — But in fact there exists, above the State, a teaching magisterium in the Catholic Church and in the Supreme Pontiff. Therefore the errors which the Catholic Church condemns, the State also ought to condemn, and it ought to accept the teaching magisterium of the Church.

Fourth objection. The right of the citizens, for whom it is easy to reject erroneous doctrines, is not harmed by liberty of teaching. But that which harms the rights of no one, ought to be permitted. Therefore liberty of teaching ought to be permitted.

I respond. I deny the *major*. For proof of this, I respond in the first place that, even granting that each and every person were able to detect the insidious devices of sophists or those who err, a right to this aggression would not thereby be something to be admitted; just as there ought not to be admitted a right in an unjust aggressor, even if there were the means for repelling his violence in the innocent, whose power to repel injury does not diminish the injustice of the aggressor.—I respond secondly, that it is false that it is easy for all to avoid the tricks of sophists, particularly when the sophisms favor the passions: in fact, we see that men—I speak not only of coarse folk, but of clever men as well—are every day entangled in false doctrines.

Fifth objection. The Church herself desires liberty of teaching, and demands that it be conceded to her from the State by right. Therefore liberty of teaching, which is good in the religious order, is not able not to be good in the civil order.

I respond. I distinguish the *antecedent:* The Church desires true liberty of teaching, *I concede;* she desires false liberty of teaching, about which our whole question is concerned, *I deny.* The Church has never opposed herself to the liberty of truth, but rightly opposes herself to the liberty, or more correctly the license, of error. But justly does she claim absolutely for herself the liberty of teaching, because she is the mistress of truth, whatever be the desire or aversion of her adversaries.—But concerning the liberty of teaching taken in the sense of the adversaries, the Church desires it in the same manner in which she desires the liberty of cult: namely, insofar as it is most unjust that the magisterium of the Church, which is the instrument of truth, is excluded from that liberty which is conceded to error through civil laws. Concerning this matter, let us hear our most holy lord Pope Pius IX, in his Letter of 19 July 1875 to Felice Dupanloup, bishop of Orléans, about the liberty of teaching which the Catholics in France had sought and received in the year 1875 from the French government:

> Although it is to the disadvantage of the eternal laws of justice and of right reason itself, that true and false be had in the same condition, and equal rights be granted to both, yet since the iniquity of the times has transferred right (which is proper by its very nature to the true alone) to the false; and, the word *liberty* being sufficiently unsuitable, has granted to it the power of proposing, publishing, and teaching its fictions; We judge you, Venerable Brother, to have made an effort, altogether skillfully and advantageously, to adapt this venom forced upon civil society into a remedy for it. Indeed,

if it is lawful for anyone of unsound mind to advance fantasies upon the public by means of the laws, and to avail himself of the same also to defend and relate the dogmas of science; there plainly is no reason at hand, why it ought not to be lawful for the truth: nor is there a reason why any person whatever, although he be a follower of fables and a hater of truth—unless he were entirely mad—would be able to deny to it the perspicuity of this right. To this ineluctable strength of argument there accedes no small degree of firmness, whether from the reproach proposed by You with respect to the impediment—to the detriment of science—cast upon so many talented minds, of setting forth their ideas; or from the facts attested to by experience, of the inclination—begotten by the captivity of truth—of letters and the higher disciplines; and also of the impudence, with which principles most pernicious not only to religion, but also to the human community, are even now published. These losses, if they are to be lamented in the license by which error everywhere is proposed to the people, certainly are to be considered deadly things in the instruction of youth and young men, in which the very root of human society is so corrupted, that it is capable only of poisoned fruits, which at length lead it, already ill, ruined, and prostrated, to dissolution.

ARTICLE 5
On the Subordination of the State to the Church

I. Nature of the question. A religious society, of which sort is the Catholic Church, lives in the company of civil society, such that the spiritual power of the Roman Pontiff is as it were in contact with the civil power, and they who are civilly subjects of the temporal authority are simultaneously subjects of ecclesiastical authority. It is commonly conceded that the civil authority, within the limits of its ends, is independent of the Church, in that manner in which we say the Church, with respect to its end, is independent of any civil authority. But it is wholly impossible that two societies should exist at once with equal independence, that is, without mutual subordination to one another; consequently, it is necessary that either the Church be subordinate to the civil State, or the civil State to the Church. Behold the question, concerning which we have said many things in Articles 61 and 63, and whose solution we give in this final article, so that there might more clearly be seen the notion of ethnarchy which belongs to the Catholic Church. Let the conclusion therefore be stated:

II. In no wise is the Catholic Church subordinate to the civil State, but the civil State of its nature is subordinate to the Catholic Church. This proposition is easily proved, if there are recalled to mind the principles which we made known in the preceding Chapter. For the notion or nature of the subordination of societies ought to be taken absolutely from the end: for, seeing that the nature of the society arises from the end to which it is ordered, where the ends of two societies are subordinated, the societies equally ought to be subordinated; and a society whose end is subordinate to the end of a higher society, is also subordinated to that other. These are the principles, without which there consists nothing anymore firm in determining the nature of society. But the end of civil society and the end of religious society are ordered to one another, and the end of civil society is subordinated to the end of the Catholic Church, and not *vice versa*. Therefore in no wise is the Catholic Church subordinate to the civil state, but the civil state of its nature is subordinate to the Catholic Church. The *minor* is proved.

The end of civil society and the end of religious society are ordered to one another. For man is composed from soul and body, and, as man, is a part of society. But civil society properly looks to the exterior perfection of man, because it is not able to penetrate into the interior things of conscience, and what is more, because it considers man living in this life, it has care chiefly for his temporal perfection; whereas the Catholic Church, as a spiritual society, is ordered rather to the perfection of the soul and directs men to eternal felicity. But although these things are true, yet it is true that man neither is able nor ought to be divided, but just as the soul is for the perfection of the body and the body is for the perfection of the soul, so equally corporeal perfection — to which the civil State directly attends — and spiritual perfection — which the Church of Christ bountifully imparts — both ought to provide for the whole man. Therefore the ends of both societies, although distinct amongst themselves, yet agree in one common end, which is the *man to be perfected;* and consequently, these ends are ordered to one another.

The end of civil society is subordinated to the end of the Catholic Church, and not vice versa. Indeed, nothing forbids that man, as a composite of soul and body, not procure for himself, in an upright manner, all those things which coincide for living this life comfortably. Nevertheless, it is irrational and repulsive to submit the soul to the body in such a manner that it is the body's slave, and esteems less his intellectual perfection, so that in his body he leads a life according to the fashion of brute animals; but the body ought to be subservient to the soul. — It savors of dementia, moreover, to think that man should be solicitous of temporal felicity — which felicity he must lose, whether he will it or not — and not think of attaining eternal happiness: *For what doth it profit a man, if he gain the whole world, and suffer the loss of his own soul? Or what exchange shall a man give for his soul?* (Mt 16:26). *For we have not here a lasting city, but we seek one that is to come* (Heb 13:14). Therefore, whatever man seeks in this life, whatever he searches out for himself in civil society and from civil society, he either seeks perversely or ought to order to the spiritual and eternal perfection of the soul. Because, therefore, the end of the Church is the interior and eternal perfection of man, but the end of civil society is his external and temporal perfection, the end of the Church is not subordinated to that of civil society, but rather the latter to the former.

III. The Catholic Church is an ethnarchic society. Before I prove that the Catholic Church truly is an ethnarchic society, and consequently that there is in it a true ethnarchy, I think it worthwhile to take a moment and put forward the doctrine of St Thomas concerning Christ, insofar as He is the Head of all men:

> There is this difference between the natural head of man and the mystical body of the Church, that the members of the natural body are all together; but the members of the mystical body are not all together: not with respect to the *esse* of nature, because the body of the Church is constituted from men, who have existed from the beginning of the world even to its end; neither according to the *esse* of grace, for, of those even who are in one time, some lack grace, to be had later, while others already possess it. Thus therefore, the members of the mystical body are taken, not only according as they are in act, but also according as they are in

potency. Yet there are some in potency who are never reduced to act; whereas there are some who are reduced to act at some time or other. And this occurs according to a threefold grade: the *first* of which is through *faith;* the *second* through *charity* of the way; the *third* through the *fruition* of the *patria*. Thus, therefore, it should be said, that taking it generally according to the whole of the world's time, Christ is the head of all men, but according to diverse grades. For firstly and chiefly is He head of those who are united to Him in act through glory; secondly, of those are united in act to Him through charity; thirdly, of those who are united in act to Him through faith; fourthly, of those who are only united to Him in potency not yet reduced to act, which yet is to be reduced to act according to divine predestination; fifthly, of those who are united to Him in potency, which potency is never reduced to act: as men living in this world, who are not predestined, who yet, receding from this age, entirely cease to be members of Christ, because they are no longer in potency, as to be united to Christ.[8]

From these principles, our thesis is easily proved. Indeed the Catholic Church encompasses all nations, whether in act or in potency, as we have heard from St Thomas; furthermore, it is of its nature a doctrinal society, and possesses an infallible magisterium in the matters which look to dogmas and morals; it is a society whose invisible head is Christ Himself, at once God and man; whose visible head is the Supreme Roman Pontiff, exalted with supernatural dignity, subject to no man, having civil powers subordinate to him, and directed, by the special assistance of the Holy Ghost, to the salvation of nations. In the Church, therefore, you have *universality*, you have *doctrinal magisterium*, you have dignity and *supereminence*: all the things, namely, which are required for an *ethnarchy*, that is, for valid authority over all peoples or nations. — This wisest kind of politics prevailed, to the good of peoples, in the Middle Ages, that is, when truly Christian peoples and kings received and venerated, in the Roman Pontiff, the Vicar of Christ — whose name, as Isaiah says, is *Wonderful, Counsellor, God the Mighty, the Father of the world to come, the Prince of Peace* (Is 9:6).

---

8   *ST* III, q. 8, a. 3.

12

Against Political Iconoclasm
Nathaniel Gotcher

There are many Catholics today who deny the necessity of promoting a Catholic political order. This denial is manifest in two strains of thought that sometimes coincide. The first is the idea that political order is amoral and pragmatic. It is primarily concerned with the material prosperity and security necessary for each person to pursue his goals. It may not legislate morality except insofar as it is clear that a given action harms another person by inhibiting his goals. The teaching of moral virtue above and beyond this is properly in the scope of ecclesiastical structures and individual families—in other words, moral formation belongs to the Church and the Family, not the State. The second idea is that political order itself is immoral and corrupt. Even the pragmatic concern for prosperity and security is tinged with the wickedness of men in power. Instead, religious institutions and private philanthropy ought to be in charge of the distribution of material goods so that the practice of charity renders the State unnecessary and frees us from the bondage of worldly political order.

What unites both strains of thought is a sort of political iconoclasm. Iconoclasts hold that any representation of God (or nature) in art is either idolatry or blasphemy, either the worship of false gods or a false worship of the true God. To political iconoclasts, any attempt to fashion a political order according to Christian principles will either lead to a worship of the state (idolatry) or a corruption of Christianity (blasphemy). This is because they misunderstand the nature of politics and the relationship of nature and grace that informs the Catholic understanding of all human activity. While nature is indeed subject to corruption, the reality of the Incarnation means that nature is perfectible by grace. Christ's redemptive act cascades down from the Cross into every dry rivulet of human activity, including politics.

God's Image and Human Nature

In the creation account in the book of Genesis, we read: "Then God said: let us make man in our image, after our likeness" (Gen 1:26). But what is this image, this likeness? What is human nature? According to Catholic dogma, God is Father, Son, and Holy Spirit. In the act of self-contemplation, God generates the Image of Himself, the Word that perfectly expresses Who He is and is Spoken to Himself. Understanding Himself, He knows Himself and loves Himself. In the abundance of this love, God conceived all things in His mind and spoke His Word to bring them into existence, creating all things in heaven and on earth and below the earth. Everything that is made came to be through the Word, and everything therefore bears the mark of God's mind. Because of this, all creation reflects and reveals God in some way. God desired that this revelation be received and so created man in His image, with a mind capable of contemplating Him through His revelations. This is the foundation of the Christian understanding of human nature.

Human nature reflects God's image through the faculty of reason. The single faculty of reason is used in three modes: artistic reason, practical reason, and contemplative reason. Reason is the ability to know order, and the three modes of reasoning correspond to the three kinds of order that it knows.

Artistic reason consists in man's ability to imitate and perfect nature, to shape and order the material world toward some good, reflecting God's own creative activity. This is realized through the reasoned making of artifacts and the guiding of the operations of nature. Man uses artistic reason to cultivate vegetation, make furniture and buildings, cure diseases, cook and prepare food, depict nature through drawing or sculpture, create musical harmonies, and guide his body in dance and sport. While each art has its own end (the artifact that is made or the perfected operation), artistic reason illuminates our understanding of nature by the reasoned ordering of things and reveals the image of God as creator present in humanity.

Practical reason (of which prudence is the virtuous habit) is the ability to guide human activity toward some good by the development of virtue. In contrast to artistic reason, which shapes and orders nature external to man, practical reason is concerned with the internal ordering of the human soul. By reflecting on the goods toward which we act, we can understand the relationship of these goods to each other, distinguishing us from animals. While artistic reason understands the useful and pleasant goods of the arts, practical reason understands the moral goods to which our behavior is ordered. This reflects God's own perfect goodness, which defines all His activity. Because we can communicate with each other about these goods and support each other in virtue, it is natural for us to form societies in which to practice virtue.

Contemplative reason is the ability to understand God through His creative activity, the order of reality. Because we were made to contemplate God, we call this man's "final end" or purpose. The Church holds that it is possible to know something about God through natural reason by reflecting on what man perceives through his senses. By our own power (that is, in the order of nature), this understanding of God is indirect because it is discerned through His creation. But God in his wisdom desires to reveal himself more directly so that we might know Him more perfectly and not through a reflection. By our own power this is impossible, but by God's intervention this "supernatural" contemplation can be achieved. This "supernatural" final end is the fulfillment of God's plan for human nature.

Human nature is made in the Image of God because of man's rational soul. And human reason is *artistic, political, and philosophical,* reflecting God's Beauty, Goodness, and Truth. These modes of reasoning have an order among themselves whereby the lower modes are understood more completely in the higher modes. Thus it is through practical reason that we can understand how art contributes to the development of a just and virtuous society, and it is through contemplative reason that we can understand how the political life contributes to man's final end, the contemplation of God. Art allows an insight into the human soul and so supports and finds its fulfillment in politics. Political life allows for the flourishing of the soul in community, the greatest natural reality by which we can contemplate God. This indirect contemplation is perfected and elevated by grace toward the final end of man, the direct contemplation of God in the Beatific Vision. By this account, both art and political life are natural and ordered not only to man's earthly happiness, but also to our heavenly destiny.

The Fall and the Corruption of Nature

Human nature, however, became subject to corruption through sin. St Athanasius teaches that creation is corruptible by nature, but God made man in His image to transcend this corruption. Man's fall was a rejection of the image of God within him and an embrace of natural corruption, which ultimately meant death. Before death, however, the threefold reasoning of human nature was obscured. By misunderstanding God's revelation through nature, man lost sight of his final end. He began to worship false gods, attributing to creatures what was proper to the creator. Without clarity about his final end, he began to lose the moral habits that form the human soul. Human political arrangements became fraught with the *libido dominandi*, the lust for power, and material prosperity became society's end. The representation of creation and the divine in art became grotesque and confused. Man, at war with God, found himself at war with creation and indeed with his own nature.

But what God has joined, man may not divide. God's image remained imprinted upon human nature, though badly damaged, and man was still capable of recognizing and pursuing his natural final end. In pagan cultures, the idea that some personal being created the universe and was owed worship remained intact, though their conception of this being was flawed. Pagan societies were organized around the worship of this being (and the other powers of nature), reflecting in some poor way the virtuous organization of society for the contemplation of the true God. Art served the religious rituals around which society was organized. Human nature could not escape the Image of God, no matter how blind it was.

Even in the blindness, some societies developed inklings of true artistic, practical, and contemplative reason. In particular, the Greek philosophical tradition pierced through the haze of natural corruption and presented to the world a clearer picture of art, virtue, and natural contemplation. Even with this philosophic light, Greek culture and its Roman successor were not free from natural corruption. Dante does not place even Aristotle and Plato in Paradise, but rather in Limbo, which, though a place of natural contemplation of God, is in Hell.

But God, in his wisdom, did not abandon man to his fallen nature. Within the chaos of false religion, God chose to reveal himself directly and form a society based on true contemplation so that the path to supernatural contemplation could be restored. His chosen people, the descendants of Abraham, Isaac, and Jacob, were the recipients of this revelation through various covenants. To counteract the deception of fallen human nature, God gave them prophets to reveal the truth of His place in their lives. He gave them a moral and ritual law to form the basis of their society and art. The revelation of God to Israel was written down in scripture, and the Word of God became the central focus of this religion.

The Incarnation and the Restoration of the Image

In order to complete the restoration of the image of God in human nature, the Word of God "was made flesh and dwelt among us" (Jn 1:14). The Incarnation is the central claim of Christianity. Knowing that His image was obscured in human nature, God chose to reveal himself perfectly to us precisely through human nature. The Word of God that was spoken to create all things, the Image of God that formed the basis for human nature and was generated by God's self-contemplation, the very Son of God revealed Himself definitively by entering his creation, taking on human nature to remake human nature. In the Incarnation, God completed the work of "making man in our own image according to our likeness." This act of God to perfect human nature is what we call grace and is the only path to perfect and direct contemplation of God, the Beatific Vision, our final end.

Grace perfects all of human nature. Not only is contemplative reason restored, but practical and artistic reason as well. The philosophical, political, and artistic tradition of the pagans, once dangerous, could now be illuminated by grace. The prime mover of Aristotle was shown to be the Triune God in whose image we are made. The common life of virtue in a city was shown to be a foreshadowing of the New Jerusalem, the City of God. The beauty of proportion in the human figure and in human artifacts was shown to be the shadow of God's own perfection revealed in the Word made flesh.

The Word made Flesh, Jesus Christ, gave us His Universal Church so that we could participate in the Incarnation and receive this grace. It is only by the action of Christ through his Church that nature is perfected by grace and in particular through the sacramental life. Christ uses water, oil, bread, and wine to enact the life of grace in man. Baptism is not merely a natural symbol of a supernatural washing; it is precisely through the natural washing that the supernatural grace is given. In the same way, anointing in Confirmation and eating in Holy Communion are not merely a natural anointing and eating but the way in which we receive supernatural health and nourishment. The sacraments give us a first taste of our final end, the attainment of human perfection.

The grace of the sacramental life then transforms us to see not only water, oil, bread, and wine as fulfilled in the final contemplation of God, but the rest of creation as well. In the new sacramental order of nature, gold and silver are made into fitting vessels for Christ's Body and Blood in the Eucharist. Stone, wood, metal, and glass are used to build God's Temple here on earth, a vision of God's people gathered to worship Him in heaven. Every human art is illuminated by grace and the natural ordering of artistic reason takes on a supernatural character. The representation of God in worship is no longer an idol but an icon.

The various iconoclastic movements since the Incarnation have been a denial of the restoration of nature. The iconoclasts feared nature, so long a deceiver, but there is no deception when we have seen God's body. Nature is not to be feared but perfected through the grace available to us in Christ's Incarnation. The Church rightly condemns iconoclasm as an affront to the Incarnate Word, but if this is true of our artistic reason by which we represent God and His creation through art, how much more so of our practical reason by which the very order of our lives is ordered according to the image of God?

Restoring the Nature of Politics

The highest use of our practical reason is the practice of politics, the ordering of a "complete" society toward a shared life of peace. This requires justice, that each have what he needs to live in harmony with every other person. This harmony, the common good, is brought to completion through communal religion, giving God His due which is the purpose toward which all human activity on earth is to be directed. God intended man to live in communities where each receives what he ought to have, and all human activity was ordered toward ensuring this so that everyone might contemplate God. The need for a just ordering of society is not precipitated by the fall but is a part of human nature as such. God's own Trinitarian life is one of a multiplicity of persons in perfect unity of being. Man, made in His image, must himself be ordered to a unity of persons. Political order, therefore, is natural to man.

In order to practice politics, our practical reason must be able to understand what is just and the proper ordering of the hierarchy of goods. This is precisely what the corruption of human nature in the fall obscured. The sensual pleasures, like the objects closest to us in a dimly lit room, are the most immediately evident goods. In a fallen world, they take on undue importance, against the goods of physical and spiritual well-being. The light of nature is often strong enough to see the goods of physical well-being, but without sufficient light, these are understood as being opposed to nobler goods, such as friendship and truth. These noble goods can be perceived through reason, but it requires the development of virtues, intellectual habits that light our way to higher goods. Since our practical reason, the understanding of intrinsic human activity, is itself corrupted by the fall, these intellectual habits, even where highly developed, are prone to failure.

Political iconoclasm is the belief that anything better than a fallen political order is impossible in this world and that such a political order is at best a necessary evil and at worst an evil to be overcome. Wishing to reduce this evil, political iconoclasts either attempt to limit political ordering to what is absolutely necessary for society to avoid chaos, or they wish to do away with political order altogether. The Church is seen as the society of grace, parallel to the society of nature. The Church can form individual Christians by grace, but grace merely protects the Christian from the influence of the fallen society of nature. It has no direct interaction with the political life. To the political iconoclast, the individual person, as the locus of virtue and receiver of grace, is a better safeguard of justice than a fallen political order. Either fallen political nature must be tolerated for pragmatic reasons, or it must be totally replaced by the Church.

But if political order is natural to man, and the common good is the highest good, then the restoration of politics through grace is the proper context of the salvation of souls, which is the highest law. The purpose of grace is to transform *all* of human nature. The sacramental life can not only guide the soul of the individual to more closely conform to God's image, it can also shape the political life of societies so that God's place in society is clearer. It is not only our artistic reason and therefore art that is reordered to our supernatural end. Our practical reason that guides how we live is transformed so that we, in society, no longer act in corruption but in imitation of Christ.

Before the Incarnation, the Israelites were forbidden graven images, but they were also warned against serving an earthly king, that is, forming a political order in imitation of those societies that surrounded them. Not only would such a king become a tyrant because of the corruption of nature, but God's own kingship, the true order of nature over His people, would be obscured. Since Christ's Incarnation, the nature of God's kingship has been revealed, and earthly political rule can be seen in this context instead of as a power in its own right. While the work of grace is not fully complete before Christ's Second Coming, and corruption will always be partially present in every human endeavor, man's political nature informed by grace is the closest earthly society can come to properly reflecting God's image. It is therefore absolutely necessary that Catholics promote a political order that gives the Church and its sacramental life, our source of grace, its proper place as the guiding institution, in short, the soul of society. It is not merely one of many voluntary associations that limit the corruption of political nature through the promotion of natural virtue. If we depend on our nature to save our nature, we are worse than lost. God has given us His Word to enlighten our politics as well as our art. Let us not destroy his gift through a misguided political iconoclasm.

13

Integralism Today[*]

Edmund Waldstein, O.Cist.

In the Catholic Church old debates that might seem to have been left behind are constantly returning. Thus, the debate in the nineteenth and early twentieth centuries between "liberal" Catholics and their opponents, sometimes called "integralists," has recently given signs of revival. One such sign is a seminar offered at Harvard Law School entitled "Law and Catholic Thought: Liberalism and Integralism." The seminar's co-teachers can be seen as representing liberalism (Princeton University's Professor Robert P. George) and integralism (Harvard's Professor Adrian Vermeule) respectively. George is certainly not a "liberal" Catholic in the sense in which that term is opposed to "conservative" — he is indeed one of the standard bearers of conservatism in the American Catholic Church. But he is a liberal as opposed to an integralist, because he thinks that political authority exists for the sake of the protection of individual rights, that one of the most important of those rights is the right of religious liberty, and that political authority should therefore not officially favor one religious confession more than others. Vermeule, on the other hand, is an integralist in the sense that he sees political authority as ordered to the common good of human life, that rendering God true worship is essential to that common good, and that political authority therefore has the duty of recognizing and promoting the true religion.[1]

---

[*] This essay originally appeared in *Church Life Journal*. My thanks to Artur Sebastian Rosman for permission to reprint it here.

[1] For two of Vermeule's contributions to *The Josias*, see *Integralism and the Common Good*, vol. 1: *Family, City, and State*, chs. 25 and 26.

Spiritual and Temporal Power

One way of seeing the debate between Catholic liberalism and integralism is as an argument over the proper response of the Church to the secularization of the modern world. One of the most sophisticated accounts of how the modern world was secularized and what exactly is *meant* by secularization is that developed by the philosopher Charles Taylor,[2] and so it will be helpful to summarize the main lines of Taylor's argument. Taylor distinguishes three main meanings that people give to secularization. The first comes out of the secularization theory of nineteenth and early twentieth century sociologists such as Max Weber and Émile Durkheim. They argued that modernization involves a differentiation of various spheres of social life and—more particularly—their separation from religion. Thus, political life was once ordered toward and by God, but now it supposedly follows its "own inherent rationality" without reference to the divine. And a similar point can be made about the economic and artistic spheres—they too are differentiated into autonomous spheres with their own internal rationality, separate from religion. This very process of differentiation of various public spheres was what Weber, Durkheim, and classical sociology primarily meant by "secularization." On their view, this differentiation led to a banishing of religion into the private realm. And this in turn led inevitably, they argued, to a decline in religious practice and belief. Such decline is the second meaning of "secularization." To those two meanings, Taylor adds a third, in which he is primarily interested: secularization can also mean that the *conditions of belief* have changed in the modern world. Whereas in premodern Europe it was nearly impossible *not* to believe in God, in the modern "West" belief in God is one among several options, and perhaps an embattled option.

Taylor disagrees with classical secularization theory on several points. First, following the work of José Casanova,[3] he denies that differentiation of various social spheres necessarily involves a privatization of religion. Rather, he argues, religion can develop into one of several "public" spheres alongside politics, economics, culture, sports, etc. But, more importantly, he disagrees that secularization in the sense of differentiation is strongly correlated with secularization

[2] *A Secular Age* (Cambridge, MA: The Belknap Press of Harvard University Press, 2007).

[3] *Public Religions in the Modern World* (Chicago: University of Chicago Press, 1994).

in the sense of decline of belief and practice. He points to a number of examples where the differentiation on the contrary occurred simultaneously with an *increase* in religious practice—such as in the United States during the Second Great Awakening, or Poland in the twentieth century.[4]

Nevertheless, Taylor does agree with his predecessors in seeing some connection between the different kinds of secularization. He argues that in fact differentiation of social spheres in the West allowed the conditions of belief to change, opening up alternatives to religious belief. And that opening up of options was a condition for the decline of religious belief and practice that did take place in some societies. So, there is an indirect connection between the first meaning of secularization (differentiation of social spheres) and second (decline in religious faith and practice) mediated by the third (change in the conditions of belief). Still, Taylor thinks that the first and third kinds of secularization are irreversible, but the second (decline of religious belief) need not be. He even thinks that attempts at reversing developments of the first kind are counterproductive and actually facilitate the second.

Taylor sees attempts at reversing the differentiation of social spheres as taking two different forms, depending on how far social differentiation is to be overcome. There are two basic forms, because there are three basic constellations of social spheres. The first is what Taylor (somewhat confusingly) terms the "paleo-Durkheimian" arrangement of "baroque" Catholic states, in which the Catholic faith is supposed to form all of social life. The second constellation is a "neo-Durkheimian" one in which there is no official religion, but the political action of the citizens is informed by a broad religious consensus across various denominations—this was the case in the United States when a broad Protestant consensus informed their politics. Finally, the third constellation is when politics has become fully unhooked from religion. Taylor sees this as already holding in much of the West, and of being its inevitable future. In this final arrangement the differentiation of different social spheres leads to an "unbundling" of different areas of life *within* individual

---

4   See Paweł Rojek, "The Polish Romantic Messianism of Saint John Paul II," *Church Life Journal*, June 12, 2018.

persons: public religious worship, private devotion, sexual ethics, works of mercy for others, and political action are no longer linked together but become separate. Thus, a contemporary Catholic person in Western Europe might attend church for Christmas services, baptisms, weddings, and funerals; for her private meditation she might follow a Westernized form of Buddhist practice; in her sexual ethics she might be a post-Freudian; in her charitable work she might support some secular society for aiding refugees; and in politics she might support a (traditionally anticlerical) left-liberal party. Taylor admits that something is lost in such unbundling, but he also thinks that certain valuable freedoms are gained. As a soft-Hegelian neomodernist, Taylor thinks that it is not our task to cry over spilled milk, but rather to make the best of what the development of human consciousness has given us.[5]

But Catholics who wish to adhere without reservation to the teachings of the Church on faith *and* morals cannot fully accept such an unbundling. And here Taylor's two forms of reaction to differentiation come in. There are those who wish to return to a neo-Durkheimian settlement of partial differentiation, and there are those who wish instead to restore something more like the paleo-Durkheimian *ancien régime*. Robert George and Catholic proponents of classical liberalism in general fall into the first group: they desire a restoration of a "moderate" liberal society in which a broad consensus exists among believers of various denominations and religions on the dignity of the human person, and in which political institutions are understood as being for the sake of defending that dignity and the rights that follow from it. On the other hand, Adrian Vermeule, and Catholic integralists more generally, wish to establish something more like the paleo-Durkheimian arrangement of the Baroque confessional state. Or, perhaps even more radically, they wish to work towards something like High Medieval Christendom. In that arrangement, as Andrew Willard Jones has masterfully shown,[6] it makes no sense to distinguish Church and state as separate spheres at all; rather, there was one single kingdom in

---

5   See Taylor's *Lectio Magistralis*, "The Life of the Church in a Secular Age," given on March 5, 2015 at the Pontifical Gregorian University; video on YouTube.

6   *Before Church and State: A Study of Social Order in the Sacramental Kingdom of St Louis IX* (Steubenville, OH: Emmaus Academic, 2017).

which spiritual and temporal authorities cooperated. Thinkers who promote such an integration do not necessarily want to emulate the Middle Ages in other respects. Vermeule, for instance, argues for further development of a robust administrative state, of a sort that St Louis IX could never have imagined. But the crucial point is that integralists want an ordered relation of temporal and spiritual power in the deliberate pursuit of the good for human beings.

Catholic liberals argue that their view of things was accepted by the Church in the Second Vatican Council's declaration *Dignitatis Humanae*, which accepted the ideal of religious liberty, arguing that it was entailed by the nature of truth which "cannot impose itself except by virtue of its own truth" (§1). But integralists can counter with the work of the philosopher Thomas Pink, who has argued that the traditional teaching of the Church, requiring temporal powers to recognize and promote the true Faith, is irreformable, and that (properly understood) *Dignitatis Humanae* did not deny that teaching. Moreover, we integralists argue that the nature of human action demands integralism. All political agents, whether they admit it or not, imply some definite conception of the good for man in their action. As Leo Strauss used to tell his students,[7] all political action is concerned with change or preservation. When it is concerned with change it is concerned with change for the *better*. When it is concerned with preservation it is concerned with preventing change for the *worse*. But the concepts of *better* and *worse* imply a concept of the *good*. Therefore, all political action is concerned with the good. The Weberian account of separate spheres of social activity, each acting according to its own inherent rationality, conceals more than it reveals of modern social life. There is not and cannot be a neutral "political rationality" that reduces politics to a technique of achieving certain penultimate objectives. For, such penultimate objectives can only become objectives pursued by human beings when they are ordered to an (implicit) ultimate objective. And if the ultimate objective is not the true end of man, the City of God, then it will be a false end, the diabolical city.[8]

---

7 The recordings from a 1966 course on Plato's *Meno* may be accessed at https://archive.org/details/PlatosMeno1119660503.

8 See D. C. Schindler, *Freedom from Reality: The Diabolical Character of Modern Liberty* (Notre Dame, IN: University of Notre Dame Press, 2017).

Catholic liberals might argue that this stark alternative can be dissolved by recalling the distinction between nature and grace. Human beings are ordered by nature toward the temporal good of a virtuous common life. This natural good can be understood in abstraction from their further order toward supernatural participation in God's life, which they receive through grace. Through the natural law, written in their hearts, human beings can understand what conduces to the natural good, and what contradicts it. Thus, the Catholic liberal can argue, it is possible to have political institutions which are founded on the natural law, which are respectful of supernatural revelation, as one among many religious confessions, without confessing a religion.

But this defense of moderate liberalism neglects a crucial truth. Nature (including human nature) was created good, but it was wounded by the fall and made subject to the devil. Only through Christ can human nature be healed of its wounds, liberated from the devil, and freed to achieve even its natural end. As Tom Pink argues,[9] such liberation takes place through conversion and Baptism. Every part of the world has to be converted and exorcised in order to liberate it from demonic power. This includes political institutions. As long as political institutions attempt to remain "neutral" towards the Church of Christ, they will in fact be under the power of the Prince of this World. As the Second Vatican Council put it in the *Pastoral Constitution on the Church in the Modern World*: "When the structure of [social] affairs is flawed by the consequences of sin, man, already born with a bent toward evil, finds there new inducements to sin, which cannot be overcome without strenuous efforts and the assistance of grace" (§25).

In a way this is the truth confusedly indicated by the classical secularization theory of Weber and Durkheim. Secularization in the sense of the separation of social spheres from religion acts against the practice of the true religion. By doing so it acts not only against supernatural virtue, but against natural virtue as well. If one looks at the world today it is not difficult to see the influence of the Prince of this World: in the unjust distribution of wealth, in the exploitation of the poor, in the dominance of usurers, in

---

9 See chapter 19.

the reckless pollution of the natural environment, in the slaughter of millions of innocents in abortion clinics, in unspeakable sexual perversions, in the lying propaganda of progress, and in so much more. To fight the spiritual battle in which we are engaged therefore includes fighting against the separation of social spheres from religion, which hands those spheres over to such influence. Taylor would claim that such a struggle is useless; the historical process is irreversible. But Taylor's opinion rests on an unreasonable reification of history. Human social life is formed by the ends that we pursue in common. Which ends we pursue are certainly formed by our common habits, traditions, technologies, and experiences, but they are also formed by example, witness, persuasion, and decision. If our social life today is ordered to the wrong ends, it is not too late to correct it. Today, as at any time, the Gospel of Christ has the power to transform every part of human life.

14

Integralism and the Logic of the Cross[*]

Edmund Waldstein, O.Cist.

Catholic integralism is the position that politics should be ordered to the common good of human life, both temporal and spiritual, and that temporal and spiritual authority ought therefore to have an ordered relation. As a consequence, it rejects modern liberal understandings of freedom.

In his article "The Integralist Mirroring of Liberal Ideals,"[1] Timothy Troutner strongly objects to the integralist position. Troutner argues that integralists in reacting to liberalism become liberalism's mirror image. Liberalism, he claims, is understandable as a reaction to real errors in Christendom, and promoted, though in a distorted way, the precious Christian truths of the goodness of liberty and equality that Christendom had forgotten. In simply rejecting liberalism as a deception of the Antichrist, Troutner argues, integralists end up defending indefensible crimes of Christendom, and condemning important truths associated with liberalism. Integralists commit a fatal error, Troutner thinks, in attempting to attain spiritual ends by means of coercive, temporal power. In this, he suggests they play the role of the devil. Just as the devil tempted Christ in the desert with the kingdoms of the world, so integralists tempt the Church with the use of worldly power. But the power

---

[*] This essay originally appeared in *Church Life Journal*. My thanks to Artur Sebastian Rosman for permission to reprint it here. The author wish to thank the members of various integralist organizations on the internet for assistance in composing this essay. Special thanks to: S. B., S. D., T. D., A. F., J. F., N. G., P. I., J. K., E. M., C. P., P. J. S., Z. T., and T. G. A. W. *Viribus unitis.*

[1] *Church Life Journal*, March 8, 2019.

that the Church uses should be quite different, he maintains. Just as Christ rejected the devil's temptation and chose to win his victory through the self-emptying sacrifice of the Cross, so too the Church must strive for the spiritual end with spiritual means, with a power that takes its form from Christ's kenotic love.

Troutner's conclusion that integralism must be rejected by Catholics is, however, false. The arguments that he uses to support it are based on exaggerations and misunderstandings. He tries to distinguish his own understanding of freedom and equality from the liberal understanding. But he does not distinguish them enough. For Troutner, as for liberals, freedom and equality are opposed to hierarchy and obedience. Whereas, in reality, true freedom and true equality *depend* on hierarchy and on obedience.

Troutner accuses integralists of uncritically accepting everything about Christendom that liberals reject, thus blinding their eyes to the errors of Christendom. But integralists have always distinguished abuses of power in Christendom from its proper uses. It is Troutner who uncritically accepts liberal rejections of the use of temporal power for spiritual ends *an sich*. Troutner manifests here a view of temporal power as so deformed by *libido dominandi* that it can never be used for good ends. On Troutner's view, grace does not heal, elevate, and perfect man's political nature, but rather replaces it with an inclination to a vague and inconsistent anarchism. Moreover, Troutner's contention that integralists promote a worldly understanding of power not formed by Christ's kenotic love misunderstands both the form of power in Christendom and (more importantly) Christ's love. Christ's self-emptying in the Incarnation and the Crucifixion is meant to restore and elevate the hierarchy of creation wounded by sin, not to replace it with egalitarianism. Nor was the Church's juridical understanding of herself in Christendom an imitation of worldly power, unaffected by Christ's *kenosis*. In fact, the very opposite is the case: the form of temporal politics in Christendom was a conscious imitation of the hierarchy of the Church and the rules of the monastic orders. And the ruler was always understood as an image of Christ, bound to *give* himself for the common good of his commonwealth just as Christ offered himself for the Church.

I am grateful for Troutner's article, because it gives me the opportunity to clarify the properly theological character of integralism. I will do so by considering the following points: the liberal understanding of freedom and equality as a reactionary rejection of the goods of hierarchy (I), the goodness of created hierarchy (II), the wounding of that hierarchy through sin (III), the restoration and elevation of it through Christ (IV), the Christological form of politics in Christendom (V), and finally the incoherence of Troutner's Christian anarchism (VI).

I. Liberalism's Reactionary Rejection of Hierarchy

The modern liberal project has always aimed at overcoming unjust inequality and servitude. Liberals have understood the special privileges of aristocratic classes as a form of unjust domination that has to be steadily overcome in favor of equal civil and domestic liberty for all. Each person should have as much liberty as is consistent with the same liberty in others. In this, liberalism promotes in a half-hearted way—moderated by cautious procedures and indirect mechanisms[2]—the same program of liberation that has been pursued in a direct and violent way by revolutionary and totalitarian leftism. Two of the most eloquent recent defenses of this program are Helena Rosenblatt's *The Lost History of Liberalism* (Princeton, 2018) and Corey Robin's *The Reactionary Mind* (Oxford, 2017).

Rosenblatt's book is a history of liberalism from a frankly liberal perspective. She attempts to defend liberalism against critics who see it as individualistic and egotistical, and as undermining virtue and religion. The liberal tradition, she argues, is founded on the ideal of the ancient virtue of generous and public-spirited liberality, purified of its aristocratic element. Apart from a few marginal libertarian cranks, she argues, the liberal tradition—the tradition of Constant, Tocqueville, and Lincoln—has always aimed at the public good, convinced that the abolition of privilege and the establishment of civil and domestic liberty serves that good, and fosters true virtue. Liberals, she argues, have not been against religion as such, but have only opposed reactionary forms of religion such as

---

[2] See Adrian Vermeule, "Liberalism and the Invisible Hand," *American Affairs*, vol. 3, n. 1 (Spring 2019), https://americanaffairsjournal.org/2019/02/liberalism-and-the-invisible-hand/.

the Catholic Church which by teaching the goodness of hierarchy and obedience has always given ideological cover to tyranny.

Robin's book is a strident defense of the same program of liberation in the form of an attack on the reactionary conservatism that has always opposed it. "Since the modern era began," Robin writes, "men and women in subordinate positions have marched against their superiors in the state, church, workplace, and other hierarchical institutions." Robin sees this series of rebellions of subjects against their rulers — the bourgeoisie against the nobles, peasants against landowners, workers against industrialists, wives against husbands, and so on — as fully just. Conversely, the reactionary response has always been unjust. It has been the response of those who, enjoying an unjust share of power and liberty, seek to defend that share. Reactionaries have always clothed their propaganda in high-sounding, public-spirited words, but this has always been a pure concoction of lies. The original defense of hierarchy, Robin perceptively notes, was in terms of "ancient and medieval ideas of an orderly universe, in which permanent hierarchies of power reflected the eternal structure of the cosmos."[3] Later reactionaries were to modify such justifications somewhat, due to the decline of their plausibility after the antiteleological Scientific Revolution, but the original justification remains the foundation of reactionary thought. Again, like Rosenblatt, Robin sees the Catholic Church, with her hierarchical understanding of Divine Order, as being one of the chief culprits in spinning the web of reactionary lies.

As an integralist I am convinced that Rosenblatt and Robin are in error. Creation truly does reflect the goodness of the Creator through the wonderful harmony of hierarchy — an order of goods, an order of beings, an order of rulers and subjects. And human affairs are indeed best when they reflect that order; when they are composed of many parts each subordinated to the other, the lower obeying the higher in humble obedience, the higher helping the lower in loving condescension. Rightly understood, freedom and equality are true goods. As rational beings, men are capable of understanding their good and pursuing it by their own will:

---

3 Cf. John Brungardt, "Ah, to Live in a Cosmos Again!," *Church Life Journal*, September 19, 2018.

true freedom. As beings of the same specific nature, men are all called to participate in the same common good: true equality. But freedom and equality are goods that depend on hierarchy and rule, obedience and humility. "If you remain with my teaching," our Lord says, "then you are truly my disciples and you will know the truth, and the truth will set you free" (John 8:32). True liberty is not opposed to hierarchy and obedience; it depends on obedience to the hierarchy of truth and goodness. And the same is true of equality: "You are my friends if you do what I tell you to do. No longer do I call you slaves, because the slave does not know what his master is doing; but I call you friends, because I made known to you all that I heard from my Father" (Jn 15:14–15). Jesus raises his disciples from slavery to a quasi-equality with God, so that they can even call him a friend. But this quasi-equality depends on submissive obedience to the commands of the Lord. It is only in losing our lives in this obedience that we find our true lives and reach our deepest desires. Indeed, the great wonder of this quasi-equality depends on a more fundamental *inequality*. It is because God, as the shoreless ocean of perfect happiness,[4] is so infinitely higher than us that his condescension in calling us into the friendship of his Trinitarian life is so marvelous.

I admit, of course, that in human affairs the good of hierarchy has often been abused. Rulers have often exploited their subjects for selfish advantage rather than aiding them to attain to the common good. And, indeed, the world has seen many false hierarchies—such as chattel slavery[5]—founded on unjust principles. But the abuse of something does not take away its proper use.

Liberalism is a reactionary program in Troutner's sense of the word. In reacting to the abuses of hierarchy, liberalism sees hierarchy itself as evil. This inevitably backfires. By misunderstanding liberty and equality as opposed to hierarchy, liberals deprive those whom they would liberate of true liberty, true equality, and truly common goods. The result is a tyranny worse than that which came before.

---

4 See Graham Ward, "The Unimaginable," *Church Life Journal*, June 26, 2018.
5 See Katie Walker Grimes, "From Slavery to Incarceration," *Church Life Journal*, March 7, 2019.

II. The Glory of God and Goodness of Cosmic Hierarchy

God is infinitely and perfectly happy. He is the absolute fullness of being, the shoreless ocean of perfection, the entirely satisfying good. And he possesses his infinite being, perfection, and goodness by an unspeakably joyful act of self-comprehension—an act of the most intense and complete life, all at once, undivided, and undistended, and yet eternal. In this eternal instant of his happiness he expresses his self-comprehension in an interior Word, a Word Who so faithfully expresses the Divine comprehension that he is himself God: God the Son. The eternal Son is not a second god, but the one and only God. The Father looks at the Son and sees in him the perfect image of his life, sharing indeed the very same act of infinitely happy life. And the Son looks at the Father and sees in him the source of that infinitely good and joyful life that he is. And Father and Son love each other with a boundlessly intense love. This love they express to each other by breathing together an eternal sigh of love—a sign, a kiss, an embrace, a gift: the Holy Spirit.[6] So perfectly does the Holy Spirit express the Divine love, that he is himself the one God.

Father, Son, and Holy Spirit are the infinite happiness of the divine life shared, given, and received in perfect unity. In them perfect necessity coincides with something like freedom, and perfect equality coincides with a holy order of subordination. The Trinitarian processions are entirely necessary; the Father *cannot but* generate the Son, and Father and Son *cannot but* breathe the Holy Spirit. And yet these processions are altogether personal and (as it were) *voluntary* acts—in this sense they are free. The Persons of the Blessed Trinity are entirely equal, since each *is* the One God. And yet there must be an "order" among them, since, as St Thomas Aquinas teaches, "where plurality exists without order, confusion exists."[7] Order consists in the relation of many to one beginning. The beginning here is the Father. Not a beginning in time—since Son and Spirit are equally eternal—but a beginning in procession. And this order from the beginning implies subordination, as St John Henry Newman says: "the very idea of order implies the idea of the

---

6 See Paul J. Griffiths, "Advent Flesh?," *Church Life Journal*, December 5, 2018.
7 *ST* I, q. 42, a. 3, sed contra.

subordinate... a subordination exists between Person and Person, and this is the incommunicable glory of the God of Grace."[8] The Son is subordinate to the Father, and the Holy Spirit is subordinate to Father and Son. Newman calls the order of the Divine Persons "glory," because order or harmony is one of the essential properties of beauty. The order of the Divine Persons is the greatest and most piercing of beauties, and therefore the most luminous glory. Son and Spirit love their subordination in this order. They never stand on their dignity or assert their rights. Joseph Ratzinger writes of the Son that he is "a completely open being, a being 'from' and 'towards,' that nowhere clings to itself and nowhere stands on its own."[9] The same is true of the Holy Spirit.

Although the persons of the Blessed Trinity lack nothing, yet by a wholly gratuitous outpouring of their goodness they decide to create creatures, who participate by way of similitude in their Creator. They create the intellectual light of the angels — pure spirits so great that they exceed in natural perfection the whole of the visible world. Each angel by a single infused thought knows more than all human philosophers of all the ages together. Each one reflects by its unique nature some ray of the Divine light, and thereby glorifies the Creator. These spirits are incomparably more numerous than the trillions upon trillions of visible stars. And they are all unequal — from the highest seraph to the lowest angel: a holy order of holy orders, holy principalities, *hierarchies* ordered by and toward their origin and end: the *Hierā Archē*, the Holy Beginning of all.

Each angel is like a universe on its own, and yet the unity of order between them is the highest natural good in which they share. God wills that they be bound together in this order, with the higher ruling the lower, and the lower submitting to the higher. The harmonious unity of order in this countless multitude of spiritual creatures is a more perfect reflection of the divine goodness, a more perfect glorification of God, than any angelic nature taken by itself. The order of the angels is a ravishingly beautiful symphony of spiritual life. As Dionysius writes, the celestial orders through their "mutual indwellings" and "the providences of the higher

---

8   *Sermons Preached on Various Occasions*, Sermon 11, "Order, the Witness and Instrument of Unity."

9   Ratzinger, *Introduction to Christianity*, 134.

for those beneath them" are "Evangelists of the Divine Silence," revealing him in whom they participate.[10]

In this order each good angel loves his subordination to his superiors and to the whole order. Their delight in the reflection of God in the common good of their order, and in their contemplation of him in their natural knowledge, would have already been a very great happiness. But God wished to raise them to a greater happiness still. By grace he gives those who accept it a share in his Divine life, an unmediated Vision of his essence. And so the angelic hierarchies stand before him, beholding his face, and crying out in an ecstasy of love and wonder: "Holy, holy, holy is the Lord God of hosts" (Is 6:3).

Here again there is a kind of equality, for each angel enjoys the same common good, but it is an equality that depends on the inequality of their hierarchical order. The spiritual symphony whereby the angels proclaim the Divine Silence is entirely determined in all its acts and motions, and yet this is a completely voluntary and personal determination—in a sense, it is freedom.

Next comes the material and visible creation: the galaxies and stars, and then the Earth with its oceans and mountains, and its living creatures, plants, and animals, who in their unknowing lives still show some trace of the beauty of their Creator. And then comes man who is the bridge between the material and spiritual worlds: a body vivified by a spiritual soul. The visible and the invisible are therefore a single order. It is this order which is the greatest manifestation of God outside of himself, and it is what he principally intends in creation. As Beatrice puts it in Dante's *Paradiso*, the order that things have among themselves is "the form that makes the world resemble God." Spiritual creatures find their perfection and happiness in submitting to this order; in being subject to other creatures; in being, like the Divine Son (to use Ratzinger's words again), completely open beings, beings "from" and "towards," that nowhere cling to themselves and nowhere stand on their own.

Man comes to knowledge of the whole of which he is a part, and the Creator to which he is ordered, indirectly. His soul is at first dark and ignorant, all its knowledge coming from the impressions of its bodily senses. The other visible things are for his sake;

---

10 See Dionysius the Areopagite, *On the Divine Names*, chapter 4.

they are words spoken to man by God to communicate himself to the human mind: "what is his and invisible, his eternal power and divinity, has been perceived by the mind through what he has made" (Rom 1:20). But, wounded by sin, it is only with great difficulty that man can come to knowledge. He must first master his lower passions and purify his thoughts by the moral virtues, and then ascend by reasoning to the intellectual virtue of wisdom. He establishes thereby a hierarchical order between body and soul and between the various faculties of the soul, with everything ruled by the noblest faculty: reason. The virtuous man becomes a microcosm, reflecting in his soul the order of the whole of creation. And by subduing, naming, and cultivating the irrational creatures he brings them up into fuller participation in that order.

This order is reflected in an even greater way in the communities in which men seek their good together: first in the family, and the tribe or village, and then in the complete community of the polity. The polity is practically necessary for human beings to attain to virtue. Here too, a hierarchical order of rulers and subjects is fitting. Unlike the angelic hierarchies, which are given by nature, human hierarchies have to be constructed by human reason. Unlike the angels, human beings are equal in their essential nature. Their hierarchies are therefore in one respect an even better reflection of the order of the Divine Persons: subordination to natural equals. The construction of human hierarchy is therefore not a tragic necessity, but a great good — the highest and most godlike intrinsic practical good of human beings. It is a life which imitates Heaven. By submitting to such hierarchical order, men are educated to become like the Eternal Son, beings entirely "from" and "toward," who do not stand on their own dignity or oppose their rights to the common good.

The intrinsic common good of political life is called "peace"; it is a beautiful symphony of virtuous life. My fellow integralist Jose Mena well described peace as not merely "a condition in which we agree not to go to war," but "the harmonious activity of God's creation working together within the order of divine providence for the good of all and the worship of God."[11] Peace is "bustling"

---

[11] Jose Mena, "After Liberalism: Towards a Politics of the Common Good," *Fare Forward*, December 16, 2020, http://farefwd.com/index.php/2020/12/16/after-liberalism/.

and "fruitful," and manifests itself in all the virtuous actions of mutual care.

A good person loves his subordination to the common good of peace. He finds his dignity in obeying his rulers for the sake of a good in which both he and they share, in cooperating with those of his own rank in common subordination to that good, and in helping his subjects to attain to it. There is here a kind of freedom—for each is enabled to achieve the true good which he really wants. And there is a kind of equality—for each shares in the same common good. But such freedom and such equality depend for their very existence on obedience and inequality.

III. Lucifer's Proto-Liberal Rebellion Against Hierarchy

The common good of order to which creatures are meant to submit is a greater good for them than any private good. But for creatures to love that good more than their private good requires a certain self-transcendence. The origin of sin is in a refusal of that self-transcendence, a refusal to submit to a higher good. Lucifer, the Morning Star of creation, the highest being in the order of nature, was too proud to submit himself to the common good:

> How wise thou wast, how peerlessly fair ... a cherub thou shouldst be, thy wings outstretched in protection ... From the day of thy creation all was perfect in thee, till thou didst prove false ... A heart made proud by its own beauty, wisdom ruined through its own dazzling brightness. (Ezek 28:12–17)

The sin of Lucifer is a refusal of the common good, because that good is hierarchical and demands subordination.

As Charles De Koninck explains, Lucifer felt injured in his dignity by the invitation to participate in a good common to many.[12] Lucifer's exalted nature, and the high freedom that it gave him, were not enough to secure him, since freedom is good only to the extent that it submits itself to order. To quote De Koninck: "The dignity of the created person is not without ties, and the purpose of our liberty is not to overcome these ties, but to free us by strengthening them. These ties are the principal cause of our dignity. Liberty

---

12   De Koninck, *Primacy*, Collins trans., 11.

itself is not a guarantee of dignity and of practical truth."[13] And he refers to the following words of St Thomas Aquinas: "Aversion from God has the nature of an end, inasmuch as it is sought for under the appearance of liberty, according to Jeremiah 2:20: For a long time you have broken the yoke, you have broken bonds, and you have said, 'I will not serve.'"[14] Lucifer's sin was therefore a proto-liberal rebellion against hierarchy and obedience.

After having ruined himself by rebelling against God, Lucifer tempts others into rebellion with him. By tempting Adam into Original Sin, he brings the whole human race into his rebellion. Adam's and Eve's sin in the Garden is a sin of disobedience, a failure to submit to the order established by God for their common good. Instead of becoming free thereby, they become the slaves of sin, unable to attain the good that they truly desire. From the sin of our first parents onward a shadow lies across the course of human events. Human beings rebel against God and worship false idols, and then their relations among themselves are corrupted by *libido dominandi*, the lust of domination. Subjects rebel against their rulers, and rulers tyrannize over their subjects and exploit them for private advantage, rather than guiding them to participation in the common good.

IV. The Restoration of Hierarchy in the *Kenosis* of the Cross

Since original sin was rebellion against hierarchy, our Lord's work of salvation is the exact opposite. He, the Eternal Son, God from God, Light from Light, enters into his own creation, taking on the form of a slave in order to heal disobedience through obedience: "Even though he was the son, he learned obedience from his sufferings; and, made perfect, he became for all who obey him the cause of everlasting salvation" (Heb 5:8–9). As the eternal Son he was always obedient to the Father, but in his suffering he "learned" obedience in our nature.

Jesus is not a proto-Jacobin revolutionary who comes to liberate subjects from submission to their rulers. On the contrary, he is the obedient one who comes to teach obedience. Certainly, he also comes to comfort the poor and the afflicted, to call tyrants to

[13] De Koninck, 12–13.
[14] *ST* III, q. 8, a. 7.

conversion, and to heal the wounds caused by the abuse of hierarchy through a preferential option for the poor and miserable. Therefore, the tyrants of his time saw him as a dangerous revolutionary. But they were in error. As St Quodvultdeus says about (and to) Herod:

> When they tell of one who is born a king, Herod is disturbed. To save his kingdom he resolves to kill him, though if he would have faith in the child, he himself would reign in peace in this life and for ever in the life to come. Why are you afraid, Herod, when you hear of the birth of a king? He does not come to drive you out, but to conquer the devil.

As long as he is a tyrant who exploits the poor and weak, Herod should indeed fear Christ who comes to save the poor and oppressed. But as a tyrant Herod is himself a rebel. If he were to start ruling for the common good, his power would be legitimate, and he would receive his authority from God. In that case he would have nothing to fear from our Lord. Indeed, as the First Epistle of St Peter teaches, the Gospel is a call to all subjects to obey their rulers:

> For love of the Lord, then, bow to every kind of human authority; to the king, who enjoys the chief power, and to the magistrates who hold his commission to punish criminals and encourage honest men. To silence, by honest living, the ignorant chatter of fools; that is what God expects of you. Free men, but the liberty you enjoy is not to be made a pretext for wrong-doing; it is to be used in God's service. Give all men their due; to the brethren, your love; to God, your reverence; to the king, due honor. You who are slaves must be submissive to your masters, and show all respect, not only to those who are kind and considerate, but to those who are hard to please. It does a man credit when he bears undeserved ill treatment with the thought of God in his heart . . . Indeed, you are engaged to this by the call of Christ; he suffered for our sakes, and left you his own example; you were to follow in his footsteps . . . You, too, who are wives must be submissive to your husbands . . . It may be God's will that we should suffer for doing right; better that, than for doing wrong. It was thus that Christ died as a ransom, paid once for all, on behalf of our sins, he the innocent for us the guilty, so as to present us in God's sight . . . He sits, now, at the right hand of God, annihilating

death, to make us heirs of eternal life; he has taken his journey to heaven, with all the angels and powers and princedoms made subject under his feet. (1 Pet 2:13–3:22)

The program of obedience sketched out here is the opposite of the program of liberation described by the likes of Rosenblatt and Robin.

Troutner is right to indicate that Christ in his first coming did not use any coercive measures to lead men towards their end, but this is because he was winning the interior grace necessary for them to obey. He never denies the legitimate use of coercion in a world wounded by sin and vice. And, indeed, his apostles make use of coercive measures in the early Church. They wield the spiritual sword of excommunication, and they hand evildoers over to other powers for temporal punishment. St Peter delivers Ananias and Sapphira to the punitive power of God for attempting to deceive the Church (Acts 5). St Paul urges the Corinthians to excommunicate a man guilty of incest and hand him over to the devil for bodily punishment: "When you are assembled, and my spirit is present, with the power of our Lord Jesus, you are to deliver this man to Satan for the destruction of the flesh, that his spirit may be saved in the day of the Lord Jesus" (1 Cor 5:4–5).

Troutner rightly points out that our Lord still resembles a slaughtered lamb in the visions of the Apocalypse, bearing the wounds that are the sign of the mild humility of his first coming. But Troutner fails to mention that the same lamb will come again in glory at the end of days and consign all who reject his salvation to the punishment of eternal fire: "For if the word spoken by the angels proved certain, and every transgression and disobedience got its just punishment, how shall we escape if we neglect so great a salvation?" (Heb 2:2–3). Contrary to what Troutner implies, the humility of Christ in his self-emptying Incarnation and Passion does not destroy the nature of political power; it presupposes, heals, perfects, and elevates it.

V. Christ and the Form of Christendom

Troutner claims that the integration of spiritual and temporal power in medieval Christendom obscured the nature of the Church. By seeing herself as a juridical *societas perfecta* (complete society), she lost sight of her true nature. She begins to resemble worldly powers, no longer reflecting her Christological "form." We have already seen in the preceding section that Troutner's understanding of the Christological form is defective. The form of Christ's saving acts does not in fact exclude all coercive uses of power. But there is another error in Troutner's claim. It is not true that the medieval Church formed herself on the model of worldly power. The obverse is true: the temporal powers of Christendom modeled themselves on the hierarchy of the Church and the rules of the monastic orders. Of course, medieval Christendom included many different political arrangements and theories, and I do not mean to defend them all. But I do wish to defend some of its most characteristic forms. I want to defend the ideal of a hierarchical society in which elements of freedom and equality depend on hierarchies of inequality and subordination. And, I want to defend the authoritative ideal of the relation of temporal and spiritual power taught by popes such as St Gregory VII and Innocent III.

The barbarian tribes who conquered the Western Roman Empire had traditionally been bound together by blood-solidarity in what Francis Fukuyama calls "segmentary, tribal institutions."[15] This blood-solidarity broke down "usually within a couple of generations after a barbarian tribe's conversion to Christianity." What replaced it were relations of fealty between lords and vassals, modeled in certain respects on monastic vows, and, even more importantly, what Andrew Jones calls "networks of counsel and aid," which went far beyond the networks of fealty and were based on the understanding of Christian charity as a form of friendship.[16]

Perhaps no document is more useful for understanding the political ideals of Christendom than the *Rule* of St Benedict of Nursia. The *Rule* is written not for complete political communities, but for monasteries, and yet its influence on medieval political life and jurisprudence was profound.

The monastic community described by St Benedict is a strictly hierarchical order, in which every monk has an exactly defined place in a scale that ranges from the abbot through all the rest of the

---

15 *The Origins of Political Order, from Prehuman Times to the French Revolution* (New York: Farrar, Straus and Giroux, 2011), 107.
16 See Jones, *Before Church and State*, 249–74, 339–69.

monks ranked by the time of entry, down to the monk or novice who was last to enter: "He who shall have come into the monastery at the second hour of a day shall know himself to be junior to him who came at the first hour of that day, of whatever age or dignity he may be" (RB 63). Those who rank lower are to honor and obey those who rank higher and address them as *Nonnus* (Reverend Father), while the higher ranked are to love those below them, and condescend to call them *Frater* (Brother). Already here we see a certain equality that depends on hierarchy. If a slave enters the monastery, and later his former master joins as well, the slave ranks higher than the one who was his master: "For whether slaves or freemen we are all one in Christ and under the one Lord bear equal rank of subjection" (RB 2). Moreover, each monk contributes to the common good of the monastery, and all can make their voices heard in chapter: "We have said that *all* are to be called to counsel because it is often to the younger that the Lord reveals what is better" (RB 3).

The abbot is to be obeyed in everything, and to be called *Dominus* (Lord) and *Abbas* (Father), because "he is regarded as the vicar of Christ in the monastery." The abbot is to rule his monastery with wisdom and gentleness. He is to apply punishments both corporal (beatings) and spiritual (exclusion from common prayer and meals). In administering these punishments the abbot has to be mindful of different dispositions:

> Suiting his actions to circumstances, mingling gentleness with severity, let him show now the rigor of a master, now the loving affection of a father; in other words, he should sternly reprove the undisciplined and the restless; the obedient and the meek and the patient ones, on the other hand, he ought rather to entreat to advance in holiness; but such, however, as are not amenable to correction and are contemptuous of authority, we charge him to rebuke and punish. Let him not shut his eyes to the faults of offenders; but as soon as they make their appearance, let him do his utmost to pluck them out by the roots, remembering the fate of Heli, the priest of Silo. (RB 2)

But he must also be mindful not to punish too severely "lest, seeking too vigorously to cleanse off the rust, he may break the vessel" (RB 64).

Integralism and the Logic of the Cross

Is the "form" of the abbot's power as described by St Benedict too worldly? Is he a victim of what Troutner calls "cognitive dissonance" in using punishments to help his monks to conform themselves to a crucified Lord? Surely not. The form of abbatial authority is truly Christological. The use of punishment in the *Rule* is a reaction to some violation of the peace, meant to lead monks back to Christ, and the witness of monastic saints throughout the centuries testifies to its wisdom. The goal is to lead sinners to true freedom:

> If anything somewhat severe be laid down in this rule, as reason may dictate, in order to amend faults or preserve charity, do not straightway depart full of fear from the way of salvation, which way cannot be entered upon except by beginnings which are difficult. But when one shall have advanced in this manner of life and in faith, he shall run with his heart enlarged and with an unspeakable sweetness of love on the way of God's commandments. (RB, Prologue)

As Andrew Jones has shown in *Before Church and State*, the use of coercive power in Christendom was seen precisely along the lines of punishment in Benedict's *Rule*. The two swords, temporal and spiritual, were seen as being necessary to punish those who rebelled against the peace, and the more they were successful in leading Christians back to Christ, the less they had to be used.

The rulers of Christendom were seen as being—like abbots—vicars of Christ. Ernst Kantorowicz, in his masterpiece *The King's Two Bodies*, gives a wealth of detail on the Christological understanding of medieval kingship. The king was seen as the principle of the order of peace in his kingdom, bound to serve it, and bound even to give his life for it as Christ did for the Church. For example, he quotes Cardinal Piccolomini, later Pope Pius II, as follows: "The prince himself, the head of the mystical body of the *respublica*, is held to sacrifice his life whenever the commonweal demands it."

The great medieval king-saints were particularly praised for their Christlike devotion to the poor and wretched. Every Holy Thursday they would symbolize that devotion by washing the feet of twelve poor men with their own hands. In their almsgiving and in their punishment of tyrannical lords, these kings were to remedy the wounds caused by abuses of inequality.

The forms of medieval representation, such as the Estates General, the Parliament, and the Cortes, were meant, like the monastic chapter, to allow different ranks of the social order to contribute to deliberation about the common good. Thus, there were forms of equality imbedded in a society of unequals. Society itself was meant to mirror the life of the Blessed Trinity with laity, secular clergy, and monks; or king, lords, and commons representing Father, Son, and Holy Ghost. In their hierarchical orders of obedience they were meant to grow in virtue and devotion to the common good, becoming conformed to the Son of God, beings entirely "from" and "toward."

It is certainly true that Christendom did not always live up to such ideals. There were many abuses. But Troutner makes no distinction between abusive and legitimate uses of temporal power. It would be wearisome to go through the examples of the uses of power that Troutner mentions, and distinguish abuses from proper uses.[17] The point that I want to make here is a more fundamental one: power has good uses. Troutner quotes a passage from Augustine's *De Trinitate* in which Augustine teaches that the devil is to be conquered not by power, but by justice. But Troutner omits the immediately following sentence in which Augustine clarifies the point: "Not that power is to be shunned as though it were something evil; but the order must be preserved, whereby justice is *before* it."[18] The point is that justice *precedes* power, not that power has no role. When power is preceded by justice it can become a good, albeit secondary, instrument to be used prudently in defending the peace and leading those who have strayed back to the right path. Rulers must be careful not to scrape off the rust too violently, lest they break the vessel. But they must also be mindful of Heli, the priest of Silo (Eli of Shiloh), who neglected to punish his sons, to the great detriment of the common good of Israel.

VI. Against Troutner's Christian Anarchism

Having rejected integralism, Troutner is not willing simply to capitulate to liberalism. He proposes another model for a nonliberal Catholic politics: namely the Catholic Worker Movement of

---

17 See, inter alia, Pink, "What is the Catholic doctrine of religious liberty?"; Waldstein, "Tarnishing the Splendor of Truth."

18 *De Trinitate*, XIII,13, emphasis added.

Dorothy Day.[19] The idea is to work practically at the local level to help the needy, combat oppression, and embody as much as possible the principles of charity, justice, and the universal destination of goods. Troutner recognizes the limits of such local communities. But his hope is that they can become "workshops for imagining, along with non-Catholics of good will, an end to capitalism and the replacement of liberal democracy with something that preserves its achievements."

Now, Dorothy Day was certainly an admirable woman, full of love for God and his beloved poor. But her movement is not an adequate model for Catholic politics. Day was an anarchist and a pacifist, deeply formed before her conversion by revolutionary leftism. This helped her to see certain kinds of injustice very clearly. And we have much to learn from her denunciations of capitalist exploitation. But it also prevented her from adequately understanding the goods of hierarchy and obedience, and the legitimate uses of coercion in fostering the common good. She tried to base her movement on the Sermon on the Mount. But her interpretation of those verses was incomplete, because she did not see clearly enough how they are to be read in the light of other parts of the New Testament.

To illustrate what I mean, recall the anecdote from Day's autobiography, *The Long Loneliness*, cited at the end of chapter 7. Day recalls how various opportunities of hospitality were taken advantage of by people who selfishly coopted them — and, it seems, no one was able or willing to take steps against the freeloaders because of a sort of passive noninterventionist mentality. Contrast this description with the *Rule* of St Benedict as described above. Superficially, Day's approach might seem more faithful to Matthew 5:40 ("And if any man will sue thee at the law, and take away thy coat, let him have thy cloak also"). But one must read such passages more carefully and in a wider context. When Jesus himself was struck on the face by the servant of the High Priest, he did not turn the other cheek, but rebuked the unjust action with sharp words (Jn 18:22–23). Much less did he turn *other people's* cheeks. In reality, the approach of the *Rule* of St Benedict is more faithful

---

19 See Casey Mullaney, "What Is the Catholic Worker Movement?," *Church Life Journal*, November 20, 2017.

to the Gospel. To allow thieves to thieve with impunity is good neither for those whom they wrong nor for the thieves themselves. A moderate use of coercion against such injustices can help to lead people to virtue and the restoration of the beauty of hierarchy in their souls.

Day was deeply influenced by her friend Peter Maurin. Maurin had been a member of *Le Sillon*, the Catholic democratic movement, condemned by Pope St Pius X in *Notre charge apostolique*. Pius X particularly condemns the *Sillon*'s liberal egalitarianism. He points out that a community of persons needs authority to direct them to the common good, and that in a world wounded by sin this authority needs coercive power to oppose "the selfishness of the wicked." And he shows that obedience to such authority does not degrade man but exalts him, since it is, "in the final analysis, obedience to God."

We integralists seek true freedom and true equality in obedience to God and in obedience to our fellow creatures for the sake of God. This is the logic of the Cross: raised up towards Heaven on the vertical trunk of that lifegiving tree, we open our arms wide in fraternal charity, allowing our hands to be nailed in holy obedience to its horizontal branches. We strive with confidence to conform human life to the pattern of heavenly hierarchies, convinced that, however imperfectly, our common life can be suffused with harmony and beauty—men, women, and children of every degree submitting in joy and delight to the common good in which they all share, raising by their common life a hymn of praise to the triune God. And we are convinced that however daunting the task, however violent the powers that oppose us, nothing that we do will be in vain. Every movement towards the freedom of obedience and the joy of the common good will be taken up and perfected in the New Jerusalem that is to come.

15*

The Politics of Hell

Urban Hannon

Let's start with a little guided meditation. I want you to imagine a society—a society made up of self-absorbed, atomized individuals—a society in which the various members tolerate each other, because they know they need each other, but only so that each of them can achieve his own private ambitions and desires—a society, moreover, that is in open rebellion against its own origins. Sound familiar yet?

Now I want you to imagine that, once upon a time, this society had been noble, and civil, and good, but that its citizens—especially its elite citizens—out of a disordered sense of pride, effected a revolution against that received ancient order. Imagine, if you will, that this revolution had some ironic consequences, such as that, in the name of liberating themselves from being subject to any official king, these citizens wound up creating for themselves an even more oppressive and authoritarian regime—and that their honorable hierarchy, which in their pettiness they would have liked to dissolve altogether, was merely replaced by a dishonorable hierarchy—that they traded an ordered harmony for hostile power relations, and a common good for private vices.

Now imagine that this populace—who, again, hate their own heritage and devote all their time and energy to contradicting it, loudly—is in fact deeply unsatisfied, frustrated, lonely, sad. And yet imagine that, despite their unhappiness in this society, they also live in constant, ever-growing fear—fear that this society of theirs, and everything it stands for, is on the verge of defeat.

* This lecture was delivered at the Pro Civitate Dei summer school in La Londe-les-Maures, France, on June 12, 2022.

Imagine, finally, that this hysterical anxiety of theirs makes them even more odious and offensive and obnoxious.

Probably by now you are not having to imagine, because unfortunately what I have been describing is not imaginary. This is a society—or at least, a "society"—which is very real, which is all around us, and with which we are forced to interact on a daily basis. I am speaking, of course, of the society of Satan and his demons. This is a talk about the politics of hell.

Fr Serge-Thomas Bonino—a Dominican friar of the Toulouse province and my professor at the Angelicum, and probably the world's foremost expert on the angelology of St Thomas Aquinas—teaches in Italian and publishes almost exclusively in French, but his one book that is presently available in English translation is relevant to our topic today: *Angels and Demons*, of no-not-that-*Angels-and-Demons* fame. Even more relevant, for those who have French, is an essay Fr Bonino wrote in *Revue Thomiste* back in 2013, "Les écailles de Léviathan: ou de l'organisation de la société des démons selon les théologiens du treizième siécle": "The Scales of Leviathan: or, On the Organization of the Demons' Society according to Thirteenth-Century Theologians." I was blessed to take a course with him this past semester on evil, the final *dispensa* for which ended up coming in at exactly 666 kilobytes (I don't think he planned that but I also wouldn't put it past him)—as well as one on Satan and the demons, fittingly located in Room 6, which you might remember as the name of Christine Taylor's 2006 horror movie about devil-worshipping doctors. All of this just to say: I will be borrowing heavily from Fr Bonino in this lecture—which is not to imply that he would necessarily endorse all of its integralist conclusions—and if you are interested in learning more about these things after today there is no better man to turn to than Fr Bonino. Thus concludes the acknowledgements section of this talk.

As we turn to consider the demons themselves, I should warn you that we will not really be getting to their politics proper until the second half of this lecture. I hope it is fair to assume that I am not speaking to a room of professional angelologists, so we will have a good amount of ground to cover on our way there, so that we can appreciate what we will find when we arrive. I think it is best to begin by situating demonology within the whole of Christian theology, because there is always a risk of exaggerating the importance of Satan, or of becoming inordinately curious about the workings of the underworld. Don't get me wrong: The demons are very real, and so is spiritual warfare. But, it turns out, indulging a morbid fascination with the devil is a great way to lose in that spiritual warfare. To steal St John the Divine's phrase from his letters to the churches in the Apocalypse: Beware of "scrutinizing the depths of Satan." The demons have their place in our Catholic doctrine, therefore, but it is important to be clear about what that place is, and not to let them leave it. Here is how Fr Bonino began our course this year:

> The Catholic Church's teaching on Satan and the demons is not at all the center of Christian revelation. It is a side teaching, a marginal doctrine, that is, a peripheral truth in the hierarchy of revealed truths. It needs to remain so. A preaching of the Christian faith obsessed with the devil would be completely unbalanced. Indeed, the doctrine on Satan must be subordinated to and integrated with the most fundamental truths of the faith: the mystery of God and of his loving plans brought about by the victory of Christ, which frees believers from the powers of evil. Therefore, Satan's place in the Christian faith is precisely under the feet of the risen Christ.

End quote, and mic drop. Now, obviously I would not be talking about the politics of hell today if I didn't think there was something valuable for us to learn from it. But the point is that our interest needs to be mortified, limited to what we can know from the science of metaphysics and from *sacra doctrina*, and exclusively ordered to our Christian beatitude and the glory of God.

Allora, to understand the demons' politics, which is part of what they do, first we need to know something about the demons' nature and condition, which is part of what they are. *Agere sequitur esse*, right?: "Action follows being," second act follows on first act. We'll take two different paths to try to get there: from above, and from the side—that is, by considering what these spiritual substances are in general, and by contrasting the demons with their angelic counterparts. Let's take the first one first, because it is always better to treat common things before particular ones, or else you end up just having to repeat yourself. (That, by the way—short side rant here—is why in the *Summa* St Thomas considers the divine essence before he considers the processions of the divine persons, *De Deo Uno* before *De Deo Trino*. It was fashionable in the twentieth century to complain that St Thomas was thereby subordinating the Most Holy Trinity to merely philosophical questions about God's simplicity and goodness and perfection and infinity and so forth, but the truth is that St Thomas was just better at methodology than his critics. If he had started with the persons, then in treating the Father he'd have had to talk about the Father's simplicity and goodness etc., and then have more articles later about the Son's simplicity and goodness etc., and then again for the Holy Spirit. It should have been obvious that he is beginning not with some deist rationalist God of the philosophers, but rather with what the three divine persons—Father, Son, and Holy Spirit—have in common.)

So then, when it comes to the angels and demons, to "angels" considered indifferently, what do they have in common? We get a first clue from St Thomas' preferred name for them: not "angels," which he usually reserves just for the lowest of the choirs, but rather—a term and an idea that originates in Aristotle—"separated substances." Separated, one might rightly wonder, from what? And the answer, in a word, is: matter. The angels are substances (analogically but truly), beings which exist in themselves and not in another. But unlike any of the substances we experience here below, they have no matter whatsoever, but are pure form. St Bonaventure would object to this, and indeed he tried to find some kind of non-bodily "spiritual matter" for the angels to have to distinguish them from the totally immaterial God, but St Thomas will have none of it, since this spiritual matter of Bonaventure's in principle cannot play the metaphysical role he would need it to play. We can't enter into the details of that *De Ente et Essentia* argument (it's in number 70, if you would like to check it yourself). But in the Thomistic picture—the correct picture—that I am sketching for you today, the angels are going to be totally immaterial. They are still infinitely inferior to God, because their angelic simplicity does not reach to the distinction of being and essence. But in terms of essence itself, the angels really are immaterial and simple.

The Politics of Hell

They are forms, and so minds, and so, by Boethius' famous definition, persons. Each one is "an individual substance of a rational nature"—or, better, an individual substance which also just *is* a rational nature—or an intellectual nature, to be more precise. For each of the angels is a species and indeed a genus unto himself, since matter is precisely what multiplies individual instances of a particular species, and the matter-form distinction is the basis of the genus-difference distinction. Lacking matter, every angel is individual and species and genus unto himself, and in the angel there is no real difference between these. It would be as though "James" and "rational" and "animal" were all identical and coextensive—in reality if not in concept—which is wild to try to wrap your mind around. Therefore, the words "angel" and "seraphim" and "separated substance" and incredibly even "substance" itself, when applied to them, do not correspond to essential kinds of things, a common sort of nature shared among many of them. Instead, these names are just convenient designators for us as we try to talk about all of these spirits who are simpler and higher than we are in the great chain of being. Our human knowledge is proportioned to sensible stuff, and so when we think or speak about angels we are already out of our depth, and we cannot see or say precisely what each of them is. So we speak in generalizations, even while knowing that there is nothing general in any of their natures, but only in the order of our minds. This was perhaps the greatest improvement Aristotle made over Plato: the insight that knowledge is in the mode of the knower, which does not necessarily correspond to the mode of the thing known. We men understand and speak of angels as though they were composed of genus and species, but that tells you something about how we think, not about how they are. For each of them is absolutely unique, and completely exhausts what he is, in a way that no individual man or dog or oak could totally actualize all the potencies of its species. In terms of his nature, therefore, every angel is simple and even relatively infinite and, in the proper sense, perfect.

As for the relations between these perfect substances, since each is a species unto himself, no two are alike, and—see *Metaphysics* Book Eight—therefore no two are equal. Each one is either higher or lower than any other one, such that they all come together to form a great linear hierarchy, a single-file line from the highest seraph down to the lowest guardian angel, with an innumerable multitude in between. On the subject of that multitude: One of the rare times that St Thomas Aquinas criticizes Aristotle is over the number of these separated substances. Aristotle had been far too stingy in estimating that number, admitting only as many angels as there were distinct and irreducible kinds of motion, each one, he thought, initiated by a different separate substance. In the *De Substantiis Separatis*, St Thomas prefers Plato's much more generous reckoning of the number of angels, going so far as to describe Plato as representing the *via sufficientior*, in contradistinction to Aristotle's *via manifestior*. Aristotle may proceed along "the more manifest way," taking us by the hand and leading us step by step from things that are better known to us to their lesser-known implications. But Plato offers "the more sufficient way," harder to see along but arriving at a more sweeping view of the truth of things—in this case, the enormity of the heavenly host.

St Thomas quotes the prophet Daniel for a scriptural warrant here, who says of the Ancient of Days, "Thousands of thousands ministered to him, and ten thousand times a hundred thousand stood before him." St Thomas reasons that, in creating, God intends chiefly the perfection of the universe, and so, the more perfect something is, the more of it we ought to expect to find in the created universe. But spirits are more perfect than bodies, so there will be even more angels in creation than there are corporeal substances—maybe vastly more. We might also think of the "myriads of angels" from Hebrews—or of the Church Fathers' taking the one lost sheep to be mankind, in comparison with the ninety-nine angels. In fact, "number," properly speaking, cannot apply to angels anyway, since number follows upon dimensive quantity which presupposes matter. And so the separated substances are strictly numberless. As Thomas quotes Denys as saying of the angels: "Many are the blessed armies of the supernal minds, exceeding the weak and constricted measure of our material numbers."

What, then, does this numberless hierarchy do—or, we should ask instead: What is it supposed to do? Here we turn from our consideration of separated substances in general to a quick consideration

The Politics of Hell

of the good angels in particular, because we want to understand the demons and our weak intellects tend to appreciate things more by contrast with their opposites, but also because evil can only be understood indirectly, in relation to the good. The good angels live peacefully in their hierarchy, etymologically their "sacred principate," where St Thomas defines "principate" as "one multitude ordered in one way under the government of a prince." In this case, of course, the prince of the hierarchy is God himself. Now the angels have three functions in their hierarchy, for the sake of those below them in line: to purge or cleanse, to illumine or enlighten, and to perfect or unite to God. St Thomas receives this threefold procedure from St Denys the Areopagite—the "Pseudo-Dionysius," if you like, and I do not—from his great treatise on the angels *The Celestial Hierarchy*. (Fun fact: The word "hierarchy" seems to have been invented by St Denys himself in this very work.) You might recognize this triad from more modern spirituality literature, which tries to divvy up people's Christian progress into the purgative way, the illuminative way, and the unitive way. I'll be honest with you: I usually find such attempts unhelpful, too narcissistic and too experientialist, trying to make a science of something that just isn't scientific, wanting to discern—or impose—a set of universalizable phenomena upon the spiritual life, which doesn't work, and isn't the point. But I flag it here just to note that the origin of the purgative, illuminative, and unitive is precisely the angelic hierarchy—and then the ecclesiastical sacraments that are our human participation in it. The good angels are constantly communicating God's goodness to those further down the hierarchy, drawing them further up and further into the happiness of God, by purifying, enlightening, and perfecting those entrusted to their care.

What form this action takes depends upon where exactly the angel falls in rank. St Denys had turned to scripture to learn about the various classes of angels within their overall ordering—to Isaiah, Ezekiel, Colossians, Ephesians, Jude—and so it is to St Denys that we owe the traditional nine choirs of angels: three hierarchies, each with three orders within them: seraphim, cherubim, thrones; then dominions, virtues, powers; and finally principalities, archangels, and angels. You might remember the scene from Canto

28 of Dante's *Paradiso*, where Beatrice recalls that St Gregory the Great had arrived into heaven, beheld the angelic orders, and been forced to admit that Denys was right and he was wrong, since he—Gregory—had switched the virtues and the principalities. "*Di sé medesmo rise,*" Beatrice says: "He smiled at his mistake." But St Thomas is nicer than Dante, and he gives St Gregory the Great a way to save face by saying that both accounts are reasonable and that they might even amount to different words for the same teaching.

We will leave aside the details of the incredibly intricate bureaucracy of this ninefold order, which Fr Bonino joked would be the envy even of the Italian administrative state. In fact St Thomas says that, if we knew the angels perfectly, we would know it to be even more intricate, because rather than nine generalized choirs, in which the higher ones tend to look up to God and the lower ones tend to look down for creation, we would see that every single angel has his own particular role to play in the hierarchy. Nonetheless, do notice that the word "choir" is especially appropriate here, since the noblest work of all the angels—even more important than their purifying, illuminating, perfecting—is the *laus perennis*, the praise of God. The action of the good angels is first and foremost a liturgical action—as ours is meant to be too. And indeed, it is for the sake of God's glory that the higher angels assist those subject to them in the hierarchy, inviting them to worship God and enabling them to do so as beautifully as possible.

We turn, at last, to the demons themselves. I will not say too much here about the fall of the demons, which—in better ages that could sustain serious speculative theology—was always the subject of controversy. For those who are interested in additional reading, I think St Thomas' best treatment of the demons' fall, which corrects certain problems in his earlier attempt from the *Prima Pars* of the *Summa*, comes in Question 16, Article 4 of the *De Malo*, his *Disputed Questions on Evil*. Suffice it to say that Thomas presents all the separated substances as having been created in grace, with a first moment of natural knowledge and love for God, and after this another moment in which the angels charitably accepted, and the demons pridefully rejected, the call to a supernatural knowledge and love of God. Fr Bonino explains the devil's motivation thus:

The Politics of Hell

Satan, in his pride, considered the conditions [of this supernatural invitation] humiliating. He regarded them as evil and therefore preferred to stick to the enjoyment of his own natural perfection insofar as, first, it belongs to him by right of nature as if he were its master, and, second, it distinguishes him from others. He preferred to remain first in the lower order instead of becoming one among others in the higher order. He has experienced the drama of the little boy who has to leave elementary school, where he is the senior, the "boss," to move on to sixth grade where he would become the smallest among the big boys.

And so Satan spurned God's invitation to a supernatural destiny, in a kind of diabolical version of Peter Pan Syndrome, with the other rebel angels as his Lost Boys. As punishment for this narcissism — ever since that moment of perfect, eternal demerit — the demons have experienced the pain of loss: the deprivation of the beatific vision and friendship with God, which is the only true happiness. Additionally, as further consequences of that most capital punishment, the demons' intellects also have been darkened vis-à-vis supernatural knowledge; their wills have been made obstinate; they have suffered grief in the resistance of their wills to the way things are (Fr Bonino says that they are "allergic to reality"); and they have been cast into hell and the earth's dark atmosphere as places of punishment for their original — and perpetual — sin.

What is surprising, however — and what will be especially pertinent to the demons' political arrangements — is just how much stayed the same for the demons despite their fall. Their natures, in fact, are entirely intact. I'm sure everyone here is familiar with the Thomistic adage "grace perfects nature," but the flipside of that is that sin does not destroy nature either — for us or for the demons. Both grace and sin are accidental modifications of a stable underlying substance. Otherwise, if grace were to replace nature rather than perfecting it, then among other absurd consequences, converting to the faith would actually be bad for me, because the *me* there would cease to exist and give way to some totally different person who would step in to take my place. This is not what the tradition means by "putting off the old man." Now it's true that grace, as a participation in the divine life of the Most Holy Trinity, is actually nobler in its essence than the human soul. Nevertheless, in its mode of being it is still just an accident, a quality—an "entitative *habitus*," if you like—existing in the substance that is man. So likewise, sin is an accidental corruption, not an essential one. This is not to downplay how bad it is: All of our blessedness or wretchedness is a matter of accidents. Only God is happy just by his essence. But it is to say that sin leaves intact the underlying nature of the sinner. And so, whatever the demons possessed by nature in that first prelapsarian moment of grace, they still have today in their state of punishment. St Thomas constantly repeats this Dionysian principle from the *Celestial Hierarchy*: "Certain gifts were bestowed upon the demons which, we say, have not been changed at all, but remain whole and most splendid"—"*integra et splendidissima*."

The demons are morally bad, therefore, but still naturally good. The reason for this goes back to St Augustine: Good and evil are not symmetrical. We do not inhabit a dualistic world, with equal and opposite forces of light and darkness warring against each other. On the contrary, all that is, inasmuch as it is, is good. Evil is merely a perversion, a corruption, the privation of a due good in a subject that ought to have it. And so the demons cannot be evil through and through, because evil is a parasite, and it cannot exist except in a good host. Evil is a perversion, and there cannot be a perversion that is not a perversion *of* something. In the case of the demons, that something is their good nature, and its good natural powers. They are putting these talents to awful ends, but the talents themselves persist. As St Thomas says, "Although [the demons] do not have the purity that is through grace, nevertheless they have *purity of nature*"—"*puritas naturae*." But being implies order, and therefore something of their original order remains for them as well. We arrive, at last, at the politics of hell.

The primary place where St Thomas Aquinas discusses the political order of the demons is in the *Summa Theologiae*, *Prima Pars*, Question 109. As I hope you know already, the *Prima Pars* is about God—specifically, the divine essence, the distinction of divine persons, and the procession of creatures from him. Unsurprisingly, Question 109 falls in the third of those, on the procession of creatures, and more precisely within the final division of that part, on the divine governance of creatures. This question has four articles: Article 1 asks whether there are orders among the demons; Article 2, whether there is authority, or precedence, among them; Article 3, whether they illumine one another; and Article 4, whether they are subject to the authority of the good angels. Let's take each in turn.

The first article asks of the order of hell *utrum sit*, "whether it is," whether the demons have any politics at all. The casual reader of the *Summa* might find that he relates to the objectors more intuitively than usual with this article, since there seem to be good reasons for believing that the demons' fall from grace would also be a fall from sociability. It is true, of course, that the will of the demons is permanently perverted, and that they are thus incapable of a genuine communion with others. It is also true that the further one descends away from God, the principle of unity, the less cohesion and the more anarchy one will find. Still, anarchy is like evil — indeed, it just is evil in the realm of political order — and so it can never exist in a pure form. Anarchy must always presume some sort of society as its subject. As Fr Bonino says,

> The idea of chaos or of absolute anarchy is as contradictory as the idea of absolute evil. As evil is a parasite on the good, so anarchy is a parasite on order. If ever anarchy were to triumph, it would immediately self-destruct, like Samson under the ruins of his own victory. In the world of the demons, therefore, there remains a certain order which, in the midst of disaster, continues to bear witness to the goodness and wisdom of God. Thus, according to St Thomas, the demonic world retains the structure of the various angelic orders from which the rebellious angels fell.

Now, the original hierarchy of the angels according to nature was meant to be fulfilled and perfected in the hierarchy of grace — and, unlike us men whose heavenly glory will depend upon our charity over the extended course of this life, for the angels God distributed grace and thus glory simply according to the proportions of their natures, so that, for the good angels, their hierarchy now corresponds exactly to their hierarchy at creation, only without the would-be-demons in between them. The demons, of course, have definitively fallen from that order of grace. But St Thomas teaches that the gifts of grace provide the formal element of the angelic hierarchy, and natural gifts the material element. Once again, grace perfects what nature disposes. And so the demons, the fallen angels, keep exactly the same order vis-à-vis their fellow demons that they had before the fall, because those natural dispositions, that matter for the hierarchy, has endured unchanged. Fr Bonino compared this unfulfilled demonic ordering to the foundations of a house whose construction has been halted for lack of money. And this, by the way, makes some sense out of St Paul's continuing to refer to the demons by the names of the angelic choirs: "For our wrestling is not against flesh and blood, but against principalities and powers," etc. According to St Thomas, those are the orders to which these demons first belonged, and from which they fell.

There is some question as to whether this ladder of demonic descent still deserves the name "hierarchy." After all, as we have seen already, "hierarchy" means precisely a *holy* principate. But the demons are not holy, and neither, especially, is their satanic prince. Nevertheless, St Thomas is still willing to extend the term "hierarchy" to them, not because the demons' own wills are holy, abused as these wills are for the sake of evil, but rather because the one who has ordered the demons from their creation is holy: God himself. Moreover, even after their fall, God uses these demonic orders for his own holy ends: to prove the saints and increase their merits, and to exact his divine justice upon the wicked. Even the demons are accounted for in St Paul's saying that all things work together for the good of those who love God. And so the demons—despite themselves and their own wicked intentions—somehow still inhabit a hierarchy. There is a twofold ordering of the Inferno: under Satan internally, and under God according to their integration into the general order of divine providence—and this latter satisfies for the definition of "hierarchy."

Thus everything is still in place, in the demons' social arrangements, and yet nothing is quite the same. Fr Bonino suggests two analogies for this phenomenon which are more familiar to our experience:

> In a corpse, all order, all structure does not disappear immediately [after death]. Although the soul, the principle of unity for the macrostructure, is absent, nevertheless the microstructures retain

The Politics of Hell

their nature, their respective properties as well as their interactions. However, the processes carried out by the microstructures are no longer in the service of the life of the organic whole. Or—to take a less macabre comparison—the collapse of the central political power at the end of the Carolingian Empire did not bring about the disappearance of all social life, but only caused its parceling out and feudalization, with many small local powers. The same happens with the society of the demons. When these angels freely reject their supernatural purpose, still their natural structures, which derive from the ontological relations between the pure spirits, do not disappear. They remain, however, mutilated and perverted.

Even bad men are political animals, and even bad angels are—granted, not animals, but—still political. Their society has an internal coherence and thus a form of unity, meaning that it is undivided in itself and divided from all others. And lest anyone should worry that this is all just Neoplatonists imposing their neurotic cosmic ordering on everything they can imagine, remember that our Lord himself referred to the City of Evil as a "kingdom"—a βασιλεία, in the Greek, or "*regnum*."

Article 2 of Question 109 concerns the king of this kingdom: the devil, or Satan. Just as the demons' nature guarantees them some preservation of hierarchy, so it also guarantees them some preservation of headship. The reason, once again, is that *agere sequitur esse*: "Action follows being"—and since the demons exist in an order, they will act in an order. Satan was the highest of the angels who fell. Whether he was the highest of the angels simply speaking has always been up for debate, with St Thomas saying probably, but with some Franciscan theologians especially preferring to have Satan as merely the highest of the cherubim so that they might exempt all the fiery loving seraphim from sin—but at the very least we can say that Satan was the loftiest relative to the rest who sinned with him. He sits at the head of their hierarchy, and so he will act at the head of their hierarchy.

He is even, in some way, the cause of the sin of the rest—not by compulsion, which would make their choice involuntary and thus not a choice at all, but by suggestion or exhortation. Recall St John's imagery of the dragon sweeping away a third of the stars with its tail—and thus one third as the traditional number of angels who fell: less than half, since sin is against their natural inclination and nature prevails most of the time—but still no meager sum, especially given what we have said already about the innumerable multitudes of separated substances. And all these hordes of demons look to Satan, their model and inspiration, as their master. As St Peter says in his second epistle, "By whom one has been overcome, of him he is also a slave." There is a kind of perverse Fourth Way principle here, with the devil as first in the genus of rebel angels, and so, by his example, the cause of the rest of the genus.

St Augustine and St Thomas go so far as to speak of the devil's prelacy as a sick imitation of Christ's own. Of course with Satan there is no effective ontological link to his demons (or to the damned among men)—he is not the cause of their being, nor does he share his life with them, the way Christ shares his very Sonship by grace. Satan's is only a moral causality, an evil exemplarity. Still, there is a sort of asymmetrical parallelism between Christ and his Church, on the one hand, and Satan and the City of Evil, on the other. Jesus even refers to "the devil and his angels," paralleling our Lord's own good angels. The tradition calls this the *corpus diaboli*, in explicit comparison and contradistinction to the Mystical Body of Christ.

We might think, for example, of the great tympanum of the Premonstratensian church of Sainte-Foy in Conques—the carving of the Last Judgment above the portal of that perfect eleventh-century Romanesque Church, just a few hours' drive from here in Occitania along the Camino de Santiago (or *Chemin de Saint-Jacques*), which probably showed up in your high school art history book. In the center of the scene is Christ as Judge, ruling over heaven and earth, but in the lower-right corner is Satan, towering over the underworld in a way that recalls—but pathetically—the majesty of Christ in heaven. Satan is crowned and seated on a throne, directing spirits and souls with his arms—but unlike Christ, with his heavenly halo and mandorla, gesturing in both directions so as to sift according to justice, Satan points only downward into his own fiery kingdom. Christ is robed in glory and attended by angel acolytes; Satan is naked and encircled by snakes. He is not a copy of Christ, but a caricature. All evil can do is ape the good.

The Politics of Hell

Two important objections arise concerning Satan's authority. First, if Satan is the greatest sinner among them, falling from the highest height and taking the rest down with him, then why is he rewarded by providence with getting to be their king? To this St Thomas answers that being a leader in evil is "not unto the good of the [leader], but rather unto [his] evil, because since to do evil especially pertains to misery, to excel in evil is to be [even] more miserable." And so, even if he cannot see it this way, Satan's rule is really a punishment, greatly contributing to his unhappiness, now and especially at the end of the world.

The second objection is this: Why would any demon choose Satan as his leader rather than God? After all, since the demons' principal characteristic is their pride, would they not prefer to be subject to one who is infinitely greater, since it seems that much more insulting to pride to have to serve one who is so inferior? As Fr Bonino puts it, "It is far more humiliating for the proud to submit to a subordinate superior than to the supreme superior. It is more mortifying for the young parochial vicar to obey the petty commands of a dull pastor than to carry out orders received directly from the Holy Father!" St Thomas responds as follows:

> All else being equal, [it is true that] the proud would rather be subject to a superior than to an inferior. But if he should be able to obtain some excellence under an inferior, which he could not obtain from the superior, then he would rather choose to be subject to the inferior than to the superior. And therefore it was not against the pride of the demons that they chose to be subject to an inferior, consenting to his authority, willing to have him as their prince and leader precisely so that they might obtain their ultimate beatitude by [their own] natural power—especially because in the order of nature they were already subject to the supreme angel even then.

Thus, although Satan harbors the illusion that he is like God, an end for others, really the lower demons submit to him not for that reason, but only because they think that submitting to Satan will let each of them become the ultimate end for himself. They too want to be like God, totally self-sufficient. "*Non serviam!*" is not just the slogan of their rebellion against the old order, but it is also the animating political philosophy of their new order itself. They are not seeking together the common good of the City of Evil, but rather each one is seeking only the affirmation of his own excellence and interest. As far as the demons are concerned, theirs is merely a kingdom of convenience.

Now, you might think that such coordinated self-interest would not be a very strong basis for political unity. You would be right. There is no true concord in the infernal kingdom, for *concordia* means "a union of hearts," and the anti-social principle of pride breeds only discord. As Fr Bonino says, "Pride nurtures a constant preference for its own good to the disregard of the common good." One thing that does help to unite the demons, however, is their common enemy. They forge a "social contract," as it were, in order to wage war more effectively against God and man. Thus St Thomas writes in the reply to an objection:

> The concord of the demons, whereby some obey others, is not from any friendship that they have among themselves; but from their common wickedness, by which they hate men, and fight against the justice of God. For it is proper [also] to wicked men that they should join themselves to one another and be subject to those whom they perceive to be stronger, for carrying out each his own individual wickedness.

Among the demons, therefore, there is no mutual affection. There is no internal and moral concord based on civic friendship, but only an external and instrumental alliance. Again Fr Bonino: "As we know, external politics is an excellent diversion when there are serious domestic political problems. Sacred union against the external enemy is a remedy against internal political divisions. Thus hatred against God and men brings the demons together, and leads them to moderate their hatred of each other." Of course this is no true political common good, but only a collectively self-interested compact of the sort one might find among a band of thieves. Satan is not so much a monarch as a mob boss.

All of this is the story the demons tell themselves about why they tolerate Satan and one another. They believe that such political bonds are optional but ultimately advantageous. Each one thinks that this social contract will eventually help him to get what he wants for himself—namely to become his own principle of happiness, and to offend God by causing the damnation of men. As Fr Bonino puts it, "The unity of the society of demons is founded, from the point of view of subjective intentions, on a convergence of misunderstood interests: a caricature of the common good." But in fact there is a deeper, truer reason why the demons are united in a society: divine wisdom. St Thomas quotes the book of Wisdom, which tells how this wisdom "reaches from end to end mightily, and disposes all things sweetly." Such wisdom, Thomas says, "leaves nothing in the universe inordinate," or without order. As Fr Bonino writes, "This type of society is viable not so much in virtue of a very unstable balance of interests as in virtue of the permanence within it of a fundamentally good nature, which, although it may be thwarted or even denied, is nonetheless present and a source of what can be positive in the permanence of this society." Thus the kingdom of hell is ultimately founded not upon the injustice of the demons, but upon the justice of God, ordering all things by nature and his providential care.

The third article of our Question 109 asks whether the demons can illumine each other. To understand the difficulty, remember the threefold act of the angelic hierarchy: purging, illumining, perfecting. Now, obviously the demons are not purging or perfecting their inferiors, purifying them or uniting them to God. But it is less clear with regard to the illuminative way, because the demons really can communicate with one another. They can and do share truths among themselves. However, the answer must be that such communication is not true illumination, for, explains St Thomas, "Illumination properly is the manifestation of truth according as it is ordered to God, who illumines every intellect." But the demons' speech to one another is meant to lead rather away from God, and thus it ends in greater darkness, not illumination. Theirs is not a communion of minds in the truth they behold, unto its source in the First Truth. They are not contemplating and handing on the things contemplated. Instead they have only a practical aim: to transmit useful information to coordinate their actions more effectively, so that they might exclude men from the illumined divinization from which they have already definitively excluded themselves. "The intention from which this communication arises is always perverse," Fr Bonino says: "It is consummated by the evil designs of the devil who is always trying to divert others from God, whereas illumination is a communication of truth that comes from God and whose purpose is to lead to God." Demonic speech, therefore, is not illuminative. It is not even speculative. It is a mere calculation of efficiency: "the primacy of the practical" taken to its most evil extreme.

Article 4, the last of our question, is about the relation between angels and demons. Granted the demons have a hierarchy of their own, how does it stand in regard to the graced angelic hierarchy of the celestial choirs? This is a consoling consideration: All authority comes from God, and so the closer anyone is to God, the more influence that one will have over others. As such, the good angels rule over the bad, because they are nearer to God, participating more fully in his royal majesty. This is just how the cosmic hierarchy plays itself out.

The angels' authority over the demons is real even now, but it will become especially manifest on the last day, when St Michael and the glorious armies of heaven march in full force, when the City of Evil is unequivocally defeated, and Satan and his subjects are banished to hell for eternity. We are living now in the last days, as indeed Christians have been ever since the Word was made flesh and dwelt among us—and the demons are not stupid. Deep down they suspect that their days are numbered, that the war will come to an end, and not in their favor—and the dread and anger of this realization makes them act out with ever greater ferocity. "Woe to you, O earth and sea," we read in Revelation: "because the devil is come down unto you, having great wrath, knowing that he hath but a short time"—after which he "shall be tormented day and night for ever and ever." We are witnessing the death throes of the *corpus diaboli* upon the earth.

This final article, about the angels' power over the demons, makes sense out of why this question on the society of hell is included in the section of the *Prima Pars* on divine governance, which might have stuck you as unusual when I first mentioned it. Not even the demons, in their rival city, escape the government of

The Politics of Hell

God. "If I descend into hell, thou art present," chants the Psalmist. Of course the demons do not formally participate in the good of the whole creation, since their entire wills are fixed against it, but materially they cannot escape. All that they do, in their coordinated rebellion, is still ultimately directed by God through his angels. Thus any evil that the angels permit—whether from demons or from men—is always for the sake of some good that follows it. In St Thomas' phrase, the angels are "ministers of divine wisdom." Moreover—and this should be especially comforting, and a nice place to conclude our consideration of the politics of hell—even the very lowest of the guardian angels, even yours or mine, can rule over Satan himself, because "the power of divine justice to which the good angels cleave is stronger than the natural power of the [demons]." Thank God.

I would like for us to return to our thought experiment from the very beginning, now—I hope—with a greater understanding of its implications. I had asked you to imagine a society—a society made up of self-absorbed, atomized individuals—a society in which the various members tolerate each other, because they know they need each other, but only so that each of them can achieve his own private ambitions and desires—a society, moreover, that is in open rebellion against its own origins. Then I asked you to imagine that, once upon a time, this society had been noble, and civil, and good, but that its citizens—especially its elite citizens—out of a disordered sense of pride, effected a revolution against that received ancient order. Next I had you imagine that this revolution had some ironic consequences, such as that, in the name of liberating themselves from being subject to any official king, these citizens wound up creating for themselves an even more oppressive and authoritarian regime—and that their honorable hierarchy, which in their pettiness they would have liked to dissolve altogether, was merely replaced by a dishonorable hierarchy—that they traded an ordered harmony for hostile power relations, and a common good for private vices. You further imagined that this populace—who, again, hate their own heritage and devote all their time and energy to contradicting it, loudly—is in fact deeply unsatisfied, frustrated, lonely, sad. And yet you imagined that, despite their unhappiness in this society, they also live in constant, ever-growing fear—fear that this society of theirs, and everything it stands for, is on the verge of defeat. You imagined, finally, that this hysterical anxiety of theirs makes them even more odious and offensive and obnoxious.

I used to think that St Thomas Aquinas had never addressed liberalism in his political writings, living, as he did, several centuries before the Enlightenment. I was wrong. He treats it carefully and critically in the text we have just considered: *Prima Pars* Question 109, on the political arrangement of the demons. It is terrifying how similar St Thomas' account of the politics of hell is to Immanuel Kant's account of the ideal government. Kant even refers to such a state as being perfect for "a population of demons," secured with general laws for conserving their common accord, laws that pit particular sentiments against each other, so that they might procedurally neutralize the proud egoistic dispositions of each individual. "Kant is here at antipodes with the political thought of St Thomas Aquinas," remarks Fr Bonino. As I expect everyone here will know well, St Thomas teaches that society arises from the natural sociability of man expressed in civic friendship and ordered to his temporal common good, itself ordered to his spiritual common good attained in and through the Roman Church. It is the Catholic alternative to Kant's Lutheran individualist state of nature, in—another Protestant's catchphrase—a war of all against all.

It is the angelic alternative to Kant's republican rule for a race of demons. For in St Thomas' Dionysian worldview, the angelic hierarchy is to serve as the archetype of our human societies, both political and ecclesiastical. James Madison was wrong, therefore, that "If men were angels, no government would be necessary." As we have seen, the angels have an elaborate government, and theirs is meant to be the model for ours. But alas, too often of late, our states have taken the demons for their political inspiration instead, with our citizens driven only by a narcissistic search for their private interest, rejecting all reference to a common good of the moral order, beginning with the transcendent common good which is God himself. Granted, there are dissimilarities here as well: Unlike the angels, our societies are not founded upon essential inequalities, since all men share a single species; and unlike the demons, no human society is definitively fixed in its rejection of God. Nonetheless, the similarities are pronounced, and they are not accidental. Liberalism has traded a hierarchy unto God for an every-man-for-himself tyranny.

We will conclude with one final quotation from Fr Serge-Thomas Bonino:

> The demonic society offers us an interesting theoretical model, for thinking about the not-always-theoretical possibility of a society that either rejects or disregards any reference to the objective moral good, and merely ensures a more or less peaceful coexistence among individuals who are deemed evil and guided solely by the pursuit of self-interest. Reflection on the demonic city confirms our contemporary experience: Such a society is feasible! It survives by virtue of a certain "a-moral," unjust, and precarious balance that is established between the subjective interests of each of the individuals involved. However, this society survives above all and most profoundly because the natural tendencies that lead each being toward the objective good of its own nature remain active in it, though disavowed and opposed on the reflective level.

In other words—what is old hat for us by now—liberalism survives by exploiting pre-liberal resources, the resources of the very metaphysical order and natural law that it speculatively denies.

By grace, St Thomas teaches, we are to be taken up into the orders of the angels, perhaps filling out the places in the celestial hierarchy vacated through the fall. And so our politics should be practicing for that ascent, and indeed helping to accomplish it, by ordering us together toward our true good. Whereas liberalism prepares our souls to be slotted into the demonic order of hell, of which it is an alarmingly accurate imitation. May our better angels prevail.

Regina Angelorum, ora pro nobis. Omnes angeli Dei, orate pro nobis.

16

St Bernard and the Theology of Crusade

J. Marlow Gazzoli

On Easter Sunday in 1146 at Vézelay, King Louis VII took the Cross of crusade. He had announced to his court at Christmas his intention to go to Jerusalem, and it was decided that the court would meet again at Vézelay, with those who would take the Cross doing so at Easter.[1] Meanwhile the city of Edessa had fallen at the end of 1144. The bishop of Jabala, Syria, came to the papal court in November 1145 and informed Pope Eugenius III of the predicament of the Church in the East. On 1 December 1145 the pontiff published for the first time *Quantum praedecessores nostri* in which he called for a crusade. However, this had not reached France by Christmas when Louis made public his intention.[2] Otto of Freising says that Louis wanted to go on Crusade because his brother Philip had died before he could fulfil his own vow to do so and that this is why Louis gathered his court.[3] When the pope's letter did reach France, King Louis wrote back to him, and the pope gave a favorable reply. On 1 March 1146 Pope Eugenius published a second version of *Quantum praedecessores nostri* which named Bernard, abbot of Clairvaux, as the preacher of the Crusade.[4]

---

1 Odo of Deuil, *De profectione Ludovici VII in orientem: The Journey of Louis VII to the East*, trans. and ed. Virginia Gingerick Berry (New York: Norton, 1948), 6–9.

2 John G. Rowe, "The Origins of the Second Crusade: Pope Eugenius III, Bernard of Clairvaux and Louis VII of France," in *The Second Crusade and the Cistercians*, ed. Michael Gervers (New York: St Martin's Press, 1992), 79–80, 82–83.

3 Otto of Freising and Rahewin, *The Deeds of Frederick Barbarossa*, trans. Charles Christopher Mierow and Richard Emery (New York: W. W. Norton, 1966), 70.

4 Rowe, 84; Odo, 8–9.

St Bernard and the Theology of Crusade

Easter came on 31 March 1146 and at Vézelay Louis and his nobles took up the Crosses which had been sent by the pope himself. So many were present that they had to relocate to a field outside the town, and it was there that Bernard addressed the crowds, the king at his side. Bernard incited so many that they ran out of Crosses; Bernard tore his own clothes to make more.[5] As he continued to preach around Vézelay, many miracles were reported and more took up the Cross. Rowe writes of Bernard's preaching at Vézelay: "It was one of St Bernard's more glittering performances. Armed with the papal letter of authorization and reading where appropriate from *Quantum praedecessores nostri*, Bernard spoke out on behalf of the Crusade as only he could speak. The response was overwhelming."[6] St Bernard even went to Germany and enlisted the king and nobles there to join, something Pope Eugenius had not even countenanced.[7] However, St Bernard's success in preaching did not translate into success in battle. Once the Crusader forces had gathered in Jerusalem in 1148, they decided to attack Damascus, but the siege failed and with it the Crusade. Louis returned to France the following year. The failure reflected poorly on the pope who had called for it, and Bernard lost influence with the pope, who had been a Cistercian before his election.[8]

The idea of a holy abbot, who would later be declared a saint and Doctor of the Church, preaching a Crusade may seem out of place, especially to the inhabitants of the modern world, who think of Christ as more of a figure of peace than of war. Indeed, Bernard himself was at first unsure of the Second Crusade; Evans writes, "Bernard's involvement was slowly won. At first Bernard was reluctant, taking the view that Christian energies should be concentrated upon the needs of the flock at home and not upon problems at the interface with Islam. But he became convinced despite himself that it was his duty to support the venture and a committed Bernard never did things by halves."[9] There is the temptation to think of

---

5 Ibid.
6 Rowe, 84; Odo, 8–11.
7 Odo, 12–13; G. R. Evans, *Bernard of Clairvaux* (New York: Oxford University Press, 2000), 16–17.
8 Evans, 17, 19.
9 Ibid., 16.

Bernard as a product of a medieval and unenlightened mindset. However, such views do not do justice to the intellect and theology of St Bernard of Clairvaux. Indeed, one can find in his writings a theology of crusade consistent with Christian principles of just war. Through an analysis of his writings on the subject, in particular his letters and the treatises *De laude novae militiae* and *De consideratione*, I will make explicit the theology of crusade implicit in the works of St Bernard of Clairvaux.

In articulating a theology of crusade, Bernard is drawing on the work of St Augustine, the father of Christian just war theory. Writing in his *De civitate Dei*, St Augustine says that there are exceptions to the divine prohibition against killing. These include instances where God commands the death of someone or the waging of war or when a hangman executes a criminal condemned by the State. To kill on the order of another to whom obedience is due, says Augustine, is not really to kill but to be an instrument of him who orders.[10] Writing specifically about war, he says, "The wise man, they say, will wage just wars."[11] For Augustine, if a war is just, the wise man must fight it as a matter of course; necessity binds him. If there were no just wars, then the wise man would never fight wars. What compels him to fight the just war is the injustice committed. Augustine writes, "For it is the injustice of the opposing side that lays on the wise man the duty of waging wars; and this injustice is assuredly to be deplored by a human being, since it is the injustice of human beings, *even though no necessity for war should arise from it.*"[12] Thus it is the presence of injustice in the world that compels the wise man to fight. What makes a war just is its opposition to injustice.

This question of war and killing was also one of the questions medieval Christians considered. The Gospels make clear that being a soldier is not problematic in itself, something St Bernard was well aware of.[13] Rather than speaking in terms of injustice, says

10 Augustine of Hippo, *Concerning the City of God against the Pagans*, trans. Henry Bettenson (London: Penguin, 2003), I.21.
11 Ibid., XIX.7.
12 Ibid. Emphasis mine.
13 Evans, *Bernard*, 167–68; Bernard of Clairvaux, *Liber ad Milites Templi de laude novae militiae*, in *Tractatus et opuscula*, eds. Jean Leclerq and Henri Rochais, vol. 3 of *Sancti Bernardi Opera* (Rome: Editiones Cistercienses, 1963), 5 (English: *In Praise of the New Knighthood*, trans. Conrad Greenia, in *Treatises III*, vol. 7 of *The Works*

St Bernard and the Theology of Crusade

Evans, "another route by which the Christian may escape from the dilemma that he may not kill but must sometimes fight is to see legitimate warfare in terms of defending the faith."[14] Thus Bernard says that the heretic and the infidel should be fought, though the infidel is to be fought to keep the peace. While Evans mentions Augustine, saying that his view allowed for offensive war to right wrongs,[15] she does not examine the relationship between Bernard and Augustine in any depth. However, rather than presenting the defense of the Faith as an alternative, it fits in with the injustice model of St Augustine. Indeed, attacks against the Church and the spiritual order are greater causes than human injustice. In this way, then, Bernard uses the principles of Augustine to defend crusades. First, a crusade is waged as a war against injustice, the injustice done to God and His Church by the infidels. Second, the crusader fights at the command of God through His vicar on Earth, the pope. Bernard expresses this in two ways: First, by referring to the crusaders as doing God's will and acting as His functionaries, and second, by giving the authority over crusades to the pope.

Having considered the broad outlines for a just war, we can turn to how St Bernard works to specifically identify crusades as just, looking mainly at his treatise on the Knights Templar with reference to his letters, especially his letter to the people of England exhorting them to Crusade.[16] St Bernard wrote the *De laude novae militiae* in response to a request from Hugh of Payns, founder and Grand Master of the Knights Templar, which suggests a date of composition before Hugh's death in 1136,[17] who asked the

---

of Bernard of Clairvaux [Kalamazoo, MI: Cistercian Publications, 1977]). References are to the section numbers of the text. Both the Latin and English were consulted, but the work is referred to under the Latin title, except when notes from the English edition are cited. All direct quotations come from the Latin with my own translation, compared against the English.

14 Evans, *Bernard*, 168.
15 Ibid.
16 Bernard of Clairvaux, *Letter 391*, in *The Letters of St Bernard of Clairvaux*, trans. Bruno Scott James (London: Burns Oates, 1953), 1–2. Letters are cited using the numbering and division of sections used by James. Where appropriate, the traditional numbering of the letter is given in brackets. In the case of *Letter 391*, James says that it is the same as Bernard's letter to the bishops of eastern France [363] (James, 463).
17 Malcolm Barber, *The New Knighthood: A History of the Order of the Temple* (Cambridge: Cambridge University Press, 1995), 44. Barber himself dates the work to sometime in the early part of the decade (xxi).

Cistercian abbot to write something for the Knights, "a sermon of exhortation," so that, "since I cannot brandish the lance, I might brandish the pen against the hostile tyranny, since you assert that it would be no small help to you, if I animate with letters those whom I cannot with arms."[18] In the opening salutation to Hugh, Bernard refers to 2 Tim 4:7, "I have fought the good fight" (*Bonum certamen certavi*),[19] thus identifying the cause of the Knights Templar with the *bonum certamen* of the Christian faith. He also does this in ascribing the title *Miles Christi* to Hugh, which comes from the same Epistle of St Paul (2:3).[20] Thus at the very beginning of the work the two principles of just war are present. The fight of the Templars is the fight of Christ, so it is just, and they are the soldiers of Christ who fight at the command of Justice Himself.

The exhortation proper begins with an explicit identification of the work of the Knights with the work of Christ. Just as Christ came into the Holy Land to fight the "princes of darkness" (*tenebrarum principes*), so now are His knights fighting those who serve the same princes.[21] Bernard is not speaking in a metaphorical sense. He calls the Muslims "the attendants of the same" (*ipsorum satellites*), the *ipsorum* referring to *tenebrarum principes*.[22] He makes this same identification of the Muslims as the servants of the Devil in his letter to the English people, in which he says that it is the Devil himself who is behind the attack on the Holy Land.[23] So the Knights are fighting the very same war which Christ Himself fought, the most just of wars.[24] Furthermore, in calling the Muslims *satellites* of the *tenebrarum principes*, Bernard is setting up a contrast with the Knights, who are the servants of the Light, which "shines in the darkness, and the darkness did not comprehend It" (*in tenebris lucet, et tenebrae non*

---

18 Bernard, *De laude*, Prol.; *In Praise*, 127n1. *Exhortationis sermonem, et adversus hostilem tyrannidem, quia lanceam non liceret, stilum vibrarem, asserens vobis non parum fore adiutorii, si quos armis non possum, litteris animarem.*
19 Bernard, *De laude*, Prol.; 213n5.
20 Bernard, Prol.; *In Praise*, 127n1.
21 Bernard, *De laude*, 1.
22 Ibid.
23 Bernard, *Letter 391*, 2.
24 See Bernard, *De laude*, 5. Bernard argues that since the Gospel allows Christians to serve as soldiers, then there is no reason why soldiery in defense of the Holy Land could be forbidden, for such soldiers have the best claim to soldiery.

comprehenderunt).[25] The Light is fighting these forces of darkness "in the hand of His powerful men" (*in manu fortium suorum*), the Knights Templar.[26] Christ is acting through the Knights, "even now making the redemption of His people, and again raising a horn of salvation for us in the house of David His servant" (*faciens etiam nunc redemptionem plebis suae, et rursum erigens cornu salutis nobis in domo David pueri sui*).[27] Throughout this first passage, St Bernard refers to the *Benedictus*, the canticle of Zacharias in the Gospel of St Luke,[28] which Zacharias sings at the circumcision of his son St John the Baptist. This canticle tells of God fulfilling His promise of redemption to the people of Israel and of the special role John will have to play in this (Lk 1:57–79). Thus St Bernard is setting up the Knights as a latter day John the Baptist, who will, just as St John did, go before the face of the Lord to prepare His paths (Lk 1:76). This identifies their military action as a way of bringing about the salvation of souls and righting the injustice of fallen man. Moreover, this identification of the Knights as a second John the Baptist shows them to be the servants of God, prophets of the All-High (Lk 1:76) who will give testimony to the Light (Jn 1:7).

St Bernard emphasizes the novelty of the knighthood espoused by the Knights Templar. The work begins, "A new type of knighthood is heard which has recently emerged on the Earth." The novelty lies in the fact that they fight in both the physical and the spiritual realms. To do one or the other is not remarkable, says St Bernard, but to do both is praiseworthy, especially because of its novelty.[29] The Knights Templar are thus *milites Christi* in both the allegorical and the quite literal sense. They would rather die for Christ than live, and this should not be surprising given what St Bernard says about such a death: to die in battle is to die a martyr, and such a good death is better than victory. Moreover, he says that to die in battle is better than to die in bed, since the former is a more glorious death.[30] Beginning with St Stephen the Protomartyr, the

25 John 1:5.
26 Bernard, *De laude*, 1.
27 Ibid.
28 Bernard, *In Praise*, 127nn1, 5–6.
29 Bernard, *De laude*, 1. *Novum militiae genus ortum nuper auditur in terris.*
30 *De laude*, 1–2.

martyrs of the Church were those who were killed by the ruling authorities for professing the Christian faith. Needless to say, such a martyrdom is strikingly different from the martyrdom suggested by St Bernard. Whereas the martyrs of the early Church are put to a death which they accept, the Knights are engaged in bloody battle, killing those who would send them to Christ. Thus St Bernard is drawing on the premise that the Knights are doing the salvific work of Christ, and this leads to the conclusion that to die doing this work of Christ is to die for the Faith, to die a martyr. Moreover, in speaking of glory, Bernard is not speaking of human glory. To die a martyr, in battle or not, is to die a glorious death in that it gives glory to God, more so than death in one's bed.

St Bernard contrasts at length the new knighthood of the Knights Templar with the worldly knighthood of their contemporaries. Indeed, while the Templars are *militia* ("knighthood"), the worldly knights are *malitia* ("badness"),[31] an effective and amusing rhetorical ploy on Bernard's part. The worldly knight is at much greater risk in battle, since he faces the loss not only of his body but also of his soul. "O truly holy and safe militia, and absolutely free from that twofold danger, by which that type of men is frequently endangered, whensoever Christ is not the cause of their fighting."[32] To fight for a just cause is good, but to fight for ill is always wrong, just as the sin of murder weighs down both those who die and those who conquer, since to conquer in sin is no victory at all. "If the cause of the fighter had been good, the end of his fight will not be bad, just as the end will not be judged good, where the cause is not good, and an unjust intention.... But if you prevail and by the will of either conquering or of avenging peradventure kill a man, you live a homicide. Moreover, it is not profitable for the dead or the living, for the conqueror or the conquered to be a homicide."[33] Even self-defense is scorned by Bernard since the soul is of greater

---

31 *De laude*, 3.
32 *De laude*, 2. *O vere sancta et tuta militia, atque a duplici illo periculo prorsus libera, quo id hominum genus solet frequenter periclitari, ubi dumtaxat Christus non est causa militandi.*
33 *De laude*, 2. *Si bona fuerit causa pugnantis, pugnae exitus malus esse non poterit, sicut nec bonus iudicabitur finis, ubi causa non bona, et intentio non recta praecesserit.... Quod si praevales, et voluntate superandi vel vindicandi forte occidis hominem, vivis homicida. Non autem expedit sive mortuo, sive vivo, sive victori, sive victo esse homicidam.*

worth than the body. To kill in self-defense, he writes, "indeed, I would not have called this a good victory, since of the two evils, to die in the body is lighter than to die in the soul."[34] The greater gravity of the death of the soul also justifies war against the enemies of the Church. If it is just to fight those who kill the bodies unjustly, how much more just is it to kill those who kill the souls with error and false religion. Thus worldly knighthood brings sin, death, and everlasting pain. Bernard even mocks these knights who preen and dress up; they are not even competent knights, and despite the prick of their conscience, their vice leads them to war.[35]

This idea of judging knights on moral criteria predates the formation of the military orders. This development began in the eleventh century and was greatly influenced by the Peace of God and Truce of God movements.[36] Consequently, the moral taxonomization of knights was a common idea starting from the mid-eleventh century, and the resulting ill-will towards enemies of peace demanded that violence be justified as defense. "Accordingly," writes Grabois, "the 'good' knights were those who fought in order to protect the churches, the poor and the oppressed."[37] While this taxonomization began in the eleventh, it became fully developed in the twelfth century. Thus in writing the *De laude*, Bernard is framing the Templars within an already existent moral framework. Grabois writes, "His original contribution to the idea resided in his interpretation of this dichotomy."[38] In the context of the Crusade, this sets up the worldly knights as models of the type of injustice just wars are waged against. Bernard plays off this to show the Knights Templar as fighters of injustice, particularly injustice against God and the Church.

In contrast to the *malitia*, the Knights Templar, however, do not sin in killing the enemies of Christ and do not fear death. Killing and being killed for Christ merits eternal glory, not eternal

---

34 *De laude*, 2. ...*ne hanc quidem bonam dixerim victoriam, cum de duobus malis, in corpore quam in anima mori levius sit.*
35 *De laude*, 3.
36 Aryeh Grabois, "*Militia* and *Malitia*: The Bernardine Vision of Chivalry," in *The Second Crusade and the Cistercians*, 50–51.
37 Grabois, 50–51.
38 Grabois, 52, 54.

damnation. St Bernard writes: "By the former he surely acquires for Christ, by the latter Christ is acquired, Who surely and graciously accepts the death of His enemy for vengeance and more graciously offers Himself to the soldier for consolation."[39] Thus if the knight kills, it is for Christ, and if he dies, it is for his own benefit as he goes to Christ. It is not a man which he kills but evil, *non homicida, sed...malicida* ("not homicide, but...malicide").[40] In making this distinction, Bernard is again going back to Augustine. Just wars are waged against injustice, and this is what Bernard means when he says that this is malicide rather than homicide. One interpretation would suggest that the enemy of Christ's Church has somehow ceased to be a person. However, such a reading is not correct when one considers what St Bernard has to say about the Jews. In his letter to England, he specifically enjoins the English not to persecute the Jews in any way, citing the Psalms. Dispersed and subject to the rule of Christians, they serve as living reminders of Christ's death and man's redemption. Trusting in the words of St Paul, the Christian should wait for the eventual conversion and salvation of the Jews, but until then their physical death only avails them unto spiritual death. Tolerance should likewise be applied to the pagans if they were subject to Christians and not engaged in war against them. Bernard considers the acts of tolerating the Jews and killing the Muslims two sides of the same piety.[41] Thus when St Bernard says that the knight is not killing man but evil, he is hearkening back to the principle annunciated by Augustine that he who kills under obedience does not kill. The knight on Crusade is not guilty of the sin of murder because he fights injustice by the command of God through the pope.

Nevertheless, Bernard writes, "In the death of the pagan does the Christian glory because Christ is glorified,"[42] but this must be read with what follows: "In the death of the Christian, the liberality of the king is opened, when the soldier to be rewarded is led out. Then the just man will rejoice over him, when he will

---

39 Bernard, *De laude*, 4. *Hinc quippe Christo, inde Christus acquiritur, qui nimirum et libenter accipit hostis mortem pro ultione, et libentius praebet seipsum militi pro consolatione.*
40 Ibid.
41 Bernard, *Letter 391*, 6.
42 Id., *De laude*, 4. *In morte pagani christianus gloriatur, quia Christus glorificatur.*

have seen punishment."[43] God's justice is manifested both in the punishment of the wicked and in the reward of His fallen,[44] and this is what gives glory to Christ and why the Christian rejoices: because the justice of God is established and the injustice of sin is removed. This is why Bernard says, "He is plainly the vindicator of Christ against those who do evil, and he is reckoned the defender of Christians."[45] Thus for Bernard the Knights Templar, and by extension all crusaders, are the servants of God, captains in His army, fighting by His command, and a crusade is a war fought by His will.[46]

While defending a crusade as a just war seems to modern eyes to be an expansion of just war theory, Bernard does not go as far as St Augustine. For Augustine it is the presence of injustice that merits the waging of war; a just war does not have to be purely defensive. Bernard, on the other hand, says that the pagans are to be killed only if it is necessary to stop the persecution of Christians. He writes, "Now, however, it is better that they be killed than that the rod of sinners be left over the lot of the just, lest the just perchance extend their hands to iniquity."[47] Thus Bernard limits the extent of just war more strictly than Augustine. A crusade, therefore, is a defensive war waged to defend the souls of Christians under attack by infidels. So, rather than an expansion of the grounds of just war, Bernard is actually limiting the grounds for just war proposed by Augustine, such that Bernard's theology of crusade can be said to place more emphasis on mercy than Augustine's theory places emphasis on justice.

The two principles of the crusade as a just war (it is against injustice and ordered by God) also appear in Bernard's letters, written during the preaching of the Crusade and after its failure, and in his *De consideratione*, written for Pope Eugenius after the Crusade.

43 Ibid. *In morte christiani, Regis liberalitas aperitur, cum miles remunerandus educitur. Porro super illo laetabitur iustus, cum viderit vindictam.*
44 Ibid.
45 Ibid. *Plane Christi vindex in his qui male agunt, et defensor christianorum reputatur.*
46 See Bernard, Letter 399 [256], 4: "Do all in your power to see that his will is done on earth as it is in heaven."
47 Bernard, *De laude*, 4. *Nunc autem melius est ut occidantur, quam certe relinquatur virga peccatorum super sortem iustorum, ne forte extendant iusti ad iniquitatem manus suas.* See above for what he says about Jews and pagans in his letter to England.

After Louis announced his intention to go on Crusade at Christmas 1145, Bernard wrote to Pope Eugenius concerning a French bishop whom Eugenius had disciplined. In rebuking the pontiff, Bernard also says that the situation could poorly affect Louis in "the good work which he has so wholeheartedly begun *under your encouragement*."[48] Likewise, in another letter to Eugenius, after the failure of the Second Crusade,[49] he calls upon the pope to aid the Eastern Church and defend the Holy Land, a job which falls to him specifically as pope.[50] Bernard writes, "In this second passion of Christ we must draw those two swords that were drawn during the first passion. *And who is there to draw them but you? ... You hold the position of Peter, and you ought also to have his zeal.*"[51] Saying that Christ is being crucified again in Jerusalem, Bernard implores the pope that, while others ignore it, he cannot who is in the place of Peter. Indeed, Bernard says that the love of God and His Church cannot but impel Eugenius, as pope, to call for a Crusade.[52]

Bernard's letter to the people of England is particularly relevant for it is a record of how Bernard preached the Crusade. Given that it is addressed to the people, it does not touch on the authority of the pope in a crusade. However, it is full of references to the crusade as just and to the crusaders as doing the will of God. Bernard begins the letter by saying that he writes to England of the Crusade because he is concerned for their salvation. As mentioned above, he identifies the Muslims as soldiers of the Devil. He speaks of the many sinners the Holy Land has converted since its reconquest by the Christians and how this infuriates the Devil. "The evil one sees this and is enraged, he gnashes his teeth and withers away in fury."[53] Thus the Devil inspires the Muslims to attack the Holy Land. Of course, says Bernard, God could stop them without the help of men, but He does not do so out of mercy for His people, offering them the Crusade as a path to sanctification. Bernard writes, "For God has pity on his people and on those who have

---

[48] Bernard, *Letter 323 [247]*, 1–2. Emphasis mine.
[49] James (470) disagrees with the previous dating to 1146, saying the contents of the letter show it was written in 1150.
[50] Bernard, *Letter 399 [256]*, 1–2.
[51] *Letter 399*, 1–2. Emphasis mine.
[52] *Letter 399*, 2.
[53] *Letter 391*, 1–3.

grievously fallen away and has prepared for them a means of salvation."[54] Thus the Crusade is not the act of a vengeful God but of a merciful and loving one. As in *De laude*, Bernard castigates the worldly knights and bids them fight for Christians instead of against them. Echoing the *De laude* he writes, "O mighty soldiers, O men of war, you have a cause for which you can fight without danger to your souls; a cause in which to conquer is glorious and for which to die is gain."[55] And if they do not join the Crusade for the sake of God, Bernard bids them join the Crusade for their own sakes, to obtain everlasting life.[56] Thus in this letter Bernard presents the Crusade as war of justice: to undo the injustice of the Muslims and to aid in the justification of Christians.

In *De consideratione* Bernard compares the crusaders of the Second Crusade with the other tribes of Israel when they fought against the tribe of Benjamin. Even though they fought a just war by God's command, they twice did not succeed. Bernard writes, "And so just men went into a just battle, the first time with God's approval and the second time at his command, and still they failed."[57] In this work, Bernard places the responsibility to call a crusade on the pope alone. Speaking of the failed Crusade, Bernard says, "We rushed into this, not aimlessly but at your command, or rather, through you at God's command."[58] But just as Moses failed in bringing the Jews to the promised land because of their sins, so Eugenius cannot be held responsible for the failure of the Crusade. When Bernard asks how a crusade can be known to be God's will, he says it is the authority of the pope which makes this known. "You answer for me and for yourself, according to what you have heard and seen, or certainly according to your inspiration from God."[59] Indeed, it is the pope alone who has the authority and responsibility to call for a crusade. Bernard writes, "Now, if important affairs should be considered by important men, who is

54 Letter 391, 3.
55 Letter 391, 3-4.
56 Letter 391, 5.
57 Bernard of Clairvaux, *Five Books On Consideration: Advice to a Pope*, trans. John D. Anderson and Elizabeth T. Keenan, vol. 13 of *The Works of Bernard of Clairvaux* (Kalamazoo, MI: Cistercian Publications, 1976), II.3.
58 Bernard, *On Consideration*, II.1.
59 *On Consideration*, II.2-3.

as competent as you to consider this matter, since you have no equal in all the world? It is for you to do this according to the wisdom and power given you from above."[60] Thus not only are the Crusaders directly fighting as the soldiers and servants of God, they are also indirectly under His authority for they fight at the command of the Supreme Pontiff.

Thus there are two principles at the heart of Bernard's theology of crusade. First, a crusade is a war waged against injustice done to God and His Church. Second, a crusade is waged by the authority of God, which is manifested by the command of the Roman Pontiff. In articulating his theology of crusade, Bernard is drawing on the just war tradition of Augustine and on the growing moral critique of medieval chivalry. While the idea of crusades has become unpopular in recent centuries, Bernard's justification is perfectly in keeping with the just war tradition of Augustine. Indeed, the principles Bernard annunciates are more limiting than those of Augustine, since a crusade must be defensive. Nevertheless, based on the principles of Augustine, Bernard argues convincingly that a crusade is a form of just war, if not the highest form, since it is directly in the service of God Himself.

---

60 *On Consideration*, II.4.

17

The Catholic State: Anachronism, Archenemy, or Archetype?

Peter Kwasniewski

It is assumed by many that the age-old problem of Church-State relations, a problem that grew ever more intense from the Reformation period through the so-called Enlightenment, has been uneasily resolved, *de facto* and *de iure,* in favor of democratic pluralism and a benign liberal ideology to which even the Church has found it possible to reconcile herself, in exchange for common recognition of basic human rights. From this perspective, Vatican II's *Dignitatis Humanae* is taken as the turning-point in Catholic social teaching, which had traditionally emphasized the Catholic confessional State as the ideal, and the non-Catholic or pluralistic state as an evil that prudence could tolerate but never approve.

Careful students of the Church's Magisterium have found this view a troubling simplification. If the Church has, in fact, changed so consistent, long-standing, and significant a teaching, what does this mean for doctrinal continuity with the past? To paraphrase Pope Benedict XVI, can a Church be trusted who changes her mind on matters of such weight, lauding as modern progress that which she condemned as godless apostasy only a few decades earlier? Moreover, is reconciliation with the aggressive secularism of the Enlightenment really as easy as blessing democracy while adding a few stern reminders about the need for religious underpinnings? Finally, if the Fathers of Vatican II had truly wanted a sea-change in Catholic political doctrine, how can one explain the persistent qualifications and footnotes — in conciliar documents, in the encyclicals of John Paul II, in the new *Catechism*, in doctrinal interventions of the CDF — that refer the reader to the unambiguous formulations of Pius IX, Leo XIII, Pius XI, Pius XII, and John XXIII? One begins to suspect that we are not dealing with any substantive doctrinal change, but rather with a rhetorically palatable, diplomatic reclothing of the same substance. Yet this also raises questions of its own. How can one respond to the common objection that such a reclothing amounts to a repudiation or a contradiction?

To help sort through these matters, I will define the concept of "the Catholic state." Then I will turn to Vatican II and, drawing chiefly upon *Gaudium et Spes* and *Apostolicam Actuositatem*, establish that the essence of the doctrine is restated by the Council, albeit in terms believed to be more adapted to the present historical situation. (I do not take up here the question of whether this attempt at a new formulation has been successful either in transmitting true doctrine to Catholics or in opening those outside the Church to her beneficent influence; I think not, but to elaborate on that skepticism would be the task of another article.) I will show that it is impossible to repudiate the ideal of the Catholic state without implicitly repudiating the claims of Jesus Christ and His Church over mankind as a whole and in each individual. A society and government imbued with reverence for the divine law is the full, natural embodiment of the Faith in the midst of the world Christ redeemed and wishes to save (cf. Jn 3:17).

What is a Catholic State and How Does It Arise?

Materially, a Catholic state is a sovereign political entity made up of a people predominantly Catholic in profession. Formally, it is defined as a nation with a regime or government whose constitution commits it to the support of the one true Faith, whose laws are in harmony with the teaching of the Magisterium on faith and morals, and whose policies implement Catholic social teaching to the widest extent possible.

The Catholic state is the natural, organic outcome of the Faith when it is fully *lived* by a people. As Russell Hittinger reminds us,

The Catholic State: Anachronism, Archenemy, or Archetype?

the Second Vatican Council's Pastoral Constitution on the Church in the Modern World *Gaudium et Spes* in § 43 invites the laity to make it a matter of conscience "that the divine law be impressed on the affairs of the earthly city" (*ut lex divina in civitatis terrenae vita inscribatur*). When this is done consistently, on a broad scale, over some length of time, the natural and proper result is a Catholic society, culture, and state. The Church and her faith will be, for the majority of citizens, the point of reference for understanding themselves and the world, the framework of their daily lives, customs, arts, letters, festivities, rituals. She will be the dominant presence in the life of the individual as in the life of the community. This has never ceased to be the ideal towards which the Church strives. In an address to the Tenth International Congress of Historical Sciences in Rome in 1955, Pope Pius XII stated:

> While the Church and State have known hours and years of conflict, there were also from the time of Constantine the Great until the contemporary era and even recently, tranquil periods, often quite long ones, during which they collaborated with full understanding in the education of the same people. The Church does not hide the fact that she considers such collaboration normal, and that she regards the unity of the people in the true religion and the unanimity of action between herself and the State as ideal.[1]

This, too, is the teaching of the Second Vatican Council's Decree on the Apostolate of the Laity, *Apostolicam Actuositatem* (1965). The Fathers first recognize the "intrinsic value" of temporal realities, and then note how easily they can be perverted to the harm of

---

1 See Msgr. Fenton's illuminating commentary in Michael Davies, *The Second Vatican Council and Religious Liberty* (Long Prairie, MN: Neumann Press, 1992), 179–81. The statement of Lefebvre that Davies quotes on p. 181 is surely exaggerated, since it fails to recognize the equally constant teaching of the popes that the *least* right of the Church is freedom to perform her mission without interference, e.g., freedom to appoint bishops, freedom of communication between the bishops and the pope, freedom of promulgation and publication of documents, and freedom to influence laws, customs, and constitutions. As we know, the Church in modern times has rarely been given even this minimal freedom by supposedly Catholic states; one need only think of France or Austria. Hence the demand in *DH* for a rigorous respect of "the freedom of the Church" is anything but an empty phrase or a meek compromise. See Russell Hittinger, "How to Read *Dignitatis Humanae* on Establishment of Religion," available at http://www.secondspring.co.uk/articles/hittinger.htm.

mankind, and finally issue a call to Christians, especially laity, to transform the temporal order according to the Gospel—without, of course, attempting a mistaken fusion of temporal and spiritual societies (as occurred, for example, in the caesaropapism of Byzantium, the Erastianism of some Western nation-states, and the Gallicanism and Josephinism of the Enlightenment). Here are the words of the Council:

> The whole Church must work vigorously in order that men may become capable of rectifying the distortion of the temporal order and directing it to God through Christ. Pastors must clearly state the principles concerning the purpose of creation and the use of temporal things and must offer the moral and spiritual aids by which the temporal order may be renewed in Christ. (§7)

The same document defines the "apostolate in the social milieu" as "the effort to infuse a Christian spirit into the mentality, customs, laws, and structures of the community in which one lives" (§13). Note that *laws* and *structures* are very clearly specified here; we are not talking merely about attitudes, social graces, and public demonstrations of piety, but also the very content and manner of political life taking their bearings from Christ and His Church. In §14, Catholics are urged to take an active interest in the reconstruction and perfection of civil society according to unchanging principles, so that citizens may be prepared for receiving the Gospel. In giving this advice the Council was doing no more than echoing Pope Leo XIII, who frequently made such exhortations—as when, in the Encyclical *Immortale Dei*, he encourages the faithful "to use their best endeavors... to infuse, as it were, into all the veins of the State the healthy sap and blood of Christian wisdom and virtue."

Why Is a Catholic State Desirable?

Since the Catholic Faith is revealed by God as the one true religion from which derives not only spiritual perfection (which is the decisive thing for our eternal destiny) but also the highest moral, intellectual, and cultural perfection achievable by man, it is desirable that this Faith become the sovereign, pervasive principle of the public life of a people, just as it should be the principle of the personal life of its adherents.[2] In this way, more men will be perfected with the full complement of virtues and more souls will attain the heavenly reward promised by Christ to those who believe in Him. Put negatively, to the degree that a society, culture, and state are non-Catholic (or worse, anti-Catholic), to that degree perfection in virtue is less likely among citizens, and the number of souls in danger of damnation greater. For a *non*-Catholic society, culture, or state to be a good thing in itself, the Catholic Faith would have to be false. Because the Faith is true, however, the only "end game" scenario as far as Christians are concerned is a converted nation of explicitly Christian institutions, deliberately working hand in hand with the hierarchy of the Church.

The common good of any political community is twofold: the extrinsic common good, God; the intrinsic common good, namely, true peace, the "tranquility of order," which is achieved by the study of truth, the impartial administration of justice, and a fitting provision and distribution of earthly goods—all of which contribute to what may be called social happiness. Now, in a Catholic society, the extrinsic common good is all the more easily and widely attained due to adherence to the true religion that furnishes the sovereign and infallible means for attaining it. Moreover, the study of truth will be a promotion of naturally knowable as well as revealed truth, with the repression of natural and supernatural errors. The administration of justice will conform to Catholic moral teaching. Marriage and family law will be regulated according to the principles of natural and divine law, and parents, *not* the state, will be regarded as the primary educators of their children. Material goods will be traded, bought, sold, provided, in the context of a strong juridical order inspired by the principles of Catholic social teaching. All of these elements pertain to the true common good of a Catholic society. It is therefore the duty of government officials, in line with the teaching of *Dignitatis Humanae*, to ensure that this common good is zealously guarded from harm, without, at the same time, attempting to interfere with the private religious

---

2 On this point and the former (the definition of a Catholic culture, society, and state), see Thomas Storck, *Foundations of a Catholic Political Order*, second ed. (Waterloo, ON: Arouca Press, 2022).

acts of non-Catholics,[3] or altogether excluding a limited public exercise of that right where public order and the common welfare of the people do not demand its restraint.[4]

Notwithstanding the obvious benefits of a thoroughly Catholic society and regime, we need to consider a corresponding danger that tends to arise and grow almost imperceptibly, as the history of Europe proves in a dramatic fashion. After centuries have passed from the time of a nation's initial conversion, it is possible that the Faith will be taken for granted; that many citizens will be poorly educated, being Catholics more by custom (often trustingly accepted and sincerely practiced) than by instruction and zealous conviction. There is thus great danger of a slow drift into an increasingly worldly mentality, as well as the perversion and corruption of citizens by errors in faith or morals spread by persuasive and "charismatic" representatives of sects that manage to gain entrance into that society. A Catholic government that really holds the common good of its people at heart is therefore obliged to limit severely the public activities of such sectarians and the public expressions of their beliefs (e.g., to prohibit entry of such people or the publication of their pamphlets), while at the same time continuing to promote, in every way possible, such religious institutions as families, parishes, monasteries, schools, and hospitals that keep the Faith alive and well in the hearts of the people.

Further Definitions and a Corollary

A non-Catholic state may be defined as one that is, or claims to be, officially neutral vis-à-vis the Church, recognizing civilly its special laws as binding on its own members,[5] and allowing it full freedom

---

3 This private exercise is equivalent to acts of intellect and will that can be externalized in the family forum. As soon as they are brought into the political or public forum, they become subject to the governance of the state for the same reason that any human act does.

4 For further clarifications, see the chapter and appendix on religious freedom in Storck's *Foundations of a Catholic Political Order*.

5 The U.S.A. is an anti-Catholic state to the extent that it allows Catholics to get divorced (and, *a fortiori*, to be civilly remarried) or have abortions when this ought to be illegal unless they formally apostatize, even as in some European countries Catholics and Protestants are legally obliged to pay church taxes until and unless they renounce their church membership. A State that permits Catholics routinely to break their solemn oaths and promises is a State that, in its official capacity, considers anything religious or

of ministry. There are, of course, varying degrees of neutrality, ranging from "warm" to "cold." The general philosophical framework of such a state is liberalism: *de facto* recognition of pluralism and the toleration of all views compatible with basic public order (as construed by current officeholders). An anti-Catholic state may be defined as one that denies the Catholic Church those rights that are due to her as a perfect society with a divine mandate, or, in a worst case scenario, actively persecutes and penalizes her members.

A corollary: to the extent that modern democracies place limits on all *formal* intersection between the Catholic Faith and the ordering of political society and temporal affairs, to this extent they are both anti-Catholic and tyrannical. The goal of the Enlightenment social contract theorists was to design a society from which the Catholic Church was effectively excluded, a society therefore "free" to reject with impunity all rules of faith and morals. Hence, we find a consistent exclusion of practicing Catholics from social contract experiments—one need only read Hobbes's *Leviathan*, Locke's *Letter Concerning Toleration*, Samuel Adams's *Report to the Boston Town Meeting*, and countless other examples from the eighteenth century.[6] It follows that when Catholics *are* permitted to live within such societies or under such regimes, it is virtually at the cost of renouncing the social dynamism and authoritative structure of the Faith itself. No less a churchman than Archbishop Charles Chaput has recognized this dark logic in John F. Kennedy's Address to the Greater Houston Ministerial Association in 1960, and in the continual stream of U.S. "Catholic" politicians who, abusing the noble title of conscience, throw their support behind sexual immorality and the slaughter of the unborn. At its root, the social contract demands a common creed of relativism and public indifference to the highest things.

---

spiritual to be mumbo-jumbo with no discernible public, objective meaning or value. A solemn oath or promise means nothing to such a State and can be treated as dissoluble or non-existent.

6 From Adams's *Report to the Boston Town Meeting* (1772): "Mr. Locke has asserted and proved, beyond the possibility of contradiction on any solid ground, that such toleration ought to be extended to all whose doctrines are not subversive of society. The only sects which he thinks ought to be, and which by all wise laws are excluded from such toleration, are those who teach doctrines subversive of the civil government under which they live. The Roman Catholics or Papists are [thereby] excluded..."

What, then, of the Second Vatican Council's Declaration on Religious Liberty *Dignitatis Humanae*—what kind of State, or what range of States, is this declaration addressing? Both its textual genesis and its internal preoccupations show us that *Dignitatis Humanae* is addressed to the two situations that had become dominant in the contemporary world: non-Catholic liberal pluralistic States (e.g., the United States) and anti-Catholic ideological States (e.g., Soviet Union, China). As Russell Hittinger convincingly argues in his book *The First Grace*, the declaration never takes up in a systematic way the question of a "normative" Catholic State, being content to mention it in passing:

> If, in view of peculiar circumstances obtaining among peoples, special civil recognition is given to one religious community in the constitutional order of society, it is at the same time imperative that the right of all citizens and religious communities to religious freedom should be recognized and made effective in practice.

Yet surely the declaration's unqualified reaffirmation that "it [the teaching on religious freedom] leaves untouched traditional Catholic doctrine on the moral duty of men and societies toward the true religion and toward the one Church of Christ" can only be construed as support for the possibility, desirability, and ideality of such a state, regardless of what some authors or promoters of the document may have wished it might have said or may have personally believed.[7] The final document neither excludes the Catholic confessional State nor omits to mention those essential limitations on, or norms for, the public expression of religious belief—limitations and norms that at least imply the traditional teaching.[8]

What Is At Stake

In an age of confusion, it is very important that we correctly conceptualize the political question—that is, the one central question on which everything else hinges. The political question *par*

---

[7] See Rev. Brian W. Harrison, "Is John Courtney Murray a Reliable Interpreter of *Dignitatis Humanae*?," available at http://www.rtforum.org/lt/lt33.html.

[8] Here we refer to the function in *Dignitatis Humanae* of concepts such as "due (or just) public order," "common good," and "the objective moral law," with respect to the exercise of any and every civil liberty—even those claimed to be rooted in human nature and pertaining directly to human dignity.

The Catholic State: Anachronism, Archenemy, or Archetype?

excellence is this: What is the status or place of the Catholic Church within a civil society and its regime?[9] The "thesis," i.e., the norm, the ideal, is nothing less than a fully Catholic culture, in which all the arts, economic life, and government are thoroughly "baptized." The pragmatic situation of pluralism (also called the "hypothesis") is any partially or scarcely Catholic culture, whose arts, economics, and government are determined by principles that vary from being merely compatible with, to being violently against, the Catholic Faith. Such a civil society will be imperfect according to both natural and supernatural criteria, and its existence can only be tolerated, never approved in itself or as a model.

What are the implications of abandoning the "thesis"? The three fundamental forces motivating the Christian in the world are the theological virtues of faith, hope, and charity. Whenever, therefore, the goal of a thoroughly converted (that is, Catholic) culture and state is no longer aspired to—even if only remotely, by sighs and prayers, when its realization seems humanly impossible—then sadly, it must be the case that faith, hope, and charity are no longer the operative principles of life. They are replaced by worldly prudence, a heavenless horizon, a human love that contradicts the missionary impulse of charity. To let go of the Gospel as the norm for *everything human* is to consign oneself and society to the mediocre exercise of mediocre virtues, at best; and given human sinfulness, it may also mean throwing open the house to the expert exercise of inhuman vices, as modern political history has shown all too vividly.

We are living in an era characterized by profound unrest: the increasing rationalism of science fueling technological barbarism, the increasing irrationalism of non-Christian religions feeding horrific violence, the increasing secularization of Western societies driving them to the brink of insanity as every perversion and aberration is not only permitted but celebrated. We must not underestimate the extent to which false ideas in philosophy, religion, and politics have brought about this world situation, nor the extent of Catholics' complicity in it by their willingness to listen to the

---

9 Cf. Pierre Manent's penetrating remarks along these lines in *An Intellectual History of Liberalism*, trans. Rebecca Balinski (Princeton, NJ: Princeton University Press, 1994).

siren song of the Enlightenment, luring us with empty promises of a universally respectful and benevolent, value-neutral, open-ended social order where religion would be the special preserve of the sovereign individual conscience—and never would the Catholic Faith be the public principle of social cohesion, moral orientation, intellectual light, and spiritual vitality. As the wake-up call becomes increasingly shrill, it is high time for us to rise from the drugged sleep of modernity and embrace a fully *Catholic*, fully *traditional* vision of the political order and the common good. It may not be our privilege to see such an order rise up from the ashes of the corrupt West, but we can be sure as steel that it will not arise from ideologies, principles, and practices that find their historical origins in the sworn enemies of the Catholic Church.

III
RELIGIOUS LIBERTY

18

Religious Liberty in the Light of Tradition

Edmund Waldstein, O.Cist.[1]

Of all the documents of the Second Vatican Council the one that has most determined the official relations of the postconciliar Church with the world is the Declaration on Religious Liberty, *Dignitatis Humanae*. The official diplomacy of the Holy See in the decades since Vatican II has largely been concerned with the defense of religious liberty. In the last years immediately following the Council the defense was mounted against atheistic communism in Central Europe, and later it was taken up against militant Islam in the Near East, and "the dictatorship of relativism" in the West.

Moreover, no other document marks the transition between the "preconciliar" and the "postconciliar" Church more than *Dignitatis Humanae*. For while the postconciliar Church presents herself as the passionate defender of religious liberty, the preconciliar Church of the "Pian Age" (1789–1962) seemed to be the implacable enemy of such liberty. A chief concern of Vatican II was to overcome the antagonism between the Church and modernity, an antagonism symbolized at the dawn of modernity by the Galileo affair, and which had taken violent political form in the French Revolution. Instead of merely condemning the errors of modern liberalism,

---

1 An earlier version of this chapter was presented to Una Voce Austria, Vienna, November 18, 2013; my thanks to Stephan Csernohorszky and Benedikt Hensellek for the invitation. I also thank Gregor Hochreiter and Felix Mayrhofer for their comments on the German version, and Alan Fimister, Thomas Pink, Rev. Thomas Crean, O.P., Peter Escalante, Matthew J. Peterson, John Ruplinger, Gabriel Sanchez, Andrew Strain, Christopher Zehnder, Peter Kwasniewski, and the backroom of *The Josias* for helpful discussions.

Vatican II wished to uncover the positive elements and authentic human concerns expressed therein. The Council wanted to show how the Church could make these positive elements her own, purifying and elevating them through the influence of grace.[2] Religious liberty was seen as a key point in this transition, because freedom of conscience, and therefore of religion, was an important concern of the Enlightenment and of the bourgeois liberalism of the nineteenth century, and the opposition of the nineteenth-century popes to this freedom was one of the sources of liberal anticlericalism.[3]

The change in the Church's attitude toward modernity seems especially clear in the matter of religious liberty. In fact, there seems to be a direct contradiction between the teaching of the Council and the teachings of the popes of the nineteenth century on this point. If one compares the central affirmation of *Dignitatis Humanae* with, for example, the section on religious freedom in Bl. Pius IX's *Quanta Cura* the contradiction seems obvious. Thus *Dignitatis Humanae*:

> This Vatican Council declares that the human person has a right to religious freedom. This freedom means that all men are to be immune from coercion on the part of individuals or of social groups and of any human power, in such wise that no one is to be forced to act in a manner contrary to his own beliefs, whether privately or publicly, whether alone or in association with others, within due limits.[4]

And thus *Quanta Cura*:

> From which totally false idea of social government they do not fear to foster that erroneous opinion, most fatal in its effects on the Catholic Church and the salvation of souls, called by Our

[2] See Pope Benedict XVI, "*Expergiscere Homo*: Address to the College of Cardinals and the Roman Curia," December 22, 2005, in *Acta Apostolicae Sedis* 95,1 (2006) 40–53; www.vatican.va/holy_father/benedict_xvi/speeches/2005/december/documents/hf_ben_xvi_spe_20051222_roman-curia_en.html.

[3] See Martin Rhonheimer, *Christentum und säkularer Staat* (Freiburg: Herder, 32012), 134–39, 143; Eberhard Schockenhoff, "Das Recht, ungehindert die Wahrheit zu suchen: Die Erklärung über die Religionsfreiheit *Dignitatis humanae*," in Jan-Heiner Tück (ed.), *Erinnerung an die Zukunft: Das Zweite Vatikanische Konzil*, 2nd ed. (Freiburg: Herder, 2013), 702.

[4] *Dignitatis Humanae* 2, in *Acta Apostolicae Sedis* 58 (1966): 929–46, at 930; translation: www.vatican.va/archive/hist_councils/ii_vatican_council/documents/vat-ii_decl_19651207_dignitatis-humanae_en.html.

Predecessor, Gregory XVI, an "insanity" [*deliramentum*], viz., that "liberty of conscience and worship is each man's personal right, which ought to be legally proclaimed and asserted in every rightly constituted society; and that a right resides in the citizens to an absolute liberty, which should be restrained by no authority whether ecclesiastical or civil, whereby they may be able openly and publicly to manifest and declare any of their ideas whatever, either by word of mouth, by the press, or in any other way."[5]

Does not Vatican II here affirm precisely that which Pius IX, citing Gregory XVI, calls a *deliramentum*? This ostensible contradiction made *Dignitatis Humanae* the most controversial document at the Council. So many doubts were raised about the first three schemata that Pope Paul VI decided to delay voting on it, moving the vote from the third to the fourth and final session of the Council.[6] At this session, a large group of council fathers protested, begging the pope with the very greatest urgency ("*instanter, instantius, instantissimus*") to reverse his decision, lest public opinion turn against the Council.[7] Nevertheless, the vote did not take place till the very end of the last session.[8]

After the Council the question of the relation of *Dignitatis Humanae* to previous teachings remained controversial.[9] Any interpretation of *Dignitatis Humanae* has to deal with this question, and interpreters have proposed various approaches that all give different answers to the question—from the assertion of a radical break with tradition to that of complete continuity with tradition. I shall now consider several answers that I consider inadequate before turning to an explanation and defense of the answer proposed by the English philosopher Thomas Pink. According to Pink there is continuity at the level of principles, but discontinuity at the level of Church policy toward the state. He shows this first by giving

---

5   Pope Pius IX, *Quanta Cura*, in Herbert Vaughan, ed., *The Year of Preparation for the Vatican Council: Including the Original and English of the Encyclical and Syllabus, and of the Papal Documents Connected with its Convocation* (London: Burns, Oates, and Co., 1869), iv-xx, at viii.

6   See Pietro Pavan, *Einleitung zur Erklärung über die Religionsfreiheit*, in *Lexikon für Theologie und Kirche*, 2nd ed., Ergänzungsband II (Freiburg: Herder, 1967), 706-7.

7   See Pavan, *Einleitung*, 706.

8   See Pavan, *Einleitung*, 709-11.

9   See Schockenhoff, "Das Recht," 703.

a new interpretation of the condemnation of religious freedom on the part of the popes of the Pian Age, showing its roots in counter-Reformation political theology. And then he applies key distinctions taken from that analysis to *Dignitatis Humanae*.

After explaining Pink's thesis, I shall further explicate it by a brief glance at the history of the relation of temporal and spiritual power in Church history. I shall then conclude by examining the theological concerns of some of the conciliar theologians who influenced *Dignitatis Humanae*.

I. Inadequate Interpretations of *Dignitatis Humanae*

Hermeneutics

In his Christmas address to the Roman Curia in 2005, Pope Benedict XVI spoke of a "hermeneutic of discontinuity and rupture" which led to a misunderstanding of Vatican II.[10] Since the Council did indeed wish to reform the Church's relations to the modern world, the impression could easily be formed that a break had been made with tradition—as though the Church could simply abandon what she had previously authoritatively taught. Pope Benedict contrasts this with a correct hermeneutic, a "hermeneutic of reform, of renewal in the continuity of the one subject-Church."[11] This hermeneutic starts with the principle of the Church's continuity through time, but allows for discontinuities at the level of policy, discipline, and the mode of expressing certain teachings.[12] For the explication of this hermeneutic Pope Benedict cites Pope John XXIII's address at the opening of Vatican II, in which Pope John defined the task of the Council as formulating the "unchanging" doctrine in a new historical situation, without changing its meaning.[13]

The hermeneutic of rupture

The hermeneutic of rupture has often been applied to *Dignitatis Humanae*. Non-theologians, such as legal scholars and political

---

10 Benedict XVI, "*Expergiscere Homo*," 46.
11 Benedict XVI, "*Expergiscere Homo*," 46.
12 See Chad C. Pecknold, "Pope Benedict's Hermeneutic of Continuity: Very Theological Reflections on Theological Method," presentation at *Reform and Renewal: Vatican II After 50 Years*, Symposium at The Catholic University of America, Washington DC, September 26–29, 2012; online at YouTube.
13 Benedict XVI, "*Expergiscere Homo*," 47.

scientists, have had no scruples in seeing a contradiction between *Dignitatis Humanae* and previous teachings.[14] But even many theologians have taken this route as well, and have come up with different explanations as to how such a rupture might be possible. "Progressive" theologians have often defended the idea of rupture by a minimalist view of the authority of Church teaching. According to them the condemnation of religious freedom, for example *Quanta Cura*, was not an infallible exercise of the Petrine Office, and was therefore reformable. They argue that only the most solemn definitions of the Magisterium are infallible, and that many "authentic" teachings of the Church are not finally binding. Thus Reinhold Sebott, S.J., argues as follows: "If we do not consider *Quanta Cura* infallible, then of course we will not consider a great many other magisterial decisions infallible. Only very few teachings can be described as dogmas in the strict sense."[15]

Such positions have been used not only to justify a hermeneutic of rupture in the reading of Vatican II, but also to put into question much of the Church's teaching with regard to faith and morals. Thus many theologians used this position to question the condemnation of artificial contraception in Pope Paul VI's encyclical *Humanae Vitae*. Pope Paul clearly wanted his teaching to be binding on the faithful, but many theologians denied that it could have binding character.[16] Sebott himself brings up the example of Pope John Paul II's apostolic letter *Ordinatio Sacerdotalis* (1994). Pope John Paul wished to definitively end the discussion on the ordination of women in that letter, but according to Sebott the letter was not infallible, and therefore the discussion cannot be considered closed.[17] Such an exaggerated minimalism with regard to Church teaching

---

14 See Schockenhoff, "Das Recht," 623–25. Schockenhoff mentions Ernst-Wolfgang Böckenförde, Klaus Schatz, Franz Xaver Bischof, and Josef Insensee as examples.

15 "Wenn man QC (*Quanta cura*) nicht als unfehlbar qualifiziert, dann wird man natürlich auch eine Menge anderer Lehrentscheidungen nicht als unfehlbar qualifizieren dürfen. Der Kreis des Dogmas muss also sehr eng gezogen werden." Reinhold Sebott, "*Dignitatis humanae* und *Quanta cura*: Die Verurteilung der Religionsfreiheit vor dem Zweiten Vatikanischen Konzil," in P. Boekholt and I. Riedel-Spangenberger, eds., *Iustitia et Modestia* (Munich: Don Bosco Verlag, 1998), 183–92, at 192.

16 See Janet E. Smith, *Humanae Vitae, a Generation Later* (Washington: Catholic University of America Press, 1998), especially 155–69.

17 Sebott, "*Dignitatis Humanae*," 192.

cannot be reconciled with the teachings of numerous popes and councils on the binding character of the ordinary and universal Magisterium of the Church.[18] Supporters of minimalism often give apparent examples of discontinuity in Church teaching to support their views, but none of the examples are un-controversial.[19]

"Traditionalists" such as the French Archbishop Marcel Lefebvre, on the other hand, were convinced that the condemnation of religious liberty by the popes of the nineteenth century was forever binding, and that therefore the teaching of the Council was wrong. Lefebvre submitted his argument to the Congregation for the Doctrine of the Faith in the form of *dubia*,[20] and his dissatisfaction with the Congregation's response[21] was a decisive factor in his decision, carried out on June 30, 1988, to consecrate four bishops without papal mandate, thus incurring excommunication *latae sententiae*.[22] Lefebvre's position was somewhat paradoxical, as the then prefect of the Congregation for the Doctrine of the Faith, Joseph Cardinal Ratzinger, pointed out: by putting his own private interpretation of previous Church teachings above the Church's official interpretation of her teaching he was giving up precisely the principle of fidelity to Church doctrine that he wanted to defend.[23]

But Lefebvre was surely right about this much: the question of religious liberty is not merely a disciplinary question; it is a moral

18 See Congregation for the Doctrine of the Faith, "Doctrinal Commentary on the Concluding Formula of the *Professio Fidei*," www.vatican.va/roman_curia/congregations/cfaith/documents/rc_con_cfaith_doc_1998_professio-fidei_en.html.

19 See Avery Cardinal Dulles, "Development or Reversal?," in *First Things* (October 2005): 53–61.

20 Marcel Lefebvre, "Dubia sur la Déclaration conciliaire sur la liberté religieuse, présentés à la S. C. R. pour la Doctrine de la Foi," Ecône, November 6, 1985, online at http://lacriseintegriste.typepad.fr/dubia.pdf; English translation: *Religious Liberty Questioned* (Kansas City: Angelus Press, 2001).

21 Congregation for the Doctrine of the Faith, "Liberté religieuse: Réponse aux Dubia présentés par S. E. Mgr Lefebvre," Rome, March 9, 1987: https://lacriseintegriste.typepad.fr/weblog/1987/03/r%C3%A9ponses-de-la-congr%C3%A9gation-pour-la-doctrine-de-la-foi-aux-dubia-pr%C3%A9sent%C3%A9s-par-mgr-lefebvre.html.

22 See the documentation collected at the website *La crise intégriste*: http://lacriseintegriste.typepad.fr/weblog/le-dialogue-avec-jeanpaul-ii-19781987.html and http://lacriseintegriste.typepad.fr/weblog/le-schisme-19882000.html.

23 "En fournissant une interprétation personnelle des textes du Magistère, vous feriez paradoxalement preuve de ce libéralisme que vous combattez si fortement, et agiriez contre le but que vous poursuivez." Letter of Joseph Cardinal Ratzinger to Archbishop Marcel Lefebvre, July 28, 1987: http://lacriseintegriste.typepad.fr/weblog/1987/07/lettre-du-car.html.

question on which the Church has taught authoritatively. Klaus Obenauer, a theologian sympathetic to traditionalism, recently pointed out that the teaching of the Council of Constance, according to which the Church has the right to hand heretics over to the "secular arm" for punishment, was solemnly confirmed by Pope Martin V. He is unable to see how that teaching can be consistent with *Dignitatis Humanae* and concludes:

> The question is raised as to how DH can stand with respect to centuries of authoritative teaching, and of canonically prescribed practice, according to which there is no right to the practice (especially the public practice) of dissent. I say the question is *raised*, and to the present hour the question has not been answered.[24]

The hermeneutic of continuity at all levels

At the opposite extreme from the hermeneutic of rupture is a hermeneutic of continuity at all levels. Thomas Storck, an expert on Catholic Social Teaching, uses such a hermeneutic of continuity.[25] Storck bases his reading on the explicit assertion in the preamble of *Dignitatis Humanae* that it does not mean to change traditional Catholic teaching on the duties of societies toward the true religion: "Religious freedom, in turn, which men demand as necessary to fulfill their duty to worship God, has to do with immunity from coercion in civil society. Therefore it leaves untouched traditional Catholic doctrine on the moral duty of men and societies toward the true religion and toward the one Church of Christ."[26]

Among the duties of societies toward true religion, Storck includes the limiting of the spread of false religions by way of censorship and such measures, as called for by the nineteenth-century

---

24 "Es stellt sich eben die Frage, wie DH [*Dignitatis humanae*] ankommen soll gegen die über Jahrhunderte verbindlich vorgetragene Lehre, und zwar vor dem Hintergrund kirchenamtlich gestützter Praxis, wonach es gerade kein natürliches Recht gibt, (zumal öffentlich) unbehelligt von der staatlichen Gewalt das Dissidententum zu praktizieren. Ich sage: 'es stellt sich die Frage, wie.' Und beantwortet ist die bis zur Stunde nicht." Klaus Obenauer, "Piusbruderschaft: Der angehaltene Zug—oder: Wie bekommt man das Signal wieder auf Grün?" www.katholisches.info/2012/11/21/piusbruderschaft-der-angehaltene-zug-oder-wie-bekommt-man-das-signal-wieder-auf-grun.

25 Some other examples are mentioned by Schockenhoff ("Das Recht," 727–28), including Arthur Utz, Robert Spaemann, Basile Valuet, and Betrand de Margerie.

26 *Dignitatis Humanae* 1; cf. Thomas Storck, *Foundations of a Catholic Political Order*, 2nd ed. (Waterloo, ON: Arouca Press, 2022), 36–37.

popes.²⁷ Thus Storck moves the apparent contradiction into *Dignitatis Humanae* itself. But he finds a key to understanding why the contradiction is only apparent by his interpretation of the "due limits" on religious freedom mentioned in the central statement of *Dignitatis Humanae* 2: "no one is to be forced to act in a manner contrary to his own beliefs, whether privately or publicly, whether alone or in association with others, *within due limits.*" *Dignitatis Humanae* 7 further explicates these limits. The exercise of religious liberty must include "respect both for the rights of others and for their own duties toward others and for the common welfare [*bonum commune*] of all." The state is required to preserve "genuine public peace, which comes about when men live together in good order and in true justice" and "public morality." Storck argues that preservation of the *bonum commune* of a Christian society would in practice allow for very heavy restrictions on religious freedom:

> the "just requirements of public order," the "due limits," and considerations of the rights of others and of the common good vary considerably from society to society, and...in a society overwhelmingly and traditionally Catholic they could easily include restrictions, and even an outright prohibition, on the public activities of non-Catholic sects, particularly on their proselytizing activities.²⁸

According to Storck, the condemnation of religious freedom in earlier ages of the Church was not the complete denial of *any* such right, but rather the denial of an *unlimited* right.²⁹ On his interpretation previous teachings were not concerned with the private right of persons to believe what they thought to be true, but rather precisely with the necessity for public order of limiting the spread of false religion:

> A non-Catholic has the real political right, even in a Catholic state, to privately profess his own religion and privately meet with his co-religionists; in a liberal regime he has a right to considerably

---

27 Storck, *Foundations*, 27–34.
28 Storck, *Foundations*, 38.
29 Storck, *Foundations*, 38: "Man's religious liberty is real and the Council's Declaration is not false or heretical; [it is] simply that the right to exercise such freedom is not the same in every place and time."

more freedom. In both cases the freedom is real, [it is] simply that the "requirements of public order" and especially of the common good differ.[30]

I do not think that Storck's thesis can be maintained. First, I think it does not do justice to the full scope of preconciliar teaching on coercion in religious matters. As Thomas Pink has shown, and as I will explain in section 3 below, previous teaching justified not only restrictions on the public activity of false religion, but also coercing heretics to return to the true faith. A second problem with Storck's thesis is that it does not do justice to the decisiveness with which *Dignitatis Humanae* denies the state any native authority in matters of religion. It grounds this lack of authority in the transcendence of religious matters over the temporal order:

> The religious acts whereby men, in private and in public and out of a sense of personal conviction, direct their lives to God transcend by their very nature the order of terrestrial and temporal affairs. Government therefore ought indeed to take account of the religious life of the citizenry and show it favor, since the function of government is to make provision for the common welfare. However, *it would clearly transgress the limits set to its power, were it to presume to command or inhibit acts that are religious.*[31]

This seems to exclude precisely the sort of limitation of false religion *for the sake of the temporal common good* that Storck wants to uphold.

The hermeneutic of reform in continuity

On Pope Benedict's hermeneutic principle one ought not to expect a contradiction between the documents of Vatican II and previous teaching, but neither ought one to expect complete continuity. One ought rather to expect reform. "Basic decisions, therefore, continue to be well-grounded, whereas the way they are applied to new contexts can change."[32] Pope Benedict explicitly applies this hermeneutic principle to *Dignitatis Humanae*:

---

30 Storck, *Foundations*, 38–39.
31 *Dignitatis Humanae* 3; emphasis added.
32 "Expergiscere Homo," 50.

Thus, for example, if religious freedom were to be considered an expression of the human inability to discover the truth and thus become a canonization of relativism, then this social and historical necessity is raised inappropriately to the metaphysical level and thus stripped of its true meaning. Consequently, it cannot be accepted by those who believe that the human person is capable of knowing the truth about God and, on the basis of the inner dignity of the truth, is bound to this knowledge. It is quite different, on the other hand, to perceive religious freedom as a need that derives from human coexistence, or indeed, as an intrinsic consequence of the truth that cannot be externally imposed but that the person must adopt only through the process of conviction.[33]

Pope Benedict thus shows that there is no direct contradiction between *Dignitatis Humanae* and, for example, *Quanta Cura*, since "religious freedom" means something quite different in those two documents.[34] Nevertheless, Pope Benedict's interpretation leaves some open questions, since it does not explain the continuity at the level of "basic decisions" and the discontinuity at the level of application to "new contexts" in detail.

A number of theologians have tried to apply Pope Benedict's principles to a detailed interpretation of *Dignitatis Humanae*. It turns out that distinguishing the two levels is not as easy as it might appear at first. I shall now examine two attempts that I find inadequate before turning (in the next section) to Thomas Pink's solution.

Eberhard Schockenhoff explicitly invokes Pope Benedict XVI's address in his interpretation. But I claim that his reading in the end falls back into a hermeneutic of rupture. Schockenhoff does see "lines of continuity" between *Dignitatis Humanae* and previous teaching on the relation of freedom and truth, but he does not limit discontinuity to the application to a new context:

> The truth does not lie simply at the mean between continuity and discontinuity. Even at the hermeneutic deep-level, the level at which the Council tries to come to an appropriate mediation of truth and freedom, there is an unmistakable change of perspective.... At any rate, it does not suffice to assert an unbroken continuity in the

33 Ibid.
34 Cf. Schockenhoff, "Das Recht," 729.

development of Church teaching on a theological or philosophical/ethical level of principle and to admit a change only with regard to the application of these principles to altered historical situations.[35]

According to Schockenhoff the Church in *Dignitatis Humanae* adopted the "hard core" of modern liberal rights as her own.[36] He sees this as a paradigm shift in the Church's understanding of the relation of truth and freedom, and the relation of human subjectivity and truth.[37] Moreover, he argues that this paradigm shift has implications for the relation of truth and freedom in the Church herself—the pastors of the Church should eschew the coercive use of teaching authority, and should use a more dialogical mode of teaching. As we shall see below, this position is hard to square with the solemn teaching of the Council of Trent, according to which the Church ought to impose sanctions on the baptized to help preserve them in the faith.

Martin Rhonheimer's interpretation is similar to Schockenhoff's, but he sees slightly more continuity and slightly less discontinuity. He does see continuity at the level of principles in the relation of truth and freedom. He even admits that the Church can coerce her members with sanctions (even ones that have "temporal" consequences),[38] but he denies that the Church can make use of the state as *brachium saeculare* for such coercion. He thinks that *Dignitatis Humanae* corrects previous teaching on "the mission and function of the state."[39] While certain previous popes taught that

---

35 "Dennoch liegt die Wahrheit nicht einfach in der Mitte zwischen Kontinuität und Diskontinuität. Denn auch auf der hermeneutischen Tiefenebene, auf der das Konzil sich um eine angemessene Vermittlung von Wahrheit und Freiheit bemüht, ist ein Perspektivenwechsel unverkennbar.... Jedenfalls reicht es nicht aus, auf einer theologischen oder philosophisch-ethischen Prinzipienebene eine ungebrochene Kontinuität kirchlicher Lehrentwicklung zu behaupten und nur hinsichtlich der Anwendung dieser Prinzipien auf veränderte geschichtliche Situationen einen Wandel zuzugeben." Schockenhoff, "Das Recht," 734.

36 Eberhard Schockenhoff, *Erlöste Freiheit: Worauf es im Christentum ankommt* (Freiburg: Herder, 2012), 15.

37 Schockenhoff, *Erlöste Freiheit*, 42–45; idem, "Das Recht," 733–34.

38 Martin Rhonheimer, "*Dignitatis Humanae*—Not a Mere Question of Church Policy: A Response to Thomas Pink," *Nova et Vetera* Eng. ed. 12.2 (2014): 445–70, at 454–55.

39 Martin Rhonheimer, "Benedict XVI's 'Hermeneutic of Reform' and Religious Freedom," *Nova et Vetera* Eng. ed. 9.4 (2011): 1029–54; idem, *Christentum und säkularer Staat*, especially 156–63; cf. also idem, "*Dignitatis Humanae*—Not a Mere Question."

the state must subordinate itself to the Church, *Dignitatis Humanae* denies this and demands a legitimate secularity for the state. This is not a break with principles derived from Sacred Scripture or the Apostolic tradition, which according to Rhonheimer "suggest a separation between the political and religious spheres."[40] But it is a break with earlier and less perfect applications of those principles. Rhonheimer argues that *Dignitatis Humanae* stands at the end of a long process through which the Church rediscovers the original meaning of Jesus's distinction between the things that are Caesar's and the things that are God's, and for the first time sees its full implications.[41] I will return to Rhonheimer's subtle argumentation below when I consider the history of the relations of spiritual and temporal power. At this point it suffices to indicate that the teaching according to which the Church can make use of the state as secular arm has a great deal more authority than Rhonheimer is willing to admit. Think for example of Pope Martin V's confirmation of the Council of Constance's teaching on the secular arm mentioned above.[42]

II. Thomas Pink's Breakthrough

The English philosopher Thomas Pink has developed a superior account of *Dignitatis Humanae*'s continuity and discontinuity with previous teaching.[43] Pink is an expert on the philosophy of Thomas Hobbes (1588–1679), and it was Hobbes that led him to a new

---

40 Rhonheimer, "Benedict XVI's 'Hermeneutic of Reform,'" 1032.

41 See especially Rhonheimer, *Christentum und säkularer Staat*, 33–191.

42 See Klaus Obenauer, "Piusbruderschaft: Der angehaltene Zug." Obenauer cites Denzinger/Hünermann (42nd ed.) 1272: "Item, utrum credat, quod inoboedientia sive contumacia excommunicatorum crescente, praelati vel eorum vicarii in spiritualibus habeant potestatem aggravandi et reaggravandi, interdictum ponendi et brachium saeculare invocandi; et quod illis censuris per inferiores sit oboediendum."

43 See the works by Thomas Pink already cited: "What is the Catholic doctrine of religious liberty?" and "Conscience and Coercion," as well as "The Right to Religious Liberty and the Coercion of Belief: A Note on *Dignitatis Humanae*," in John Keown and Robert P. George, eds., *Reason, Morality, and Law: The Philosophy of John Finnis* (Oxford: Oxford University Press, 2013), 427–42; "The Interpretation of *Dignitatis Humanae*: A Reply to Martin Rhonheimer," *Nova et Vetera* Eng. ed. 11.1 (2013): 77–121; "Jacques Maritain and the Problem of Church and State," Lecture, Mundelein, October 2013, www.academia.edu/8576510/Jacques_Maritain_and_the_problem_of_Church_and_State; "Suárez and Bellarmine on the Church as Coercive Lawgiver," Lecture, Bologna, December 2013, www.academia.edu/8577465/Suárez_and_Bellarmine_on_the_Church_as_Coercive_Lawgiver.

approach to the problem since one of Hobbes's main concerns in *Leviathan* was to refute the Catholic claim according to which the Church has its own coercive authority independent of the state.[44] The two main defenders of the Catholic position in Hobbes's time were Robert Bellarmine and Francisco Suárez, and so Pink studied their arguments. He noticed that they pose the question of coercion in religious matters in terms quite different from those used today. Today it is usual to see the question of freedom and coercion in religion as a question of the competence of the state: does the state have the authority to use coercion in religious matters or not? Moreover, the coercion in question is thought of as coercion of public actions, not of the interior act of faith itself.[45] But Bellarmine and Suárez do not treat the question of religious coercion in the first place as a question of the competence of the state; they treat it as a question of the competence of the Church, since they see the Church as a *societas perfecta* (a complete community) with its own coercive authority—an authority to promulgate binding laws and enforce them with sanctions. The Church, the Mystical Body of Christ and Communion of Saints, is of course much more than a juridical *societas perfecta*, but this juridical character is essential to her as well. Church laws are therefore not merely rules of a voluntary society, which would only bind so long as one wished to remain within the society. Rather, Church law is genuine coercive law, binding on all her members.[46]

Everyone who has become a member of the Body of Christ through Baptism is thereby forever subject to the law of the Church. Baptism does not "expire" when someone apostatizes or falls into heresy or schism. The Church can therefore continue to demand that the baptized keep their baptismal vows and the other duties flowing from baptism. And the Church can back this demand up with sanctions.[47] The Council of Trent explicitly taught that the Church as a genuine coercive authority can impose not only spiritual sanctions (such as excommunication), but also temporal sanctions. Against a thesis of Erasmus, who thought that baptized

---

44 See Pink, "Suárez and Bellarmine," 187.
45 Pink, "What is the Catholic Doctrine," 1–2.
46 Pink, "Suárez and Bellarmine," 187–88.
47 Pink, "Suárez and Bellarmine," 188. The implications of this truth and of its nearly universal denial today are taken up in detail in the next chapter.

children ought not to be forced to keep their vows when grown up, Trent promulgated the following canon:

> If anyone says that when they grow up, those baptized as little children should be asked whether they wish to affirm what their godparents promised in their name when they were baptized; and that, when they reply that they have no such wish, they should be left to their own decision and not, in the meantime, be coerced by any penalty into the Christian life, except that they be barred from the reception of the Eucharist and the other sacraments, until they have a change of heart: let him be anathema.[48]

One of the main obligations that flows from Baptism is the obligation to believe. According to the traditional teaching it belongs to the essence of faith that Baptism be free, and no one can therefore be coerced into Baptism; the Church has always condemned forced Baptisms.[49] But once a person has received the supernatural virtue of faith through Baptism, he is obliged to keep the faith. For this reason St Thomas Aquinas, to take one prominent example, teaches that although the unbaptized can never be forced to accept the Christian faith, heretics who have fallen away from the true faith can and ought to be coerced back into accepting it.[50] Pope Pius VI confirmed this view, explicitly citing St Thomas, in the Brief *Quod Aliquantum* (1791):

> We must distinguish between those who have always been outside the Church, namely infidels and Jews, and those who have subjected themselves to her through Baptism. The former ought not to be compelled to profess the Catholic Faith, the latter however are to be coerced (*sunt cogendi*). St Thomas proves this with his usual solidity.[51]

During the Counter Reformation such teachings were used to justify coercing Protestants to accept the Catholic faith. Since

---

48   Council of Trent, Session VII, *Decree on Baptism*, canon 14, March 3, 1547; citation following Pink, "What is the Catholic Doctrine," 16; for the Latin text, see Denzinger/Hünermann 1627.
49   Cf. *Dignitatis Humanae* 11–12 with many citations of patristic and magisterial texts.
50   See *ST* II-II, q. 10, a. 8.
51   Pius VI, *Quod Aliquantum*, in *Brefs et instructions de notre Saint Père le Pape Pie VI*, vol. 1 (Rome, 1797), 132; cf. Rhonheimer, "Benedict XVI's Hermeneutic," 1036.

there is only one Baptism, baptized Protestants are subject to the jurisdiction of the Catholic Church.[52] As Pink points out, one can of course question the prudence and morality of the inquisitorial methods of applying this teaching, but such questioning need not necessarily entail a rejection of the teaching itself.[53]

The idea that persons should be coerced not only in their external actions but even in the very act of faith itself is unusual today. Pink shows that the influence of the philosophies of Hobbes and Locke have had an important role in making such an idea seem strange. Hobbes and Locke argue that such coercion ought to be forbidden *de jure* because it is impossible *de facto*.[54] But according to scholastic philosophy legal coercion has a pedagogical function,[55] and therefore it can help persons to accept the truth. Since Baptism infuses the virtue of faith, coercion need not necessarily lead to hypocrisy. Coercion can force the baptized to examine the evidence of the faith.

In exercising coercion the Church has historically made use of the right to use the temporal power as an instrument or organ (secular arm). This does not, however, imply that the temporal power was seen as having a native jurisdiction in religious matters. Insofar as the temporal power acts as an instrument of the Church it is precisely *not* acting on its native authority. In the nineteenth century this distinction was very emphatically taught by Pope Leo XIII:

> The Almighty, therefore, has given the charge of the human race to two powers, the ecclesiastical and the civil, the one being set over divine, and the other over human, things.... Whatever, therefore in things human is of a sacred character, whatever belongs either of its own nature or by reason of the end to which it is referred, to the salvation of souls, or to the worship of God, is subject to the power and judgment of the Church. Whatever is to be ranged under the civil and political order is rightly subject to the civil authority.[56]

---

52 See Pink, "Suárez and Bellarmine," 188.
53 Pink, "What is the Catholic Doctrine," 26; cf. E. Waldstein, "Tarnishing the Splendor of Truth."
54 Pink, "What is the Catholic Doctrine," 6.
55 See Pink, "What is the Catholic Doctrine," 6–9; cf. Michel Therrien, "Law, Liberty, and Virtue: A Thomistic Defense for the Pedagogical Character of Law," Dissertation, Fribourg, 2007.
56 Pope Leo XIII, *Immortale Dei*, in *Acta Sancta Sedis* 18 (1885): 11, 14.

Thus the temporal power has *no authority whatsoever* in religious matters. Nevertheless, this does not exclude the temporal power acting as an agent of the Church in such matters.

In the light of this distinction, Pink can show the continuity of *Dignitatis Humanae* with previous teaching. For previous teaching would agree that in religion everyone should be "immune from coercion on the part of individuals or of social groups and of any human power" (*Dignitatis Humanae* § 2) if "human power" is taken to mean worldly or temporal power. Thus *Dignitatis Humanae* § 3 is entirely traditional when it teaches that "religious acts" "transcend by their very nature the order of *terrestrial* and *temporal* affairs," and that the state would "transgress the limits set to its power," were it to command or forbid such acts.[57]

But such a statement about the limits of the authority of the temporal power in no way restricts the authority of the Church. For *Dignitatis Humanae* explicitly states that it is treating of "immunity from coercion in civil society" and leaving untouched traditional teaching on duties toward the Church, and therefore by implication the rights of the Church.[58] So on Pink's reading, *Dignitatis Humanae* is treating *only* of the state's own task and authority derived from natural law, *not* on any additional task that it might receive as agent of the Church. It is simply *not treating* of the authority of the Church to coerce the baptized even with the assistance of the secular arm. Pink sees this reading confirmed in the fact that a number of council fathers wanted a passage inserted affirming "as compatible with religious liberty that the Church use sanctions to impose her doctrine and discipline on those subject to her,"[59] but the Conciliar Commission rejected this request for the following reason: "This (proposal) is not admitted, since ecclesial obligation or right is not treated here, nor is the question of freedom within the Church herself."[60]

But, Pink argues, by not mentioning the right of the Church to make use of the state as secular arm, *Dignitatis Humanae* changes

---

57 See Pink, "What is the Catholic Doctrine," 45 and passim.
58 *Dignitatis Humanae* 1.
59 Pink, "What is the Catholic Doctrine," 34.
60 *Acta Synodalia Sacrosancti Concilii Oecumenici Vaticani II* (Rome, 1970–1980), vol. 4, pars 6, 763; trans. following Pink, "What is the Catholic Doctrine" 34.

Church policy. That is, the Church no longer makes use of that right; she no longer authorizes the temporal power to act as her agent:

> the Church's present and evident refusal to license such coercion by states on her authority... is... made evident by *Dignitatis Humanae* in itself; by the Church's subsequent diplomatic policy toward states, which now excludes state coercion to support Catholicism; and by the absence from the 1983 *Code of Canon Law* of the requirement on the state to act as a coercive agent that the 1917 *Code* had contained.... *Dignitatis Humanae* constitutes a great reform in the policy of the Catholic Church. For the first time since late antiquity, the state is no longer directed to act as the Church's agent to enforce and defend her jurisdiction.[61]

This is a change not in doctrinal principles, but in their disciplinary application to particular historical circumstances. Thus Pink does indeed use a "hermeneutic of reform"—he shows continuity at the level of principles, but discontinuity at the level of application to circumstances.

Pink's position can thus be summarized as follows:

- There is a right to religious liberty.
- This right means that no worldly power has the authority to coerce persons to religious acts, or to prevent them from practicing religion within the limits of public order.
- The Church as the spiritual power has the authority to coerce the baptized (and only the baptized) to keep their baptismal vows.
- For this purpose the Church can make use of temporal power as an instrument or agent.
- *Dignitatis Humanae* treats of religious freedom only in relation to the temporal power.
- Practically *Dignitatis Humanae* represents a change in Church policy, since the Church no longer makes use of her right to use the temporal power as an instrument.

I consider Pink's case very strong indeed, but it is to be expected that there will be opposition to it from those who have expounded other interpretations. Thus Martin Rhonheimer has defended his own interpretation against Pink. According to Rhonheimer the

---

61 Pink, "Conscience and Coercion."

traditional teaching, according to which the Church can make use of the temporal power as its instrument for coercing the baptized in religious matters, has "no roots in Scripture, nor in the Apostolic Tradition or in the Fathers,"[62] and was therefore reformable, and was in fact "definitively and with sound theological reasons abandoned by Vatican II."[63] Rhonheimer tries to establish this by an appeal to the history of Church-state relations, which he claims Pink "disregards."[64] In order to defend Pink against Rhonheimer I will now give a brief summary of the relations between the Church and the temporal power. I will base this summary in large part on Rhonheimer's own research,[65] but will draw conclusions very different from his.

III. Spiritual and Temporal Power: A Glance at History

The ancient world did not distinguish between spiritual and worldly power. In the Greek city-states and later in Rome, the worship of the gods was an important element of political or imperial life, and was therefore considered to fall under political or imperial authority. Aristotle considers worship to be an essential function of the *polis*: "Fifthly, or rather first, there must be a care of religion, which is commonly called worship."[66] Although the Romans distinguished between *res divina* and *res publica*, these two were not conceived of as distinct powers with distinct ends;[67] the function of divine worship was largely to secure political/imperial success.[68] Ancient Israel reversed this order; the worship of God is the primary thing to which all of life is subordinated. But here too there was no distinction between spiritual and temporal power.[69]

62 Rhonheimer, "*Dignitatis Humanae*—Not a Mere Question," 447.
63 Ibid.
64 Ibid.
65 As presented above all in the first part of *Christentum und säkularer Staat*.
66 Aristotle, *Politics* VII,8 (1328b13), trans. Benjamin Jowett.
67 See Itai Gradel, *Emperor Worship and Roman Religion* (Oxford: Oxford University Press, 2002), 4–6.
68 See Numa Denis Fustel de Coulange's enduring nineteenth-century classic, *The Ancient City: A Study on the Religion, Laws, and Institutions of Greece and Rome*, trans. Willard Small (Boston: Lee and Shepard, 1877).
69 See Rémi Brague, *The Law of God: The Philosophical History of an Idea*, trans. Lydia G. Cochrane (Chicago: University of Chicago Press, 2007), ch. 4.

The distinction between spiritual and temporal or worldly power was an innovation of Christianity. And, as Rhonheimer argues, it was able to make this distinction because Christianity is a religion of redemption.[70] Christianity did not deny the legitimacy of the existing political order, it recognized therein an authority founded in God's creation and granted by His providence. But like any part of creation it saw the political as wounded by sin and in need of healing in the present, and, in the eschatological future, of elevation, fulfillment, and transcendence by a higher form of communal life. The order of creation was seen as a good, but temporary and preliminary order—a sign of a yet better order to come. The Lord's famous dictum according to which one must render unto Caesar the things that are Caesar's, but unto God the things that are God's (Mt 22:21) did not at all conform to expectations about the Messiah. The Messiah was expected to end Roman rule and reestablish the rule of God. But Jesus does not immediately destroy the existing order; instead He plants the kingdom of God as a seed that is to grow in the midst of the existing order. Only at His triumphant return at the end of time will He replace earthly powers with the New Jerusalem.

In the time between the Ascension and the Second Coming of the Lord, Christians have to care both for the "temporal"—that is, passing, preliminary—goods, and for the imperishable eternal goods of the kingdom of God. Very soon a distinction was made within the Church herself between the Apostles whose responsibility was primarily for the ministry of the word of God, and the deacons who had the duty of caring for temporal matters (see Acts 6).

The early Christians had a somewhat ambivalent attitude toward the power of the Roman emperor. On the one hand his authority is recognized as given by God for the punishment of evildoers (cf. Romans 13:1-8) and the securing of a peace that makes it easier for Christians to live a pious life and preach the Gospel (cf. 1 Tim 2:1-4).[71] On the other hand, the Book of Revelation portrays Rome as a new Babylon that unjustly sheds the blood

---

70   Rhonheimer, *Christentum und säkularer Staat*, 36-44.
71   Cf. Rhonheimer, 40-44.

Religious Liberty

of the martyrs. The early Church Fathers demanded an end of persecution and a granting of religious freedom to Christians.[72]

After Constantine ended the persecution of Christians, Christianity was at risk of being instrumentalized, of being given the function of securing the safety of the empire that once belonged to the pagan gods. The Church Fathers, especially St Ambrose and St Athanasius, protested against this attempt to subordinate the Church to worldly power.[73] They insisted on two principles: first, "the primacy of the spiritual over the earthly/worldly affairs," and second, "the ordering of all earthly/worldly affairs to the heavenly and eternal.[74] The Fathers understood these principles to allow to the temporal power a role in helping to preserve the true faith. Thus the imperial power was used to suppress the Arian heresy.[75] Rhonheimer considers the "enthusiasm" with which the Fathers saw worldly power as an instrument of orthodoxy problematic and "astonishing," but his astonishment rests on a *petitio principii*.[76] It is only because Rhonheimer first interprets the direct New Testament derivation of worldly power from God as "sovereignty" and "independence of religious claims to ordering authority"[77] that the patristic willingness to make use of the state as an instrument for the suppression of heresy seems wrong to him. But one should rather take the patristic application of New Testament principles as an authoritative guide to the meaning of those principles.

The sack of Rome by the Visigoths in 410 seemed to many Romans to be a refutation of Christianity. Clearly Christianity was not able fulfill the classic function of religion: preserving the city from catastrophe. St Augustine answered this argument in his great work *The City of God*. The true religion does not exist for the sake of securing the transitory order of this world, but rather for the sake of building up the City of God, which will only be fully realized after the passing of this world. The City of God is founded on a love of God that leads its citizens to contempt for

---

72 See Rhonheimer, 42–43.
73 See Rhonheimer, 49.
74 Rhonheimer, 46: "der Primat des Spirituellen über das Irdisch-Weltliche...die Hinordnung alles Irdisch-Weltliche auf das Himmlische und Ewige."
75 See Rhonheimer, 49, 51.
76 Rhonheimer, 49.
77 Rhonheimer, 41.

themselves, counting all earthly things as worthless.[78] Thus God allows "temporal" catastrophes to disturb the reign of Christian rulers, in this way teaching all not to serve God for the sake of worldly advantages (*Civ. Dei* V,25). Augustine argues that temporal goods ought to be ordered to eternal ones (*Civ. Dei* XIX,17), but that this ordering will never be achieved entirely harmoniously till the second coming of the Lord. For, there is a second city here on earth in addition to the city of God—the *civitas terrena*, the earthly city. This city is founded on a love of self to the contempt of God (*Civ. Dei* XIV,28). And these two cities are in conflict. Although both cities are (for different reasons) interested in conserving temporal peace, so that a limited cooperation between them in temporal matters is possible (*Civ. Dei* XIX,17), nevertheless, this cannot be taken as allowing for a neutral temporal realm, as Rhonheimer would have it;[79] the earthly city is *always* opposed to true religion.[80] Thus Augustine argues that it is fitting for temporal things to be ordered by Christian rulers.[81] And these rulers ought not to be neutral in religious matters. Rather they should promote the true religion and even punish heretics.[82] Justice consists in giving each his own; thus no society is just that does not give God the worship due to Him (*Civ. Dei* XIX,21).[83]

Since Christian rulers must see to it that society gives God His due, it might seem that they must of themselves have a certain authority in spiritual matters, that is, an episcopal authority. But this idea was rejected by the Church. In 494 Pope St Gelasius I taught that the royal power and priestly authority are two distinct principles, both instituted by God, and that the subordination of

---

78 Cf. *De Civitate Dei* XIV,28; hereafter cited parenthetically as *Civ. Dei*.
79 Rhonheimer, *Christentum und säkularer Staat*, 55.
80 See Rowland, "Augustinian and Thomist Engagements with the World," especially 446–49; E. J. Hutchinson, "Whose Augustine? Which Augustinianism?," *The Calvinist International*, August 2014: http://calvinistinternational.com/2014/08/14/whose-augustine-augustinianism; Donald X. Burt, *Friendship and Society: An Introduction to Augustine's Practical Philosophy* (Grand Rapids: Eerdmans, 2009), 200–27.
81 See Rowland, "Augustinian and Thomist Engagements," 448.
82 Rowland, "Augustinian and Thomist Engagements," 448–49; Burt, *Friendship and Society*, 200–27.
83 "Hence, when a man does not serve God, what justice can we ascribe to him...? And if there is no justice in such an individual, certainly there can be none in a community composed of such persons" (trans. Marcus Dodds).

temporal to spiritual good implies that the temporal rulers must be subject to the priestly authority in matters that concern eternal salvation.[84]

But Christian rulers both in the Byzantine Empire, and, after the *translatio imperii* of 800, in the Holy Roman Empire, did not always accept the Gelasian teaching. In the West a conflict between pope and emperor developed that came to a head in the High Middle Ages in the Investiture Controversy. The popes from St Gregory VII to Boniface VIII developed previous teaching on the relation of the two powers, and taught that the subordination of the temporal under the spiritual ought to be preserved by a *juridical* subordination of worldly under priestly authority. Priestly authority is seen not just as *auctoritas*, but as a genuine *potestas*, a coercive power. Rhonheimer argues that calling the priestly authority *potestas* is contrary to the actual meaning of Gelasian dyarchy,[85] but one can also see it as a development of what was implicit in previous teaching. If one considers the very high degree of magisterial authority with which the *plenitudo potestas* of the pope was taught from St Gregory VII's *Dictatus Papae* (1075) to Boniface VIII's *Unam Sanctam* (1302), then it is simply not possible to reject this development as illegitimate.[86]

Unam Sanctam conceives of the *potestas* of the pope as a *direct* authority, at least when it is a question of using temporal power for directly spiritual purposes. In such matters the sword is drawn "at the will and sufferance of the priest."[87] But when it is a question of temporal matters that are only indirectly ordered to the spiritual, it is not clear whether the pope's power is direct or indirect (*potestas indirecta*). Giles of Rome, who gave an important theoretical defense of the claims of *Unam Sanctam*, argued that the pope's authority was direct even in such matters.[88] But since he goes on

---

84   Gelasius I, *Famuli Vestrae Pietatis*, https://sourcebooks.fordham.edu/source/gelasius1.asp.
85   Rhonheimer, *Christentum und säkularer Staat*, 75.
86   On the theological note of the teaching of *Unam Sanctam*, see Steven Wedgeworth, "Happy Anniversary *Unam Sanctam*," *The Calvinist International*, November 2013, http://calvinistinternational.com/2013/11/18/happy-anniversary-unam-sanctam.
87   Boniface VIII, *Unam Sanctam*, https://sourcebooks.fordham.edu/source/b8-unam.asp.
88   See, for example, *De ecclesiastica potestate*, II,6: "terrena ... potestas et secundum se et secundum sua, potestati ecclesiastice subdatur" (*Giles of Rome's "On Ecclesiastical Power"*).

to argue that this authority while direct is not "immediate and executory,"[89] his theory is basically indistinguishable from the theory of *potestas indirecta,* according to which the Church can only intervene in temporal affairs *ratione peccati,* that is, in order to forbid or punish sin. Giles explains the relation of spiritual to temporal by a number of analogies, including the analogy of soul and body. Just as the body has its own needs (food, drink, etc.), but exists finally for the sake of the soul and is thus subject to the soul, so temporal things have their own necessities but are finally for the sake of spiritual things, and temporal rulers must thus be subject to the pope, the supreme spiritual ruler.[90]

The claims of the popes in the High Middle Ages were supported by various reform movements in the Church such as the Cluniacs, Cistercians, Norbertines, and Dominicans. All of these movements were concerned with emphasizing the primacy of the spiritual and combating worldliness within the Church.[91]

Especially from the fourteenth century onwards, new powers opposed themselves to the papal claims—the territorial rulers, who were slowly developing the beginnings of nation-states. With lamentable myopia the popes had at first supported the territorial rulers as a balance to the power of the emperor, but soon these rulers proved themselves more dangerous enemies than the emperor. King Philip the Fair of France, for example, was able to prevail in his struggles with Pope Boniface VIII. After the death of Boniface and his short-lived successor, Pope Clement V, began the "Babylonian Captivity" of the popes in Avignon.[92] After the popes returned to Rome, they were politically integrated into the newly revived system of Italian city-states—in a manner practically incompatible with the two sword theory of the High Middle Ages.[93]

While the great Church reform movements of the High Middle Ages, from the Cluniacs to the Dominicans, were supporters of the papacy (excepting the Albigensians and the antipapal wing

---

[89] *De ecclesiastica potestate,* III.

[90] *De ecclesiastica potestate,* I,7.

[91] See Christopher Dawson, *The Formation of Christendom* (San Francisco: Ignatius Press, 2008 [1965]), 216–27; *The Dividing of Christendom* (San Francisco: Ignatius Press, 2008 [1965]), 30, 38.

[92] Dawson, *The Dividing,* 41–43.

[93] Dawson, *The Dividing,* 53–56.

of the Franciscans), the reform movements of the Late Middle Ages and the Renaissance became increasingly antipapal.[94] This development reached a climax in the Protestant Reformation. The Reformers turned on the pope and allied themselves with the territorial rulers. The "Magisterial Reformation" of Luther and Calvin gave the Christian "magistrate," i.e., the territorial ruler, a competence in certain religious matters independent of the clergy. This autonomous competence of the magistracy was based on new theological principles that completely reconceived the relation of worldly and spiritual power.

Calvin (following Luther) distinguished sharply between an invisible kingdom in consciences of the elect, in which there was complete freedom from coercion and each believer was subjected to Christ, the only king and priest, without any intermediary, on the one hand, and, on the other, a visible external kingdom. The visible kingdom was concerned not only with "worldly" matters in the old sense, but also with external acts of religion. Calvin places *both* the magistrates *and* the preachers of the Word in the *external* kingdom.[95] The preachers are concerned with persuading people, whereas the magistrates are concerned with coercing their external actions, including their religious actions.[96]

The Reformers thus rejected the Catholic teaching defined as early as the Fourth Synod of Toledo according to which the Church has the right to coerce the baptized to keep the faith, since on their account no visible authority whatever can have any authority over conscience. Moreover, they see coercive authority over external acts of religion as belonging not to priests — which they don't think exist — nor even to preachers, but rather to the magistrates.

The Reformers' rejection of Catholic teaching on these points is rooted in a new theology of grace, or rather a rejection of the traditional distinction between grace and nature. The Catholic attitude toward "temporal" affairs is rooted in a view of nature as a *temporary* order of being, due to be perfected and in a sense

---

94 See Dawson, *The Dividing*, 30, 42–43.
95 See Steven Wedgeworth and Peter Escalante, "John Calvin and the Two Kingdoms," Part 2, *The Calvinist International*, May 2012, http://calvinistinternational.com/2012/05/29/calvin-2k-2.
96 Wedgeworth and Escalante, "John Calvin."

replaced by a better, permanent order, a super-nature to be established by grace. On the Catholic view the created natures of things are good. By sin they are wounded, but not destroyed. Christ comes to heal and reestablish nature. But not only to reestablish it the way it was before the Fall; Christ elevates nature, granting a better kind of being, a supernatural being. And in fact nature was always intended as a sign and preparation for the supernatural. So, for example, marriage is a communion of persons that flows from nature and is good. But in the second coming of Christ marriage is shown to have been only a temporary reality, a sign of the wedding of Christ and His bride the Church. Everything that was good in marriage will be present in a more eminent mode in the union of Christ and His bride, but natural marriage itself will be no more (cf. Mt 22:30). Nature is thus a shadow and image of the reality that is to come through grace. The natures of things are not destroyed by grace, but they are so transformed that much that belonged to them before is transcended and replaced by that of which it was the image. In the present time, though, both realities are present at once; the new reality of grace is present as a seed alongside the old reality of nature. Thus the Wedding of the Lamb is present as a seed in the Church's union with Christ in the Sacraments, but this union now exists alongside natural marriage. And natural marriage is now elevated by grace to be a sacrament—an effective sign of the perfect that is to come. But higher than sacramental marriage is consecrated virginity, because virginity is not merely a sign of the coming reality, but an anticipation of that reality—the consecrated virgin already lives the form of life that the blessed will have in Heaven (although she still lacks the perfect union of the beatific vision).

Calvin rejected the Catholic distinction between nature and the supernatural. On Calvin's account there is only nature. In the beginning nature was so perfect that man had true happiness, beatitude. But this perfection was possessed in an insecure mode; it could still be lost. And it was lost through sin. The grace of Christ restores the original perfection of man. The eschatological fulfillment is nothing more than the restoration in an unlosable mode of the very same beatitude that man already enjoyed in Eden. On Calvin's account, grace does *not* elevate nature to a supernatural level, and thus nature is *not* a temporary reality meant to serve as a sign of a better reality to come.[97] This is the reason for Calvin's rejection of Catholic teaching on the evangelical counsels of poverty, chastity, and obedience, which to him must seem an unwarranted rejection of God's good order of creation.[98] And this is the explanation of the (from a Catholic perspective) exaggerated value put on worldly affairs and "ordinary life" in Protestant culture.[99]

One of the main ideals of the reform movements of the High Middle Ages was *contemptus mundi* (contempt for the world), or *fuga saeculi* (flight from the world)—understood not only as contempt for the disorder of the fallen world and for the demonic powers and the *civitas terrena* over which they rule, but also as a healthy disregard for the passing goods of the preliminary order of things. This relative contempt for the preliminary corresponded to the demand that the temporal power be subject to the spiritual power. Thus St Bernard of Clairvaux's *De Consideratione* already contains the two sword theory that Pope Boniface VIII was later to adopt.[100] But since the Reformers of the sixteenth century rejected the ideal of *contemptus mundi*, it makes sense that they demanded the autonomy of worldly rulers.[101] The Catholic dualism of nature and grace corresponds to an integralist vision of the relation of spiritual and worldly power, whereas the Protestant monism of nature corresponds to an independence of worldly power from clerical authority.

The Reformation led at first to the formation of so-called "confessional states." Calvinist confessional states were famed for moral rigorism. Since they did not recognize life according to the Evangelical Counsels as a *status perfectionis*, they expected moral perfection from everyone. The great success of Calvinist discipline in forming prosperous and militarily powerful societies led to their imitation in Catholic countries. The confessional states quickly

97 See Peter Escalante, "Two Ends or Two Kingdoms?," *The Calvinist International*, April 2013, http://calvinistinternational.com/2013/04/08/two-ends-or-two-kingdoms.
98 See Escalante, "Two Ends."
99 See Charles Taylor, *Sources of the Self* (Cambridge, MA: Harvard University Press, 1989), Part III: "The Affirmation of Ordinary Life."
100 See Rhonheimer, *Christentum und säkularer Staat*, 76–78.
101 See Escalante, "Two Ends."

developed into the first sovereign territorial states in the modern sense. Often religion was practically degraded to a means of civil discipline.[102] Paradoxically this contributed to the secularization of the Western world.[103] At first in the Netherlands, and then at the end of the eighteenth century in North America, states were formed that claimed to be neutral in religious matters. They wanted to limit themselves to the preservation of outward peace, leaving each person to worship whatsoever he pleased so long as he could agree on common rules of commercial life and public security with everyone else.[104]

The complete secularization of the state was not at all the intention of the Reformers. But it would not have been possible without their distinction between the visible and the invisible kingdom, their exaltation of the freedom of conscience, and their exaggerated regard for natural goods. These positions were conditions for the development of the European Enlightenment. The Enlightenment began in the sixteenth century with a new ideal of progress through scientific/technological domination of nature. As Pope Benedict XVI has emphasized, this ideal was from the beginning a secularization of Christian hope:

> Up to that time, the recovery of what man had lost through the expulsion from Paradise was expected from faith in Jesus Christ: herein lay "redemption." Now, this "redemption," the restoration of the lost "Paradise" is no longer expected from faith, but from the newly discovered link between science and praxis. It is not that faith is simply denied; rather it is displaced onto another level—that of purely private and otherworldly affairs—and at the same time it becomes somehow irrelevant for the world.[105]

This ideology came to see nature as an inert mechanistic mass without inner teleology, a mere object for arbitrary manipulation by human power. In the political realm it led to a thorough secularization of public life. In Protestant countries this development was relatively peaceful. But in Catholic countries it involved a passionate

102 Taylor, *A Secular Age*, chapter 2: "The Rise of the Disciplinary Society."
103 See Brad Gregory, *The Unintended Reformation: How a Religious Revolution Secularized Society* (Cambridge, MA: Belknap Press of Harvard University Press, 2012).
104 Gregory, *Unintended Reformation*, 160–72.
105 Pope Benedict XVI, *Spe Salvi* 17.

struggle between the "enlightened" and the forces of "ignorance and superstition." The *philosophes* considered the Catholic Church to be an enemy of material progress because of her commitment to asceticism and *contemptus mundi*, and an enemy of freedom because she punished heretics and censored books. Thus in Catholic countries a passionate anticlericalism developed which had its first political success in the violent persecution of the Church in the French Revolution. In the nineteenth century anticlerical liberals and reactionary restorationists alternated in the governments of Europe. In the twentieth century, totalitarian, anticlerical regimes developed, whether they were communist and officially atheist as in Russia, or nationalist and neopagan as in Germany.[106]

In the Catholic Counter-Reformation, theologians such as Francisco Suárez and St Robert Bellarmine had responded to the claims of the confessional state with detailed expositions of the Catholic teaching, according to which the worldly power can act in religious matters only as an organ of the spiritual power.[107] But in the following centuries, in which the nation-states consolidated their monopoly on coercive power, this teaching came to be less and less understood. Although Pope Leo XIII returned to this teaching in the nineteenth century, teaching it authoritatively in the encyclical *Immortale Dei*,[108] his teaching was often misunderstood, so that many nineteenth-century Catholics — including such luminaries as Bishop Ketteler of Mainz — did not think that the Church had true coercive authority of her own.[109] Thus Thomas Pink summarizes the situation immediately before Vatican II as follows:

> And so we arrive at the view of religious coercion current before the Second Vatican Council, one that still shapes much post-conciliar "traditionalist" opinion. Religious coercion is really the business of the state. There is no question of the state coercing belief or private practice. But the state must publicly recognize the Catholic faith as true and restrict the public presence of other

---

106 See Michael Burleigh, *Earthly Powers: The Clash of Religion and Politics in Europe from the French Revolution to the Great War* (New York: Harper Perennial, 2007); *Sacred Causes: The Clash of Religion and Politics, from the Great War to the War on Terror* (New York: HarperCollins, 2007).
107 See Pink, "Suárez and Bellarmine"; cf. Part II above.
108 See Part II above.
109 See Pink, "Conscience and Coercion."

religions. That behind all this state activity lay another authority, the Church, truly coercive in her own right — whose authority in the case of the baptized extended to coercing even private religious belief and practice — tended to be forgotten.[110]

IV. The Concerns of the Conciliar Theologians

Dignitatis Humanae begins with an optimistic reading of one of the signs of the times: "A sense of the dignity of the human person has been impressing itself more and more deeply on the consciousness of contemporary man."[111] A footnote referring to Pope Pius XII's famous Christmas Radio Message of 1944 shows that the Council fathers had a very specific development in mind — a change that had come about through the experience of the totalitarian dictatorships of the twentieth century. This experience seemed to make a *rapprochement* between the Church and modernity possible: suddenly it seemed that the enmity between the Church and modernity that had been so pronounced since the Enlightenment might come to an end. At the beginning of the twentieth century much of public opinion still considered the Church to be an enemy of progress and freedom, but after the World Wars opinion had shifted, and many saw the Church as a moral beacon that had stood strong against irrational slaughter and destructive ideology. In Western Europe especially, the experience of a totalitarianism that had wanted to entirely subordinate the human person to this-worldly goals made many think that it was necessary to recover a sense of the dignity of the human person as a creation of God with a transcendent destiny. Within the Church many thought that this new atmosphere presented a chance to reconvert the world to Christianity.[112]

Although the 1950s did not quite see the mass conversions that some expected, nevertheless the Church enjoyed unusual prestige. In many parts of Western Europe, Christian social-democratic parties came to power. Many of these were influenced by the thought of the French philosopher and convert Jacques Maritain.[113]

110 Pink, "Conscience and Coercion."
111 *Dignitatis Humanae* 1.
112 See Edmund Waldstein, "The Papacy Against the False Gospel of Progress," *Sancrucensis*, February 22, 2013.
113 See Alan Fimister, *Robert Schuman: Neo-Scholastic Humanism and the Reunification of Europe* (Brussels: Peter Lang, 2008).

Maritain had recognized the opportunity for an antitotalitarian reaction quite early. In the 1920s he had been an integralist and a supporter of *Action Française*,[114] but in the '30s he promoted a democratic philosophy based on respect for the dignity of man as an image of God. In *Integral Humanism* (1936) he argued for a new form of the relation of Church and state suitable to the modern age. He tried to show that the principle of the distinction between spiritual and worldly power, and the primacy of the former, could be realized in different ways at different times. In the Middle Ages the Church's exercise of *potestas indirecta* over the worldly power was appropriate to the stage of development mankind had then reached. But with mankind at its current stage of development it would be better for the Church to give up the exercise of such a *potestas*, and exert only a moral influence on political life.[115] Maritain's theory was meant to enable him to propose a new model of Church-state relations without rejecting traditional teaching.

In the United States of America a somewhat analogous development was taking place. In the nineteenth and early twentieth centuries American Catholics had been considered un-American, since their European political theology seemed irreconcilable with the principles of the American Republic. In the 1950s the Jesuit John Courtney Murray tried to prove the compatibility of Catholicism and American political philosophy. Murray acted as advisor to the Catholic presidential candidate John F. Kennedy. Kennedy's election to the presidency in 1960 seemed to Murray and many American Catholics to represent the acceptance of such compatibility on the part of the American public.[116]

Murray argued for an even stricter separation of Church and state than Maritain. Murray founds this separation on a strict distinction between nature and grace—the state as a community rooted in natural law has a different end from the Church, the Church's end being given by grace. As the Murray scholar Leon Hooper, S.J., put it, in a passage discussed earlier in chapter 6:

---

114 Fimister, *Robert Schuman*, 106–8.
115 See Pink, "Jacques Maritain"; Fimister, *Robert Schuman*, 113–25.
116 See Thomas W. O'Brien, *John Courtney Murray in a Cold War Context* (Lanham, MD: University Press of America, 2004), 65–66, 100, and passim.

> [In] this world there are two sources of moral authority. Early on these were for Murray the state and the church, or, more generally, the natural law and the revealed law. Later they became civil societies and religious communities, or the secular and the sacred. Each of the two orders is differently based (in creation and redemption) and is directed toward different ends (civic friendship and eternal beatitude). Each can legitimately claim its own autonomy.[117]

From these principles Murray argues for a consistent neutrality of the state in religious matters.[118]

Against the background of the developments exemplified by Maritain and Murray, one can understand the widespread opinion in the Church in the run-up to the Second Vatican Council that the Church had to reformulate her teachings in a manner suitable to the modern age in order to take the great opportunity the times offered her. In one of his last speeches as pope, Pope Benedict XVI recalled the atmosphere at the time of the beginning of the Council with the following words:

> There was an incredible sense of expectation.... [W]e knew that the relationship between the Church and the modern period, right from the outset, had been slightly fraught, beginning with the Church's error in the case of Galileo Galilei; we were looking to correct this mistaken start and to rediscover the union between the Church and the best forces of the world, so as to open up humanity's future, to open up true progress.[119]

The question of the Church's stance towards progress was a central question of the Council. *The Pastoral Constitution on the Church in the Modern World, Gaudium et Spes*, addressed this problem with a certain ambivalence. Consider the following passages:

> Sacred Scripture teaches the human family what the experience of the ages confirms: that while human progress is a great advantage

---

117 Leon Hooper, General Introduction to *John Courtney Murray, Religious Liberty: Catholic Struggles with Pluralism*, ed. Leon Hooper (Louisville, KY: Westminster/John Knox Press, 1993), 25; citation following Schindler, *Heart of the World*, 77.

118 See Schindler, *Heart of the World*, ch. 1.

119 Pope Benedict XVI, "*E' per me un dono*," Address to Parish Priests and the Clergy of Rome, February 14, 2013: http://www.vatican.va/holy_father/benedict_xvi/speeches/2013/february/documents/hf_ben-xvi_spe_20130214_clero-roma_en.html.

Religious Liberty

to man, it brings with it a strong temptation.... That is why Christ's Church, trusting in the design of the Creator, acknowledges that human progress can serve man's true happiness, yet she cannot help echoing the Apostle's warning: "Be not conformed to this world" (Rom 12:2). Here by the world is meant that spirit of vanity and malice which transforms into an instrument of sin those human energies intended for the service of God and man.... While earthly progress must be carefully distinguished from the growth of Christ's kingdom, to the extent that the former can contribute to the better ordering of human society, it is of vital concern to the kingdom of God.[120]

Gaudium et Spes was trying to strike a delicate balance. It was trying, as it were, to subvert the Enlightenment idea of progress, to use the language of progress but give it a new meaning.

The danger here was that the opposite would happen: that Enlightenment ideas would subvert the teachings of the Church, making of them a metaphor for innerworldly progress. This was the danger of "modernism," which had been condemned as far back as 1907. In order to avoid this danger it was necessary to give an exact account of the relation of nature and grace. The French conciliar theologian Henri de Lubac, S.J., one of the main authors of *Gaudium et Spes*, tried to develop the implications of the scholastic principle *gratia non destruit naturam, sed eam supponit et perficit et elevat* (grace does not destroy nature, but presupposes, perfects, and elevates it). He argued that the relative disregard for natural goods in the Catholic *contemptus mundi* does not imply a reduction or a poisoning of human culture, but on the contrary allows for a truly noble development of culture in view of the coming elevation and sublation of human nature.[121]

In the aftermath of the Council, in his preface to a German translation of *Augustinisme et théologie moderne*, de Lubac complained of a "rising tide of immanentism" that was trying to "dissolve the

---

120 *Gaudium et Spes* 37; 39.
121 Cf. Pope Benedict XVI, Address to Representatives from the World of Culture, Collège des Bernardins, Paris, September 12, 2008: http://www.vatican.va/holy_father/benedict_xvi/speeches/2008/september/documents/hf_ben-xvi_spe_20080912_parigi-cultura_en.html; cf. idem, *Spe Salvi* 13–15, noting the references to de Lubac in 13–14.

Church into the world,"[122] and against which de Lubac wanted to preserve the distinction between nature and grace. Before and during the Council, however, he saw the danger as coming primarily from the other direction—from those who made that distinction too sharp, separating nature and grace too much.[123] This is the problem that we saw in John Courtney Murray. While de Lubac recognized this problem clearly, recent work by theologians such as Steven Long suggests that he misidentified its roots. De Lubac argued that the problem lay in the idea of "pure nature" ordered to a natural end intelligible in abstraction from grace. But Long has convincingly argued that the real problem lies in a conception of nature that is not theonomic enough, a conception that makes nature appear as a closed system indifferent toward the divine. De Lubac's misidentification of the root of the problem leads him to postulate a natural desire for a supernatural end, an idea that tends towards a monism of grace.[124]

As we saw in Calvin's case, a monistic view of the relation of nature and grace leads to exaggeratedly dualistic view of the relation of Church and state, and so it is no surprise that de Lubac's slight tendency toward a monism of grace leads him to exaggerate the autonomy of the state. Thus already in 1932 de Lubac denied that the state ought to be juridically subordinated to the Church, arguing that just as grace transforms nature from within, the Church should inspire the state through the hearts of its citizens, but without giving it external commands:

> The law of the relations between nature and grace, in its generality, is everywhere the same. It is from within that grace seizes nature, and, far from diminishing nature, raises it up, in order to make it serve its (grace's) own ends. It is from within that faith transforms reason, that the Church influences the state. As

---

122 Henri de Lubac, *Die Freiheit Gnade*, I. *Das Erbe Augustins*, trans. Hans Urs von Balthasar (Einsiedeln: Johannes Verlag, 1971), Vorwort des Verfassers zur deutschen Ausgabe, 9-11.

123 De Lubac, *Das Erbe Augustins*, 7-8.

124 See Steven A. Long, *Natura Pura: On the Recovery of Nature in the Doctrine of Grace* (New York: Fordham University Press, 2010). While I agree with Long's main thesis, I think that he exaggerates certain points. See Edmund Waldstein, "De Lubac and His Critics Make the Same Error."

the messenger of Christ, the Church is not the guardian of the state; on the contrary she ennobles the state, inspiring it to be a Christian state and thereby more human.[125]

De Lubac thus went further than Maritain, whose disciple Charles Journet he cites unfavorably, since de Lubac considers a *potestas indirecta* of the Church over temporal affairs illegitimate at all times.[126]

In the debates on *Dignitatis Humanae*, old-fashioned traditionalists such as Cardinal Siri of Genoa were on one side, and various proponents of a new approach were on the other. But the proponents of a new approach had very different conceptions of what that approach should look like. Jacques Maritain's approach had many influential proponents including Pope Paul VI himself, who had translated Maritain's *Integral Humanism* into Italian,[127] and Charles Cardinal Journet, Maritain's favorite student.[128] Fr John Courtney Murray was himself involved in drafting *Dignitatis Humanae* as a peritus, and his theory was promoted by the American bishops.[129] Henri de Lubac was also involved as a *peritus*, and his concerns were shared by several bishops including de Lubac's friend the then Archbishop of Krakow, Karol Wojtyła.[130]

The supporters of Maritain and de Lubac were united in thinking that an "Americanist" dualism such as that promoted by Murray was inadequate. They wanted the text to argue from the duty of man toward the truth, an approach that Murray thought incoherent.[131] But Maritainians and de Lubacians could agree neither on de Lubac's rejection of *potestas indirecta* nor on Maritain's theory of different epochs. The solution to which they came was simply to bracket the question of the relation of Church and state, and

---

125   Henri de Lubac, "Le Pouvoir de l'église en matière temporelle," *Revue de Sciences Religieuses* 12 (1932): 329–54, at 343–44, citation and translation following Schindler, *Heart of the World*, 78.

126   See Bryan C. Hollon, *Everything is Sacred: Spiritual Exegesis in the Political Theology of Henri de Lubac* (Cambridge: James Clarke, 2009), 41–46.

127   Fimister, *Robert Schuman*, 101.

128   See Pink, "Jacques Maritain."

129   See O'Brien, *John Courtney Murray*, 100–104.

130   See Massimo Serretti, "I due amici che fecero la 'rivoluzione' del Concilio Vaticano II," in *IlSussidiario*, October 12, 2012, www.ilsussidiario.net/News/Cultura/2012/10/12/LA-STORIA-I-due-amici-che-fecero-la-rivoluzione-del-Concilio-Vaticano-II/328529.

131   Schindler, *Heart of the World*, 61.

simply to treat of religious liberty in relation to the state's native powers, showing how such liberty is founded in the dignity of man's transcendent end. This solution, probably suggested by Cardinal Journet,[132] is expressed above all in the following passage of *Dignitatis Humanae* §1 that I have already quoted:

> Religious freedom...which men demand as necessary to fulfill their duty to worship God, has to do with immunity from coercion in civil society. Therefore it leaves untouched traditional Catholic doctrine on the moral duty of men and societies toward the true religion and toward the one Church of Christ.

This solution enabled the postconciliar Church to engage in an energetic defense of religious liberty around the globe without giving up the continuity of her teaching. But since *Dignitatis Humanae* did not explain its solution clearly enough to avoid the *impression* of discontinuity, it contributed to a crisis of authority in postconciliar theology.[133]

---

132   See Pink, "Jacques Maritain."
133   See John Conley, "Religious Freedom as Catholic Crisis," in *The Human Person and a Culture of Freedom*, ed. Peter A. Pagan Aguiar and Terese Auer (Washington, DC: American Maritain Association/CUA Press, 2009), 226–41.

19

Vatican II and Crisis in the Theology of Baptism

Thomas Pink

1. Vatican II and Theological Crisis in the Church

Leo XIII's magisterial teaching in *Immortale Dei* is clear. The gospel requires that the state recognize the truth of Catholicism and unite to the Church in a single Christian community as body to the Church's soul, legally privileging Catholicism as the true religion.[1] This magisterial teaching is now generally rejected within the Church—not in opposing magisterial teaching but through what I shall refer to as "official theology." Official statements that do not themselves carry any magisterial authority—that come from office-holders within the Church but which merely express a prevailing theological opinion—constantly suggest, against Leo XIII, that the true ideal is for the state to be separate from the Church and to remain effectively neutral in matters of religion.

We have then a conflict between magisterial teaching and official theology—between what the formal teaching of the Church obliges us to believe, and prevailing theological opinion in official circles. But does this conflict, about this particular issue, really matter? Since there is little actual prospect of the kind of Church-state unity that Leo XIII required, it is tempting to think that the issue of the desirability of such a unity is no more than academic. But that would be a mistake. This conflict between magisterial teaching and

---

1 See especially *Immortale Dei* 13–14: "The Almighty, therefore, has given the charge of the human race to two coercive authorities [*potestates*], the ecclesiastical and the civil, the one being set over divine, and the other over human, things... There must, accordingly, exist between these two authorities a certain orderly connection, which may be compared to the union of the soul and body in man."

current official theology about Church and state is not isolated or without significance. It is one central expression of a wider crisis of erroneous official theology within the modern Church. This is a revolution in the official theology of grace and baptism—and that involves at its root a deficient conception of the Fall. The new official theology does not just oppose magisterial teaching on Church and state, but on many other matters too—such as the very necessity of the sacraments for salvation.

This revolution in official theology is not obviously and explicitly taught by the magisterium at Vatican II, and does in fact involve clear conflict with magisterial teaching of that very Council. But the revolution is a crisis of the Second Vatican Council nonetheless. It arose in the period of the Council, and has been deepened by official actions, by and under Paul VI and his successors, that constantly invoke that very Council.

This revolution in the official theology of baptism is having dire consequences. It is sapping the Church's mission from within. It lies at the heart of the current crisis over *Amoris Laetitia* and the indissolubility of marriage. The *Amoris Laetitia* crisis is not isolated. It is an instance of a type—a crisis very much of the Second Vatican Council, and the revolutionary change in official theology following that Council. Until the deeply questionable nature of that new theology is clearly identified and understood, there will be more crises of this type; in other words, the underlying crisis of the Council will continue.

2. Official Theology

Many have debated whether Vatican II involves a crisis within magisterial teaching itself. Does *Dignitatis Humanae* teach magisterially in a way that conflicts with the earlier magisterium, such as that of *Quanta Cura* or *Immortale Dei*? I have argued that at least in respect of *Dignitatis Humanae*, Vatican II does not involve a crisis of that kind, in the very integrity of the magisterium itself, but it is not my intention to argue the matter further here.[2] Others

---

2 See especially my "The Interpretation of *Dignitatis Humanae*: A Reply to Martin Rhonheimer," *Nova et Vetera* Eng. ed. 11.1 (2013): 77–121 and "*Dignitatis Humanae*: Continuity after Leo XIII," in *Dignitatis Humanae Colloquium*, Dialogos Institute, vol. 1, ed. Thomas Crean OP and Alan Fimister (Dialogos Institute, 2017): 105–46.

claim that a crisis of magisterial teaching is occurring within the postconciliar period—such as between *Amoris Laetitia*, with the subsequent papal clarification of it in the *Acta Apostolicae Sedis*, and *Familiaris Consortio*. Now that may or may not be so. But I shall also not attempt to resolve the question of whether the postconciliar magisterium has been consistent.

My immediate subject here is rather different. For whether or not there has been a crisis within the magisterium itself, it is anyway overwhelmingly clear that Vatican II has been followed by a serious crisis of another kind—a crisis not of magisterial teaching, but of *official theology*, and of which *Amoris Laetitia* and the officially promoted theology surrounding it is certainly a part. Whether or not Vatican II or the period since has seen contradiction at the level of the magisterium, it has very definitely seen such contradiction at the level of what I shall term official theology.

What is official theology? The term "official theology" is not a current term of art among Catholic theologians; but we need it to pick out something that has always existed in the life of the Church, and which plays a very important role in the day to day life of Catholics. Official theology is the Church's theological account of herself and her mission where the provision of this account is official—it involves official bodies or persons—but does not of itself impose any obligation on our belief as Catholics. Official theology may convey magisterial teaching, or it may go beyond magisterial teaching. It may even, unfortunately, obscure or even contradict magisterial teaching. But official theology is not itself a further case of magisterial teaching.

The Church constantly produces official theology. It is an ever present and essential element in the Church's life. Nowadays its existence is especially clearly advertised, because there are in the modern Church official bodies that make theological statements in the Church's name, but which disavow any claim to be teaching magisterially in so doing. Such bodies include the International Theological Commission and—as we shall discuss—the Commission for Religious Relations with the Jews. But the phenomenon is far more widespread, and far older.

Vatican II and Crisis in the Theology of Baptism

The Church constantly has to explain herself, her teaching and her practices both to Catholics and to those outside the Church. And she has to be able to do so without ipso facto teaching magisterially—without the explanation provided of itself imposing an obligation to believe based on the Church's authority. This is especially important where policy has to be followed and explained in cases where the Church does not yet feel able to determine a question magisterially, or where the officials involved anyway lack the authority to teach magisterially. Official theology is communicated in the training of clergy, through seminary manuals and lectures. It can be found in what passes as usual in sermons, homilies, and ecclesially provided devotional literature. It can be found in all manner of official explanations of liturgy or pastoral practice. It can be found especially in what is *not* said. Official theology can reveal itself in silence—in what is not treated as of significance or comment in the Church's life, as well as what is.

Not all concerning faith and morals asserted even by popes and bishops is magisterial teaching. This must be so, otherwise (for example) it would have made no sense for Pope Francis recently to have determined that the conclusions of Synods of Bishops are henceforward to possess magisterial status, when they did not before, or for theologians to distinguish between those assertions made by a pope as a theologian, and those made by him as magisterial teaching. Much here remains theologically undecided. But magisterial teaching seems to be teaching that engages on the part of the faithful something more than a mere reason for them to believe what is asserted. Magisterial teaching does not simply provide reasons but imposes obligations—of fidelity of mind and belief. These are obligations to believe with the assent of faith in the case of what is taught infallibly, or to give something distinct from the assent of faith, something termed in *Lumen Gentium* and in the 1983 Code a religious submission of intellect and will (*religiosum intellectus et voluntatis obsequium*) or of mind (*religiosum animi obsequium*), in other cases.

These obligations are given canonical form, in canons 750 to 754 in the section of the 1983 Code *De ecclesiae munere docendi*—*On the teaching function of the Church*. These canons leave much open to debate. What is a religious submission of intellect and will or of mind to fallible teaching if not the assent of faith, and is it always an obligation to belief, especially since what is taught could be false? Canons 750 to 754 have antecedents in the 1917 Code in canons 1323 to 1326 from the section *De magisterio ecclesiastico — On the magisterium of the Church*. But the language of the two Codes is importantly different. For example, the 1983 Code in canon 753 requires the faithful within their care to "adhere with a submission of mind" to the "authentic magisterium" even of fallible individual bishops or local assemblies of bishops. But the parallel canon 1326 of the 1917 Code does not impose such a requirement on the faithful explicitly, or indeed propose any other explicit obligation on the mind, but specifies simply that individual bishops and their local assemblies are "true teachers" of those within their care.

We can bypass these very important but difficult questions here, as one thing is clear. Insofar as it does impose a canonical obligation on the mind, magisterial teaching must be given by some bearer of authority, such as bishops, capable of imposing that obligation. And since it is accepted that assertions on faith and morals may be made by popes and bishops that are not magisterial, teaching that is magisterial must sufficiently manifest an intention to obligate the faithful. If canonical obligations are to be genuine obligations that really do bind morally, their imposition has to be signaled to those they seek thus to bind.

This being so, there is much theological assertion by officials of the Church that is not magisterial teaching in this sense — either because it does not clearly come from popes or bishops themselves, or because even if it does, it comes without a clear intention to teach magisterially so as to bind the intellect. All this non-magisterial assertion falls within the category of official theology. Some of this assertion ought to be believed because although the assertion of it does not itself count as a magisterial act — it might be a passage in a parish homily or newsletter — it does convey what is already magisterial teaching. But the distinction between magisterial teaching and official theology matters even in such cases. For having conveyed magisterial teaching, the very same document may go on to make claims that entirely lack magisterial backing, but without this being in any way clear to the ordinary faithful. The same homily or newsletter that faithfully communicates dogma about the Holy Spirit may contain assertions about what that same Holy Spirit has inspired that are not magisterial teaching at all, and that can perfectly well be false.

Just because magisterial teaching comes from an authority that is divinely provided for, and God is truth, we should expect magisterial teaching to exhibit a general level of consistency and truth. Nonetheless not all magisterial teaching is infallible; and how far consistency and truth can be relied on where the magisterial teaching is given fallibly is a deeply important question which the current state of the Church may be making the more pressing. But whatever may be true of magisterial teaching, official theology taken as a whole, as it has existed throughout history, is certainly not at all consistent with itself, and has over time included much falsehood. Official theology can perfectly well directly contradict not just other cases of official theology, but magisterial teaching itself or (at least) support pastoral strategies impossible to reconcile with magisterial teaching. This is certainly the case with much official theology since Vatican II. The effect of official theology that contradicts the magisterium can be disastrous. For it can detach ordinary members of the Church from the Church's own teaching — just because the ordinary faithful very naturally greatly rely for their understanding of what the Church teaches on prevailing official theology.

Moreover, the problem is not just that official theology can make positive assertions that contradict magisterial teaching. Official theology can also suppress magisterial teaching through omission. Official theology is not limited, after all, to what is explicitly pronounced. Indeed, change in official theology can come most easily through silence. Something that has long been magisterially taught, and taught as important to salvation, is no longer even mentioned. Here the influence of defective official theology can be most pernicious, just as its distance from genuine magisterial teaching is most obvious and undeniable. For silence is especially clearly not magisterial teaching in its own right. Simply failing to mention something certainly does not impose any obligation to disbelieve it, or even remove an existing obligation to believe it. But it can radically affect the life of the Church nonetheless. It can remove important elements of the faith from the consciousness of most Catholics.

Both in its pronouncements and in its silences, official theology is a part of the life of the Church that is constantly changing. Consider the following issues, where there have been marked revolutions and reversals of official theology over time, often linked to important changes in ecclesial and pastoral policy. In some cases there may never have been any actual magisterial teaching on the topic. In other cases there may have been magisterial teaching—but especially since Vatican II official theology has come to ignore and pass over it in silence, or even to contradict it.

1. We have already mentioned the issue of whether, at least ideally or in principle, the state should form a body-soul union with the Church. There is widespread official theology that ignores Leo XIII's very clear magisterium—Cardinal Ratzinger, later pope, will shortly provide us with an example. This reminds us of a number of things. First, it is alarmingly easy, at least since Vatican II, for magisterial teaching to become invisible—something that is just no longer discussed. It is not that Leo XIII's teaching is regularly clearly identified as such, and then condemned as erroneous. Some theologians are willing to make that step.[3] But more commonly, it is as if the teaching had never been given. So invisible has it become, that we even get Leo XIII feted as the alleged founder of a new form of Catholicism—"evangelical Catholicism"—that is supposed to come to its maturity at Vatican II and that supposedly includes, as a central element, the inherent goodness of the very Church-state separation that Leo XIII so clearly condemned.[4]

The prevailing official theology on Church-state separation, that Church-state separation is inherently good, is important in another way as well. Official theology may be nothing more than an official party line. It may even contradict the magisterium. But that does not

---

[3] See, for example, Martin Rhonheimer, who, in "Benedict XVI's 'Hermeneutic of Reform' and Religious Freedom," *Nova et Vetera* Eng. ed. 9.4 (2011): 1029–54, openly claims that the nineteenth century papal magisterium on Church and state was in error.

[4] For this curious interpretation, see the extensive theological journalism of George Weigel.

make it in any way optional in career terms. A friend arriving at a Roman university to study for a doctorate in the early 1990s was very clearly warned that any suggestion of "integralism" on his part in political theology would be, within ecclesial academia, career death.

2. An especially clear example of a rather dramatic silence in modern official theology about magisterial teaching relates to Trent session 7 canon 14. This is the teaching of Trent, in a canon on baptism, that fidelity to baptismal obligations, which include the central obligation to faith, is legitimately enforced on the baptized through sanctions that go beyond mere exclusion from the sacraments.[5] This was never going to be a minor matter, as this teaching supports canon law's consistent treatment to this day of heresy and apostasy in the baptized as punishable crimes, a treatment to which the early modern Church was practically committed at every level. This understanding of the canon and the dogmatic force accorded to it was quite uncontroversial from the time of Trent to Vatican II. Francisco de Toledo, the first Jesuit to be made a Cardinal and teaching theology during and immediately after Trent at the new Roman College, notes that the canon was against Erasmus, and was intended to condemn as heresy his demand for toleration of infidelity in the baptized—a view of Trent that Toledo entirely shares with the Council's first great historian, the otherwise very different antipapal Venetian Paolo Sarpi.[6] Thereafter the canon so understood is a seminary manual platitude.[7] We have here

---

5 "If anyone says that when they grow up (*cum adoleverint*), those baptized as little children should be asked whether they wish to affirm what their godparents promised in their name when they were baptized; and that, when they reply that they have no such wish, they should be left to their own decision and not, in the meantime, be coerced by any penalty into the Christian life (*suo esse arbitrio relinquendos nec alia interim poena ad christianam vitam cogendos*), except that they be barred from the reception of the Eucharist and the other sacraments, until they have a change of heart: let him be anathema." *Council of Trent*, Session 7, Decree on baptism, canon 14, March 3, 1547, in Alberigo and Tanner, eds., *Decrees of the Ecumenical Councils* (Washington, DC: Georgetown University Press, 1990), 2:686.

6 Cardinal Francisco de Toledo, *In Summam Theologiae Sancti Thomae Aquinatis Enarratio* (Rome, 1869), vol. 2, q. 10, a. 8, "An infideles sint ad fidem impellendi." For Sarpi's account and commentary on it, see Le Courayer's edition of Sarpi, *Histoire du Concile de Trente* (Amsterdam, 1751), 436.

7 Among notable theological discussions up to Vatican II, a sample which could be expanded with some ease: Billuart, *Summa Sancti Thomae* (Liege, 1746–51), in the *Tractatus de fide*, diss. V, art. II, "Utrum infideles cogendi ad fidem?"; Giovanni Perrone,

magisterial teaching conveyed under an agreed and uncontroverted interpretation in official theology over four centuries.

But after Vatican II official theology falls silent. Significantly, as with Leo XIII's teaching on Church and state, it is not as if the existence of the canon is openly admitted, and then frankly dismissed as involving doctrinal error on the part of a general council. Explicit denial of solemn teaching by an earlier general council is still (on the whole) avoided at the official level.[8] It is not even as if the canon is still generally recognized but suddenly and equally generally reinterpreted.[9] Instead the canon is simply ignored. Like a non-person in an official state photograph, it has been retouched into non-existence. Most modern Catholics have no idea that Trent passed such a dogmatic canon, or of its significance. Instead they are constantly told, as a point of official theology, the complete historical falsehood that not only does the Church now oppose any coercion of

---

Praelectiones Theologicae quas in Collegio Romano SJ habebat (Milan, 1845), vol. 7, *Tractatus de baptismo*, pp. 103–11; Hurter, *Theologiae Dogmaticae Compendium* (Innsbruck, 1908), vol. 3, Tract IX, §§ 315–16, pp. 281–82; Choupin, *Valeur des Décisions Doctrinales et Disciplinaires du Saint-Siège* (Paris, 1913), 265; "Peines ecclésiastiques: légitimité," *Dictionnaire de Théologie Catholique*, vol. 12 (Paris, 1933), 635–36; Ottaviani, *Institutiones Iuris Publici Ecclesiastici* (Rome, 1935), vol. 1, §170; Merkelbach, *Summa Theologiae Moralis* (Paris, 1938), vol. 1, §740; Ott, *Fundamentals of Catholic Dogma* (Cork, 1955), bk. 4, pt. 3, sec. 2, §6, 360.

8   Though one official spokesman for the Catholic Church in the UK, when I told him about the canon, without any hesitation at once responded: "Oh, we'll have to change that."

9   Though recently, having been reminded of the canon's (now very unwelcome) existence, John Finnis has attempted a very novel re-interpretation of his own: see "John Finnis on Thomas Pink" in Keown and George, *Reason, Morality, and Law*, 566–77. He bravely claims, against history and four centuries of theological consensus to the contrary, that the canon was intended not to condemn Erasmus but only to teach the legitimacy of a coercive enforcement on the baptized, not of Catholic faith, but only of some duties under natural law (such as, for example, some general duty of justice: see 574–75). But this reading has nothing to do with anything discussed at Trent, as the Council *Acta* make very clear. Obviously some natural law duties can be enforced—think of the duty not to kill—but the Council fathers and theologians at Trent never worried themselves over some notional heresy that denied this. The condemnable view discussed in debates about canon 14 at Trent is always Erasmus's—that *faith* not be enforced on the baptized. And it is this view that everyone at the Council who gave an opinion condemned—as *falsus*, *haereticus* or *damnandus*—without any debate to the contrary. I discuss Finnis's highly eccentric interpretation of Trent in more detail in "John Finnis's Alternative History of Trent," online at www.academia.edu/37861294/John_Finnis_Alternative_History_of_Trent. In its anachronisms and misreadings of the *Acta* of Trent, Finnis's interpretation is a beautiful example of just how anxious today's "conservative" Catholicism is to "reconstruct" aspects of the Church's past that do not suit its own novel and very "postconciliar" theology.

the act of faith, but that she has "always done so." And this is indeed just false. Coercion of the act of faith has only ever been opposed by the magisterium in principle and without exception for the case of the unbaptized, who as unbaptized are not bound by any baptismal obligation to fidelity and who fall outside the Church's jurisdiction.

3. Is spiritual death from making an unworthy communion a real danger to be carefully guarded against in pastoral and liturgical arrangements and by other forms of ecclesial policy? Once this was indeed treated as a real danger. Before the 1970 liturgical reform *Lauda Sion* was a compulsory Sequence for Corpus Christi:

> Sumunt boni, sumunt mali;
> Sorte tamen inaequali,
> Vitae vel interitus.
> Mors est malis, vita bonis:
> Vide paris sumptionis
> Quam sit dispar exitus.[10]

Traditional liturgical readings on Holy Thursday and Corpus Christi included verses 27–29 from 1 Corinthians 11, warning of the judgment that falls on unworthy communions. How different the liturgy, and the official theology, of today! Outside the London Oratory, I have never heard this passage from *Lauda Sion* sung at an ordinary parish Corpus Christi Mass;[11] and verses 27–29 are now entirely omitted from the lectionary of the reformed Roman liturgy.[12] And here we see the important role of silence and oblivion within official theology. Recently I was addressing the clergy of an English diocese on the theology of ecumenism, with the ecumenical officer of the bishops' conference present. This ecumenical officer suggested that communion should be more readily available to Protestants. When asked whether any such Eucharistic sharing should, for the spiritual good of the Protestants themselves, always be preceded,

---

10 "The good, the guilty share therein, With sure increase of grace or sin, The ghostly life, or ghostly death: death to the guilty; to the good immortal life. See how one food man's joy or woe accomplisheth."

11 The Oratory aside, I have generally never heard *Lauda Sion* at all in the New Rite—except at one London parish where it was said, but in a specially shortened form, omitting just that passage about the fatal consequence of an unworthy communion.

12 See "The Omission That Haunts the Church," in Peter Kwasniewski, *The Holy Bread of Eternal Life: Restoring Eucharistic Reverence in an Age of Impiety* (Manchester, NH: Sophia Institute Press, 2020), 181–95.

as allowed for in canon law, by *penitential* sharing—because most Protestants, though prone like all of us to mortal sin, will never have confessed and received absolution, so that holy communion could be spiritually very dangerous to them—the ecumenical officer reacted with utter incomprehension and surprise. We may conclude that at least within the bishops' conference of England and Wales there is a prevailing, and highly problematic, official theology that treats unworthy communions as not a real danger at all. We shall be returning to the problems caused by this relatively new official theology. It is clearly fundamental to the crisis over *Amoris Laetitia*.

This issue of unworthy communions and their spiritual danger brings us to the importance of the liturgy and liturgical reform. Omissions within official theology are very often importantly linked to and dependent on liturgical omissions. It is very much easier for official theology to change, and even come to contradict magisterial teaching, if the liturgy has ceased to represent that teaching. The *de iure* removal from the liturgy of passages of scripture warning of unworthy communions, and the disappearance in practice of *Lauda Sion* as well, have been essential to the propagation of the new official view that unworthy communions are certainly not a real and constant danger.

4. Can children who die unbaptized before the age of reason attain the beatific vision? Or are they capable of natural happiness at best, or are they even threatened with the pain of sense? Debate exists about magisterial teaching in this area. One thing does seem clear, however. There is certainly no magisterially taught guarantee of the beatific vision. Meanwhile there have been marked shifts in official theology, as in liturgical and pastoral policy. And this case reminds us that whatever may be true of magisterial teaching, where official theology is concerned, not only can the official theology of one time contradict that of another—but the change can go back and forth, and not consistently in one direction only. Thus the high and late Middle Ages saw a shift away from an uncompromising Augustinianism to theories of natural happiness or even, in thinkers such as Cajetan, to theories of possible supernatural happiness. But then, alongside the radical Augustinianism of the Reformation, Trent saw a revival of a Catholic Augustinianism. Cajetan's view narrowly

escaped condemnation for heresy at Trent, and official theology returned to more uncompromising views, so that natural happiness was the most that could be hoped for.[13] By the seventeenth century Petavius, though a Jesuit and an opponent of Jansenism, could even maintain again that infants who die unbaptized will suffer the pain of sense.[14] And then, even before Vatican II there was a revival among some theologians of the more benign pre-Tridentine views of Cajetan and others.[15] Since Vatican II, official theology, without any direct backing from some new formal teaching of the Council—there was none—has become almost mandatorily benign, not only in optimistic preaching but in pastoral policy and related liturgical change. Friends of mine struggled at their parish with a priest who insisted, very much against their wishes, on a postponement of their child's baptism until six months after birth at the earliest—to enable their completion of a diocesan preparation course for parents. They turned to a papally instituted traditional priestly order, which baptized their child immediately.

5. Has the Church replaced Israel as the people of God—the community through which God now works human salvation and in which he is to be worshipped? That has certainly been historical Catholic teaching, still maintained in *Lumen Gentium*, a declaration of Vatican II that counts as a "dogmatic constitution." *Lumen Gentium* teaches that an old Israel according to the flesh has been succeeded "through a new and perfect covenant" by the Church as a "New Israel" of the spirit rather than the flesh, formed by "calling together from Jews and Gentiles a people that would be bound together in unity not according to the flesh but in the Spirit. This would be the new people of God" (§9). But then, on that basis, the Church has a clear public mission: to call the Jewish people away from Jewish unbelief and into the Church, exactly as Gentiles are to be called away from Gentile unbelief and into the Church. This public mission to the Jewish people was pursued by the apostles in the New Testament. And the spiritual need for it, for the sake

---

13 On attitudes to Cajetan at Trent, see "Baptême" in *Dictionnaire de Théologie Catholique*, 2:325–26.
14 Dionysius Petavius, *Dogmata Theologica*, De Deo, Bk. 9, ch. 11.
15 For brief discussion, see Ott, *Foundations of Catholic Dogma*, Bk. 2, sec. 2, §25, 113–14.

of Jewish salvation, was taught even before *Lumen Gentium* by an earlier general council, Florence.[16] This is a mission that the Church recognized and pursued right up until Vatican II. Yet despite all this, the view that the Church has any such mission is now deeply controversial within official circles. Indeed, *Lumen Gentium* and the Council of Florence notwithstanding, we shall see that such a mission of the Church appears to be denied outright in current official theology. The issue here is not whether God has a continuing concern for the Jewish people, as if God could or would ever have abandoned them. Rather, the issue is how to understand that persisting concern—and whether, for the sake of their salvation, all of humanity, Jew and Gentile alike, is called on the very same terms to baptism into the one Church, something that was even within living memory very clearly taught.

Official theology is merely that. As we have already observed, though official theology may convey magisterial teaching, it may also go beyond magisterial teaching or hide its existence or even oppose it. And since, just *as* official theology, it imposes no obligation of its own on our belief as Catholics, we should not be afraid to criticize it when its content deserves criticism—and very especially when it actually contradicts magisterial teaching. For then the default assumption must be that it is the official theology that is false, as merely a current party line that places no obligation on us to believe it, and not the magisterial teaching. Indeed, where official theology contradicts magisterial teaching, we may be under a canonical obligation not to believe the official theology.

The period since Vatican II has seen an explosion of dubious official theology—in novel positive claims that contradict both the magisterial teaching and the official theology of the past, and in novel silences that serve instead most effectively to bury that past teaching and theology. Now erroneous official theology does not of itself threaten the consistency of the magisterium. But it still poses a huge problem. It is tempting for a "conservative" Catholic to clutch Denzinger to themselves, and piously declaim that all is well because on this or that question "magisterial teaching has not changed," especially when there is a single passage or footnote, no

---

16 As will be discussed below.

matter how obscure, within a document of Vatican II that supports the historical magisterium. But remember: the individual Catholic's immediate exposure to "what the Church teaches" is deeply shaped by current official theology.

Denzinger is itself a partial selection of past magisterial teachings, with the selection changing significantly from edition to edition, according to official theological fashion, and by omission and not merely addition. But most ordinary Catholics do not even read Denzinger anyway. What most Catholics are immediately exposed to is official theology at its most humdrum—in conventional sermons or devotional literature at the diocesan or parish level—and so to magisterial teaching only as transmitted or even mispresented and obscured at that level. So if some part of magisterial teaching does come to be omitted from official theology, that silence will mean very effective oblivion. The ordinary Catholic will have absolutely no idea that the magisterial teaching exists at all. The teaching will have no impact on their religious life. This means that a problematic body of official theology can have dire consequences for the health of the Church and the efficacy of her mission. Even if it does turn out to be true that Vatican II has led more to a crisis of official theology than to a crisis within magisterial teaching itself, that may leave the crisis no less serious for that.

The erroneous official theology of grace and baptism that has become especially prevalent since Vatican II cannot be dismissed just as a rogue "spirit of the Council"—as nothing more than some liberal theologians on a frolic of their own. The theology may be no more than a debatable party line. But it is a party line that is common to officeholders within the Church—assumed almost without thinking by clergy "in good odor" at every level, up to that of popes and cardinals.

3. Vatican II and a Revolution in the Official Theology of Baptism

Vatican II may not have introduced any new teaching about baptism in its formal magisterium. But even so, the Council event is deeply associated with a revolution in baptism's official theology.

Aspects of this revolution were already occurring before the Council, in some cases with roots going back to the nineteenth century. The Council event deepened or confirmed these theological changes. Other aspects of the revolution involved official liturgical changes brought about thanks to the Council. These liturgical changes were not in general directly called for by any document of the Council. But they were introduced by Paul VI in the name of applying the Council, and opposition to them is characteristically treated in official circles as opposition to the Council.

So we can with some justification talk of Vatican II as lying at the center of a revolution in the official theology of baptism. This revolution in official theology is extensive, has had a very great impact on everyday Catholic belief and practice, and seems in almost every respect deeply problematic, as overtly inconsistent with or at least involving a compromising silence about what has long been the clear magisterial teaching of the Church.

The dominion of the devil

The first and most important change has to do with how the Church now presents the Fall and original sin, and what the Church is doing when through baptism she releases us from the guilt of original sin. The Church's historical teaching is clear. The Fall has delivered the world, in so far as it is fallen, to the devil as its prince. The guilt of original sin involves, therefore, subjection to the dominion of the devil. This is vividly stated by the Council of Florence in its decree for the Copts. Faith in Christ, and baptism, in freeing us from original sin, free us from subjection to the devil:

> [The Council] firmly believes, professes and preaches that never was anyone, conceived by a man and a woman, liberated from the devil's dominion except by faith in our Lord Jesus Christ, the mediator between God and humanity, who was conceived without sin, was born and died.[17]

And:

> With regard to children, since the danger of death is often present and the only remedy available to them is the sacrament of baptism by which they are snatched away from the dominion of the devil and adopted as children of God, it admonishes that

---

17 Council of Florence, Session 11, Bull of Union with the Copts, *Decrees of the Ecumenical Councils*, ed. Tanner and Alberigo, 1:575.

> sacred baptism is not to be deferred for forty or eighty days or any other period of time in accordance with the usage of some people, but it should be conferred as soon as it conveniently can; and if there is imminent danger of death, the child should be baptized straightaway without any delay, even by a lay man or a woman in the form of the church, if there is no priest, as is contained more fully in the decree on the Armenians.[18]

This equation of original sin with subjection to the dominion of the devil has long been reflected and taught in the liturgy of baptism, in the rites of both Rome and Constantinople. In the traditional Roman baptismal liturgy, we find a sequence of exorcisms that directly represent baptism's role as releasing us from the devil's possession. Thus: "Go forth from him (her), unclean spirit, and give place to the Holy Spirit, the Paraclete." And again:

> I exorcise thee, unclean spirit, in the name of the Father ✠ and of the Son, ✠ and of the Holy ✠ Spirit, that thou goest out and depart from this servant of God, N. For He commands thee, accursed one, Who walked upon the sea, and stretched out His right hand to Peter about to sink. Therefore, accursed devil, acknowledge thy sentence, and give honor to the living and true God: give honor to Jesus Christ His Son, and to the Holy Spirit; and depart from this servant of God, N., because God and our Lord Jesus Christ have vouchsafed to call him (her) to His holy grace and benediction and to the font of Baptism.

And again: "And this sign of the holy Cross, which we make upon his (her) forehead, do thou, accursed devil, never dare to violate." And finally:

> I exorcise thee, every unclean spirit, in the name of God the Father ✠ Almighty, in the name of Jesus ✠ Christ, His Son, our Lord and Judge, and in the power of the Holy ✠ Spirit, that thou depart from this creature of God N., which our Lord hath deigned to call unto His holy temple, that it may be made the temple of the living God, and that the Holy Spirit may dwell therein.

That baptism constitutes our liberation by Christ from the dominion of the devil is not denied outright in official documents of

---

[18] Ibid., 576.

the postconciliar Church. Indeed, the 1992 Catechism refers to the doctrine in at least two places. In §1237 it links the doctrine to the practice of baptismal exorcism: "Since baptism signifies liberation from sin and from its instigator the devil, one or more exorcisms are pronounced over the candidate." And in §1250 the Catechism characterizes baptism as a liberation from "the power of darkness": "Born with a fallen human nature and tainted by original sin, children also have need of the new birth in baptism to be freed from the power of darkness and brought into the realm of the freedom of the children of God, to which all men are called."

Now the magisterial teaching is that baptism is not only a sign of our deliverance from the dominion of the devil, but necessary to its effecting. Until the child is actually baptized, the child still remains, with fallen humanity, under the devil's dominion. The traditional exorcisms present this exactly, calling on the devil to depart *now*, with the child's baptism.

But there is another theology of the matter, one which treats the baptism as a sign of a deliverance from diabolic dominion that, thanks to Christ's coming, has in effect already happened—a liberation that the child does not have to wait until actual baptism to enjoy. And this theology is left open in the new rite of baptism introduced by Paul VI in 1970. Granted, the new rite still speaks of release *from original sin* as effected by baptism. But original sin is no longer liturgically presented as implying continued subjection to the devil. The former multiple and very unambiguous exorcisms are all removed, to be replaced by a single new prayer, which reads:

> Almighty and ever-living God, you sent your only Son into the world to cast out the power of Satan, spirit of evil, to rescue man from the kingdom of darkness, and bring him into the splendor of your kingdom of light. We pray for this child: set him (her) free from original sin, make him (her) a temple of your glory, and send your Holy Spirit to dwell with him (her). We ask this through Christ our Lord.

The difference is obvious. The new prayer is simply a prayer that God release the child from original sin. It is no longer explicitly commanding the devil to depart the child and abandon his dominion of it *now*. In fact the devil's departure is not commanded at all. Which is why the new rite's so-called "exorcism" is not really a genuine formula of exorcism. The destruction of the power of the devil is associated in the prayer not with the devil's departure from the child only at the moment of its baptism, but rather with Christ's coming into the world. Any clear statement that, even after the coming of Christ, the child until actually baptized remains under the dominion of the devil—a devil whose departure has then to be explicitly commanded—has been removed.

This change is associated with a wider one. The traditional forms of blessing for liturgical use of natural elements such as water and oil also involve exorcism. Within a fallen world, natural elements require release from the dominion of the devil before they can be appropriated and used by the Church as holy water or holy oil. Take this exorcism that initiates the blessing of the oil of the sick in the traditional liturgy for the Chrism Mass:

> I exorcise thee, thou most unclean spirit, and every incursion of Satan, and every phantasm: in the name of the Father, and of the Son, and of the Holy Spirit: do thou depart from this oil, so that it may become a spiritual unguent for strengthening the temple of the living God; so that the Holy Spirit may dwell therein, by the name of God the Father almighty, and by the name of his well-beloved Son our Lord Jesus Christ, who will come to judge the living and the dead and the world by fire.

These exorcisms have likewise been removed from blessings in the new Roman liturgy. The message is clear. Blessings need only give thanks to God for a world that is good. There is no need of exorcism to remove a persisting diabolic dominion over a world that, though by nature good, is also fallen. The traditional Roman liturgy with its formulae of exorcism for baptism and for blessings is now seen by many modern theologians as problematic and as having required reform just because, unlike the new, its forms for baptism and blessing really do contain genuine exorcisms of the devil—commands addressed to the devil that he depart from an unbaptized child or from natural elements.[19]

19 For further discussion of postconciliar theological opposition to such exorcisms, see the important article by Uwe Michael Lang, "Theologies of Blessing: Origins and Characteristics of *De benedictionibus* (1984)," *Antiphon* 15.1 (2011): 27–46, especially at 35–36. Lang is rightly critical of this opposition: "The act of blessing [in the reformed

Baptism is not now generally explained to Catholics as release from diabolic dominion. That idea of baptism may have been taught by the Council of Florence, and it may still lurk in those just cited Catechism paragraphs. But it plays no role in the Church's current pastoral life. That the fallen world and the unconverted within it are still subject to the devil is simply not part of the Church's current official theology. It is a conception of the world that many contemporary Catholics would find alien and even shocking—and which has been carefully removed from the reformed baptismal liturgy. Diabolic dominion over a fallen world is not now presented in the Church's baptismal liturgy, is not pastorally communicated in parish homiletics, and—as we are about to see—does not inform the current policy of the Church. The issue is not (yet) the reality of the devil or of original sin, none of which is generally denied.[20] It has instead to do with what the existence of the devil and original sin imply for the Church's relation to an unconverted world.

If the fallen world—the world of the unconverted and unbaptized—really does lie under the dominion of the devil, then the consequence is clear. The Church cannot really live at peace with

postconciliar liturgy] consists above all in the recognition and proclamation of the goodness of created things and of the loving care of their Creator. The apotropaic aspect of blessing, that is, to protect against the influences of evil and of the Evil One, is largely absent. Lessi-Ariosto considers this aspect of blessings a remainder of a pessimistic worldview that does not take into account the goodness of God's creation, but it could be asked whether such a position does not underestimate the consequences of original sin. The theological rationale for this claims to be biblical, but would appear to be oblivious of the fact that Christ himself, in the Gospel of John, speaks of 'the prince of this world' (Jn 12:31, 14:30, 16:11)... Daniel Van Slyke has noted that 'any view that discounts the influence of evil in favor of an insistence on the goodness of creation can be accused of an optimism that verges on naïveté.' It would seem to be—and I suggest this here for the purpose of further exploration—that the relegation of apotropaic blessings has less to do with biblical *ressourcement* than with modern theologians such as Edward Schillebeeckx OP (1914-2009) and Karl Rahner SJ (1904-1984), who considered the whole created world already endowed with or permeated by divine grace. Their notion of 'sacramentality' is extended to the whole of creation, and so the specific nature of the sacraments is lost: the sacraments and, by consequence, the sacramentals are mere manifestations that make explicit what already takes place" (44-45). I obviously share Lang's view.

20 The reality of the devil or of original sin may not be openly denied at least within the English church. But official theologies can be highly local. The official theology of the Flemish church is more radical. One Flemish priest, a retired academic of the Catholic University of Leuven, at a baptism in Leuven where this writer was a godparent, would not use even the New Rite's "exorcism," as being supposedly theologically erroneous and outmoded—nor, I was assured, would other Flemish clergy.

the world until it is converted. The Church can no more live at peace with the unconverted world than she can live at peace with the devil. Central to the Church's relation to the unconverted world must be a commitment to spiritual confrontation, where the only way out of the ensuing spiritual conflict is the world's conversion.

And this is Christ's own message, who presents his mission as centrally involving conflict between a converted and an unconverted world—between the world of the baptized and the world of the unbaptized—with the mission to baptize as both crystallization of this conflict, and the only means to victory in it.

> I came to cast fire upon the earth; and would that it were already kindled! I have a baptism to be baptized with; and how I am constrained until it is accomplished! Do you think that I have come to give peace on earth? No, I tell you, but rather division... (Lk 12:49–51)

Baptism then is not a source of harmony and solidarity with the as yet unconverted world, but precisely in so far as the world is not yet converted, a source of spiritual conflict with it.

But what instead if the dominion of the devil has already, thanks to the coming of Christ, been effectively removed, so that at some eschatological level, even the unconverted world—the world of the unbaptized—is already released from the devil's power? Perhaps through the coming of Christ the world, though fallen, is already marked, even prior to baptism and incorporation within the visible Church, by a Christianity that, to use the Rahnerian expression, is "anonymous."[21] Even the unconverted world is somehow already released from diabolic dominion and, albeit implicitly rather than explicitly, already committed to the supernatural end. Then the relation of the Church even to the unconverted world need not be one of conflict. Even prior to the world's conversion, the Church's primary relation to the world can already be one of dialogic harmony.

The traditional liturgy of exorcism, in baptisms and in blessings, stands in contradiction to this benign conception of the situation of the unconverted world. It presents the unconverted world as still in the possession of Christ's and humanity's deadly enemy. Without

---

21 For a succinct account, see Peter Kwasniewski, "Karl Rahner and the Unspoken Framework of (Much of) Modern Theology," *OnePeterFive*, July 27, 2022.

the world's baptism and its conversion, there can be no articles of peace—no stable dialogic harmony. But a benign conception of the unconverted world and of the Church's relation to it is plainly now dominant in official theology, and the traditional liturgy's unwelcome contradiction has been comprehensively suppressed. The duty to convert the world is constantly subordinated to the pursuit of harmony with it. This subordination of conversion to dialogic harmony is a central feature of postconciliar official theology.

The issue does not of course affect only baptism but generalizes from it. For though baptism initiates a life of grace that detaches us from the devil, that grace can be lost through mortal sin. To prevent such loss and then as remedy for its occurrence, we need the other sacraments, and not the Eucharist alone but that condition of the Eucharist's worthy reception once grace has been lost—the sacrament of penance—without which communion threatens to bring with it not liberation but a confirming of spiritual death and diabolic dominion. And the needed combination of these sacraments is largely lacking not just among the unbaptized but in many communities of the baptized. Eucharist and penance are lacking in the Protestant world. But in effect penance is also lacking among many modern Catholics, who regularly take communion without ever going to confession—something with alarming implications, according to traditional magisterial teaching, for the internal life of increasingly large parts of the Church. For communion without confession is liable to drive us further from the life of grace, and so even further under the dominion of the devil, and there are important effects of this detachment very apparent in the life of the contemporary Church, as we shall see.

Baptism, the conversion of the state, and the Church as coercive potestas

If the fallen world is under the devil's dominion, and is in inevitable spiritual conflict with the Church until it is converted, then to remove the conflict no part of the world can be excluded from that conversion.

The Church's magisterium has long taught that the need for conversion includes the state. Even if individuals are Christian privately, that does not guarantee the health of the political community. For we do not pursue the communal good simply as private individuals, but as members of a community, through public institutions—and spiritual sickness can arise as much in public life as in private.[22]

Now the state is divinely established just as is the Church, though each in a different way. While the authority of the Church is based on a law of the New Covenant that is supernatural and revealed, state authority is based on natural law. But just as much as the Church, the state is a form of community and authority that is divinely instituted so that humanity may flourish. This means that it is fundamental to Catholic teaching that harmony between Church and state must be possible, at least in principle. How could God not provide for harmony between two authorities each of which he has ordained and instituted?

But if the Church can only coexist harmoniously with a nature that has been removed from the devil's dominion through baptism and conversion, that must be true in particular for communal authority in its natural form—the state. For the state too, like the rest of nature, is affected by the Fall. This allows for no political neutral space. The state too must be rescued from the dominion of the devil, and brought into the Church, so that it publicly commits itself to Christ. Otherwise, if unconverted, the state will degrade from the proper order of nature. So the Church has clearly taught, not least through the magisterium of the nineteenth century popes. These popes taught, with clarity and, we are now beginning to see, with foresight too, that the conversion of private individuals is not enough. Unless the state itself is converted, and recognizes Christ politically and publicly, natural law as it concerns the public good and public justice will, thanks to the Fall, cease to be clearly recognized and applied: "Where religion has been removed from civil society, and the doctrine and authority of divine revelation repudiated, the genuine notion itself of justice and human right is darkened and lost."[23] And:

---

[22] For more on the nature and role of the state, and the consequent need for the state's conversion, see my "In Defence of Catholic Integralism," online at *Public Discourse*, www.thepublicdiscourse.com/2018/08/39362/.

[23] Pius IX, *Quanta Cura* 4.

Therefore the law of Christ ought to prevail in human society and be the guide and teacher *of public as well as of private life*. Since this is so by divine decree, and no man may with impunity contravene it, it is an evil thing for any state where Christianity does not hold the place that belongs to it. When Jesus Christ is absent, *human reason fails*, being bereft of its chief protection and light, and the very end is lost sight of, for which, under God's providence, human society has been built up. This end is the obtaining by the members of society of natural good through the aid of civil unity, though always in harmony with the perfect and eternal good which is above nature. *But when men's minds are clouded*, both rulers and ruled go astray, for they have no safe line to follow nor end to aim at.[24]

That degradation of the political community will guarantee not only the moral ruin of the state, but its enmity to the gospel, tied as the life of the gospel is to observance of the natural law—a law of which the devil is an unrelenting enemy.

The Church's involvement in spiritual warfare within a temporal order that is fallen is also fundamental to the nature of the Church herself, and has long determined magisterial teaching about that nature. The Church has been given by Christ himself the authority to protect the supreme good of religion. But locked as she is in a spiritual conflict within a fallen world, the Church is under attack both from without and also from within—from her own sinful and often recalcitrant members. So she must be able to protect the good of her community from those attacks. She must be able to discourage wrongdoing by her members that threatens the spiritual good of the Christian community she serves. And she must also be able to prevent spiritually damaging intrusions into that community by opponents from without. So the Church, just as much as the state, must be a *potestas* or coercive authority. Just as the state must be able to use law to protect the political community, so the Church must be able to use law to protect the ecclesial community. The Church has been given by Christ the sovereign authority to make laws and to enforce those laws within her jurisdiction by legitimate threats of punishment that to be effective must include temporal as well as spiritual sanctions.

24 Leo XIII, *Tametsi Futura*, 8.

Subjection to the Church's jurisdiction, as the magisterium teaches and as the 1983 *Code of Canon Law* continues to claim, comes with baptism. So at Trent, as we have already seen, and elsewhere, the magisterium has clearly taught that baptism subjects the baptized to a coercive jurisdiction, that of the Church, with obligations to fidelity on the baptized that may be enforced—where breach of those obligations is genuinely culpable, and where enforcement really is necessary to protect the religious good of the Church's community. Because the state itself needs to be converted, baptismal obligations can take political and public as well as private form. Officials of a state that is publicly Christian can be bound by their baptism to exercise their office so as to support the mission of the Church. In particular the officials of a publicly Christian state can be bound to assist the Church in the exercise of her jurisdiction, as canon 2198 of the 1917 *Code of Canon Law* still insisted.[25] Baptism obligates the rulers of a Christian state to act as body to the Church's soul—to form a single Christian community where, in religious matters, the state helps as secular arm (*brachium saeculare*) to enforce the law of the Church.

This theory of the Church as *potestas* for the good of religion and of the need for a soul-body union of Church and state is a longstanding part of the Church's magisterium. At its heart is the teaching that baptism has a juridical character fundamental to the nature of the Church herself. It is baptism that provides the Church as *potestas* with her coercive jurisdiction, and then obligates officials of a publicly Christian state to support that jurisdiction when called on by the Church to do so. Baptism then is the basis for the legitimacy of a soul-body union of the Church with that of the state, where in matters of religion the state may act as agent or secular arm of the Church as *potestas* for the good of religion.

Vatican II was careful not to contradict this teaching. According to the official *relationes* that interpreted *Dignitatis Humanae* to the Council fathers at Vatican II, the declaration does not in any way deny the Church's status as *potestas* for religion, and addresses only the authority of the state when detached from any

---

25 *Code of Canon Law* (1917), can. 2198: "Offences against the law of the Church alone, are, of their nature, within the cognizance of the ecclesiastical authority alone, which, when it judges it necessary or opportune, can claim the help of the secular arm."

union with the Church, and so acting only on its own authority as *potestas* for the civil order.²⁶ The 1983 *Code of Canon Law* also still clearly presents the Church as a *potestas*. The Code clearly asserts that the Church has a jurisdiction over the baptized, with the authority to enforce that jurisdiction with threats of temporal as well as spiritual punishment.²⁷

Nevertheless the idea of the Church as a *potestas* is decreasingly taken seriously in official theology. In practice a model prevails of the Church as, in effect, a voluntary society, and with this comes a conception of canonical obligations as really no more than membership rules. All that culpable breach of them really merits is not some genuine form of punishment, but simple loss of membership. With this comes a view of Church-state separation not as a regrettable evil, as Leo XIII viewed it, but as a positive good.

Consider Joseph Ratzinger, who when writing as a cardinal defended both the idea of the Church as a voluntary society whose authority is purely moral, and the desirability of Church-state separation. Not only is the entry of unbaptized adults into the Church treated by him as an entirely voluntary matter—which was always taught—but continued fidelity in the baptized is treated by him

---

26 See this *relatio* of September 1965, issued to the Council fathers just before the final vote: "For the schema rests on the traditional doctrine of a distinction between a double order of human life, that is sacred and profane, civil and religious. In modern times Leo XIII has wonderfully expounded and developed this doctrine, teaching more clearly than ever before that there are two societies, and so two legal orders, and two coercive authorities (*potestates*), each divinely constituted but in a different way, that is by natural law and by the positive law of Christ. *As the nature of religious liberty rests on this distinction of orders*, so the distinction provides a means to preserving it against the confusions which history has frequently produced" (Vatican II, *Acta Synodalia* 4.1, 193). And at the same time, emphasizing that coercion on the authority of the Church in the order of religion to enforce her jurisdiction is not being addressed by the declaration: "Therefore this question of religious liberty, *since it has to do with the civil order, is to be distinguished from other questions which are of a theological order*. The first of these is of the nature and extent of that evangelical liberty by which Christ has liberated us (Gal 5,1); *the other has to do with relations between freedom and authority within the Church herself*" (Vatican II, *Acta Synodalia* 4.1, 185).

27 See especially can. 1311: "The Church has the innate and proper right to coerce (*coercere*) offending members of the Christian faithful (*christifideles*) with punitive sanctions (*poenalibus sanctionibus*)" (*christifideles* being defined in can. 204 as the baptized). Sanctions can extend to temporal penalties, as per can. 1312: "The law can establish other expiatory penalties which deprive a member of the Christian faithful of some spiritual or temporal good and which are consistent with the supernatural purpose of the Church."

as entirely voluntary too, which Trent formally denied. Moreover, the use of civil penalties by a Christian state to enforce ecclesial law is condemned by Ratzinger—despite the fact that such use was called for by General Councils such as Lateran IV and Trent:

> This community in its turn, the Church, understands itself as a final moral authority which however *depends on voluntary adherence* and is entitled only to spiritual *but not to civil penalties*, precisely because it does not have the status the state has of being accepted by all as something given in advance... This is not in any way to dispute the fact that this balance has often enough been disturbed, *that in the middle ages and in the early modern period things often reached the point of Church and state in fact blending into one another in a way that falsified the faith's claim to truth and turned it into a compulsion so that it became a caricature of what was really intended*... With this the fundamental task of the Church's political stance, as I understand it, has been defined; its aim must be to maintain this balance of a dual system as the foundation of freedom. Hence the Church must make claims and demands on public law and cannot simply retreat into the private sphere. Hence it must also take care on the other hand *that Church and state remain separated and that belonging to the Church clearly retains its voluntary character*.[28]

Contrast here the magisterial teaching of Leo XIII, who condemned "the fatal theory of the need of separation between Church and State" in *Libertas Praestantissimum* (at §18). Leo XIII clearly taught also that the Church is not a voluntary society with mere membership rules, but, just as much as the state, is a *societas perfecta*—a sovereign *potestas* or coercive lawgiver:

> Others oppose not the existence of the Church, nor indeed could they; yet they despoil her of the nature and rights of a perfect society, and maintain that it does not belong to her to legislate, to judge, or to punish, but only to exhort, to advise, and to rule her subjects in accordance with their own consent and will. By such opinion they pervert the nature of this divine society, and attenuate and narrow its authority, its office of teacher, and its whole

---

28 "Theology and the Church's Political Stance," in Joseph Ratzinger, *Church, Ecumenism, and Politics: New Essays in Ecclesiology* (New York: Crossroad, 1988), 161; my emphases.

efficiency; and at the same time they aggrandize the power of the civil government to such extent as to subject the Church of God to the empire and sway of the State, like any voluntary association of citizens. To refute completely such teaching, the arguments often used by the defenders of Christianity, and set forth by us, especially in the encyclical letter *Immortale Dei* (§12) [where the Church is taught to be a genuine *potestas*], are of great avail; for by those arguments it is proved that, by a divine provision, all the rights which essentially belong to a society that is legitimate, supreme, and perfect in all its parts exist in the Church.[29]

Modern official theology assumes that the state should be religiously neutral because it also assumes that this public neutrality will be entirely consistent with harmony between Church and state. We see the general model of dialogic harmony with the unconverted world applied to an unconverted state in particular.

The idea that Church and state can live in harmony without the state's conversion was influentially supported even before Vatican II by Jacques Maritain. It was central to the new political theology that Maritain was developing in the decades before the council, especially in *Man and the State*. On juridical questions Maritain was a more orthodox Catholic than Ratzinger. Unlike Ratzinger, he did not attack as outright error the magisterium's teaching that the Church herself is a *potestas* entitled under appropriate circumstances to use the state as her coercive agent. Instead Maritain adopted a subtler view. By contrast to Ratzinger, Maritain admitted that such use by the Church of the state, far from "falsifying the faith's claim to truth" as Ratzinger supposed, had in its time—the Middle Ages—been fully legitimate. But then Maritain made a crucial claim. Thanks to a supposed progress of the gospel, and human spiritual advancement, it was no longer a condition of harmony between Church and state that the state should be publicly Christian. Maritain allowed that previously, under the more spiritually primitive conditions of the past, in what he termed the *sacral* age of medieval Europe, it had been necessary for the good of religion for the state to convert, and for the political community to be a community of the baptized. Harmony between Church and

---

29 *Libertas Praestanstissimum* 40.

state did once require a soul-body union of them that was then entirely legitimate, just as Leo XIII had taught. But we now lived in what Maritain termed a *secular* age. And in this new secular age, supposedly thanks to a progress of the gospel, the Church could now live in harmony with the state without requiring the state's conversion into a Christian state. Harmony could obtain without a shared religion, simply within a shared framework of natural law. In Maritainian political theology, under conditions of modernity the political community can now somehow escape the dominion of the devil without needing to be converted.[30]

The Church's ever-increasing conflict with secular states suggests, alas, that such escape may not be available—and that the secular age may not constitute spiritual advance at all. The issue, let me emphasize, is not whether a soul-body union of Church and state is now realizable. Clearly under modern conditions there is simply no prospect of such a union. The issue, rather, is what we must expect from a state that is no longer publicly committed to the truth of Christianity in its laws and policies. What the nineteenth century popes taught us to expect in such a case is clearly what we are now getting—not harmony with the Church, but deepening spiritual conflict, and a conflict moreover that, just as those popes predicted, is rooted in the state's denial of natural law, especially as it concerns marriage and the right to life.

The efficacy of grace—through or apart from explicit faith and visible participation in baptism and other sacraments

Even before Vatican II the magisterium taught that salvation is possible, at least in principle, even for those who are not Catholic. Pius XII taught that non-Catholics may be related to the Church through some kind of unconscious desire, and implied that this may be a (less than certain) help to their salvation:

> As you know, venerable brethren, from the very beginning of our pontificate, we have committed to the protection and guidance of heaven those who do not belong to the visible body of the Catholic Church, solemnly declaring that after the example of the Good

---

30 For more detailed discussion of Maritain, see my "Jacques Maritain and the Problem of Church and State," *The Thomist* 79 (2015): 1–42.

Shepherd we desire nothing more ardently than that they may have life and have it more abundantly. Imploring the prayers of the whole Church we wish to repeat this solemn declaration in this encyclical letter in which we have proclaimed the praises of the "great and glorious Body of Christ" and from a heart overflowing with love we ask each and every one of them to correspond to the interior movements of grace, and to seek to withdraw *from that state in which they cannot be sure of their salvation*. For even though by an unconscious desire and longing they have a certain relationship with the Mystical Body of the Redeemer, *they still remain deprived of those many heavenly gifts and helps which can only be enjoyed in the Catholic Church*.[31]

But even if a chance of salvation is offered to all, this hope was always accompanied by equally magisterial warnings of the kind provided by Pius XII here—that detachment from the visible Church is spiritually highly dangerous, not just for the non-baptized but also for those who, though baptized, lack the fullness of the faith in communion with the Church and, most importantly, the further sacraments of Eucharist and penance. Such detachment might not remove the very possibility of salvation. But it will still endanger salvation. Certainly, God is not bound by his own sacraments. But the magisterium has historically taken care to remind us not to presume on God's not being bound.

The current official theology on this matter is now very different. This author knows through direct testimony that a Protestant cleric was quite recently discouraged at the topmost level of the Church from becoming Catholic. Ecumenical dialogue is no longer consistently treated in official circles as Vatican II's *Unitatis Redintegratio* still treats it, as a path to genuine unity under Peter within the one Church for whole ecclesial communities separated from her that is parallel to, and not in any way opposed to, the other path of individual reception. Rather, ecumenical dialogue is often treated in practice as a substitute for genuine unity, as if its real purpose were merely to initiate harmonious coexistence between a plurality of "Christian churches" that nevertheless remain separated. Just because the outcome being aimed at is a harmonious coexistence without real unity, ecumenical dialogue is even treated in some

---

31 *Mystici Corporis* 103.

quarters as if it were somehow inconsistent with also encouraging individual receptions. For the open pursuit of individual receptions might threaten the harmony of this coexistence.

And so we arrive at a form of "zombie" ecumenism that effectively blocks the path to Christian unity rather than providing it. The ecumenism is a "zombie" form, because although it appears living, it is really dead, serving not to end but to preserve the existing separateness of Christian bodies, and to do so precisely through its prioritization of harmonious coexistence above all else. This degenerate ecumenism just provides complacent support for a status quo. In particular it blocks any public encouragement of individual receptions, just because such public encouragement would threaten that status quo. The possible spiritual loss to (and even loss *of*) those who are denied "those many heavenly gifts and helps which can only be enjoyed in the Catholic Church" no longer matters.

Complacent presumption on God's mercy in official theology extends beyond the other sacraments to baptism itself. In historic magisterial teaching, because all need to be rescued from the dominion of the devil, and because the New Covenant provides but one sure means of rescue that applies to all—baptism—therefore *all* are called to baptism, and the Church's mission to convert and baptize is a mission to all peoples. There is no alternative covenant or way of salvation available. The Church is indeed exactly as the magisterium in *Lumen Gentium* describes her: the New Israel replacing the Israel of old, for Jew and Gentile alike.

But that is no longer the view taken in modern official theology. One body in particular—the practitioners of Torah-based rabbinical Judaism—is treated as somehow exempt from the call to baptism and visible unity within the one Church. The issue here is not that we are now being allowed at least to hope for salvation even apart from membership in the visible Church. As we have seen, some magisterial license for such a hope might not be new, though certainly any license given was only for hope, not complacency. The problem is that in the case of Judaism, hope is now being replaced by complacency—a complacency that is supposedly divinely sanctioned. Where the Jewish people are concerned, a public mission to convert and baptize is now being officially excluded.

It is very important to note that a mission to the Jews is not being excluded just as a matter of temporary or local prudence. For example, given the appalling persecution of the Jewish people, a persecution that took a radically murderous form in modern times, and the disgraceful participation of Christians in that persecution, it could be argued that missionary work specifically and overtly directed at the Jewish people might in our particular context be counterproductive as offensive or intimidating.[32] But this is not the way a mission to the Jews is being excluded. It is being excluded in principle, as if such exclusion were supposedly dictated in some way by the very nature of the Church and her mission, and by the terms of a supposedly different mission divinely given to Judaism apart from the Church.

It is impossible to reconcile the rejection of a mission to the Jews on this supposedly principled and quite general basis with the practice of the apostles themselves—the model and origination of the Church's mission. Such a rejection is also opposed by the Council of Florence that not only teaches the universality of the call to and need for baptism, but specifically condemns any continued reliance for salvation on the ceremonies of the Old Law.[33] And, as we have already seen, an ecclesial mission to Jew and Gentile alike is taught by *Lumen Gentium*. The new official theology has therefore to be accompanied by much alternative history—by much silence about or outright denial of the Church's past commitment to such a mission to the Jewish people, as if right up until Vatican II whole religious communities had not been dedicated to it.

This rejection of a public mission to the Jews is accompanied by continued lip-service to the universality of Christ's saving covenant. That is, official theology tends still to deny any dual covenant theory—the clearly heretical position that the Jewish people have a saving covenant distinct from that offered by Christ to the Gentiles through baptism into the Church. But while the doctrinal content of dual covenant theology is still officially rejected, nonetheless a

[32] One might wonder whether all such evangelization would be quite as counterproductive as is often supposed—but we need not debate this here.

[33] See the Council of Florence, Bull of Union with the Copts, *Decrees of the Ecumenical Councils*, 1:576; and then, citing Florence, Pius XII in *Mystici Corporis*: "On the Cross then the Old Law died, soon to be buried and to be a bearer of death, in order to give way to the New Testament of which Christ had chosen the Apostles as qualified ministers."

pastoral program presupposing that content is being adopted. And with that pastoral program, the content of dual covenant theology still slips in at least at the margins of theological expression, again at the very highest levels of the Church. Take Judaism's denial of Christ's identity as the savior of all mankind. If dual covenant theology is false, this denial must be a very serious error and so an evil which God, as the author of truth and no deceiver, must permit but not directly will. Yet Joseph Ratzinger, writing when pope but as a private theologian, associates this error with a supposed distinctive mission for the Jews — as if their rejection of Christ were not opposed to God's salvific will for them, as it surely must be, but were somehow an expression of it:

> In this regard, the question of *Israel's mission* has always been present in the background. We realize today with horror how many misunderstandings with grave consequences have weighed down our history. Yet a new reflection can acknowledge that the beginnings of a correct understanding have always been there, waiting to be rediscovered, however deep the shadows.[34]

What is this mission, special as Israel's "own mission," as Ratzinger terms it?[35] Certainly not to respond here and now through conversion and baptism to Christ's universal saving call. For Israel's "mission" implies, on Ratzinger's understanding, that by her very nature the Church really has no public mission of her own to convert and baptize the Jewish people as she has to convert and baptize the Gentiles. What of the inconvenient truth that the apostles themselves began with and always maintained a public mission to their fellow Jews? Ratzinger equivocates, rather unconvincingly:

> But it was becoming increasingly clear that the evangelization of the Gentiles was now the disciples' particular task — thanks above all to the special commission given to Paul as a duty and a grace.[36]

But this really is misleading. St Paul's own prioritization of a mission to the Gentiles hardly excluded even in his case a public call to Jewish conversion as well; and, as special to him, this prioritization

---

34 Joseph Ratzinger, *Jesus of Nazareth: Holy Week* (San Francisco: Ignatius Press, 2011), 44.
35 Ratzinger, 46.
36 Ibid.

Religious Liberty

had nothing whatsoever to do with what Ratzinger implies—a supposed general detachment of the apostles as a whole from a public mission to all humanity, to Jew and Gentile alike.

Romans chapter 11 is a famous proclamation of God's continuing concern for the Jewish people, and of God's determination to remain faithful to his promise of salvation for them. It predicts the persistence of Judaism as a religion rejecting Christianity until the end times, when the mission to the Gentiles is finally concluded. Now when St Paul writes that at that time "so all Israel will be saved" (Rom 11:26), he seems to have meant, at least, that all that is left of Judaism at that time will then be converted and saved. But that does not guarantee a route to salvation for practitioners of Judaism living now that is independent of faith in Christ and baptism as Gentile salvation is not. Nor does St Paul seem to have envisaged such a route. After all, St Paul claims in that same chapter that he advertises his own ministry to the Gentiles to make his fellow Jews jealous of what the Gentiles are being offered "and thereby save some of them."[37]

Ratzinger, however, does take this chapter to exclude, on scriptural grounds, any mission to the Jews here and now. Quoting a theological speculation of Hildegard Brem, Ratzinger concludes:

> In the light of Romans 11:25, the Church must not concern herself with the conversion of the Jews, since she must wait for the time fixed for this by God, "until the full number of the Gentiles come in" (Rom 11:25).[38]

But this is effectively to admit dual covenant theology in some form. However much, or little, actual baptism may matter here and now to the salvation of an individual Gentile, it is being treated as *especially* irrelevant to the salvation of an individual Jew. Even if Christ is still supposed to be in some way savior for Jew and Gentile alike, baptism clearly does not matter to Jewish salvation as it matters to Gentile salvation. For where the Jewish people are

---

[37] "Now I am speaking to you Gentiles. Inasmuch as I am an apostle to the Gentiles, I magnify my ministry in order to make my fellow Jews jealous, and thus save some of them" (Rom 11:13–14). And the Jews are described as to be grafted back into salvation "if they do not persist in their unbelief" (Rom 11:23).

[38] Ratzinger, *Jesus of Nazareth: Holy Week*, 45.

concerned, the Church is specifically forbidden *by the very terms of her mission* openly to encourage it. Contrary to *Lumen Gentium*, the Church is not after all in the business of calling "together from Jews and Gentiles a people that would be bound together in unity not according to the flesh but in the Spirit" — a new and universal people of God to replace the old Israel of the flesh.

This is part of a wider phenomenon. Even when the letter of magisterial teaching is still preserved by official theology, at least for a while, its pastoral implications are often abandoned in Church policy — where this is necessary to avoid some especially unwanted conflict with an unconverted world. And then, inevitably, official theology begins to compromise or elide that past magisterial teaching.

Summary: the sacraments as salvation theatre

We see official theology omitting or even denying magisterial teaching about baptism — and in ways that consistently underplay the implications of the Fall. The need for baptism for salvation is soft-pedalled, its role in subjecting the baptized to the jurisdiction of a *potestas* is effectively denied, as are its political implications — baptism's clear involvement of the state. In all of this it is assumed that, even prior to baptism and real conversion, somehow the world is already released from the dominion of the devil and oriented towards salvation, so that, as with Maritain's new vision of Church-state relations, harmony with the world no longer presupposes its conversion.

Of course, if this official theology is taken seriously, there arises an obvious question about the point of *actual* membership in the Church and *actual* participation in her sacramental life. This threatens to become a form of salvation theatre, at best a merely representative sign of salvation, where what actually saves us is some invisible and universal supernatural orientation eschatologically linked to Christ. As one Italian priest preached in my hearing to his congregation in Verona in September 2016, participation in penance and the Eucharist is simply a sign of something Christ has already achieved. For we are all *già salvati* — all already saved.

This is a transformation in the Church's official theology of baptism, and in clear conflict with the historical magisterium. At the heart of it lies a vision of the Church's relation to the unconverted world—be it the world of the state, of non-Catholic Christian communities, or of non-Christian religions and of Judaism in particular—as primarily directed at attaining spiritual harmony, and so as excluding spiritual conflict, and to this end as prioritizing dialogic harmony over conversion, and even in some cases (the state and the Jewish people) as precluding conversion altogether. Central to this vision of harmonious coexistence with an unconverted world is the abandonment of any conception of the world as still, until its conversion, lying under diabolic dominion.

4. Church and State—and the Operation of Grace to Heal

How far can the operation of grace really be detached from visible membership of the Church? Is receipt of the sacraments no more than a form of salvation theatre—the representation of a communication of grace that is really effected independently? This is the fundamental issue, to which the relationship between baptism and release from diabolic dominion is key. Is baptism the means by which we are liberated from the devil's power, or a mere sign of a liberation that occurs independently of actual baptism—that has, in effect, already happened?

While the Church allows for the possibility of salvation even of the unbaptized, the magisterium has never treated visible membership of the Church and actual participation in her sacramental life as a matter of indifference. Hope has certainly been offered, but not the comfort of complacency. But perhaps the historical magisterium was just wrong. Perhaps modern official complacency is really warranted, and we have to draw the lesson of a New Pentecost—that for her entire history until Vatican II the Church was consistently betraying her own gospel by trusting insufficiently in the divine mercy.

How consistent though is such a theory of the New Pentecost with the doctrine that revelation was complete with the death of the last apostle—and that the Church was equipped by Christ from the very beginning to preach that revelation without error, preserving it faithfully without adding to it? For if we are all living, only now, through a New Pentecost, it would seem that for centuries, from the very beginning until the last Council, the Church was woefully in error about her own mission, and that only now after two millennia does she understand that mission aright—a mission that, it now appears, may even leave actual membership in her and actual reception of her sacraments as things of symbolic significance only, and no more than elaborate salvation theatre.

At this point someone might raise an important difficulty. We are debating how grace is made present and effective in human life to save us—whether in a way that significantly depends on actual receipt of the sacraments of the Church, or in a way that is largely assured independently of them. But who can tell with precision who is saved and who is not? So whilst the theory of invisible salvation may seem presumptuous, opposing skepticism might seem equally presumptuous too.

But in fact the operation of grace is not entirely hidden from us. For the same grace that elevates us to the supernatural end also operates to heal nature and to repair the moral damage done to human nature by the Fall. Grace repairs, in particular, the damage done by sin to the human will and intellect. Here the operation of grace is far more visible—and in a way that suggests a significant dependence for its operation on membership in the visible Church and actual and worthy participation in her sacraments.

The Fall did not remove the natural law entirely from human nature. We retain an understanding of its foundations, that goodness should be pursued, evil avoided. We also remain capable of doing good and avoiding evil at the level of natural morality. But sin, original and actual, has still done real damage. As Aquinas noted, without the help of grace we cannot now avoid all serious wrongdoing. And even our understanding of the detail of the moral law may be impaired, so that at certain times and places particular groups or societies of people might cease to understand that, for example, theft is wrong, or that innocents should not be killed. Such failure to acknowledge even the content of the natural law, Aquinas notes, can affect the political order. In a fallen world, states may pass laws that conflict with, and reflect a failure to understand, important parts of natural law.[39]

39   See *ST* I-II, q. 94, a. 6 and q. 109, a. 2.

So grace operates at two levels—to raise us above nature, and to repair nature. And its operation to repair nature is by no means invisible. Where we find failure not only to apply the natural law, but even to acknowledge important parts of its content, then we can empirically determine that grace is not operating effectively. And such evidence becomes plentiful precisely when whole human societies are detached from the Church, or where groups of people remain visibly members, but collectively abandon worthy participation in her sacramental life—as where the habit of communion without confession becomes typical. We arrive at the phenomenon of widespread dissent, both outside the Church and in the postconciliar period within the Church as well, from the natural law concerning human life and marriage

As for private individuals, so for political communities as well—as the nineteenth century popes consistently predicted. It is with the operation of grace to heal that, as we have seen, the political teaching of the nineteenth century popes was immediately concerned. Thanks to the Fall, humanity in general is threatened with a degradation of its nature—and the political community is in no way exempt from this threat. The popes were quite explicit that at the political level grace would reliably operate to heal nature only through a genuine conversion of the political community, and its membership and participation in the life of the Church at the public level. Without that conversion, as Leo XIII predicted, "human reason fails" in relation to the public good. Secularization of political life has led only to ever increasing levels of state denial and violation of those parts of the natural law that are central to issues of life and death—marriage and respect for the right to life of the innocent. The political community is returning in its public life to the dominion of the devil—an allegiance that opposes it to natural law and therefore also to the mission of the Church. There is indeed no neutral space.

What stops the Church from living in a stable harmony with an unconverted world? Ultimately, of course, for as long as the world does remain unconverted, *Christ himself* is the obstacle, given the unconverted world's subjection to the devil, and the devil's enmity with Christ. But the unconverted world is at war too with the law of its own created nature—the natural law, conformity to which is basic and essential to any conformity to Christ. Without a restoration of respect for natural law, which can come only through the healing grace of Christ, there can be no harmony between Church and world. The case of the secular state shows, with particular clarity, that the Church cannot expect any such harmony without conversion.

5. The Pursuit of Harmony with the Unconverted World

The Church's ultimate goal is harmony with all mankind—with a world both as God's creation and as redeemed by Christ. According to the new official theology, however, not only is this harmony to be aimed at—but it is supposed to be attainable already, even without the world's conversion. Yet we can now clearly see, and the magisterium has historically taught, that such harmony is not possible. The Church cannot coexist in spiritual peace with the dominion of the devil.

Nevertheless, because the new official theology dictates this arrangement, the contemporary Church still persists in her pursuit of harmony without conversion. What then if, as it must, this pursuit consistently proves unsuccessful? The one lesson the new official theology will not allow to be drawn is the traditional one; that harmony with the unconverted world is impossible precisely because the world is unconverted.

Since, where attaining harmony between Church and world is concerned, the world's non-conversion is nowadays not supposed to be a problem, the modern official theology encourages the idea that the solution must instead lie in the other way left open—not in a transformation of the world, through its conversion, but rather in a transformation of the Church. The new pastoral program of the Church towards the unconverted—the program of the New Pentecost—is supposed to be one of a stable dialogic harmony, a harmony no longer dependent on conversion. When the harmony fails to arise, renewed effort must be made to find remaining obstacles to it that can safely be removed—no longer from the side of the world, through its conversion, but from the Church's side. To prevent conflict, then, the Church will increasingly attempt to adapt herself to the unconverted world, where she thinks she somehow can, and especially at the level of pastoral policy.

The first to go will be any conflict-producing prioritization of conversion. The strict doctrinal letter behind that mission to convert may still be respected—but in cases where conflict is particularly feared, the pastoral commitment to that mission will be rapidly ended, and may even be ended on grounds of alleged principle, and not some simple temporary prudence. Lip-service continues to be paid to the universality of the Church's mission—but this universality can still be thoroughly contradicted at the pastoral level.

Thus in a 2015 statement on the fiftieth anniversary of *Nostra Aetate*, the Church's Commission for Religious Relations with the Jews still excludes dual covenant theology at the level of doctrine:

> Since God has never revoked his covenant with his people Israel, there cannot be different paths or approaches to God's salvation. The theory that there may be two different paths to salvation, the Jewish path without Christ and the path with the Christ, whom Christians believe is Jesus of Nazareth, would in fact endanger the foundations of Christian faith. Confessing the universal and therefore also exclusive mediation of salvation through Jesus Christ belongs to the core of Christian faith.[40]

Now, surely, if Christ's saving covenant is universal, and the body by which Christ saves is the Church, the Church's public mission must include, at least in principle, a call to the Jewish people. Yet, the Commission urges that, as a matter of *principle*, the Church's public mission excludes any such call—simply because the Jewish people's self-identity depends on not being converted.

> It is easy to understand that the so-called "mission to the Jews" is a very delicate and sensitive matter for Jews because, in their eyes, it involves the very existence of the Jewish people. This question also proves to be awkward for Christians, because for them the universal salvific significance of Jesus Christ and consequently the universal mission of the Church are of fundamental importance. The Church is therefore obliged to view evangelization to Jews,

---

40 "'The gifts and the calling of God are irrevocable' (Rom 11:29): A Reflection on Theological Questions Pertaining to Catholic–Jewish Relations on the Occasion of the 50th Anniversary of *Nostra Aetate* (No. 4)," December 10, 2015, n. 35.

who believe in the one God, in a different manner from that to people of other religions and worldviews. In concrete terms this means that the Catholic Church neither conducts nor supports any specific institutional mission work directed towards Jews. While there is a *principled* rejection of an institutional Jewish mission, Christians are nonetheless called to bear witness to their faith in Jesus Christ also to Jews, although they should do so in a humble and sensitive manner, acknowledging that Jews are bearers of God's Word, and particularly in view of the great tragedy of the Shoah.[41]

The Church does not call on Jews to convert and be baptized as she might still call on Gentiles to convert and be baptized. Does this not endanger the salvation of those unbaptized Jewish individuals passed by? It had better not do so. If giving even the impression that conversion to Christ was not needed in their case did endanger Jewish salvation in any way, abandoning a public mission to the Jews, and doing so as a matter of principle, would be an act of profound hostility to the Jewish people. The Commission's policy—the Jewish people are not to be invited to convert and be baptized as other peoples are—makes sense only on one assumption: Jewish salvation must not depend at all on conversion and baptism.

Yet the Commission still insists that the Church's mission is universal. It maintains that for Christians "the universal salvific significance of Jesus Christ and consequently the universal mission of the Church are of fundamental importance."[42] But now the Commission faces a dilemma. Jewish salvation, it seems, is radically independent of baptism and conversion. If even then the Church's mission of salvation still includes the Jews under the very same covenant as the Gentiles, the covenant offered by Christ in the New Testament cannot after all depend on actual baptism and conversion. These are mere signs of Christ's mission, not means needed to effect it. The mission of the Church involves the sacraments simply as a form of salvation theatre.

Suppose on the other hand that the Church's mission does importantly depend on the sacraments as means to effecting it.

---

41 Ibid., 40.
42 Ibid.

Then that mission cannot after all include the Jewish people. If baptism is taken to be radically dispensable in the salvation of the Jewish people but is not so for the Gentiles, this is to concede dual covenant theology in some form. There must be a different salvific deal for the two peoples, and the Church's mission, as sacrament-dependent, is to the Gentiles alone.

Notice of course one important consequence of an official theology that does ever radically detach salvation from actual conversion to Christ, whether for the case of the Jewish people alone or more generally. The spiritual conflict required to ensure conversion centrally involves confronting error about matters vital to salvation—in particular about the identity and significance of Christ himself. But if the removal of error on this point is no longer seen as vital to salvation—if the error is no longer seen clearly as spiritually dangerous, or even a real error at all—then the spiritual conflict that attempts at conversion would inevitably lead to is increasingly seen as an unnecessary evil. The attempt to convert becomes an unnecessary and offensive intolerance—something that has to be avoided in order to facilitate harmonious coexistence and the better to enable those forms of cooperation that can be common property with the unconverted world. And so we see the Church Commission concluding:

> One important goal of Jewish-Christian dialogue certainly consists in joint engagement throughout the world for justice, peace, conservation of creation, and reconciliation. In the past, it may have been that the different religions—*against the background of a narrowly understood claim to truth and a corresponding intolerance*—contributed to the incitement of conflict and confrontation. *But today religions should not be part of the problem, but part of the solution.* Only when religions engage in a successful dialogue with one another, and in that way contribute towards world peace, can this be realized also on the social and political levels.[43]

The solution to the plight of a fallen world is no longer first and foremost the public acknowledgment by all of Christ, but cooperation towards no doubt valuable but entirely secular ends. And this especially excludes pressing the religion-dividing issue of

---

43 Ibid., 46.

Christ, the very issue that a public mission to the Jewish people would raise. Suddenly, in official theology it seems, the Church's mission to convert is no longer the solution, but the very problem.

If the sacramental life of the Church is increasingly understood no longer as effecting of salvation, but instead as a form of salvation theatre, then even in relation to that sacramental life, other values—those acceptable to the unconverted world—may come to dominate. If the attempt to convert and invite into the Church's sacramental life causes offense and disharmony, then, since we are dealing with a symbol—a sign that is, strictly speaking, inessential or unimportant in itself to actually *effecting* salvation—the symbol may be sacrificed. Equally if, within the life of the Church, denial of a sacrament would be offensive and conflict-producing, then again, since unworthy receipt of the sacrament no longer threatens salvation, offence may carefully be avoided there too. The denial of communion to whole categories of people because their way of life is in public contradiction of the gospel may come to look unacceptable—especially when an unconverted world increasingly insists that the way of life is not objectionable at all, but right and liberating.

Thus the prioritization of harmony over conversion corrupts the Church's mission not only *ad extra*, but *ad intra* too. The pursuit of harmony with the world but without the world's conversion will not only stifle the Church's mission to convert those without, but weaken the internal life of the Church. And this will happen in two ways. First, in placating that world without converting it, the Church will inevitably encourage her own membership actually to conform to the unconverted world themselves. But of course, with lowering levels of worthy participation in the full sacramental life of the Church—especially through communions unaccompanied by confession—the pursuit of harmony with the unconverted will increasingly dominate the internal life of the Church herself. For the unconverted world will increasingly extend to include more and more of the Church's own members who cease to participate in her sacraments worthily, and so cease benefit from the life of grace, even in their beliefs. The unremedied consequences of sin for the human intellect—the "clouding of human reason"—will damage the internal life of the Church herself, and lead to ever increasing levels of dissent not only with revelation but with the plain content of natural law. And so we come to the crisis in the Church's treatment of marriage—the crisis of *Amoris Laetitia*.

We now see the source of the pressure to adopt pastoral programs that seem primarily designed to defuse conflict with the unconverted—and in doing so muffle the content of magisterial teaching that is conflict-threatening, even when the letter of that teaching is still respected.

A common thread emerges, linking the Church's official policy towards and theological understanding of her relations to those unconverted without to her treatment of those effectively unconverted within. Dual covenant theology is still formally denied, but a pastoral program is adopted that presupposes some form of a dual covenant—a path to salvation special to practitioners of Judaism that is left mysterious but that, at least in the here and now, bypasses the Church and baptism entirely. And then we have an internal parallel to this. The indissolubility of marriage is formally taught—but to remove conflict with the unconverted within as much as without the Church, the pastoral implications of that teaching begin to be ignored, and a pastoral program is adopted that treats marriage as in effect dissoluble. Indeed some of the same figures can be found in both programs of conflict-precluding pastoral adjustment. Walter Cardinal Kasper has denied the letter of dual covenant theology—but is a notable proponent of adopting its pastoral program. He is also a notable proponent of adopting a pastoral program that treats marriage as, in effect, dissoluble.

Inevitably in both cases the magisterial teaching itself is soon watered down. Just as official theology begins to inch towards dual covenant theology at the level of theory as it concedes to it outright in pastoral practice, so likewise concessions begin to be made in relation to marriage doctrine as well. So it is increasingly suggested, even by senior prelates, that not all sexual relations outside marriage should be classed as adultery or fornication. Some "conscientious" cases of such relations, it is even suggested, may become morally equivalent to a form of "marriage."

Much of "conservative" Catholicism has been deeply shocked by *Amoris Laetitia*, but is prone to see the problem of official theology detaching itself from the historical magisterium as a peculiarity of the current pontificate. But now we see the deeper source of the crisis, which lies in a revolution—occurring with Vatican II, though apart from any new magisterial teaching of the Council—in the official theology of the sacraments and of baptism in particular.

6. Conclusion

The revolution in the official theology of baptism is twofold. Dialogic harmony is given priority over conversion—and the sacramental life of the Church is seen as signifying of salvation accomplished, rather than something on which salvation actually depends.

There is a common root: the assumption that diabolic dominion over humanity has already been removed even in advance of baptism, and without any need for the world's conversion. That assumption is what makes the modern Church's pursuit of harmony with the world without its conversion appear feasible, and even a goal to be prioritized over conversion itself.

But the goal of harmony without conversion is not feasible at all. What reveals this is what also provides strong evidence that the operation of grace really does significantly depend on worthy participation in the sacramental life of the Church. This evidence lies in the very visible failure of grace to heal nature without nature's conversion—a failure that lies at the heart of moral conflict between the Church and an unconverted world.

Central to magisterial teaching about baptism is the grim reality, so clearly taught dogmatically at Florence, that the unconverted world remains under the dominion of the devil. Consequently, as Christ himself clearly proclaimed, baptism is a source not of harmony with the unconverted world but of spiritual confrontation of it and spiritual conflict with it—a spiritual conflict that can be ended only by the world's conversion.

The crisis of *Amoris Laetitia* is not a theological crisis of the current pontificate alone. It is not isolated, and it has parallels elsewhere that had already arisen under previous postconciliar popes. One especially glaring parallel to the pastoral muffling of the Church's marriage teaching, we have seen, is the equally serious compromising of the Church's mission publicly to call all humanity to Christ — the Church's flirtation at an official level, at least at the level of pastoral strategy and even to a degree beyond, with dual covenant theology. Both are parts of a more general crisis in official theology that has followed Vatican II. This crisis involves a revolution in understanding of the sacraments, and of baptism in particular — a revolution which immediately implicates the Church in pastoral programs that prioritize harmony over conversion, and which, to protect this prioritization at the pastoral level, inevitably compromises the Church's presentation of magisterial teaching too. Until this general crisis of official theology is generally understood for what it is, and fidelity to magisterial teaching is recovered at every level of the Church, but especially at the highest levels, the general crisis of the Vatican II period will only continue, and take new forms.

20

A Critique of John Locke's *Letter Concerning Toleration*

Derek Remus

The first three centuries of the Catholic Church's existence were a period of violent and bloody persecution at the hands of the Roman Empire—that is, the state. The Church persevered through this trial, however, and, instead of diminishing, increased in proportion to the persecutions she suffered, until at last she was granted freedom of worship and hers was made the official religion of the Empire. This was the beginning of that harmonious union between Church and state which gave rise to Christendom—a union in which the state recognized that its proper good was ordered toward a higher good, namely, eternal beatitude, and the Church, to the extent that affairs of state bore upon the salvation of souls, was solicitous about those affairs.

This union lasted throughout Europe for twelve hundred years. Then came the Protestant Reformation. The divine origin of the papacy was challenged; the religious unity of Europe was shattered; Christendom unraveled. The Church still existed, however, and the question of how governments ought to deal with her under the new order of things became an urgent problem for political philosophers.

Thomas Hobbes and Benedict Spinoza held that the head of state ought to be the head of the Church, since otherwise the citizens' loyalties would be divided.[1] John Locke, on the other hand, took an

---

[1] See Thomas Hobbes, *Leviathan*, Part IV, ch. XLIV: "Which second coming not yet being, the kingdom of God is not yet come, and we are not now under any other kings by pact but our civil sovereigns... This power regal under Christ, being challenged

Religious Liberty

apparently more benign position by calling not for the subjection of the Church to the state but for the total separation of the two powers. In his *Letter Concerning Toleration*, he said that there is no connection, and hence no conflict, between the salvation of souls and the goods of this world. Therefore, the state must grant equal status and liberty to all religions within its domain, provided that they do not teach any doctrines dangerous to the state's welfare (which doctrines would then not be, properly speaking, religious), and those religions in turn must in no way concern themselves with political affairs.

While the positions of Hobbes and Spinoza have more or less found expression historically in regimes such as those of Protestant England and the People's Republic of China,[2] the Lockean position has found perhaps no better expression than in the regime of the United States of America. Indeed, the influence of Locke on several of the American Founding Fathers with regard to the question of Church and state (not to mention several other questions) cannot be contested.[3] As a consequence, many American Catholics,

---

universally by the Pope and in particular Commonwealths by assemblies of the pastors of the place (when the Scripture gives it to none but to civil sovereigns), comes to be so passionately disputed that it putteth out the light of nature, and causeth so great a darkness in men's understanding that they see not who it is to whom they have engaged their obedience." Benedict Spinoza, *Theologico-Political Treatise*, ch. 19, entitled: "It is shown that the right over matters spiritual lies wholly with the sovereign, and that the outward forms of religion should be in accordance with public peace, if we would obey God aright."

2 I say that this is true *more or less*. The regimes enumerated do not agree with those about which Hobbes and Spinoza theorized, or (obviously) with each other in every respect.

3 As examples of this influence on one of the Founding Fathers, consider the following statements from Thomas Jefferson: "Believing with you that religion is a matter which lies solely between man and his God, that he owes account to none other for his faith or his worship, that the legislative powers of government reach actions only, and not opinions, I contemplate with sovereign reverence that act of the whole American people which declared that their legislature should 'make no law respecting an establishment of religion, or prohibiting the free exercise thereof,' thus building a wall of separation between Church and State" (Letter to the Danbury Baptist Association). "But our rulers can have authority over such natural rights only as we have submitted to them. The rights of conscience we never submitted, we could not submit. We are answerable for them to our God. The legitimate powers of government extend to such acts only as are injurious to others. But it does me no injury for my neighbor to say there are twenty gods, or no God. It neither picks my pocket nor breaks my leg" (*Notes on Virginia*, Query VII). The resemblance that the thought contained in these statements bears to Lockean thought on Church and state may not be clear in every way right now, but it will no doubt become clear as we proceed.

whether wittingly or unwittingly, tend to espouse positions on Church and state that are more or less Lockean in principle and to regard the American status of Church and state, where the state treats all religious bodies equally, as an ideal toward which the rest of the world ought to strive.

Such thinking, however, is clearly opposed to that of the Church's Magisterium. While the Magisterium teaches that the ecclesiastical and civil powers have "fixed limits within which" each "is contained, limits which are defined by the nature and special object of the province of each,"[4] these limits do not mean that there are no areas that fall within the jurisdiction of both powers or that the ends of Church and state, while distinct, have no order existing between them. On the contrary, Pope Leo XIII teaches that the state is bound by divine law to engage in the "public profession of religion ... not such religion as [men] may have a preference for, but the religion which God enjoins, and which certain and most clear marks show to be the only one true religion."[5] Pope Pius IX condemns the proposition that "it has been wisely decided by law, in some Catholic countries, that persons coming to reside therein shall enjoy the public exercise of their own peculiar worship."[6] Pope Pius XI declares that the "kingly dignity" of Christ "demands that the State should take account of the commandments of God and of Christian principles, both in making laws and in administering justice, and also in providing for the young a sound moral education."[7] All of these papal pronouncements make it clear that the Lockean position on Church and state is irreconcilable with Catholic doctrine.

In this essay, I will show that the Catholic Church is right about the relation between Church and state and that Locke is wrong. I shall do so principally through the teachings of the Common Doctor of the Church, St Thomas Aquinas. The essay will consist of three parts: 1) an exposition of Locke's position as expressed in *A Letter Concerning Toleration*; 2) an exposition and defense of the Church's position; 3) a refutation of Locke's position in light of that defense.

---

[4] Pope Leo XIII, *Immortale Dei* 13.
[5] *Immortale Dei* 6.
[6] Pope Pius IX, *Syllabus of Errors*, n. 78; also see *Quanta Cura*, the encyclical attached to the syllabus.
[7] Pope Pius XI, *Quas Primas* 32.

I. Exposition of *A Letter Concerning Toleration*

Before we examine the substance of Locke's *Letter Concerning Toleration*, we must point out two possible sources of confusion in understanding it.

First, throughout the *Letter*, Locke complains that in his day Christians are killing and persecuting each other on account of differences in belief and that they are often using the power of the state to do so. His repeated condemnation of this state of affairs can make one think that the unjustness of using the state to kill and persecute one's neighbors on account of religion is really what the *Letter* is all about. In fact, however, the main purpose of the *Letter* is to establish a general doctrine concerning the very natures of Church and state from which the unjustness of using the state to kill and persecute one's neighbors on account of religion follows as a consequence. It is this general doctrine, and not a consequence of it that happens to be true, which constitutes the real target of our attack on the *Letter*.

Second, throughout the *Letter*, Locke speaks of the "mutual toleration of *Christians* in their different professions of religion" [emphasis added].[8] This can make it seem that Locke intends the equal toleration of different religions implied by the separation of Church and state to extend only to Christian bodies. Later in the *Letter*, however, Locke speaks of toleration not only for the "different professions of religion" within Christianity but for all religions. He asks:

> Shall we suffer a Pagan to deal and trade with us, and shall we not suffer him to pray unto and worship God? If we allow the Jews to have private houses and dwellings amongst us, why should we not allow them to have synagogues?[9]

Therefore, the reason that Locke refers frequently to toleration for different *Christian* religious bodies is merely that he is writing for Europeans, nearly all of whom happen to be Christian; his principles, however, demand toleration for *all* religious bodies.[10]

---

8 John Locke, *A Letter Concerning Toleration*, in *The Second Treatise of Government and A Letter Concerning Toleration* (Mineola, NY: Dover Publications), 115.

9 Locke, 149.

10 This is, of course, under the condition that all religious bodies refrain from interfering in matters outside the proper domain of religion, as Locke conceives it. As

A Critique of John Locke's Letter Concerning Toleration

Let us now examine the substance of the *Letter*. As we have said, the central contention of the *Letter* is that the state can have no interest in the salvation of souls and that the Church can have no interest in civil affairs. Concretely, this means that the state must grant equal status and liberty to all religious bodies within its domain and that those religious bodies must in turn refrain from all intervention in affairs of state.

To show the first part of the *Letter's* central contention, namely, that the state can have no interest in the salvation of souls, Locke begins by defining the state, or commonwealth, as "a society of men constituted only for the procuring, preserving, and advancing their own civil interests."[11] By "civil interests" Locke says he means "life, liberty, health, and indolency of body; and the possession of outward things, such as money, lands, houses, furniture, and the like."[12]

If we wish to understand fully what Locke has in mind when he defines the state in this way, we must turn to his *Second Treatise of Government*, where he gives an account of how the state comes to be. Here he says that prior to the existence of the state, men are in a state of nature, that is, "a *state of perfect freedom* to order their actions, and dispose of their possessions and persons, as they think fit, within the bounds of the law of nature, without asking leave, or depending upon the will of any other man."[13] This "state of perfect freedom" belongs to all men equally, so that the state of nature is also a state of equality, "wherein all the power and jurisdiction is reciprocal, no one having more than another."[14] Further, the "state of perfect freedom" is not unlimited but is bounded by the "law of nature," which obliges every man to preserve himself and "teaches all mankind...that being all *equal and independent*, no one ought to harm another in his life, health, liberty, or possessions."[15] In other words, since all men possess the freedom to dispose of themselves as they please equally, the only limit to one man's exercise of that freedom, aside from not destroying himself,

will become clear later, there are certain religious bodies which do not refrain from doing so, and therefore, there are exceptions to the rule of toleration.

11 Locke, 118.
12 Ibid.
13 Locke, *Second Treatise of Government*, ch. II, sec. 4, p. 2.
14 Ibid.
15 *Second Treatise*, II, sec. 6, p. 3, emphasis added.

is not to hinder another man's exercise of that same freedom. Every one may do as he likes, so long as he lets others do as they like.

Most men, however, do not let others do as they like. Hence, Locke declares that while man always has the "right" to enjoy his "state of perfect freedom," his actual enjoyment of that state is "very uncertain, and constantly exposed to the invasion of others."[16] In order to make that enjoyment certain, men form a contract with each other whereby they agree to unite into a society and to create some authority upon whom they confer the power of protecting their lives, liberties, and possessions from the encroachments of others. The society thus instituted is the state. While it is true that, in entering the state, men give up certain "rights" belonging to their natural "state of perfect freedom" — most notably, the right to punish those who attempt to harm them without appeal to a higher power—, they do so only in order to enjoy the remainder of those "rights," which they value more, more securely.[17] The end of the state, therefore, is to protect those natural rights which its citizens value most and hence want to enjoy most without the interference of others. When these rights become the object of the state's protection, they become "civil interests" or "civil rights." Hence, in the *Letter*, Locke defines the state as "a society of men constituted only for the procuring, preserving, and advancing their own civil interests."

Having defined the state, Locke briefly describes the duty and power of the civil magistrate. He says that the duty of the civil magistrate is to secure the aforementioned civil interests to "the people in general and to every one of his subjects in particular" through "the impartial execution of equal laws."[18] To execute these laws, the magistrate must have the power to punish those who violate them, and to have this power, he must be "armed with the force and strength of all his subjects."[19] The power of the magistrate, therefore, "consists only in outward force."[20]

---

16 *Second Treatise*, IX, sec. 123, p. 57.

17 There are several texts in the *Second Treatise of Government* in which Locke speaks as though men leave the state of nature behind when they enter political society. Since, however, in entering political society, men give up certain natural rights in order to enjoy others more securely, it is clear that they leave the state of nature behind only in part.

18 Locke, *Letter*, 118.

19 Locke, 118.

20 Locke, 119.

In light of his definition of the state and his account of the duty and power of the civil magistrate, Locke provides four arguments for why the power of the civil magistrate does not in any way bear upon the salvation of souls.[21]

The first argument is that care of souls has not been committed to the magistrate by anyone. It has not been committed to him by God because God has not given any man the authority "to compel anyone to his religion."[22] But for the magistrate to have a care of souls would be for him to compel men to his religion, since the power of the magistrate "consists only in outward force." Care of souls has not been committed to the magistrate by the consent of the people because no one may so "abandon the care of his own salvation as blindly to leave to the choice of any other, whether prince or subject, to prescribe to him what faith or worship he shall embrace."[23] The reason for this is that "faith is not faith" without "the inward and full persuasion of the mind," which cannot be effected by making someone "blindly" follow the dictates of someone else.[24]

The second argument is that the power of the magistrate "consists only in outward force," as stated, but outward force cannot affect what one holds in the mind. Faith, however, as stated in the previous argument, demands "the inward and full persuasion of the mind." Therefore, the magistrate has no power by which he can influence the religion of his subjects. Therefore, he cannot have a care of souls.

Note that both of these arguments rely on the claim that, since the power of the magistrate "consists only in outward force," the magistrate cannot exercise care of souls in any other way than by forcing his citizens to perform acts by which they embrace the religion of the state. If we deny this claim, then the arguments fall apart.

---

21 The first three arguments immediately follow Locke's account of the power and duty of the civil magistrate and are explicitly stated to be arguments for the conclusion that civil power "neither can nor ought in any manner to be extended to the salvation of souls" (118). The fourth argument, however, does not show up till several pages later when Locke treats the duty of the magistrate "in the business of toleration" (128) in greater detail. Moreover, Locke does not explicitly refer to it as a new argument for the said conclusion, even though that is in fact what it is. The structure of the *Letter* does not always follow the best order.
22 Locke, *Letter*, 118.
23 Locke, 119.
24 Locke, 119.

Religious Liberty

The third argument is that, even if outward force could affect what one holds in the mind, that would bring about the damnation rather than the salvation of most men. For given "the variety and contradiction"[25] of the opinions of princes with regard to religion, most princes would force false religions on their subjects.

The fourth argument is that the salvation or damnation of one's neighbor in no way advances or harms one's civil interests. If one's neighbor goes to hell, one's health or money, for example, will still remain fully intact. The duty of the magistrate, however, is to secure everyone's civil interests. Therefore, matters pertaining to salvation are wholly outside of the magistrate's jurisdiction.

One might conclude from the foregoing arguments that the basis for religious toleration is the mere fact that the practice of one's religion is something outside the state's jurisdiction. Later in the *Letter*, however, Locke implies that the practice of one's religion is something more than that, namely, a natural right:

> These accusations [that assemblies of religious bodies are nurseries of factions and seditions] would soon cease if the law of toleration were once so settled that all Churches were obliged to lay down toleration as the foundation of their own liberty, and teach that *liberty of conscience is every man's natural right*, equally belonging to dissenters as to themselves.[26]

The language of "natural right" calls to mind the state of nature. Locke seems to be implying that the freedom to practice the religion which one's conscience judges to be acceptable to God is really a particular determination or expression of man's natural "state of perfect freedom." In other words, man's natural freedom to dispose of himself as he pleases implies his freedom to practice the religion of his choosing. This makes sense, if we bear in mind that the only limit to the "state of perfect freedom" is the law of nature, which forbids a man from destroying himself and from harming the "life, health, liberty" and "possessions" of others. Inasmuch as practicing the religion that one deems acceptable to God violates neither of these prescriptions of the law of nature, it must necessarily be a determination of man's "state of perfect freedom," and in particular,

---

25 Locke, 120.
26 Locke, 145–46; emphasis added.

A Critique of John Locke's Letter Concerning Toleration

one of the determinations that man does not give up when he enters political society. If this is true, then it would follow that the practice of one's religion, precisely because it in no way encroaches on other men's civil interests, is itself one of the civil interests that constitute the object of the state's protection.

Having argued that the state can have no interest in the salvation of souls, Locke then argues that churches can have no interest in affairs of state. He begins by defining a church as "a voluntary society of men, joining themselves together of their own accord in order to the public worshipping of God in such manner as they judge acceptable to Him, and effectual to the salvation of their souls."[27] As a consequence of this definition, Locke declares that each man is free to join that church "in which he believes he has found that profession and worship which is truly acceptable to God" and that he is free to leave the same church "if afterwards he discover anything either erroneous in [its] doctrine or incongruous in [its] worship."[28] Moreover, since a church comes to exist through the voluntary coming together of its members, the right of making the church's laws "can belong to none but the society itself; or at least (which is the same thing), to those whom the society by common consent has authorized thereunto."[29] In other words, the power of a church resides in the wills of its members.

When Locke says that each man is free to enter that church which he judges to be acceptable to God and to leave the same church if he later comes to think that it is unacceptable to God, he is in effect maintaining that in matters of religion each man is his own judge of what is true and false. Later, he says this explicitly: "Every man in that [religion] has the supreme and absolute authority of judging for himself."[30] Though he does not mean that an individual's judgment makes religious doctrines to be true or false, he does mean that an individual *may* and even *should* submit each doctrine to his own scrutiny before accepting it and allow for the possibility that later on, upon scrutinizing the doctrine again, he may find it to be false. This, of course, is a consequence of Locke's doctrine

---

27   Locke, 120.
28   Locke, 120.
29   Locke, 121.
30   Locke, 141.

of the natural right to liberty of conscience, according to which the practice of religion is a mere determination of man's natural "state of perfect freedom," and a man may therefore hold whatever religious doctrines and perform whatever religious activities he judges to be acceptable to God. We should note here that Locke himself is "personally" a believer and thus thinks that God has made some kind of special revelation to man, but from what we have said, he clearly thinks that this revelation is ultimately a matter solely between God and the individual and that its interpretation is subject to the individual's supreme judgment.

Locke's definition of a church helps us to see more explicitly a consideration that was implicit in his fourth argument for why the state cannot have a care of souls, namely, that the basis for the state's toleration of the religions within its domain has nothing to do with a duty of the state to worship God. If a church, as far as the state is concerned, is nothing but a voluntary society of men, then its claim to toleration cannot be based on a claim that it is of divine origin and must be accorded freedom as a requirement of divine law; rather, such a claim must be based solely on the church's status as a free society whose affairs do not jeopardize civil affairs and on the natural right of men to profess whatever religion they choose.

In his arguments for why the state has no care of souls, Locke already attempted to show that there is no connection between civil affairs and the salvation of souls,[31] inasmuch as jurisdiction over civil affairs demands the use of force, whereas jurisdiction over the salvation of souls does not (and in fact cannot). From the proposition that there is no connection between civil affairs and the salvation of souls, however, it automatically follows that churches cannot concern themselves with politics. Moreover, since the exercise of religion is really the exercise of a natural right, that is, a determination of man's natural "state of perfect freedom," religion is a purely individual affair and therefore has no bearing on political life. Therefore, just as the state has no interest in the salvation of souls, so the Church has no interest in affairs of state.

---

31 If we wish to keep Locke consistent with himself, the claim that there is no connection between civil affairs and the salvation of souls is not true absolutely, since the practice of religion is a civil interest itself. Nevertheless, the reason that the practice of religion is a civil interest is precisely that it has nothing to do with all other civil interests.

A Critique of John Locke's Letter Concerning Toleration

To conclude our discussion of the *Letter*, let us examine Locke's attitude toward the Catholic Church. One might think that a Lockean regime would be friendly toward the Catholic Church, since a Lockean regime is governed by the principle of religious toleration, and, after all, Catholicism is a religion. Moreover, about two-thirds into the *Letter*, in order to illustrate how religious opinions do not harm civil rights, Locke mentions the belief of Roman Catholics in the Real Presence of Christ in the Eucharist, asserting that even though that belief is false and absurd, Catholics do "no injury" to their neighbors by holding it.[32]

Later, however, Locke makes it clear that there are other reasons which make the Catholic Church an exception to the rule of toleration. There are cases, he says, when churches exist of which the members "arrogate to themselves...some peculiar prerogative covered over with a specious show of deceitful words."[33] As an example of such a church, Locke mentions one which holds "that faith is not to be kept with heretics" and "that kings excommunicated forfeit their crowns and kingdoms."[34] Such a church interferes with civil affairs and therefore affairs that are outside the proper domain of religion. Locke is clearly thinking of the Catholic Church here, since he is clearly thinking of those popes who in previous centuries had excommunicated certain European monarchs for persecuting the Church and then declared that their subjects no longer owed them allegiance.

Another exception to the rule of toleration, says Locke, is a church "which is constituted upon such a bottom that all those who enter into it do thereby *ipso facto* deliver themselves up to the protection and service of another prince."[35] Here Locke explicitly mentions Islam, the members of which are subject to the Mufti of Constantinople, who is himself subject to the Ottoman Emperor. Locke no doubt has the Catholic Church in mind as well, however, since in addition to being the spiritual head of the Catholic Church, the pope really is the head of a temporal dominion, namely, Vatican City and, at the time of Locke, the Papal States.

32 Locke, 140.
33 Locke, 144.
34 Locke, 144.
35 Locke, 145.

It should be emphasized that for Locke to regard the Catholic Church as an exception to the rule of toleration is perfectly consistent with his principles. For even if he is wrong about the subjection of Catholics to a foreign prince, since the pope's authority as head of Vatican City (and formerly the Papal States) is accidental to his authority as pope, it is still true that when the pope excommunicates a political ruler and absolves that ruler's subjects of the duty of allegiance toward him, he has become involved in a nation's political affairs precisely in virtue of his universal solicitude for the salvation of souls, that is, precisely in virtue of his office as pope.[36]

Moreover, an enormous part of Catholic doctrine is concerned with temporal matters—a point that Locke does not make but that certainly strengthens his case. What, for example, are the Church's teachings on marriage, education, and economics if not teachings that pertain to civil affairs? These considerations should give those Catholics pause who subscribe in principle to an essentially Lockean understanding of Church and State relations but nevertheless demand that the state grant the Church liberty. For the Catholic Church, a Lockean regime can turn out to be just as oppressive as a Hobbesian or Spinozan regime.

II. The Truth about Church and State

So much for our analysis of Locke's position. Now we shall turn to the way things really are. It is worth pointing out that our starting point will be very different from that of Locke. As we have seen, Locke's doctrine concerning Church and State relations is rooted in his belief in the centrality of civil rights. The protection of civil rights is the object of the state's jurisdiction, and the basis for religious toleration is that the practice of religion is not a threat to civil rights; in fact, the practice of religion turns out to be a civil right itself. As we shall see, Catholic doctrine concerning Church and State relations, on the other hand, is rooted in the primacy of the common good. Consequently, our defense of this doctrine will consist of the following parts: 1) an account of the nature of the common good in general and of the axiom that the common good is preferable to the private good; 2) an account of

---

[36] How this is the case will become clear later.

A Critique of John Locke's Letter Concerning Toleration

the end of the state or the political common good; 3) an account of the relation of religion to the political common good apart from revelation; 4) an account of the end of the Church established by Christ or the common good of eternal beatitude; 5) an account of how the political common good and the common good of eternal beatitude are related to each other.

1. The Primacy of the Common Good

The common good is any good which is a final cause to many. It is opposed to the private good, which is a final cause only to one. The common good is not a mere collection of private goods; rather, it is a good to many precisely by being one good numerically. This is because the common good is a cause to many not accidentally but *per se*. A cause is a cause to many accidentally when it causes each of its many effects through a distinct act, e.g., when the foot causes each of its many footprints through a distinct impression on the sand, since here the mode of causality is the same as that by which many causes produce many effects. A cause is a cause to many *per se* when it causes all of its many effects through one single act, e.g., when the sun illumines everything on a hemisphere of the earth through one single illumination. Hence, since final causes are causes by being the objects of appetite, the common good, insofar as it is a final cause to many, is the object of the appetite of a multitude precisely by being one numerical final cause. Therefore, it cannot be a mere collection of private goods, since then it would be many final causes.

Moreover, although the common good is the good of a multitude, it is not the good of that multitude "envisaged as a sort of singular,"[37] as if it did not belong to the singulars constituting the multitude. For then its belonging to the multitude would be accidental to the manyness of that multitude. The common good would then "be properly singular, or, if one wishes, it would differ from the singular good of the particulars in being the good of none of them (*nullius*)."[38] Applied to politics, such an understanding of the common good would be totalitarian, since the common good would really be the

---

[37] Charles De Koninck, *The Primacy of the Common Good against the Personalists*, in *The Writings of Charles De Koninck*, ed. and trans. Ralph McInerny (Notre Dame, IN: University of Notre Dame Press, 2009), vol. 2, p. 75.

[38] Ibid.

private good of a gigantic individual (the state), to which good the private goods of other individuals would be subservient by sheer power of force.

On the contrary, the axiom that actions belong only to supposits demands that the community pursue and enjoy the common good through the actions of the individuals that make up the community. The common good is therefore desirable for *individuals*, but in such a way that it is not diminished by the multiplicity of the individuals for whom it is desirable.

Moreover, the unity of the common good causes the individuals that pursue and enjoy it to become one "complete agent"; this does not negate the differences that exist among the individuals but rather orders "these differences to one another and to the whole."[39] Further, each individual properly pursues and enjoys the common good not merely because it is good for him but because it is good for him and for all the other individuals who pursue and enjoy it with him. Hence, as St Thomas says in *Quaestiones Disputatae de Caritate* with regard to the political common good, a good politician loves the common good not that he may have and possess it but that it may be conserved and defended.[40]

It is a *per se notum* proposition that the common good is better (more choosable) than the private good.[41] For the common good

---

[39] John Nieto, "The Axiomatic Character of the Principle that the Common Good is Preferable to the Private Good," *The Aquinas Review* 14 (2007): 109–32, at 114.

[40] See St Thomas Aquinas, *Quaestiones Disputatae de Caritate*, a. 2, c.: "Amare autem bonum alicuius civitatis ut habeatur et possideatur, non facit bonum politicum; quia sic etiam aliquis tyrannus amat bonum alicuius civitatis ut ei dominetur; quod est amare seipsum magis quam civitatem; sibi enim ipsi hoc bonum concupiscit, non civitati. Sed amare bonum civitatis ut conservetur et defendatur, hoc est vere amare civitatem; quod bonum politicum facit: in tantum quod aliqui propter bonum civitatis conservandum vel ampliandum, se periculis mortis exponant et negligant privatum bonum."

[41] More specifically, it is the kind of *per se notum* proposition called an axiom, that is, a principle which is common to all the sciences inasmuch as it is a truth about being as such or one of the concepts convertible with being. At first, one might be surprised by this, since it seems that the notion of the common good is found only in political science. Examples reveal that this is not the case, however. In the *De Anima*, Aristotle accounts for the generation of the nutritive soul by the common good of the perpetuation of the species (Bk. II, ch. 4), and in the *Metaphysics* (Bk. XII, ch. 10), he says that God is the extrinsic common good of the whole universe. As we shall see later on, the common good is present in sacred theology inasmuch as the beatific vision is a good common to all the elect. The reason for the axiomatic character of the principle of the primacy of the common good is that the good is convertible with being, and since the

is a final cause which satisfies the appetite of a multitude, whereas the private good is a final cause which satisfies the appetite of only one of the individuals in that multitude. A multitude stands to the individuals that constitute it, however, as a whole to its parts. Therefore, since every perfection is proportioned to the subject which it perfects, the good which perfects the multitude stands to the good which perfects only one of the individuals in that multitude as a whole to its parts. But the whole is greater (more) than its parts. Therefore, the good of the multitude is better and more desirable than the good of an individual in that multitude.

Put another way, the common good is diffusive of itself to more beings than the private good. But the good, insofar as it bears the notion of desirable, is diffusive of itself, and so one good is better than another insofar as it is diffusive of itself to more beings. Therefore, the common good is better and more desirable than the private good.

Thus, for example, victory is the common good of the whole army; food, sleep, and personal glory are private goods of the soldiers constituting the army. Hence, the victory of the army is superior to the food, sleep, and personal glory of the individual soldiers. The soldier should therefore love that victory more than his food, sleep, and personal glory and, if necessary, should be willing to sacrifice the latter for the sake of the former.

2. *The Common Good of the City and the Political Nature of Man*

Let us now apply what we have said about the common good in general to the common good as it exists in the state or city.[42] Here it is helpful to begin by considering how the city comes to be.

The city comes to be from the association of smaller communities which exist prior to it in time.[43] The first of these communities is the family or household, which comes to be for the sake of maintaining the species and procuring the needs of daily life, such as

---

good is good by being good to some thing, which is either one or many, the division of the good into common and private is a *per se* division of the good and therefore a division of the good insofar as the good is convertible with being.

42 While it is possible for the words "city" and "state" to have distinct connotations, they are here used interchangeably.

43 This paragraph follows closely Aristotle's discussion of the coming to be of the city in *Politics* I.2.

eating and having shelter. Then, from the association of families, the village comes to be for the sake of procuring the needs of non-daily life, such as those relating to buying and fighting. Since, however, there are needs that even the village cannot procure by itself, different villages come together and form a city, which is the perfectly self-sufficient community. Hence, as Aristotle says, the city "comes into being for the sake of living,"[44] that is, for bringing about those conditions which are necessary for the members of the city to satisfy the needs of life.

These conditions constitute the first common goods of the city, since they belong to all the members of the city as such. Note, however, that they merely constitute useful common goods, since they exist for the sake of other goods, namely, those which satisfy the needs of the individuals, families, and villages that make up the city. Nevertheless, if the citizens have a rightly ordered love for these goods, then they will love them not merely because they are good for themselves taken as individuals, but above all because they are good for the whole city, since insofar as they are good for the whole city they are more common and therefore have more fully the *ratio* of good.

Once the city exists, however, other common goods arise in it, namely, pleasant and honest ones. For although the city comes to be "for the sake of living," it "exists for the sake of living well."[45] When men have established a city and thus have the useful common goods that enable them to live, they are not content merely with living but seek to live well. To live well, however, they do not retire into their private lives as if it were there that they really find the good life and their common life were only for the sake of their private lives. Rather, because their membership in the city makes them parts of a whole, and they apprehend that the whole is greater than its parts, they seek to live well by pursuing and enjoying goods that are common to the whole city. Some of these goods are pleasant, such as public statues and music, and others are honest, such as the administration of justice and the worship of God. It is the latter which constitute the highest goods of the city and the true source

---

44 Aristotle, *Politics*, I.2.
45 Ibid.

of political happiness because, prescinding from the division of the good into common and private, it is universally true that honest goods have the *ratio* of good more than useful or pleasant goods, since only honest goods are desired on account of themselves.[46]

The honest common goods constitute the citizens' common life of virtue; they are the noble actions which the citizens can only perform in common. This is because, as is clear from the rational nature of man, the highest good of man insofar as he is an individual is activity of his soul in accordance with those virtues that govern his own affairs. Therefore, the highest good of man insofar as he is a citizen is activity of his soul in accordance with those virtues that govern his affairs as they relate to the city. Hence, Aristotle says rightly that the political community "must be regarded ... as being for the sake of noble actions" and that "those who contribute most to a partnership of this sort have a greater part in the city than those who are equal or greater in freedom and family but unequal in political virtue."[47]

From what we have said, it is clear that man is ordered toward the political life by his very nature.[48] For since the city comes to exist as a result of man's natural incapacity to provide for his needs by himself, it is clear that the city comes to exist by nature; therefore, man is inclined to enter it by nature. A further proof that man is naturally political can be taken from the fact that man alone of all the animals has the power of speech. Voice, which is common to other animals, expresses the pleasant and painful, but speech alone, since it alone expresses intellectual concepts, expresses the useful and the harmful and therefore the just and the unjust, inasmuch as the just and unjust are concerned with equality and inequality in things that are useful and harmful. But a society in which men communicate with each other regarding the useful and the harmful, the just and the unjust, and other such things, is precisely what constitutes a city. Therefore, men are by nature inclined toward participation in political life. They are naturally

---

46 See St Thomas, *ST* I, q. 5, a. 6: "... quia honestum dicitur quod per se desideratur."
47 *Politics* III.9.
48 This paragraph follows closely Aristotle's discussion of how man is by nature a political animal in *Politics* I.2 and St Thomas's commentary in *Sententia Libri Politicorum* I, Lectio 1.

ordered toward being parts of the city, and they cannot attain the full perfection proportionate to human nature unless they order themselves to the political common good.

Let us now say a few words about how men order themselves to the political common good. First, any community pursues and enjoys its good through the actions of the individuals that make up the community. This means, however, that the individuals must pursue and enjoy that good precisely as a community, that is, as individuals united in a common agency. The individuals can only be united in a common agency if there is some governing principle that directs them to order their actions toward the common good. In the state, this governing principle is the ruler, whether the ruler is a single man or a body of men.

The ruler has the duty to determine the means appropriate for the attainment of the common good. These means are the laws of the state. Hence, St Thomas defines law as a "certain ordination of reason toward the common good promulgated by him who has care of the community."[49] Therefore, the citizens order themselves toward the common good by obeying the laws. By doing so repeatedly, they acquire the virtue of legal justice, through which they are disposed determinately to order the actions of all their other virtues to the common good and to subordinate their private goods to the common good.

Here it is necessary to point out that not any dictate of the ruler has the force of law, since law by definition is ordered toward the common good. Thus, if the ruler should pass a law which is ordered toward his private good, then he has not really passed a law.

We can see more precisely how a human law that is not ordered toward the common good lacks the force of law, if we consider the relation of human law to eternal and natural law. The eternal law is the divine reason insofar as it governs the entire universe and directs it toward a common end, namely, God himself.[50] Creatures participate in the eternal law insofar as "from its impression they

---

49 ST I-II, q. 90, a. 4: "Et sic ex quatuor praedictis potest colligi definitio legis, quae nihil est aliud quam quaedam rationis ordinatio ad bonum commune, ab eo qui curam communitatis habet, promulgata."

50 God is the extrinsic common end of the universe. There is also an intrinsic common end of the universe, namely, the order of the universe.

have inclinations toward their proper acts and ends."[51] The rational creature participates in the eternal law in a more excellent way than other creatures, since not only does he have an inclination toward his proper act and end impressed on him by the eternal law, but he apprehends his proper act and end rationally, so that he is able to provide for himself the means by which he can perform his proper act and attain his proper end. The participation of the rational creature in the eternal law is called the natural law.

Now, as we have already seen, man is naturally inclined toward participation in political life. Therefore, the natural law, which commands him to pursue those things toward which he has a natural inclination and to avoid the contrary, commands him to enter political society and work for the realization of the common good. Nevertheless, the natural law specifies the way for man to work for the realization of the common good in a purely universal manner and therefore without complete determination. Therefore, in order to bring about a determinate realization of the common good, the rulers of political society must draw particular conclusions from the precepts of natural law and make particular determinations of those precepts and then promulgate these conclusions and determinations as laws. Consequently, every authentic human law is derived from the natural law, which is ordered toward the common good. Moreover, since the natural law is derived from the eternal law, a human law which undermines the common good is a violation of the divine order. This is sufficient to conclude our discussion of the political common good.

3. *The Natural Role of Religion in the State*

We have seen, then, that the end of the city is the common good of its citizens—above all, their common life of virtue. Of all the virtues pertaining to this common life, the chief one is that of religion.

Religion is the virtue by which a man orders himself to God by exhibiting due honor to Him, "to whom we ought principally to

---

51 *ST* I-II, q. 91, a. 2: "Unde cum omnia quae divinae providentiae subduntur, a lege aeterna regulentur et mensurentur, ut ex dictis patet; manifestum est quod omnia participant aliqualiter legem aeternam, inquantum scilicet ex impressione eius habent inclinationes in proprios actus et fines."

be bound" as to our first principle.[52] Religion is a potential part of justice, since through it man renders what is due to another, though not to an equal. It is the highest of the moral virtues, since it is ordered to God in a more proximate way than any of the others, and God is the ultimate end of all the moral virtues.

The duties of religion bind not only the individual man but also the state. For the state, insofar as it arises from nature, has God, the cause of nature, "for its Author."[53] Moreover, since human law is derived from natural law, and natural law participates in eternal law, it follows that the common good of the state is ordered ultimately to the common good of the whole universe, namely, God. Political power is therefore a secondary cause through which God, the first cause, orders all things to himself. Therefore, since God is the first principle and ultimate end of the state, it is a requirement of natural justice that the state worship God. Since worship of God is thus an element of the state's common life, it is necessary that the state have one religion.

Moreover, the political common good cannot be realized if the state does not worship God. For the common good of the city is the happiness of the city. It is very difficult, however, for even one man to be happy, due to the difficulty of conquering the appetites and to the contingencies of fortune. All the more difficult is it, therefore, for a whole city to be happy. Therefore, the political common good is attainable only through divine assistance. Hence, in practicing the virtue of religion, the state not only adores God as its first principle and last end but also petitions God for the happiness of the community and thanks him for the blessings he has bestowed upon the community. Since, therefore, there is one happiness of the state, it is fitting that there be one order whereby that good is brought about and thus that the state have one religion.

Note, furthermore, that without revelation, religion cannot be ordered to the attainment of anything other than temporal goods, which are ordained to the common good of the city. One may of

---

52 *ST* II-II, q. 81, a. 1: "... religio proprie importat ordinem ad Deum. Ipse enim est cui principaliter alligari debemus, tanquam indeficienti principio; ad quem etiam nostra electio assidue dirigi debet, sicut in ultimum finem; quem etiam negligenter peccando amittimus, et credendo et fidem protestando recuperare debemus."

53 *Immortale Dei* 3.

course hope for goods after death, but without revelation there is no order by which such goods may be attained. Therefore, apart from revelation, is it fitting not only that the state have one religion but also that the priests who have the care of that religion be subordinate to the political rulers.[54]

4. The Catholic Church and the Divine Common Good

Christ, however, has made accessible to all men of whatever nation a good which transcends the goods of this life and to which those goods must be ordered, namely, the divine good which is the object of eternal beatitude. It is critical to point out that the divine good is a common good; indeed, it is the most universal common good of all. The reason for this is that, as we said earlier, a good is common insofar as it is diffusive of itself to many, and therefore, one common good is more of a common good than another insofar as it is diffusive of itself to more beings. But God, the supreme good, is diffusive of Himself to every being that exists. Therefore, to see and enjoy the divine essence in eternal beatitude is to share in a common good which "most fully has the note of common good."[55] Note that this is true even though "as such the beatitude of the single person does not depend on the actual communication of this beatitude to many"; rather, it depends on "its essential communicability to many," which communicability follows simply from the supreme character of the divine good.[56] Moreover, even if only one creature were to partake of eternal beatitude, he would still share it with God. That alone would be sufficient to make eternal beatitude the most universal common good.

Those who participate in the divine common good participate in it together "according to distinct acts or offices."[57] They thus constitute a society which is analogous to a political society, that is, which contains all the perfections of a political society and

---

54 See St Thomas, *De Regno* I,15: "Quia igitur sacerdotium gentilium et totus divinorum cultus erat propter temporalia bona conquirenda, quae omnia ordinantur ad multitudinis bonum commune, cuius regi cura incumbit, convenienter sacerdotes gentilium regibus subdebantur."

55 De Koninck, *Primacy*, McInerny ed., 81.

56 De Koninck, 97.

57 *ST* III, q. 8, a. 4: "Unum autem corpus similitudinarie dicitur una multitudo ordinata in unum secundum distinctos actus sive officia."

more. Hence, Scripture speaks of the heavenly Jerusalem, and St Paul, addressing those who are members of it on earth, says, "You are fellow citizens with the saints, and the domestics of God."[58]

The angels and blessed souls, who constitute the Church Triumphant, are citizens of this celestial society fully, since they possess the divine good by beholding it as it is in itself. Nevertheless, men are made citizens of it on earth, though less perfectly, through membership in the Church Militant, by which they receive grace, a certain participation in the divine nature, in their souls.

To be good citizens of the celestial society, men must order their wills toward the divine common good and love it according to itself, that is, they must love it not for its possession by them but for its maintenance and diffusion.[59] This love is not natural to them. For just as man under the formality of earthly citizen requires that a love of the political common good be added to his will through the acquired virtue of legal justice, so man under the formality of celestial citizen requires that a love of the supernatural common good be added to his will through the infused virtue of charity. For by charity a man "loves God for Himself and his neighbors who are capable of beatitude" as himself.[60]

Just as men are ordered to the political common good through human law, men are ordered to the divine common good through divine law and, in particular, the new law or law of the Gospel. The new law, says St Thomas, is principally the "grace of the Holy Spirit."[61] In a secondary way, it comprises certain things that effect this

---

58 Eph 2:19; cf. *Quaestiones Disputatae de Caritate*, a. 2: "...ita cum homo per divinam gratiam admittatur in participationem caelestis beatitudinis, quae in visione et fruitione Dei consistit, fit quasi civis et socius illius beatae societatis, quae vocatur caelestis Ierusalem secundum illud, Ephes. II, 19: *estis cives sanctorum et domestici Dei*."

59 See *Quaestiones Disputatae de Caritate*, a. 2: "Sic igitur amare bonum quod a beatis participatur ut habeatur vel possideatur, non facit hominem bene se habentem ad beatitudinem, quia etiam mali illud bonum concupiscunt; sed amare illud bonum secundum se, ut permaneat et diffundatur, et ut nihil contra illud bonum agatur, hoc facit hominem bene se habentem ad illam societatem beatorum."

60 Ibid.: "Et haec est caritas, quae Deum per se diligit, et proximos qui sunt capaces beatitudinis, sicut seipsos."

61 *ST* I-II, q. 106, a. 1: "Id autem quod est potissimum in lege novi testamenti, et in quo tota virtus eius consistit, est gratia Spiritus Sancti, quae datur per fidem Christi... Habet tamen lex nova quaedam sicut dispositiva ad gratiam Spiritus Sancti, et ad usum huius gratiae pertinentia, quae sunt quasi secundaria in lege nova, de quibus oportuit instrui fideles Christi et verbis et scriptis, tam circa credenda quam circa agenda."

grace in the soul, namely, the Sacraments, as well as certain things "pertaining to the use of this grace," namely, certain doctrines to be believed and certain precepts to be fulfilled. The doctrines are the articles of faith, and the precepts are the Beatitudes and the Ten Commandments. We should note here that inasmuch as the new law contains the Ten Commandments, it contains the whole of the natural law as well, since the Ten Commandments are a divinely revealed reaffirmation of the natural law. This fact will be important for our discussion of the relation of the Church to the state.

Our Lord has entrusted the task of ordering men according to the new law to the Catholic Church, which He Himself instituted. The government of the Church is administered by the members of the ministerial priesthood and, in particular, by the members of the episcopate, among whom the pope, the Bishop of Rome, has primacy. To carry out this government, the priests and bishops administer the Sacraments, teach the faithful what they must believe, and direct the faithful in fulfilling the precepts of divine law. This latter they accomplish through instruction and exhortation as well as through the promulgation of ecclesiastical law, which determines divine law just as human law determines natural law.

Let us conclude our discussion of the divine common good by noting that the diffusiveness of the divine good is such that God wills all men to partake of it: "Going therefore, teach ye all nations; baptizing them in the name of the Father, and of the Son, and of the Holy Ghost."[62] Therefore, the Church has a divinely ordained duty to bring all men into her fold, and her jurisdiction transcends the distinction of nations. We now proceed to examine the relation of the Church to the state.

5. The Relation of the Church to the State

We said earlier that the state has a duty to worship God. We also said that apart from revelation, religion can only be ordered to the acquisition of temporal goods, which are ordered to the common good of the city, and that the priests ought therefore to be subject to the civil rulers. We have now seen, however, that Christ, who is God Himself, has established a religion which is

---

62 Mt 28:19.

ordered toward a higher, more universal good than the good of the city and according to which He desires all men, regardless of nation, to worship Him. This religion is that of the Catholic Church. Therefore, it follows that since the coming of Christ, the state has a duty to worship God according to the Catholic religion.

Moreover, just as the private good must be ordered toward the common good, so a lower common good must be ordered toward a higher common good; therefore, the life of political virtue, which constitutes the highest common good of the city, must be ordered toward the eternal common good of the beatific vision. Consequently, since "those to whom pertains the care of antecedent ends ought to be subjected to him to whom pertains the care of the ultimate end and be directed by his rule,"[63] it follows that whereas in states that existed prior to Christ, those who had jurisdiction over religion were rightly subject to the civil rulers, in states that exist after Christ, the civil rulers are to be subject to the rulers of the Catholic Church.[64]

This subjection of the state to the Church must be rightly understood, however. For as St Thomas says in his *In Libros Sententiarum*, there are two ways in which a superior and an inferior power can stand to each other. The first way is when

> the inferior power (*potestas*) arises wholly from the superior; and then the whole power (*virtus*) of the inferior is founded upon the power (*virtutem*) of the superior; and then simply and in all things must the superior power (*potestati*) be obeyed more than the inferior.[65]

For example, the minister of a king receives all his power from the king; therefore, his power is founded upon that of the king, and in all matters the king must be obeyed more than he. Thus, if there is ever a contradiction between what the minister orders and what the king orders, men must obey the king. The second way is when both the superior and the inferior power

---

63 *De Regno* I,15: "Sic enim ei, ad quem finis ultimi cura pertinet, subdi debent illi, ad quos pertinet cura antecedentium finium, et eius imperio dirigi."

64 Cf. ibid.: "Sed in nova lege est sacerdotium altius, per quod homines traducuntur ad bona caelestia: unde in lege Christi reges debent sacerdotibus esse subiecti."

65 *In II Sent.*, dist. 44, q. 2, a. 3, *expositio textus*: "Aut ita quod inferior potestas ex toto oriatur a superiori; et tunc tota virtus inferioris fundatur supra virtutem superioris; et tunc simpliciter et in omnibus est magis obediendum potestati superiori quam inferiori."

arise from one certain supreme power (*potestate*), which subjects one to the other according as it wishes; and thence one is not superior to the other except in these things with regard to which one is placed under the other by the supreme power (*potestate*); and in those things only must the superior be obeyed more than the inferior.[66]

It is in the latter way that the Church relates to the state as a superior to an inferior power. The power of the state does not derive from the power of the Church; rather, the power of both derives from the supreme power of God, albeit in different ways. Therefore, the state is subject to the Church only in those matters with regard to which God has ordained that it be subject to it. These matters, says St Thomas, are those things "which pertain to the salvation of the soul."[67]

We can understand more fully what St Thomas is saying here if we note that while the state must order the citizens' temporal welfare to the attainment of eternal salvation, not every temporal affair in virtue of its object affects men's attainment of salvation.[68] As we have seen in our discussion of the divine common good, salvation demands that men fulfill the requirements of the divine law, which includes all of the natural law. Often, however, within the limits of revealed and natural law, there are a diversity of means by which the state may attain its proper end. Clearly, with such matters as these, the Church has no concern and therefore no right to become involved.

There are other temporal affairs—and a great deal of them at that—which *do* affect men's attainment of salvation, since revealed and natural law do not leave open the course of action to be

---

66 Ibid.: "Potest iterum potestas superior et inferior ita se habere, quod ambae oriantur ex una quadam suprema potestate, quae unam alteri subdit secundum quod vult; et tunc una non est superior altera nisi in his quibus una supponitur alii a suprema potestate; et in illis tantum est magis obediendum superiori quam inferiori."

67 *In II Sent.*, dist. 44, q. 2, a. 3, *expositio textus*, ad 4: "...et ideo intantum saecularis potestas est sub spirituali, inquantum est ei a deo supposita, scilicet in his quae ad salutem animae pertinent; et ideo in his magis est obediendum potestati spirituali quam saeculari."

68 Note the phrase "in virtue of its object." An affair which does not pertain to the attainment of heavenly happiness in virtue of its object still pertains to it in virtue of the intention with which a man engages in it.

taken in such affairs. These affairs, such as marriage and education, belong to the jurisdiction of both the Church and the state, albeit not in the same way, since the Church is concerned with them insofar as they relate to the eternal common good, and the state is concerned with them insofar as they relate to the political common good. The state, therefore, has the duty to govern these affairs in a way such that they are capable of being ordered toward the eternal common good and to ensure that its laws concerning them are in accordance with natural and revealed law.[69]

For example, when the state dispenses marriage licenses, it must not dispense them to Catholics who have been married in a non-Catholic marriage ceremony, for, according to revealed law, such a marriage is not a real marriage. Further, the state must ensure that the Church is able to provide instruction in the Catholic faith to students in state schools. Since the existence of public buildings falls within the domain of temporal affairs, the state, at least in a Catholic country, where the religious unity of the people could be threatened by the public practice of non-Catholic religions, has the right to prohibit the building of non-Catholic churches. Further, since the state has the duty not only to safeguard civil peace (a useful common good) but also public virtue (an honest common good), the state has the right to prohibit the propagation of opinions in the press which threaten that virtue. But since, after Christ, the virtuous life to which a nation is naturally ordered is ordered to the attainment of heaven, the state also has the right to prohibit the propagation of opinions in the press which are opposed to its citizens' attainment of heaven, such as opinions that are blasphemous or constitute an attack on the Church.

The Church, for its part, has the right to insist that the state fulfill its duty to govern temporal affairs in a way such that they

---

[69] The state, of course, has the duty to ensure that its laws are in accordance with the natural law for a reason more immediately tied to the nature of the state, namely, the derivation of every authentic human law from the natural law. Therefore, the requirement after the coming of Christ that the state order its good toward the good of eternal beatitude is an additional reason the state has this duty. It is worth noting, however, that, due to man's fallen nature, it is very difficult for anyone without the assistance of divine revelation to have an error-free knowledge of the natural law. Therefore, a state that recognizes the infallibility of the Church's Magisterium is better able to fulfill its natural duty of passing laws in accordance with the natural law than a state that does not.

are conducive to the attainment of salvation. This does not mean that the Church has the physical power to coerce the state into exercising this duty, but it does mean that the Church has the moral power to do so. That is, the Church can command the state to grant it temporal assistance in some way (such as public funding for the Church's missionary work) or to refrain from passing certain laws which would violate natural or revealed law, and the state is morally obliged to listen to the Church. Moreover, in cases where the rulers of a nation are Catholic and violate the rights of the Church or the precepts of the natural law in some flagrant way and as a consequence behave tyrannically, the Church can inflict ecclesiastical penalties on those rulers, such as excommunication, and can even declare the fact that they are behaving tyrannically.[70]

It is unnecessary to do more than point out that just as there are temporal affairs which do not as such bear upon salvation, so there are ecclesiastical affairs which do not as such bear upon the temporal welfare and are thus wholly outside of the state's jurisdiction.

In sum, since the coming of Christ, the state has a duty to recognize the Catholic Church as the true religion and to worship God according to it. It has the duty to ensure that its laws do not violate the teachings of the Catholic Church, which proclaims the revealed law and the natural law in their fullness. It has the duty to promote the welfare of the Church insofar as that welfare can be promoted by temporal means. Conversely, the Catholic Church has the right to demand that the state fulfills all of these duties. None of these statements violates the distinction between Church and state, since not all temporal affairs are subject to the jurisdiction of the Church, and not all spiritual affairs are subject to the jurisdiction of the state. As for those matters that are both temporal and spiritual, the state and the Church are concerned with them in different ways, even though the way the state is concerned with them is subordinate to the way the Church is concerned with them.

---

70 This is the basis for the declarations of popes in different eras of the Church's history that the citizens of certain nations no longer owed allegiance to their rulers.

III. The Godless State

It will now be opportune, in light of what has been said in the preceding section, to reexamine the arguments of Locke's *Letter Concerning Toleration* on behalf of the thesis that the state has no care for souls and the Church has no interest in politics.

As we noted in our exposition of the *Letter*, Locke's first two arguments for why the state can have no care of souls rely on the claim that, since the power of the state "consists only in outward force," the state cannot exercise care of souls in any other way than by forcing its citizens to perform acts whereby they embrace the religion of the state. But force is incapable of affecting men's mind and will, in which true religion really consists. Therefore, the state has no competence to force its citizens to embrace its religion. Therefore, it cannot have a care of souls.

The Catholic Church agrees with Locke that it is unjust for the state to force its citizens to perform acts whereby they become members of a given religion, even if that religion is the true one, precisely for the reason that Locke gives, namely, that faith is not real without the "inward and full persuasion of the mind." As St Augustine says, "Man cannot believe otherwise than of his own will."[71] Nevertheless, in caring for souls the state can make use of force in ways which do not involve making its citizens perform acts whereby they become members of the true religion. The state in a nation where most people are Catholic, for example, can prohibit the erection of non-Catholic churches and the propagation of religious error in the press. In this way, it protects its Catholic citizens from dangers to their faith and thus, by fortifying that faith, can make its Catholic citizens more effective witnesses to the truth for its non-Catholic citizens. The state thus exercises care for the souls of both its Catholic and non-Catholic citizens, but it does not thereby force anyone to become a Catholic.

In general, Locke fails to distinguish between affecting the mind and will directly and affecting them indirectly. Only God can do the former, but men can do the latter, and one of the ways they can do it is through force. The state exemplifies this even apart from the question of religion, for the state by nature is interested in

---

71 Quoted in *Immortale Dei* 36.

certain goods of the soul, namely, those which constitute political virtue, and can force its citizens to perform certain external acts that can dispose them internally toward the acquisition of these goods. To hold otherwise would be to deny the habituating power of law. All the more, then, is Locke wrong to equate care of souls with forcing men to embrace religions against their will.

Locke's third argument for why the state cannot have a care of souls is that even if the compulsive power of the state could affect the interior dispositions of its citizens—something we have shown to be in some sense possible—the "variety and contradiction" of the opinions of most princes with regard to religion would bring about the damnation rather than the salvation of most men, since most princes would force false religions on their subjects.

To say that the state has a care of souls and that it has a duty to worship God, however, is not to say that the state may adopt whatever religion it happens to like or even judges to be true. Rather, it is to say that the state has a duty to adopt the religion which has truly been revealed by God, namely, the Catholic religion. Therefore, if a ruler imposes a false religion on his subjects, he is in no way justified in doing so by the principle that the state has a care of souls. It is true that he may in fact impose a false religion on his subjects in the name of that principle, but the fact that a principle may be abused does not nullify the principle. Moreover, as Pope Leo XIII states, "it cannot be difficult to find out which is the true religion, if only it be sought with an earnest and unbiased mind; for proofs are abundant and striking." He continues:

> We have, for example, the fulfilment of prophecies, miracles in great numbers, the rapid spread of the faith in the midst of enemies and in face of overwhelming obstacles, the witness of the martyrs, and the like. From all these it is evident that the only true religion is the one established by Jesus Christ Himself, and which He committed to His Church to protect and to propagate.[72]

So much, then, for our reply to Locke's third argument.

Locke's fourth argument rests on the premises that the state exists for the sake of protecting its citizens' "civil interests" alone

---

72 *Immortale Dei* 7.

and that the salvation or damnation of one's fellow citizens in no way advances or harms one's "civil interests." A corollary of the latter premise is that the practice of whatever religion one happens to adopt is a natural right. Closely tied to this corollary is Locke's view that the judgment of each individual is the supreme authority in matters of religion, a view which influences his definition of a church as a "voluntary society of men" who come together to worship God in the way that they see fit.

The view that the proper end of the state is the safeguarding of its citizens' individual interests alone is simply a violation of the axiom that the common good is preferable to the private good. Underlying this violation is Locke's view of man in the state of nature, where man comes into the world with the freedom to do whatever he wants with himself, provided that he does not hinder others from doing likewise. If this is so, then man's chief good is to do whatever he wants, and therefore, his chief good is himself. Consequently, he has no natural end and cannot be perfected by pursuing some good extrinsic to himself. The law of nature, far from ordering man toward a determinate end, is merely a limit which prevents one complete whole from interfering with the activity of another complete whole. Hence, man cannot have a natural inclination for political life, nor can he be perfected by pursuing the good of a whole of which he forms a part, and so it is impossible for the state to come into being for the sake of anything other than the protection of goods that are purely individual.

The view that the salvation or damnation of one's neighbor has nothing to do with one's civil interests and that religion is therefore nothing more than the exercise of man's natural right to liberty of conscience is also a violation of the axiom that the common good is preferable to the private good, since it makes religion, which is concerned with man's highest end, a purely individual affair. Again, underlying this violation is Locke's view of man in the state of nature. For if man's natural status is that of an end in himself, then the nature of divine revelation must be such as to fit with the conditions of that status. This means that even if divine revelation enjoins duties on man's conscience, from the standpoint of nature, man's exercise of those duties is simply an exercise of his natural freedom to do whatever he likes, which includes, of course, following the dictates of his conscience. In this way, moreover, conscience derives its force simply from being an expression of the individual; in no way is that force related to the conformity of conscience to objective truth. Religion thus becomes something that concerns only the individual who practices it and is therefore a private good. Moreover, since neither the political nor the religious life of man demands ordination toward a common good as to its chief good, to argue, as we have done, that the good of the state is ordered toward the good of the Church as an inferior common good to a superior common good, is absurd.

From what we have said, it is clear that underpinning Locke's rejection of the axiom that the common good is preferable to the private good is his rejection of man as ordered to an end. To respond adequately to this rejection, we would have to argue against Locke's understanding of man as a knower. For as Locke makes clear in *An Essay Concerning Human Understanding*, all man can know are particular ideas received through sensation and reflection on the operations of his internal powers, together with the complex ideas that he himself composes from those simple ideas; therefore, he cannot know what things are universally, that is, he cannot know the natures of things. But if man cannot know the natures of things, it is futile to speak of him as being naturally ordered toward an end, and all that remains for him to pursue are the sensible pleasures that arise from his perception of sensible ideas. We shall simply take it as self-evident here that man can know the natures of things and that Locke is therefore wrong; to offer a dialectical argument by which to manifest man's ability to know the natures of things would be beyond the scope of this essay.

Man, then, is not an end in himself. The highest good of the state is a common good, not a collection of private goods. Religion is not a purely individual affair but one that demands participation in an ordered multitude which has as its object the most universal common good of all. Therefore, the good of the state is ordered toward the good of the Church as an inferior common good to a superior common good, and therefore, civil affairs *are* related to the salvation of souls.

Further, while it is true that the salvation of one's neighbor does not affect one's individual civil interests by agent causality, it may affect them by final causality. In other words, my neighbor can go to hell, and my money will still be intact; my possession of that money does not depend upon his salvation as on an agent cause. But his salvation may determine in some way how I ought to use my money; perhaps his faith is weak, and I ought to buy him a good religious book which God will use as a means for strengthening his faith. Therefore, the use of my money may depend upon my neighbor's salvation as on a final cause. Therefore, the salvation or damnation of one's neighbor can in some way affect even one's individual civil interests.

Note, too, that liberty of conscience, as Locke understands it, implies a false notion of liberty. True liberty is the property of the will to choose those means appropriate to the end that reason apprehends as good. For since man is ordered toward an end, he must seek the means to attain it, and because he sees that these means "may exist or not," insofar as they depend on the activity of his will, he is *free* to choose them.[73] Therefore, any act by which man defects from his true end is a defect from true liberty. This is so even if a man's act is in accordance with the judgment of his reason but that judgment is false, since reason itself defects when it falls away from the truth. Hence, Locke's conviction that man has a natural right to act in accordance with the dictates of his conscience, regardless of whether or not his conscience is conformed to truth, is false.

We have now responded to Locke's arguments for why the state cannot have a care of souls. Further, since, as we saw in our exposition of *A Letter Concerning Toleration*, Locke's arguments for why the Church can have no interest in political affairs depend on the same principles as his arguments for why the state cannot have a care of souls, we do not need to respond to the former arguments. There are, however, several other problems with Locke's doctrine of the separation of Church and state that we should address.

First, to say that any two orders, such as the political and the ecclesiastical, have nothing to do with each other is opposed to

---

73 Pope Leo XIII, *Libertas Praestantissimum* 5 and 6.

A Critique of John Locke's Letter Concerning Toleration

the order of the universe. For God has ordained the universe to a single end, and therefore, the different orders within the universe stand in a determinate relation to each other. This would not be true, however, if certain orders in the universe are utterly irrelevant to each other.

Second, Locke's separation of temporal from spiritual affairs is simply naïve. For even if religion orders man toward a good that is not of this world, it does the ordering in *this* world. Therefore, it must of necessity make certain stipulations about how man uses the things of this world. Consequently, the very nature of religion demands that there be such things as mixed matters, that is, matters which belong to both the temporal and spiritual orders and which fall within the jurisdiction of both the state and the Church. Therefore, the state and the Church cannot help but interact with each other, if religion is to be anything real at all in the world.

Third, in Locke's doctrine of separation of Church and state, a church is defined as "a voluntary society of men, joining themselves together of their own accord in order to the public worshipping of God in such manner as they judge acceptable to Him, and effectual to the salvation of their souls." This definition, however, in effect reduces the church to a purely human institution. The state must, of course, subscribe to this definition. The position that all churches are purely human institutions, however, is just as much a judgment about religion as the position that one Church is not of purely human origin. Therefore, the separation of Church and state itself demands that the state make judgments about religious matters.

Fourth, despite his reduction of religious practice to the level of a natural right, i.e., a determination of man's natural "state of perfect freedom," Locke holds that there is such a thing as divine revelation and that "the observance of these things [prescribed by divine revelation] is the highest obligation that lies upon mankind."[74] From the standpoint of nature, the practice of religion is an exercise of man's freedom to do with himself whatever he wants, but from the standpoint of what is above nature, the practice of religion is a duty which restricts man's freedom to do with himself whatever he wants. This, in effect, introduces an opposition between the

---

74 Locke, *Letter*, 141.

natural and the supernatural orders. Such an opposition is, of course, absurd, since God is the source of both orders, and grace does not destroy nature but presupposes and perfects it.[75]

Fifth, the separation of Church and state is ultimately a rejection of God. For to say that the state must treat all religions equally is to say that the state must be indifferent to whether any of those religions has been instituted by God. But to say that the state must be indifferent to whether any of those religions has been instituted by God is to say that the state has no duty to worship God. To say that the state has no duty to worship God is to say that the state in no way depends upon God.

A deadly practical consequence follows from the proposition that the state does not depend upon God, namely, the independence of the state from the dictates of the natural law. We have seen that the natural law is simply the participation of the rational creature in the eternal law; therefore, to deny the eternal law is to deny the natural law. But to hold that the state does not depend upon God is in effect to deny the eternal law, since it is to deny that the state is a secondary cause within a plan by which God governs the universe. Therefore, it follows from the doctrine of the separation of Church and state that the law of the state in no way depends upon the natural law for its legitimacy. The state may therefore do whatever it pleases; it has no obligation to serve the common good of its citizens but is like a big individual to whose private good the goods of its citizens are subservient.

Locke himself, of course, holds that there is a God and even that the state should not tolerate atheism, inasmuch as "promises, covenants, and oaths, which are the bonds of human society, can have no hold upon an atheist."[76] Locke's reason for holding the latter thesis, however, is not because of any actual duty of the state towards God but merely because of the practical necessity of believing in God for the sake of civil stability. Yet does a state which considers itself under no obligation to maintain the good of its citizens really need to promote belief in God for the sake of

---

75   Cf. *ST* I, q. 2, a. 2, ad 1: "...sic enim fides praesupponit cognitionem naturalem, sicut gratia naturam, et ut perfectio perfectibile."

76   Locke, *Letter*, 145.

what it considers as civil stability? Could such a state not effect its own vision of stability by means of sheer force or, even better, by giving its citizens an abundance of sensual pleasure to keep them happy? It does not take much reflection to see that this is the kind of state that exists in most countries of the Western world today. Let this suffice for our refutation of the Lockean doctrine of the separation of Church and state.

Conclusion

In sum, a consideration of the true nature and purpose of the state and the Church, in light of the axiom of the primacy of the common good, leads us to the conclusion that the Catholic Church is right about the relations between Church and state. After the coming of Christ, the state has a duty to publicly profess the Catholic religion and, in the words of St Thomas, "to procure the good life of the multitude according as it is congruent with attaining celestial beatitude."[77] The Church, for its part, has the right to ensure, as far as it has the power, that the state fulfills these duties.

On the other hand, Locke's contention that the state should treat all religions within its domain equally and that the Church should stay out of politics stems from a false understanding of the nature and purpose of the state and of the Church alike, an understanding which arises from his exaltation of the private good above the common good.

A correct understanding of the principles governing the relations between the Church and the state is critical in our day, when the individualism and religious indifferentism of the doctrine of separation of Church and state have become a matter of intellectual custom for most people. If a society cannot really flourish unless it acknowledges God, then so long as the truth about Church and state is not recognized and men refuse to acknowledge that Christ is king not only of individuals but of nations, the world will not be rid of its many evils and will never attain true peace. But wherever that truth is recognized and men do acknowledge that Christ is

---

[77] *De Regno* I, 16: "Quia igitur vitae, qua in praesenti bene vivimus, finis est beatitudo caelestis, ad regis officium pertinet ea ratione vitam multitudinis bonam procurare secundum quod congruit ad caelestem beatitudinem consequendam."

king of the nations, the state will attain true political happiness, the Church will be able to exercise her mission fully, and men will enjoy happily the passing goods of life on earth as they strive with good hope to attain the eternal good of life in heaven.

Appendix: The Non-Catholic State after Christ

Having read the account of the relations between Church and state given above, one may very likely ask: is not such an account absurd given the conditions of the modern world, where numerous countries, such as the United States, contain large portions of non-Catholics and are characterized by that great achievement of contemporary man called religious pluralism?

To answer this question, let us begin by acknowledging that in many countries today the realization of the principles that we have articulated concerning the Church and the state *is* practically impossible. Therefore, it would not be prudent for the Church to insist that the governments of such countries fulfill the duties imposed on them by those principles in all their fullness. That, however, does not negate the *truth* of those principles, which are based upon the very nature of the Church and the state. No particular difficulty in implementing them can undermine their universal validity as an element of the objectively right order of things. The following quotation from Pope Leo XIII in his Encyclical *Longinqua Oceani* (On Catholicism in the United States) testifies to the absolute validity of the said principles even for a country like the United States:

> The Church amongst you, unopposed by the Constitution and government of your nation, fettered by no hostile legislation, protected against violence by the common laws and the impartiality of the tribunals, is free to live and act without hindrance. Yet, though all this is true, it would be very erroneous to draw the conclusion that in America is to be sought the type of the most desirable status of the Church, or that it would be universally lawful or expedient for State and Church to be, as in America, dissevered and divorced. The fact that Catholicity with you is in good condition, nay, is even enjoying a prosperous growth, is by all means to be attributed to the fecundity with which God has endowed His Church, in virtue of which unless

men or circumstances interfere, she spontaneously expands and propagates herself; but she would bring forth more abundant fruits if, in addition to liberty, she enjoyed the favor of the laws and the patronage of the public authority.[78]

Moreover, as we have seen, a government which holds in principle that it must treat all religions within its domain equally and that those religions must in turn refrain from any intervention in politics cannot tolerate the Catholic Church and be consistent with itself. Nor can it acknowledge its duty to ensure that its laws are in accordance with the natural law. Such a government may not realize these consequences of the doctrine of separation of Church and state at first, but after a period of time, during which it is able to develop its understanding of that doctrine, it is virtually impossible that it will not realize them. The promotion by the state of numerous forms of immorality in the United States, Canada, and several European nations, together with the more and more frequent clashes between the Catholic Church and the governments of those nations over matters such as abortion and homosexual "marriage," testifies to this. Therefore, even if it is unreasonable to expect that the governments of nations with large non-Catholic populations will recognize the Catholic Church as the true religion and the infallible interpreter of the moral law, the Catholic Church will inevitably end up suffering persecution in those nations, and the natural law will end up being abandoned.

Consequently, even in countries where it is imprudent for the Church to demand the realization of the right order governing the relations between Church and state in all its fullness, Catholics cannot feel satisfied with the lack of that realization. Therefore, they must strive to win as many non-Catholics to the Church as possible and must work to establish the proper natural basis for the right relations between Church and state by instilling in men's minds the primacy of the common good and the foundation of the state in natural law. In this way, Catholics in non-Catholic countries will do what they can to peacefully pave the way for the time when the fullness of the right order can be realized.

---

78   Pope Leo XIII, *Longinqua Oceani* 6.

CONCLUSION

An Integralist's Brag

Edmund Waldstein, O.Cist.

In 2014 I was in a doctoral seminar full of young German and Austrian moral theologians. We were discussing the problem of the "divorced and remarried." One of the young theologians brought up the example of a young woman of her acquaintance who was abandoned by her husband at the age of 25. Surely, it would be absurd that such a person should be "martyred" for the sake of a rule? I responded that to be a martyr is to be a witness to the truth. Just as Christ Himself died to witness to the truth, so we Christians are called to die (at least figuratively) for the truth. If it is really true that a sacramental marriage is indissoluble, is it not worth martyrdom? I expected the response to focus on the usual objections to the traditional understanding of indissolubility. To my surprise, on this occasion, the response focused on the notion of martyrdom. One of the theologians claimed that no one is ever actually required to suffer martyrdom. To give the witness of one's blood is a personal choice, he argued; one might feel subjectively called to do it, but one couldn't blame someone who chose to burn incense to a statue of an emperor, rather than to die; such a person, under such duress, could hardly be said to have denied Christ. I was rather astonished, though on reflection, I should not have been. If one can find a way around Matthew 19:9, then why not around Matthew 10:33?

As the conversation moved on, I continued to think about the position that had just been laid out. It seemed an example of the "weak thought" called for by the Italian philosopher Gianni Vattimo. According to Vattimo, weak thought holds to no position so absolutely as to demand martyrdom. He sees it as the only form of thought adequate to the postmodern condition. It is the sort of position that Joseph Ratzinger famously associated with the "dictatorship of relativism." Whereas "a clear faith based on the Creed of the Church" is labeled as fundamentalism, relativism seems "the only attitude that can cope with modern times." But I was not fully satisfied with this explanation. The logical outcome of relativism would seem to be a mistrust of zeal in moral causes. And yet, I knew from many other conversations how much zeal the theologians in that seminar had for causes which they saw as championing justice and truth against oppression and bigotry: feminism, antiracism, gay rights, etc. Indeed, Vattimo himself sees "weak thought" as grounding not indifference, but rather a commitment to progressive politics. But these theologians were ready to go beyond Vattimo in the absolute terms in which they spoke about justice.

Later on in the seminar, the conversation turned to "intrinsically immoral acts" (acts that are immoral simply on account of the kind of action that they are, apart from the circumstances). The usual objections to the concept of intrinsically immoral acts were raised. But then, again to my surprise, the same person who had brought up the example of the 25-year-old abandoned by her husband said that while she objected to the way the notion of intrinsically moral acts was often used to stifle moral discernment and impose repressive sexual norms, nevertheless, there were some areas in which she wished the Church would be more forthright in condemning actions as intrinsically evil. She mentioned the treatment of women in patriarchal, third-world societies as an example of such an area. This, it seemed to me, was not really compatible with "weak thought." Certain evils were indeed to be condemned absolutely—ones that directly countered the progressive movement of liberation. Here was a form of strong thought, although it was concerned not so much with immutable truths as with emerging and developing truths, since in a progressive movement, what was unobjectionable yesterday can be pure evil tomorrow.

It seemed to me that these theologians shared more with anti-Christian progressives than with the Christian tradition. But then, as the historian Tom Holland has argued, there are strong parallels between secular progressivism and Christianity, and its successive waves of reform.[1] In late antiquity, Christianity was the cause of truth, justice, and freedom. The Christian Gospel was about overcoming superstition, oppression, and vice. The deplorable *pagani*, sinister reactionaries, in thrall to false and defeated gods, were being overcome by the forces of justice and truth. Christian Reform movements throughout the ages would recall the same dynamic: seeing themselves as championing truth, justice, and freedom, against superstition, oppression, and enthrallment. The great reform movements of the Middle Ages—such as the Gregorian Reform or the Albigensian Crusade—saw themselves in such terms.

But it was not only orthodox movements who saw themselves in such terms; heretical movements did the same. The Protestant Reformation saw itself precisely as the cause of truth and freedom against ignorance, superstition, and oppression. And, indeed, the same mentality that we see in Christian reform movements is taken over in modernity by anti-Christian movements. The Enlightenment began as a movement among believing Christians, but with time its more radical proponents came to see themselves as championing reason *against* Christian pretensions of revelation. The spirit of Christian reform is turned against Christianity itself. Now it is Christianity that is ignorance, superstition, and oppression, while secular reason serves the cause of truth and liberation.

In our current era, radical postmodern versions of critical theory have executed a similar reversal on Enlightenment reason. Now the Enlightenment metanarratives of liberation and progress are exposed as masks of patriarchy, racism, and hatred of difference. The light of a new dawn of an endless play of difference will liberate all the oppressed groups of the world. The great evil that these new "woke" reformers see is the injustices inevitably imposed on the less powerful by the more powerful. Despite their general contempt for Christianity, we can still see here a trace of the Christian Gospel: "He has pulled down the dynasts from their thrones, and raised

---

[1] See *Dominion: How the Christian Revolution Remade the World* (New York: Basic Books, 2019).

up the humble" (Lk 1:52). It is this trace, however faint, that gives the woke reformation its power and attraction.

And it is this, in part, which makes current progressive ideology (despite its anti-Christian aspects) attractive to Christians such as the young moral theologians in my doctoral seminar. Human beings are political animals, and we yearn to serve great political causes of justice and liberation. But this makes it all the more vital to discern whether a given movement is based on truth or falsehood. I am deeply convinced that the current "woke" movements of political liberation are based on fundamental errors about human nature and human freedom. They therefore do not serve true human flourishing. They are destructive of true human happiness.

If I am right, how ought we as Christians to respond to the would-be liberators of our day? I believe that we can look back to models of Church engagement with the world that have fallen out of fashion in the last sixty years, models such as the Catholic Counter-Reformation. At the time of Vatican II, after the trauma of the World Wars, it seemed to many in the Church that the age of the Tridentine Counter-Reformation was over. The human community was open to a new commitment to a fundamentally Christian understanding of human dignity and natural law. A reconciliation between the Church and secular progress seemed within reach. But we no longer live in 1962. The social conditions to which the Council fathers addressed their pastoral strategies have passed for ever. Never before have we seen such blatant violations of the natural law proclaimed as moral progress—abortion, euthanasia, sexual perversions of the most insane kind, and the obliteration of sexuality itself in "gender fluidity," etc. What we need now is the sort of confidence in asserting the integral truth of the Catholic tradition, and the natural law, that the great saints of the Tridentine Reform demonstrated.

There were Catholics in the sixteenth century who wanted to water down those aspects of Catholicism most attacked by the Protestants: penance, fasting, vigils, indulgences, veneration of relics, scholasticism, and much else of the fabric of medieval Catholicism both in its popular piety and in its mystical and speculative theology. Such Catholics wanted a Catholicism that would be more in tune with the tastes of the ascendent middle classes, and whose theological light would be taken more from humanists such as Erasmus of Rotterdam than from the scholastics. But the great figures of the Counter Reformation—St Charles Borromeo, Fr Domingo Bañez, St Teresa of Avila, Pope St Pius V, St Ignatius of Loyola, and many others—took a different path. Their approach was not to water down Catholicism, but to radicalize it, to draw more deeply from the sources of the tradition so as to invigorate the present. They met the challenges of Reformation theology by showing that the truths which the Reformers saw in a partial and distorted way were more fully given in the Catholic Tradition. We must do something similar in our own day.

To me, a key aspect of this renewed confidence in Catholic truth must be political: a recovery of what I have called *integralism*, the primacy of spiritual truth for the realization of political justice. As St Augustine taught in *The City of God*, no political community can be just that does not acknowledge the true God and communally render him his due. We human beings are political animals, and we cannot hope to meet the false promise of political justice proclaimed by the woke zealots of our day, unless we can show that there is a truer justice, a fuller liberation to be found in a truly Christian politics.

Integralism holds that political action ought always to be directed towards the true good of human beings, as inscribed into our very nature by the Creator, knowable by human reason, and authoritatively interpreted by the Catholic Church. Integralism holds that the Church herself is not a voluntary association within human society, but rather a necessary society, endowed with authority by God, ordered to a yet higher good than the good of nature. And it teaches that temporal societies are called to recognize the Church for what she is, and to recognize her authority over the supernatural good, and therefore to give way to her authority in matters touching on the supernatural good, where the temporal good can be mediately directed to the eternal.

Many, even strongly committed Christians, react to integralism with an incredulous shaking of the head. It seems to them an unrealizable fantasy, irrelevant to the practical political problems facing us in our own day. I want to respond to them in the spirit of "Campion's Brag," the famous letter of my patron saint: St Edmund Campion, S.J.

When Campion entered England in 1580, Protestantism was the religion of the ascendant elites. It was the religion of the emerging middle classes with their new economic power. It was the religion of the intellectual and cultural elites—of the fashionable scholars, writers, and artists. And it was above all the religion of the Elizabethan political and bureaucratic elite. To its proponents, Protestantism was the cause of truth, justice, and freedom. Catholicism, by contrast, was to them the religion of superstition, oppression, and treason; the religion of deplorable country bumpkins, reactionary aristocrats, and malign foreign tyrants. And yet, when Campion, who was living in disguise, in constant danger of capture, wrote a letter to the Queen's Privy Council explaining his motives, he wrote with such tremendous confidence that the letter came to be known as "Campion's Brag." "I would be loth to speak anything that might sound of any insolent brag or challenge," Campion wrote, but to its readers it did indeed constitute a challenge. Campion wrote of having "such assurance" in his side of the quarrel and "evidence so impregnable" and "such courage in avouching the Majesty of Jhesus my King" that he was sure that, if given a fair hearing before three different audiences, he could persuade them all.

The first audience that Campion craved was the Lords of the Privy Council themselves, before whom he would "discourse of religion, so far as it toucheth the common weale." The second audience were all the learned Anglican divines of Oxford and Cambridge, whom he would persuade of the truth of the Catholic faith "by proofs innumerable, Scriptures, Councils, Fathers, History, natural and moral reasons." The third audience were the lawyers of England "spiritual and temporal," whom he proposed to persuade of the justice of the Catholic cause through the "common wisdom" of the English legal tradition.

I believe that the same threefold task of persuasion—political, theological/philosophical, and juridical—faces integralists today.

On the political front this means not limiting our political action to carving out "religious exemptions" from the moral insanity of progressive politics, but rather a confident and aggressive promotion of the true good and the natural law. Progressive politics is built on a foundation of lies. And this can be shown persuasively, since all human beings have the natural law written on their hearts, and can see for themselves the misery that a life in denial of truth yields. I am convinced that we can show people that abortion is the murder of innocent human beings; that unbridled capitalism and consumerism wound nature, exploit the poor, and impede true human flourishing; that the social contagion of transsexualism destroys the lives of vulnerable teenagers; that sexual perversion, promiscuity, and pornography poison the relations of the sexes, and deprive children of the stable families they need to flourish. I believe that we can show that the wasteland of loneliness and malice, so skillfully described by the greatest artists of our time, is a direct result of the pile of lies on which postmodern society is built, and that the solution is to be found in truths which most of those artists would dismiss as passé. And I believe that we can show that the fostering of strong subsidiary communities, with deep cultural identity, need not lead to xenophobia or racism, but can actually promote human flourishing.

This political task means forming what Adrian Vermeule has called "the party of nature."[2] It means recognizing that many of the political reactions to elite politics that we see in contemporary "populism" derive their strength from correctly identifying some of the lies of the elite. It means purifying populism of all that is irrational or distorted in it, turning it towards the true common good.

Far from being irrelevant fantasy, this political task can be begun with eminently practical steps that can be taken in the here and now. Vermeule himself, along with Sohrab Ahmari, Patrick Deneen, Chad Pecknold, and Gladden Pappin, have been pointing to such steps in their Substack blog *The Postliberal Order*, in which they show how unnecessary the "defensive crouch" of much opposition to progressivism is.[3] In his work at *American Affairs*, Pappin has also given us a wealth of policy proposals on such

---

2 See his essay of that title posted at *The Postliberal Order* on December 7, 2021.

3 Patrick J. Deneen, "Abandoning Defensive Crouch Conservatism," *The Postliberal Order*, November 17, 2021.

matters as industrialism, the family, and the role of the state in promoting the true good.⁴ Pappin develops the concept of "first wave integralism." This means that the integralist goals do not have to be realized all at once to be relevant to political action. A "first wave" of integralism can take small steps towards promoting virtue, the common good, and the recognition of natural law. This first wave can then be followed by second, third, and fourth waves, in which the goal of an integrally just society can be approached more closely.

The second task that Campion set himself was to persuade the learned men of England both through Scripture and the Church Fathers and also through "natural and moral reasons." That is, it was both a theological and a philosophical task. *The Josias*, the integralist website that I edit, is mostly devoted to exploring the philosophical and theological underpinnings of integralism. Those underpinnings have profound implications for the theology of the Church. The doctrine of the Church as *societas perfecta*, a complete society, ordered to the final end of human life, so central to all integralist thought, has been disastrously obscured in much recent theology. The result has been that the Church is too often reinterpreted in the light of whatever political conceptions are in fashion. Thus, the German Synodal Way has declared that authority in the Church must be reformed to conform to "the standards of a plural, open society in a democratic constitutional state." This is a complete reversal of the proper relation of the Church to political form. It is not the Church who ought to imitate the model of worldly politics; rather temporal political communities ought to imitate the Church as their exemplar.⁵ To my mind, therefore, one of the most important recent contributions to Catholic ecclesiology is *Integralism: A Manual of Political Philosophy* by Fr Thomas Crean and Prof. Alan Fimister (editiones scholasticae, 2020).

---

4   See "Corporatism for the Twenty-First Century," vol. 4, n. 1 (Spring 2020); "Affirming the American Family" (with co-author Maria Molla), vol. 3, n. 3 (Fall 2019); "Toward a Party of the State," vol. 3, n. 1 (Spring 2019).

5   See Edmund Waldstein, O.Cist., "Politics as a Sketch for the Church," *New Polity* 2.1 (February 2021): 6–32, online at https://www.academia.edu/50955708/Politics_as_a_Sketch_for_the_Church.

Conclusion

The renewal of the theology of the Church is intrinsically linked to a more general renewal of theology and philosophy. It is no secret that Catholic theology has been in crisis since Vatican II. This is not necessarily the fault of the Council documents themselves, which contain much profound theological teaching. But it is the fault of the hasty paradigm shift in Catholic theology that followed the Council. The scholastic method, with its whole framework of theological science, was abandoned, and no adequate replacement was found. While postconciliar theology certainly made some brilliant achievements (Balthasar's theological aesthetics, Ratzinger's theology of hope, Wojtyła's theology of the body, etc.), the wider trend was a catastrophic collapse of adhesion to the deposit of faith. In part, this was due to philosophical problems. Scholastic philosophy having been abandoned, many theologians thought they could find an adequate replacement in the critical philosophy of German idealism, or the postmetaphysical philosophy of Heidegger. But such philosophies are unsuited to being handmaids of theology, because they are fundamentally false. They cut theology off from reflection on the infinite ocean of unbounded reality that is the true God. A theology built on thin, Kantian ice, or shifting, Heideggerian sand cannot respond adequately to the self-revelation of God, the infinite ocean of being, perfection, goodness, and happiness, who, in an ecstasy of sheer generosity, has created rational beings to share in the joy of His Trinitarian life.

What is needed is a renewal of theology as a scholastic *scientia:* demonstrative, syllogistic, speculative, and sapiential. A theology whose soul is the word of God in Scripture and Tradition, but which makes use of solid metaphysical realism to help understand the concepts necessary for the interpretation of the word. There are a number of promising signs pointing in this direction today, including the *Sacra Doctrina Project*, to which I and a number of other integralist theologians belong.

A renewal of scholastic theology requires a renewal of metaphysical realism. And this in turn requires a renewal of the philosophy of nature. Aristotle's metaphysics — the greatest achievement of philosophical reason — is dependent on his *physics*, his hylomorphic and teleological understanding of nature. And here we touch a point that is crucial to our confrontation with the modern world view. The twin foundations of the modern world are the rejection of the authority of the Church and the rejection of teleology in nature. Modern natural science, with its reduction of nature to its metrical aspects, is not only foundational to modern technology and economics, it is also the root of the modern rejection of natural law and of metaphysics. Recovering a teleological understanding of nature is necessary to recovering an understanding of the objective good as perfective of our being. It is therefore crucial to a recovery of objective ethics and politics. What is needed is a further elaboration of the critique of the scientific revolution developed in the last century by philosophers such as Hans Jonas, Jacob Klein, and Charles De Koninck, and the development of a new natural philosophy that can synthesize the deepest insights of Aristotelianism with the true discoveries of later science.

The third of the tasks which St Edmund set himself was to persuade the lawyers of England. Recent objections to integralism have tended to focus on questions of rights and of the rule of law—juridical questions. Integralists, our critics assert, would deprive persons of the rights and liberties promised them by liberalism, which has been institutionalized in the West since (at least) the nineteenth century. Integralists, the same critics claim, are enemies of the rule of law. These charges are completely false. Hence one of the main tasks of integralism today is a revival of the great tradition of jurisprudence, with its roots in the ancient world, and its branches in the great jurists of the Middle Ages. This great juridical tradition had deep and vital insights into the true nature of law and of rights, and the foundation of both in the true good of man. These insights were rejected by liberalism, with its roots in Enlightenment misunderstandings of the relation between law and right, and between objective rights and subjective rights.

In *After Virtue*, Alasdair MacIntyre has shown the effect of the liberal concept of rights in undermining communities of virtue. He goes too far, however, when he claims that universal human rights are "fictions." The problem is not that such rights are fictions. For, in fact, there are such rights, rooted in human nature. The problem is rather how liberalism misunderstands the order between rights and law and the good.

In the great tradition of classical and medieval jurisprudence, the primary sense of "a right" is "an object of justice." What does this mean? Many modern writers have misunderstood what is meant, because they assume it means something very lofty and universal, such as an objective moral order (*right* as opposed to *wrong*). But, in fact, what the juridical tradition means by "an object of justice" is something so concrete, particular, and banal that at first glance it seems hardly worth mentioning. The virtue of justice is the firm will to give to each his due. Thus, an *object* of justice is *what is due*, the *thing or action due to another.* Thus an "objective right" is nothing more than a thing or action due to another. For example, a fair share of the spoils of battle is due to Achilles—it is his *right*. Or, money is due to the baker who gives me a loaf. The money is his *right*. Or the cantor's singing of an antiphon is due to the cathedral chapter which has appointed him—the singing of the antiphon is the chapter's *objective right*. The spoils, the money, and the singing are themselves the objective rights. That is, it is not primarily that Achilles *has* a right to the spoils, but rather that the spoils *are* his right.

Now this objective sense of right can be analogically extended to rights in a more familiar sense: subjective rights. Subjective rights are the moral powers that persons have over their objective rights. Achilles has a subjective right *to* the spoils of war. That is, no one can justly withhold them from him. Similarly, the baker has a subjective right *to* the money that is his objective right. The baker can say both "the money *is* my (objective) right," and "I have a (subjective) right *to* the money."

Why is this important? The importance becomes manifest when we ask: Which is the primary reality? Are subjective rights derived from objective rights or vice versa? The liberal answer is that subjective rights are primary. It is because we have certain subjective rights that certain things are due to us. But the true answer is that objective rights are primary. It is not because Achilles has a subjective right to the spoils that they are due to him, rather it is because the spoils are due to him that Achilles has a subjective right to them.

Religious Liberty

As integralist jurists have argued at *The Josias*, and the juridical blog associated with it, *Ius & Iustitium*, the primacy of objective rights over subjective rights is crucial to seeing the proper relation of rights and law. Since objective rights are primary, subjective rights are dependent on a prior distribution of things. This distribution is largely a matter of law. Law is the foundation of rights, the reason for rights. As St Thomas Aquinas put it, *lex est ratio juris*, law is the reason of right. Law, on this understanding, is something of reason, directed to the common good, made by the authority responsible for the common good, and promulgated. The key terms here are *reason* and *common good*. Law goes back to rational understanding of what the true common good of human communities is. Thus, the distribution of objective rights, on which subjective rights depends, goes back to a sapiential understanding of the true good. The whole order of rights, therefore, is directed to the true common good. Rights, then, are ultimately justified by the common good, and they ought to be distributed in such a way as to allow everyone in society a full participation in the common good. Because there are different levels of society, and accordingly different kinds of law—divine law and natural law, as well as the positive laws of various human communities—the task of the jurist is to understand all the different levels of law as sources of right.

The liberal understanding of rights, however, reverses the proper order. For liberal thinkers, subjective rights are the primary juridical and political reality on which everything else is founded. Subjective rights are *liberty*, they are the moral power to act without interference from another. *Because* human persons have inalienable rights to life, the possession of private property, freedom of speech, freedom of religion, etc., certain things and actions are due to them. In classical liberalism, what is due to them is primarily *negative*, that is *non-actions*—not killing a person, not interfering with or stealing their property, not limiting their freedom of expression, etc. What follows from this is that for liberals the role of law is to limit rights in order to preserve them. That is, law puts certain limits on the subjective rights of each individual, in order to secure the maximum of liberty in each compatible with the liberty of all.

Conclusion

The liberal conception of law leads to an instrumental understanding of the common good. For liberals the common good is not that in which the members of society find their flourishing and happiness, but rather an order instrumental in bringing about the liberty of all. The true goal is not an actual good, but the maximum freedom for each to determine his good. If tyranny is defined by subordinating the common good to the private good, then the liberal order is a tyranny in which everyone is a tyrant. The tyrannical face of contemporary woke progressivism is actually much more liberal than conservative liberals are willing to admit. For, societal disapproval of the way of life in which I have found my "identity" (i.e., my true self, my flourishing and happiness) limits my freedom to enjoy that identity. Hence the seemingly illiberal demand that others celebrate the lies that persons tell themselves about themselves, seen, for example, in the LGBTQI+ movement, actually follows from the liberal principle of maximalization of individual liberty.

Far from being the enemies of rights and the rule of law, integralists are the true defenders of rights and laws properly understood, and truly at the service of human flourishing and happiness.

"Campion's Brag" caused a great stir when it was circulated. Campion followed it up with a pamphlet entitled *Ten Reasons, for the Confidence with which Edmund Campion Offered his Adversaries to Dispute on Behalf of the Faith*. In the last of the ten reasons that Campion gave for his confidence he calls on many kinds of witnesses through many generations to the truth of his cause. For integralists, one group of witnesses is particularly relevant—the witness of great Christian rulers:

> I call to witness likewise Princes, Kings, Emperors, and their Commonwealths, whose own piety, and the people of their realms, and their established discipline in war and peace, were altogether founded on this our Catholic doctrine. What Theodosiuses here might I summon from the East, what Charleses from the West, what Edwards from England, what Louises from France, what Hermenegilds from Spain, Henries from Saxony, Wenceslauses from Bohemia, Leopolds from Austria, Stephens from Hungary, Josaphats from India, Dukes and Counts from all the world over, who by example, by arms, by laws, by loving care, by outlay of

money, have nourished our Church! For so Isaias foretold: *Kings shall be thy foster-fathers, and queens thy nurses.*

Integralism is an attempt to revive the great political tradition of that host of witnesses, and of the theological, philosophical, and juridical principles upon which that tradition rested. It may be that we will not be given a fair hearing, yet have we such a courage in avouching the Majesty of Jhesus our King, and such affiance in His gracious favor, and such assurance in our quarrel, that we will not be discouraged.

www.ingramcontent.com/pod-product-compliance
Lightning Source LLC
Chambersburg PA
CBHW022058150426
43195CB00008B/182